CHEQUE MATE

THE GAME OF PRINCES

CHEQUE MATE

THE GAME OF PRINCES

JEFFREY A. BAKER

Whitaker House

CHEQUE MATE: THE GAME OF PRINCES

Dr. Jeffrey A. Baker
The Baker Report
3615 W. Waters Avenue, Suite 308
Tampa, FL 33614

ISBN: 0-88368-383-0
Printed in the United States of America
Copyright © 1993 by Jeffrey A. Baker
Cover design by Rob Varela
Cover illustration by Richard Zizzi

Whitaker House
580 Pittsburgh Street
Springdale, PA 15144

2 3 4 5 6 7 8 9 10 11 / 05 04 03 02 01 00 99 98 97 96

Dedication

To the gentle spirit,
who has supported me in this project,
but more importantly,
in my life, my work, and
in the monumental struggle to expose the truth;
who, when others stopped believing,
lost the vision,
and forgot the past —
thereby surrendering the future —
alone stood with me.
For this, and so much more,
I relish the idea of our growing old together.
Marcia, thank you for being my wife.

Acknowledgements

It is impossible to thank all of the people who have made this book possible. But, there are some special people who I must remember for their vision and sacrifice.

First to Phyllis, Robert, and Belinda, who have allowed themselves to be used mightily in bringing this project from dream to reality.

I would also like to thank all of those who have paved the way for so many years for others such as myself. These are men of courage and stamina — such as Howard Phillips, Dr. Rousas John Rushdoony, Don McAlvany, and scores of others — who have dedicated their lives to restoring America. Through their endeavors and teachings I have come to many of my understandings.

To William "Bruce" Bendt, who has been my friend and confidant, and whose assistance in editing and documenting this book was invaluable.

Finally, I would like to acknowledge you, the reader, for your discernment and your desire to know the truth — even if that truth is disturbing.

CONTENTS

FOREWORD

by

Justice William Cassius Goodloe (Retired)
Supreme Court, Washington

This book is about more than good vs. evil, materialism vs. truth - it is a political, scientific, and humanistic culmination in the modern age of thoughts and ideas that began in ancient Greece. Plato looked out upon the world and thought that "return to nature" by way of population control, including infanticide, would be the solution to the evils of his time and asked why these Utopias never arrive upon the map?

Diogenes thought we should "turn and live with the animals - they are so placid and self-contained." Aristotle described his "superman of ethics," and said, "Men readily listen and are easily induced to believe that in some wonderful manner (Utopia) everybody will become everybody's friend, especially when someone is heard denouncing the evils now existing ... which are said to arise out of the possession of private property. These evils, however, arise from quite another source — the wickedness of human nature."

Plato in *Timaeus,* reported the legend of sunken Atlantis, a continent in the Western seas. This report was the cause of Bacon's conversion of Plato's Utopia in the old Atlantis to the new America of Columbus. Thus in Bacon's Utopia, he created a new society in which at last science has its proper place as master and victor in the battle of knowledge and invention over ignorance and poverty.

In *Thus Spoke Zarathuystra,* Nietzsche described Utopia but added something he thought was new - superman. "Dead are all Gods: now we will that superman lives.... I teach you superman. Man is a bridge and not a goal: what can be loved in man is that he is a transition and a destruction." Nietzsche tells us that the superman can survive only by human selection, by eugenic foresight and an ennobling education. He says the best should marry only the best; love should be left to the rabble, and the purpose of marriage is not merely reproduction, it should also be development. "Thou shalt not only propagate thyself, but propagate thyself upward! Marriage: thus I call the will of two to create that one which is more than they who created it." Zarathustra asks, "What is good? All that increases the feeling of power, the will of power, power itself, in man."

And out of all these philosophers came Adolph Hitler who not only borrowed infanticide from Plato, and the superman from Nietzsche, but added his part with the creation of a super-race — and added genocide, war, pestilence, starvation, and death chambers.

What you are about to read in the pages that follow is an unveiling of the Malthusians of modern philosophy. Today, everyone that hears about the New World Order, of the Council on Foreign Relations, the Trilateral Commission, the National Security Council, or the International Monetary Fund asks, "Who are they?" If you watch the events of today you will read about millions dying throughout the world in minor wars from Africa, to Bosnia, to Asia, to South America and other third world nations throughout the world, while the nations that could help, won't. You have read about millions starving while American farmers are paid not to grow food and farmers are going bankrupt while millions in subsidies are appropriated by Congress to prevent failures, but banks are foreclosing anyway. You will ask why hundreds of thousands of AIDS patients are allowed to die while the government labels the disease a civil rights issue instead of a public health problem. Millions of babies are aborted annually with no government interference. In sum, why are the powerful nations of the world standing while all of this is happening? The answer is revealed in this very remarkable book which brings the philosophy of Utopia and the superman up to the minute and tells us what we must do.

Jeffrey Baker is declaring war. He is defining the issues and drawing the line in the sand. In truth this is the last stage of the war between good and evil, between truth and the lie, between spiritual truth and materialism, and which side wins is up to you. He tells us what to do and how to do it. Is it too late? Not yet, but it *will* be too late if you and I continue to shrug our shoulders and say, "No one told me." *Cheque † Mate • The Game of Princes* tells you the truth. From this day forward, there can be no more excuses.

Justice William C. Goodloe (Retired)
Supreme Court, Washington

INTRODUCTION
by
William "Bruce" Bendt

I am sure that many of you, who pick up this book, are like me. You are looking for knowledge and information. Some of you are looking for answers to the problems you face daily in your homes, families, neighborhoods, jobs, churches, educational choices, governments, and a host of other dilemmas. Some of you are looking for purpose, direction, or a cause to champion. Perhaps some of you already perceive the New World Order handwriting on the wall and want to know if there is any hope.

I am also sure that many of you are looking for entertainment, while others are looking for an intellectual challenge, and are salivating at the opportunity to tear apart an argument.

Having known and worked with Jeff for several years, I can assure you that both he and I have been at all of these stages in our lives. In *Cheque † Mate · The Game of Princes* Jeff has done his homework well. You'll find knowledge and information that is both well-researched and documented, but which you've probably never seen or heard before. In addition to explaining the New World Order, Jeff offers practical answers to help you deal with problems that almost all of us are experiencing regularly.

I have read many books pointing out the handwriting on the wall, but they unfortunately have left the reader cold, with no answers. That is not the case with *Cheque † Mate · The Game of Princes*. Jeff's work is filled with hope, and yes, for those who want to do something to better themselves and the world in which they live, a cause worthy of your support.

Jeff's warm writing style and instant wit make this treatise really enjoyable. You may not agree at every point, but hopefully, you can share the sentiments of old, wise Benjamin Franklin:

> I have experienced many instances of being obliged by better information or fuller considerations, to change opinions, even on important subjects, which I once thought right but found to be otherwise. It is therefore that the older I grow the more apt I am to doubt my own judgement and to pay more respect to the judgement of others. Most men, indeed, as well as most sects in religion think themselves in possession of all truth, and that when others differ from them it is so far error.

I trust that this book will be as much of an adventure in reading, mystery, and intrigue for you as it was for my family when first we were confronted with these thoughts. Thank you, Jeff.

SECTION I

SETTING UP THE GAME

Chapter 1

My Remembrances

*I remember when America wasn't like a Norman Rockwell painting...
a Norman Rockwell painting was like America.*

A lot has changed in the United States and in the world since the carefree days of my boyhood. Unfortunately, most of the changes have not been for good. Perhaps more distressing is that change in America and the world is dramatically accelerating, and it leads each of us to wonder — will the changes we are facing continue to be dark and ominous? Are we likely in the future to live in a world and a country that more closely resembles the frightening world described by George Orwell, or will the future lead us back to the innocence and splendor of America and the world that I remember growing up in the 1950s?

Cities and towns were different in the 50s. People were different then; not that there weren't people of bad intent. I don't mean to imply that America at that time was a utopia, because it wasn't, but there was a certain quality of innocence about life. I experienced a real sense of neighborhood, growing up as a child in the northern Illinois city of Rochelle (located near the Wisconsin border). I remember with a certain fondness some of those who affected my life in that town of 8,000 people.

Mr. Karon, our next door neighbor, was a Frenchman whose parents had immigrated to America when he was a boy. He still had a heavy accent, a hearty laugh, and as I recall, an occasional whisper of bourbon on his breath.

I remember every fall he would tap all of the maple trees in the entire neighborhood and collect the sap to make maple syrup. I can remember the chill in the air and Mr. Karon standing beside a huge caldron in his back yard, singing at the top of his lungs as he boiled the maple down to syrup for days on end. That wonderful aroma of maple, mingled with the firewood, permeated the entire neighborhood. There was a sense of anticipation among the neighbors, knowing that in just a few short days they would each receive a sample of Mr. Karon's delicious homemade maple syrup.

This was a time when raking the leaves was a family holiday, of sorts. Usually, one Saturday in the fall, everyone in the neighborhood raked their leaves together. All day long the grownups raked as the children ran and played, diving gleefully into the mountains of red, auburn, and gold. As the day came to an end and we began to see the glimpses of the arrival of evening, puffs of smoke dotted Third Street as the families raked and gathered the leaves into community piles for the annual fall rite of the burning of the leaves. This was not one of those highly publicized events, where we brought in the local politicians or the media. Instead, we brought hot dogs, marshmallows, apple cider, and hot coffee.

When Mr. Kassmar's milk route was expanded to include another several blocks, the entire neighborhood celebrated with him, knowing that his wife was expecting their third child. The increased territory would mean extra income, just in time to meet the needs of their about-to-be-expanded family. He wasn't going to be able to retire to the French Riviera, but he was able to make a living in Rochelle.

We didn't have *Nintendo* games. We didn't have VCRs or CD players. Many families didn't have color televisions; in fact, many didn't even have a television. There was a gentle quality that surrounded life around my home. Neighborhoods, while being far from perfect, still possessed a sense of community and friendship.

A father taught his children how to rake leaves and throw a baseball. Most couldn't teach them how a television worked because few could afford one at that time. But dads taught their kids about life. They taught about personal accountability and honor; about responsibility and dignity; about respect for God and country. As a result, the Kassmars, the Bakers, and the other families had children who were well-behaved, polite, and well-mannered.

There was no artificial code of behavior. Rather, integrity was a way of life. Children treated adults with respect, and adults had a sense of parenting over all the children in the neighborhood. Everybody accepted his responsibility in the community. If a child misbehaved, he was just as likely to be scolded by a neighbor as he was by his own parents. Try that in today's society and you'll probably end up with a lawsuit on your hands.

While boyhood mischief existed, it was the mischievousness of *Den-*

nis the Menace or Opie Taylor. Today, boyhood mischief is all too often expressed in headlines such as "Boy Eleven Years Old Rapes Eight Year Old Girl." Mischief displayed in those days was climbing a fifty foot tower — just to see if it could be done.

It was a time when the neighborhood children played *Hide 'n' Go Seek* or *Capture the Flag*. Entertainment consisted of neighborhood picnics and impromptu block parties, instead of rock concerts featuring *Mega Death* and *Two Live Crew*.

It was a time when doors were left unlocked; when milk was delivered to coolers on the front doorstep; and when life was lived on the front porch — instead of behind curtained and burglar-barred windows.

It was a time in America when a new puppy in the family was news throughout the neighborhood. The birth of a child in a family brought neighbors together to make suppers, bake pies and cakes, and to make sure that the family was looked after while the new Mama was yet in the hospital.

In those days relatives took care of relatives. My cousin, Sherry, lived with us for several months during a rough time in her family. Nobody thought too much about it because the practice was common. In fact, it was a Baker family tradition to have each of us — my two brothers and myself — stay for two weeks with a maternal uncle in Peoria, Illinois every year.

One of my fondest childhood memories is the sights, smells, and sounds of Stangley's Market, which was only two blocks away from our home. I still remember old Mr. Stangley, standing in sawdust on the wooden floor, the big, glass-and-wood candy case as you walked in the door, and the smells of the butcher section in the back of the store. There were no elaborate locking systems or alarms on Mr. Stangley's store. There were no signs saying: "Shoplifters Will Be Prosecuted To The Fullest Extent Of The Law." I remember so often being given a dollar to go down to Stangley's Market for milk and bread, and there was always money left over for a piece or two of candy, for which Mr. Stangley seldom charged.

And I remember picking up the phone in the back room and asking the operator: "Enterprise 327, please," to ring my home when I had forgotten part of the grocery list. (Well, you know how boys can get distracted at times — don't you?)

I remember my fourth grade teacher, Mrs. Miller, who lived just down the block from us, around the corner to the right, and at the far end of the block. She lived in the second story of a huge old house. It was not uncommon for Mrs. Miller to entertain us, in her own home, with stories from her childhood and treats of cookies and Kool Aid. Teaching wasn't a job then - it was a vocation. Unlike teachers today, Mrs. Miller was never threatened with violence from her fourth grade class. Rather, she was a grandmother, for whom each of us had love and respect.

It was a time when, over the loud speaker of our school, the pledge of allegiance was read and each of us recited it proudly. A prayer was said at the beginning of each day, and a lesson read from the Bible. It was a time for children of wonderment. Teachers read great works of literature to their classes after the lunch break.

I remember wonderful Saturdays with Grandpa Baker. He would arrive late Saturday morning, pick up my brothers and me, and we would usually follow a set ritual. We would first go to what was called "the stack" at Del Monte Foods, where Grandpa had worked for about thirty years, and where he was now the manager. The stack was a place where all of the pea vines and corn husks that had become refuse from the foods packing operation were piled onto a hugh stack — so big that trucks and tractors could drive on it. These were used to feed cattle during the long winter months.

During the hot summer months, the college kids worked their way through school at the viner stations (where the pea vines, loaded with ripe juicy peas, were brought for initial processing to separate the peas from the pods and vines). It was not unusual for the students to work fourteen, sixteen, and eighteen hour days during the long summer in order to have money to pay for the next year's tuition. The area around the viner stations was buzzing with bright, young men still filled with innocence and wonder; still not too good to do summer jobs; and still not looking for the government to provide for their needs. Rather, independent people, living independently, and yet ... dependent in the community sense. Having visited the stack and viner stations, we would then be off to Harry's Sandwich Shop. This was a little hole-in-the-wall, greasy-spoon, with a Dairy Queen on the front end. It was a time when no one worried about cholesterol, meat additives, vegiburgers, and the plethora of nonsense accompanying the "healthy" lifestyle of America today. They were great, big, fat, juicy hamburgers, with cheese melted on the top. Buns were grilled to perfection, laden with green, crispy, and puckery dill pickles. The malted milk shakes were so thick and creamy and were made with real eggs. They were so delicious that they were just one-rung-on-the-ladder below heaven.

Even as my father's career with Del Monte Foods progressed and we moved to the suburbs of the tiny little town of Rochelle, life really didn't change much. Being a rural subdivision, it was our custom to go down to the creek at the end of the street, follow it along to the edges of the corn and pumpkin fields, and then to sneak into the corn fields where we built secret forts.

We followed the creek to the woods and lived bold and daring dreams, as pirates or explorers; the brave exploits of patriotic Americans were relived and created. Fantasy life in those days did not have deviant sexual overtones; rather purity, joy, and accomplishment of exploration and nobility. Even in the cold of winter, we would follow the frozen creek, in the now barren fields under gray skies, to our secret places in the woods. Here we built camp fires and told stories ... and life was good.

Yes, my childhood memories are of a sweeter, simpler America. It was a time of barefoot summers and tracking (usually with limited or no success) animals in the snows of winter. It was a time of splendid inquisition, as we did not understand how everything worked. Our lives had not been analyzed, socialized, homogenized, theorized, and ruined by false presumptions. It was a time of simple faith. We believed in America. We believed in our neighborhoods. We believed in the values and virtues of God, country, purity, and honesty.

It was a time of rolled-up blue jeans, white socks, black shoes, loose-fitting shirts, combed hair, and brightly-washed faces; a time of wholesome Americana. These remembrances still make me long for the nostalgic America that Rockwell painted.

O.K. Perhaps life then wasn't as comfortable as it is now. We didn't all have two cars or a television in every room. Not everyone was upwardly mobile; in retrospect, most of us were poor by today's standards. But we had friends and people who loved us, and we could count on one another in times of crisis. Life was good and life was happy. Somehow ... something happened in America.

Entertainment was pretty much centered around little league baseball, church, ice cream socials, picnics, Vacation Bible School, and the family vacation. Today entertainment is professional wrestling, with hideous spectacles of crude, vulgar, and obnoxious men choking each other with chains, beating each other with chairs, and crashing heads together until blood explodes from the forehead of the "good guy," with the continuation of this episode to next week. Today entertainment is centered around twisted, perverted rock stars living lives of demonic opulence in a drug culture which is obviously destroying America.

Sociologists tell us that current societal values resulted from a natural process of evolution. However, as I pick up newspapers today and read of our elderly being murdered in their homes as they sleep, by burglars taking the stereo, television, and a few dollars; as I read about eight year old girls raped by eleven year old boys; as I read of teachers being threatened and beaten in their classrooms and students killing each other for drugs; as I read of the drive-by shootings; as I read of teenagers mauled and stampeded to death at rock concerts; as I listen to the music that advocates suicide, Satanic worship (whose lyrics are absolutely degrading and vile toward women and humanity), I have to question these great social thinkers who call this societal evolution. If this is evolution — I would favor devolving.

Do you remember *Laurel and Hardy* in those great old movies? They were always in, or on the verge of, trouble. They never meant to do anything wrong. It just seemed that circumstances were overwhelming them. Little Stan was always the fall guy — whether it was his fault or not. Oliver was always mad at him. "Well, here's another nice mess you've gotten me into," he was frequently heard to say. And the reply was always the same whimper, "I'm sorry, Ollie."

In the not too distant past, those words came ringing into my remembrance as we saw Ollie North, in front of the reprobate, hypocritical Congress. They probed, pried, and attempted to shred him of his long and distinguished career. Fortunately for Ollie, he had done a little shredding of his own.

I mention Ollie, not to refuel the debate over the Iran-Contra Affair, or to re-examine his guilt or innocence, but because it is striking to me that the situation ever happened in the first place. It makes no difference whether or not he was guilty or innocent. Rather, it's the one-up-manship of Congress that needs to be looked at with scrutiny.

Politics in America today seems to have taken on an increasingly sinister nature. I don't remember all that much about government as a boy, but like the rest of life then, there was a certain honesty in government. Now, before all of you historians prove my ignorance by citing three hundred classic cases of dishonest politicians ... let me explain.

I have heard it said that the oldest profession known to man is prostitution. While that may be true, I have a sneaking suspicion that the profession was invented because they heard there was going to be a political convention in town.

Surely, some politicians were lecherous, greedy, and dishonest ... but that was different. It was at least limited, old-fashioned greed, dishonesty, and self-aggrandizement. Today, however, there seems to be an illusive, *Hidden Agenda* — some sort of grand design for creating a power elite.

As the web of this grand scheme is spun subtly and cautiously, its thin threads attach and entwine themselves around every aspect of American society, leaving us only the question — who or what will be the next victim? As Congress passes increasing anti-business and anti-worker legislation; as our school system is systematically destroyed; as government becomes more imperialistic and further insulated from the people — one has to wonder — where is all of this leading? Therefore ...

I seek not just to uncover the spider weaving the web, but to expose the web.

Chapter 2

Yorel Of Moscow

Yorel Legov remembered life as a boy, when no matter how bad things got, his family could always count on the State to be there. He mused, as he stood in the long line waiting to buy food, how different things were now. There had been food lines for a long time, but before, he always knew that he would eventually "bring home the bacon."

Now, he knew that he would not take home the bacon ... because there was none. For some time the State had taken on the role of controlling all food production through subsidies, encouraging agribusiness, using public-private partnerships, and regulating all farming through environmental protection laws (wetlands acts, streams and rivers acts, state lands acts, and a plethora of other land control acts). The production, supply, and distribution of all agricultural products, including produce, meat, dairy, and grain, had all been placed under the control of the State.

When the corporate State collapsed everything fell into chaos. As a result, bringing home the bacon (or practically anything else for that matter) was at best difficult, at worst impossible. It had all seemed like such a good idea — centralized power, planning, distribution, and the like.

"Maybe," Yorel thought, "we should have considered what would happen if the State collapsed; but at the time that possibility was just unthinkable. Everyone thought the State was forever. The State provided our jobs and regulated our pay to make sure that each was treated with at least the semblance of fairness. The State educated our children and took care of all of our needs."

Yorel was suddenly brought back to reality as the line jolted forward. However, this reality check was short-lived, as the monotony of standing in line quickly set back in. Yorel was soon moving in time backwards to his life as a boy in Moscow. That was a time when there were real neighborhoods. He knew the butcher, the baker, and the all of the families around him.

He remembered when the wife of the tailor was about to deliver her third child and the neighbors took turns preparing meals for her husband and the other two children. This was just a part of life. No one told anyone to do it — people just did it. Neighbors took care of neighbors. But now life was hard. Even the thought of taking a meal to a neighbor, or delivering firewood to an elderly couple, was unthinkable. Survival was the order of the day.

Yorel's trip down memory lane was interrupted once again as the line inched forward. Perhaps today would be different than yesterday and the day before. Perhaps today he would actually make it to the entrance of the market.

Disturbances and fights in the food lines were an everyday occurrence, as people became desperate. Yesterday, a man had been beaten severely as he first pleaded and then tried to push his way into the front of the line. His plight was not uncommon. He had a wife and four children. There had been little or no food in his house for a couple of days and his children were ill from the poor living conditions in the heatless, drafty building in which they lived. There was running water only a couple hours a day and often it wasn't clean. But even boiling water had become difficult, since electricity was only available for a few hours and usually at random times. It was very hard trying to keep even the smallest supply of sterilized water to cook enough food (if it was available) for the rest of the week. Everyone standing in line was in a similar situation. Sympathy and human kindness were now replaced with contempt and anger.

How had all this started? Yorel so vividly remembered the woods and streams, the mountains and prairies around Moscow, Idaho. In fact, his parents had immigrated to these United States from another Moscow to escape from the very conditions in which Yorel was living right now. What had happened to the American dream? "I guess," Yorel thought, "we sold it for another dream. We reached for the carrot that the State had dangled in front of us. We believed that they could provide for all of our needs. We could trade self-indulgent, individual rights for Utopia."

"Funny," Yorel thought, "throughout history men have traded off their individual liberty for utopia and every time this has been the result."

An aching sense of foreboding formed a sick feeling in the pit of his stomach. The reality of the finality and irreversibility of America's mistake settled like a death notice over Yorel — and he knew that all was lost and that the gray prison which had replaced his parent's beautiful America was permanent. The sense of dread and feeling of hopelessness was now a life sentence, and what was worse — his children now shared that life sentence, as would future generations.

History teaches us that man learns nothing from history.
Hegel

Chapter 3

The World In Brief

Life has changed. The specter of death hangs over the world from The Sudan to Ethiopia; from Somalia through the entire Middle East; and from northern Mexico to Argentina; we see the images of suffering, pain, and deprivation. We see the spreading of drought and famine. Millions of people may be on the verge of starvation, while hundreds of thousands of others are dying each and every day. I was recently told by a relief worker to Guatemala that people are actually living on the refuse in garbage dumps. It is indeed hard to imagine such poverty in this kinder and gentler world in which we now live and where all will soon be a global bliss, according to people like former President George Bush.

Even now an old adversary, cholera, is sweeping across parts of Peru and other South American nations. Cholera, the disease of poverty, is often the result of people eating the fish and drinking from polluted waters, which are also used synchronously for a laundromat, watering trough for animals, bathroom facilities, and swimming pool for every parasite known to man.

The suffering continues all across the continent of Africa. As if it weren't bad enough that the economic output of almost half a trillion people on the African continent is only roughly equal to the gross national product of Belgium, they are now also being ravaged by drought and famine.

Meanwhile, on the European continent, we have witnessed the official formation of the European Economic Community (EEC). However, all is not rosy. Great Britain is in the midst of a deep, severe, economic recession or depression. Germany's financial power has, to a large extent, been neutralized as they have now adopted the poor, illiterate orphan of East Germany.

And as the cycle of poverty, violence, greed, and ignorance continues, the world suffers. Even our very environment groans under the weight of so much avarice and ignorance in the world. As the poor often become poorer, they do whatever it takes to survive: be it cutting down trees in the Rain Forests, polluting their waters and streams with raw sewage (for lack of any place else to dispose of it), or destroying the underwater habitat off their coasts.

Such is the case in the Mediterranean, where Egyptian fishermen place enormous nets over large schools of fish, drop dynamite, and stun or kill the fish. The edible ones are kept and the inedible left to rot. Meanwhile, the underwater habitat, formerly a major tourist attraction, is destroyed.

Now having wrecked both tourism and the food chain, the poverty grows deeper and deeper. Our first reaction is to say, "Yes, they are just ignorant people doing ignorant things."

Yet, we, the sophisticated people in the United States, are no better. In the little town of Times Beach, Missouri, near my former home in St. Louis, the entire city was poisoned out of existence by toxic waste. For the first time in the history of the United States, the federal government was obliged to step in and buy out an entire town, because such massive amounts of PCBs and other toxins were dumped in the area, that the land became uninhabitable. For those of you who remember the Love Canal incident, it pales in comparison to this.

In our kinder and gentler world, homosexuals are demanding rights (which are not actually rights, but special sodomy subsidies and privileges). They violently contend for these privileges and threaten to organize massive blood donations to contaminate the U.S. blood supply if their demands are not met. An indication of their threats is shown in an article by Michael Swift, "The Homosexual Agenda," portions of which appeared in Boston's *Gay Community News:*

> We shall sodomize your sons, emblems of your feeble masculinity, of your shallow dreams and vulgar lies. We shall seduce them in your schools, in your dormitories, in your gymnasiums, in your locker rooms, in your sports arenas, in your seminaries, in your youth groups, in your movie-theatre bathrooms, in your army bunkhouses, in your truck stops, in your all male clubs, in your houses of Congress, wherever men are with men together. Your sons shall become our minions and do our bidding. They will be remade in our image. They will come to crave and adore us....
>
> All laws banning homosexual activity will be revoked. Instead legislation shall be passed which engenders love between men....

If you dare cry faggot, fairy, queer at us, we will stab you in your cowardly hearts and defile your dead puny bodies....

There will be no compromises. We are not middle-class weaklings.... Those who oppose us will be exiled.

We shall raise vast, private armies, as Mishima did, to defeat you. We shall conquer the world because warriors inspired by and banded together by homosexual love and honor are invincible as were the ancient Greek soldiers.

The family unit — spawning grounds of lies, betrayals, mediocrity, hypocrisy and violence — will be abolished. The family unit, which only dampens imagination and curbs free will, must be eliminated....

All churches who condemn us will be closed. Our only gods are handsome young men.... All that is ugly and vulgar and banal will be annihilated....

... Any man contaminated with heterosexual lust will be automatically barred from a position of influence. All males who insist on remaining stupidly heterosexual will be tried in homosexual courts of justice and will become invisible men.

We shall rewrite history, history filled and debased with your heterosexual lies and distortions. We shall portray the homosexuality of the great leaders and thinkers who have shaped the world....

We shall be victorious because we are fueled with the ferocious bitterness of the oppressed.... We too are capable of firing guns and manning the barricades of ultimate revolution.

In some cities such as Detroit, women have a one in four chance of being raped. Statistically, in the United States 75 percent of the women will be victims of violence in their life time.

Close to home in Haiti, the poverty and misery of its citizens, who earn the equivalent of $330 U.S. per year, threaten at any moment to erupt into national violence.

Since 1945, we have seen a deluge of revolution, war, murder, and mayhem inspired oftentimes by communist-led forces throughout Asia, Africa, and Latin America. We fought a bloody war in Viet Nam that was destined for failure, because it was never really fought. Just enough blood was kept flowing to insure that the conflagration continued.

The insanity also continues with the nationalist army officer, Col.

17

Mohamar Qaddafi, whose cultural revolution overthrew the monarchy government of Libya in 1969, and who became the prime minister in 1970. The Middle East is still a powder keg with Jews and Arabs at each others throats, even while officially at the bargaining table.

We have fought the now famous One Hundred Hour War in Kuwait, where the largest number of American forces since Viet Nam, was gathered. The War in the Gulf, backed by overwhelming military strength, better technology, and dramatically superior leadership, which we witnessed live, blow-by-blow, via satellite, was "successfully" prosecuted. Ramifications of the One Hundred Hour War in Kuwait are just now beginning to be analyzed. Speaking of Operation Desert Storm, then President, George Bush said:

> A new partnership of nations has begun. We stand today at
> a unique and extraordinary moment. The crisis in the Persian Gulf,
> as grave as it is, also offers a rare opportunity to move toward an
> historic period of cooperation. Out of these troubled times, our fifth
> objective — can emerge: a new era, freer from the threat of terror,
> stronger in the pursuit of justice, and more secure in the quest for
> peace. An era in which the nations of the world, east and west, north
> and south, can prosper in harmony.[1]

Look at our recent victory in the Middle East. What was it all about? Supposedly we won — but, madman Saddam Hussein is still in charge in Iraq. It seems so curious that we bait Hussein into taking Kuwait and then go to war against him. Why? Could it have been simply to establish power under the auspices of the United Nations? Is that what it was really about? Again, according to Bush: "When we are successful, and we will be, we have a real chance at this **new world order,** [emphasis mine] an order in which a credible United Nations can use its peacekeeping role to fulfill the promise and vision of the United Nations founders."[2]

The Keystone Coup in the Soviet Union, which began Monday, August 19, 1991, has been called this because it was one of the most bizarre coup attempts, if not in the history of the world, at least, in the history of the Soviet Union. First, Mikhail Sergeevich Gorbachev enjoyed tremendous global popularity, which was surpassed only by his unpopularity at home. As the former head of the KGB, Gorbachev, a master of the art of security, surrounded himself with his most competent security people. Yet, in the entire coup, his people didn't defend him and not one of his security team was killed. This strikes me as more than just a little odd.

18

Second, why would the coup leaders, all very experienced men within the apparatus of the Soviet Union (KGB Chief, Defense Minister, Prime Minister, etc.), whom Gorbachev had recently placed in power, fail to sever all outside communications? Soviet airports for domestic and international travel remained open. Potential opponents to the coup, such as Boris Yeltsin, were not arrested or even detained, and television and radio were not silenced.

Yeltsin addressed the world press from the podium of the Supreme Soviet Politburo, while the television cameras continued to roll. This drama almost appeared to be a staged event, scripted to fail, and played out in front of the world's cameras.

The American media immediately dismissed the proposition of a staged coup as ludicrous. And as usual, the American public was gullible enough to believe that all of this was being accomplished as a "breath of democracy" blowing across the once communist state. Remember the words of Mikhail Gorbachev before the Supreme Soviet Politburo on November 2, 1987:

> In October 1917 we parted with the old world, rejecting it
> once and for all. We are moving toward a **new world, [emphasis
> mine]** the world of communism. We shall never turn off that road![3]

Was it truly freedom winning over tyranny? Was it, in fact, irrepressible good triumphing over evil? Or is there perhaps another conclusion? Was it just another move in a global chess game to establish a New World Order?

The real coup was the emergence of Yeltsin, now the President of the Commonwealth of Independent States (CIS), with Gorbachev's longtime ally, Edward Shevardnadze, by his side.

According to Bush, we will live in a world that is much better, much gentler, much kinder, and much safer as a result of Bush's presidency. The facts, however, don't necessarily stack up with that opinion.

Frankly, what I see is a world that is becoming more turbulent, more dangerous, and more frightening for many people. I see constant revolutions across the world. I see the former Soviet Union as very volatile, inasmuch as, almost every one of the independent states is facing severe economic crisis, food shortages, and shortages of leadership, decency, and morality.

In Germany Nazism and the Nazi Party is on the rise again. Hundreds, perhaps thousands of immigrants are being persecuted, tortured, and in some cases, even murdered by the new fascists. To make matters worse, on April 10, 1993, the high court of Germany decided that "their constitution does not ban Germans from fighting abroad and they will join NATO air patrols over Bosnia, breaking one of the strongest taboos of post-war Germany."[4]

In Bush's kinder, gentler world, tens of thousands of innocent Chinese students were murdered in Tiananmen Square, by a government given most favored nation status by the Congress of the United States. China received this status at the urging, if not insistence, of the Bush Administration.

U.S. officials say that "Iran is close to concluding a deal with North Korea to buy a new intermediate-range missile that the Koreans are developing." The CIA reported that "the new North Korean missile represents a threat to the stability of both Asia and the Middle East."[5]

Everything seems to be changing, yet everything seems to be staying the same. I should say that it doesn't matter who gets elected or which political party is in power, the policies stay the same. One party says they are conservative. The other party says they are liberals, and, yet, as you examine the results of their policies, you find that they are, for the most part, identical. One uses a bit more radical leftist language. The other one uses more "centrist" language. Yet, both govern in exactly the same way: bigger government and more debt. Nothing has changed. How is it that no matter who you elect to office, the policies don't change? And whether there is a Democrat or Republican in office, foreign policy remains basically the same.

From the election of Clinton-Gore, resulting from Bush's "taking a dive," to the happenings in Germany, England, France, the former Soviet Union, or whatever part of the world it might be, I would refer you back to the words of Franklin Delano Roosevelt:

In politics, nothing happens by accident.
If it happens, you can bet it was planned that way.

Chapter 4

The New World Order

We are standing in the face of the greatest historical confrontation humanity has gone through,... a test of 2000 years of culture and Christian civilization, with all of its consequences for human dignity, individual rights and rights of nations... Wide circles of
American society and wide circles of the Christian community do
not realize this fully....[6]

- Pope John Paul II

Two centuries ago our forefathers brought forth a new nation; now we must join with others to bring forth a New World
Order.

Declaration of Interdependence
Signed by 32 Senators and 92 Representatives
January 30, 1976 — Washington D.C.

Now, we can see a new world coming into view. A world
in which there is a very real prospect of a new world order. In the
words of Winston Churchill, a "world order" in which the "principles of justice and fair play ... protect the weak against the strong."
A world where the United Nations, freed from cold war stalemate, is
poised to fulfill the historic vision of its founders. A world in which
freedom and respect for human rights find a home among all nations.[7]

George Bush

In Charles Dickens' *A Christmas Carol,* when visited by the Ghost
of Christmas Future, Scrooge asked if the things he saw were fixed in stone
or if they could be changed. Many men and women of divergent opinions

in this nation have a sense of foreboding about the future of America. To all but the most unaware, the phrase **New World Order,** espoused by George Bush, Mikhail Gorbachev, Pope John Paul II, and others, is well known. However, the meaning of those words, the vision embodied in them, and the effects and implications for America upon the enactment of this New World Order, are a matter of considerable dispute. In essence, however, there seem to be four basic positions concerning the New World Order.

First, many Americans believe that there is a movement toward implementation of some sort of a New World Order. While not all agree as to the amount of power or authority such a governing body will have, most (who hold this position) do agree that this New World Order will have a benign influence to one degree or another in the areas of: global environmental policies, the relationship between nations and their governments, and at least a general plan for world-wide, social planning. In other words, they agree that this New World Order will act in some capacity as a global Central Planning Agency.

Secondly, there are those who believe that the New World Order is a dark secret plot to overthrow not just constitutional America, but further, to establish a "tyrannical" rule over the entire globe.

Thirdly, there are those who believe that this is a "guided" process of societal evolution, that while being steered by wise men and women of vision, it is not a conspiracy, inasmuch as the term conspiracy has such dark and ominous tones. While those who hold to this theory of the New World Order also agree that it concerns world government presiding over the affairs of humankind, they would disagree that it is a step toward tyranny. They believe it is a conscious choice toward global peace, protection of the planet, and world-wide justice.

Finally, there is a fourth group that is simply baffled by the conflicting media reports on the subject. They are taking a wait-and-see attitude. Most Americans probably fall into this "position neutral" category.

Even among this latter group there seems to be a consensus that there is a move toward a world governing body, such as the United Nations. This position is supported by Sir Brian Urquhart, a representative to the U.N. over the past forty years, who was quoted in *Time* magazine on February 3, 1962, as saying, "We've got to stop looking at the U.N. only in terms of day-to-day emergencies and start seeing it as the only organization that can foster institutions for a global society."[8]

Since President John F. Kennedy's (JFK) assassination on November

22

23, 1963, there have been persistent rumors that ten days prior to his death, while on the campus of Columbia University, Kennedy made the following statement: "The high office of President has been used to foment a plot to destroy the Americans' freedom, and before I leave office I must inform the citizens of this plight."

Columbia University categorically denies that President John F. Kennedy was ever on their campus. William "Bruce" Bendt, who assisted me in my research, was unable to find in the federal books and records depository any records for Kennedy on November 13, 1963. *The entire day has been either omitted or removed.* It appears as if that day didn't exist in the life of JFK.

However, it is interesting to note that Kennedy did have a meeting in New York with the International Bankers just prior to the time he was reported to have made the above statement at Columbia University. In this meeting he learned that he had been lied to about Cuba and many other issues. In fact, there is substantial evidence that Kennedy was beginning to uncover an "international effort" to use the office of the President of the United States against America, and had threatened to expose this movement.

The *New York Times* is reported to have published an article several weeks after Kennedy's assassination in which Kennedy stated that the office of the Presidency had been misinformed and used concerning the Cuban Crisis. Is it possible that, like so many before him, JFK died because he began to catch a glimpse of the New World Order?

Is it possible that JFK told his brother, Bobby Kennedy, what he had learned and this information later led to Bobby Kennedy's assassination? The evidence is still inconclusive. However, there are just too many loose strings in the non-conspiracy theory surrounding the deaths of the Kennedys.

Throughout history, and throughout the history of the United States, men have espoused the same lyrical, utopian dreams. There have been, for some time in this country, those who have espoused a New World Order. *The New York Times,* July 26, 1968, reported that New York governor Nelson Rockefeller, in an address to the International Platform Association, at the Sheraton Park Hotel in New York, called for the formation of a New World Order.

In 1973 we find in the *Humanist Manifesto II* these words:

> We deplore the division of humankind on nationalistic grounds. We have reached a turning point in human history where the best option is to transcend the limits of national sovereignty and

23

to move toward the building of a world community ... a system of world law and world order based upon transnational federal government.

Compare this statement with the 1976 remark of Democratic Presidential candidate, Jimmy Carter, who said, "We must replace balance of power politics with world order politics."

Continuing right on through to January 29, 1991, when Bush said before the Congress of the United States, "What is at stake is more than one small country. It is a big idea — a **New World Order**, where diverse nations are drawn together in a common cause to achieve the universal aspirations of mankind; peace and security, freedom, and the rule of law. Such is a world worthy of our struggle, and worthy of our children's future!"

Historically, it is important to remember that the cry for a New World Order is not new, it is centuries old. According to Biblical history we see its presence at the Tower of Babel, where all men had come together to form a one-world government. Their purpose was to "build us a city and a tower, whose top *may reach* unto heaven;"[9] so that man could elect himself god. But the New World Order didn't happen.

In addition to Biblical history, Alexander the Great, the Caesars, and even the office of the papacy during the Crusades, all desired to set up a New World Order. Yet, it seems that even a New World Order based upon religion somehow devolves into nothing more than a reign of terror. The Crusades were hardly Holy Wars; rather, they were reigns of terror seeking to overthrow other reigns of terror. Still, the New World Order was not achieved. Global peace was not brokered.

Adolph Hitler's Third Reich was his New World Order. Hitler was a maniacal, demonic madman, who ordered the extermination of six to eight million Jews, countless Poles, Czechs, and other nationalities. He saw it as his duty to destroy the weak, the infirmed, and the aged because they were unable to produce for society's needs.

As we look at the reign of terror created and fostered by Vladimir Ilyrich Ulynanov Lenin and Leon Trotsky, which was carried on by Joseph Vladimir Stalin, right up through the current Soviet leadership, including Gorbachev and Yeltsin, we have witnessed the suffering and oppression of the masses.

Millions were slaughtered during the Chinese Communist Revolution and the subsequent purges under Mao Tse-tung's leadership. Multi-

24

tudes have died in the blood baths created under these socialistic systems called *communism,* whose ultimate goal was, and is, world government.

Again, even those New World Order systems based upon religion are every bit as tyrannical, demented, and blood thirsty as any other. The Islamic revolutions and fervor that spread like wildfire across the Middle East in the 1970s and 80s, wrought immense massacres for "infidel" peoples.

The Ayatollah Khomeini stated, "Islam will be victorious in all the countries of the world, and Islam and all the teachings of the Koran will prevail all over the world."[10] As we can see from his remark, religion was at the heart of these massacres.

Still, in all, with the multitude of crises facing this world, the clamor goes up, yet again, for another New World Order. History shows a recurring desire for a New World Order directed by individuals or groups with differing goals; be they benign, tyrannical, guided, or position neutral. The questions are: Will this latest, and possibly last New World Order, be yet another chamber of horrors? Will the trend toward self-destruction and tyranny continue? Most men desire to know with Ebenezer Scrooge:

Is the future set in stone, or can it be changed?

Chapter 5

The Players

> There exist on this earth, [Cardinal] Wyszynski used to say,
> only three Internationales.[11]
>
> Malachi Martin, *The Keys of This Blood*

It has long been understood that there are competing interests within the general movement supported by those who would create yet another New World Order or World Kingdom. After extensive examination, it is clear to me, that in the general sense, the emphases or components comprising this latest, and perhaps final New World Order, pertain to the areas of global economics, global politics, and global religion. I will borrow Cardinal Wyszynski's term and call these competing forces the *Internationales*.

I will refer to the leaders of these Internationales, who constitute the key players in this globalist chess game, as the *Princes*. Their objective in the game is to take these three Internationales and establish a kingship over their proposed kingdom, *The New World Order*. Each Prince is vying to become the King. The financial press, who for the sake of appearance, is often irreverent toward those individuals who control wealth and wield power, has also referred to them as Princes.[12]

Global economics is primarily the purview of the Golden Internationale; global politics is that of the Red Internationale; and finally, a global religious system falls within the domain of the Black Internationale. The Princes of these Internationales jockey for control of their area of influence and subsequent pre-eminence over the other Internationales.

As one might expect, there is created a dynamic tension between them. This tension, at times, expresses itself in petty bickering; while at other times, it expresses itself in all out war. *The Game of Princes* is made interesting in the fact that there is not only war between the Princes, within their own Internationale, but also between the other two Internationales. But

27

what makes it truly fascinating is the fact that there are no set boundaries between the Internationales. Each of these Princes can, and often does, slide effortlessly, depending on the circumstances, back-and-forth between the Internationales.

Further, it is important to understand that the Princes and their Internationales can work in conjunction with other Princes, as well as with one or both of the other Internationales, while at the same time plotting intrigue and mischief, murder and mayhem, against a member of another Internationale — or even an entire Internationale.

The Rook

As the name indicates, the Rook (or Castle) represents the Golden Internationale, and its Princes operate in the realm of finance and banking. They see castles, kingdoms, mansions, and *money* as their strength. Their control of things political is based upon the power of economic influence, illusion, and contrivance within the world of finance. It is important to understand that all political systems, including the one envisioned by the Rook, are, by their very nature, religious because every political or legal system determines the morality of the culture.

These Princes now control the Central Banks of Europe, Japan, Canada, the emerging nations around the world, and, of course, the Federal Reserve Bank (the Central Bank in the United States). Because of this unprecedented power, they are able to create ebbs and flows within economies. As each economy is *steered,* the one consistent pattern that can be seen world-wide is that they are all being driven further into debt. The Princes goal is to immerse economies further into the financial abyss which, if the pattern continues, will lead inexorably to inescapable bankruptcy. John F. Hylan, the late Mayor of New York City, on March 26, 1922, made the following remark:

> The real menace of our republic is the invisible government which, like a giant octopus, sprawls its slimy length over our city, state and nation. At the head is a small group of banking houses generally referred to as "international bankers." This little coterie of powerful international bankers virtually run our government for their own selfish ends.[13]

In addition to controlling the Central Banks of most of the world, the power of the Golden Princes continues to grow through their ability to manipulate the price of gold, silver, and other key commodities such as grains, oil, and militarily important industrial metals. Through their control of basic food commodities and economic systems, the political and moral systems of nations, and even entire hemispheres, can be directed, corrupted, and used for building their own power and accomplishing their purposes. Franklin D. Roosevelt disclosed in a letter to a close associate dated November 21, 1933: "The real truth of the matter is, as you and I know, that a financial element in the large centers has owned the government ever since the days of Andrew Jackson."[14]

While their ultimate goal is global financial control, we shall begin our look at *The Game of Princes* with the use of money as a tool to gain control of the political agenda in the United States. These men of money seek power. Raw power over people. Money can buy power only to a certain point. Beyond that, politics is sport. World politics is the ultimate *Game of Princes.*

At present both major political parties in the U.S. are also Pawns, either knowingly or unknowingly, of the Golden International. As we shall discover later, the Republican Party was early in its history co-opted and used to push the agenda of the Golden Princes (International Bankers) and became the initial party of these New World Order initiators. However, once it was publicly known that the Republican Party was the connection between Wall Street and the Golden Princes, the game began to change and new players entered.

As a result, they were then, at least temporarily, forced to share their power with others. But, like good pragmatists, the Princes of the Golden Internationale recognized that the only way to assure victory in a horse race is to own all the horses. So, they set about the task of capturing, controlling, and using the Democratic Party. The proof for these assertions will be presented later; but for now, it is important to understand that the political system of the United States is thoroughly controlled and skillfully used by the Princes of the Golden Internationale. Still today, the Democrats are being used to further the desires of the Golden Internationale. Meanwhile, the Republicans have remained the blind dupes of the Princes and will continue to be their scape goats, on those rare occasions, when a portion of their strategy is discovered.

Since before the turn of the twentieth century, the Princes of the Golden Internationale have controlled, either through direct ownership, or through surrogates, the major media sources in this country. The major sources of "information" in America are controlled by the same power structure. By their control of the major sources for the dissemination of propaganda, labeled the network news, they can control, or at the very least dramatically influence, the outcome of elections.

They began putting their power to the test with the election of Woodrow Wilson in 1912. The importance of Wilson's election was his willingness to support, and even to fight for, the creation of the Federal Reserve Board and the Federal Income Tax in 1913.

In a speech delivered by Senator William Jenner on February 23, 1954, he said:

> Today the path to total dictatorship in the United States can be laid by strictly legal means, unseen and unheard by the Congress, the President, or the people.... Outwardly we have a constitutional government. We have operating *within* our government and political system, *another* body representing another form of government, a bureaucratic elite which believes our Constitution is outmoded and is sure that it is the winning side.... All the strange developments in foreign policy agreements may be traced to this group who are going to make us over to suit their pleasure.... This political action group has its own local political support organizations, its own pressure groups, its own vested interests, its foothold within our government, and its own propaganda apparatus.[15]

Their electoral power has in the subsequent years increased, as was illustrated in the Presidential election of 1992, of the little-known, long-shot, womanizing governor, of the small southern state of Arkansas, William (Bill) Jefferson Clinton. It was, in fact, the best campaign ever waged by a candidate and the news media working in tandem.

Further, illustrative of their ability to influence the outcome of elections, is the makeup of the Congress after the 1992 elections. Even with all of the disgust of the American people toward that corrupt body of leaders, the vast majority of these elected thieves went back to office.

With all of this power — with all of this influence — the Princes have the ability to create the rise and fall of entire governments (such as that of Margaret Thatcher, who by her refusal to acquiesce to their demands that the British pound be merged with the European Community's form of monetary exchange, found herself suddenly, overwhelmingly rejected, even by

30

those within her own party).

However, lest I unintentionally leave the impression that *The Game of Princes* is a *fait accompli,* you should note that there is one major overriding problem, and several minor problems, in establishing eventual world control, through this powerful, economic, and information dissemination system.

The major problem is establishing a cause behind which all can rally. While the United States, and most of the other nations, have gone primarily socialist or communist, there are still, in the West, people who are fiercely patriotic and who refuse to surrender to a New World Order system of global socialism.

Even those who cry for a New World Order understand that there are problems with the system that is being created. Recent polls in the United States indicate that the socialist form of government, established by our own Congress, the Executive Branch (Presidency), and the vile and corrupt Judicial Branch (Supreme Court) of the United States, is at odds with, at least in theory, the beliefs of many Americans.

However, by careful control of the electoral process, there is little or no choice given to the people in the Presidential elections. It is the opinion of this writer that even the outsider, H. Ross Perot, was the Establishment's anti-establishment candidate in the 1992 elections. Instead of competing in the market place of ideas, America is offered the choice of the lesser of two, or in the case of the '92 elections, three evils; the choice then becomes — which evil will we endorse? Perhaps that explains why almost 50 percent of all Americans have historically stayed home on election day.

Couple this fatalistic understanding with the reality that many people are in a struggle — just to survive — financially, spiritually, politically, morally, and in every other way — and we can begin to see the roots of the lethargy that is engulfing America. If people are given nothing more to believe in than a socialist system of survival, the Princes lack a sufficient motivator for their movement. Simply put, money is not a good motivator.

All of this results in a general numbness and feelings of absolute powerlessness for most Americans, which is, of course, the Princes' desired result. Their plan is to lull us to sleep and to come like a thief in the night. However, if we should awaken ... then what?

Since the beginning of time, man has sought deeper meaning to life, other than just economic consequence or reward. For most of us, we simply want the power to control our lives, to live out our destinies, to raise our families, to provide our food, to put a roof over our heads, and to generally provide for ourselves through work of our choosing. There may come a point — if the alarm is sounded in time — when Americans will once again stand up and say, "No more!"

The problem for these Princes then becomes — into what would they have us invest our faith, our beliefs, our goals, and our dreams for tomorrow?

The Knight

The Knight best illustrates the Red Internationale. The Knight's driving force is his desire to overpower those around him and have his sword proclaimed as the mightiest. The Red Internationale, while primarily concerned with global politics, also serves as a home away from home for some of those individuals within the other two Internationales.

With the Rook we saw the goal was money obtained through political power, based loosely upon spiritual (albeit humanistic) values. However, with the Knight, we see *political power* as the driving force, and money more of an antecedent result. They are usually men of power, means, and influence. Their belief system ranges from humanism to earth-worship to pantheistic paganism.

The Knight, like the Rook, finds itself with glaring weaknesses. First, it is at loggerheads with the Rook because of the mechanism that drives it. There is a long and bloody history of both the Knight and Rook using and abusing each other.

Secondly, because the vision of the New World Order and power sought by the Knight is driven by forces political, which are, in fact, religious at their core, it is quite easy for it to overlook some of the economic consequences of that which it does. As a result, conflict often develops between the Princes of the Red and Golden Internationales. However, their conflicts are tempered with their commonality of purpose ... the New World Order.

Having then a similarity in purpose, they often work together and flow back and forth between the two Internationales. It is amazing the flexibility shown and acumen with which these Princes fit into almost any political, economic, and religious setting. Typically, they are players in more than one field at a time. These Princes face many problems; while attempting to maintain the secrecy of their *Hidden Agenda,* they are, at the same time, promoting it.

It is important to remember that a good share of the unsuspecting followers (the Pawns) of these groups are not schemers, but rather, utopian dreamers. They would (should the cloak of darkness or secrecy be lifted, and the horrific belief systems, goals, and vision of the Princes' New World Order be revealed) find themselves diametrically in opposition to those illumined of the world and may well abandon them. Not that this would cause the Princes' plans or schemes to go necessarily awry. However, it may slow them, in that they would have to resolidify a base of popular support.

As is almost always the case when secrecy is a must, someone — not always even someone of opposition — reveals the plan. Such was the case when Dr. Carroll Quigley, a confidant of the Princes, revealed the concepts of the New World Order, as proposed by the Knight and Rook, in his work, *Tragedy and Hope: A History Of The World In Our Time.*

Unfortunately for America, the Princes have well-insulated themselves from mass exposure to the public at large, through control of the propaganda that we call the news. I do not believe that Dan Rather, Tom Brokaw, or Peter Jennings are maniacal men with evil intent, but they see themselves as men of intellect and vision. They are, if you will, utopian dreamers so enamored with their own intelligence that they are blinded by their own "illumination," and professing themselves to be wise, they become utter fools.

I find it interesting that these enlightened media elite do not practice what they preach. None of them redistribute their wealth voluntarily to lower themselves to a national average income. None of them live in modest homes, with modest lifestyles, in an effort to give away 75 percent, 80 percent, or 90 percent of their accumulated wealth and annual earnings. In my estimation, they decide (and will continue to do so as long as the Princes control the media) what is best for humanity; that is — the rest of humanity — not themselves.

The goal of the Princes, and even many of our own political leaders, is to set up a world government based upon some version of a United Nations type organization. An article from *Time* magazine, September 17, 1990, stated that "the Bush administration would like to make the United Nations a cornerstone of its plans to construct a New World Order." Also, Jeanne Kirkpatrick, former United States Ambassador to the U.N., indicated that one of the underlying goals, of Bush's command of the U.N. forces during Desert Storm, was to prove to the world how a "reinvigorated United Nations could serve as a global policeman in the New World Order."[16]

However, with the abysmal record of that ridiculously inefficient, self-defeating, and ultimately failed organization, the chances of success, through that or any other currently existing world body, without major structural changes or short of a global crisis, are two: slim and none.

The Bishop

For us it becomes important to throw into the mix the third and final Internationale, which we will term the Bishop, because of the principle *spiritual* motivation of this player. It is the opinion of this writer, that in addition to the New Age, mystic, occultic, and "hug-a-tree" crowds, that there is yet a more encompassing religious movement. It will, and to a large extent already has, infiltrated Christianity and most major religions world-wide, through organizations such as the World Council of Churches.[17] This might be looked at as the Black Internationale.

There seem to be two main schools of thought on this subject. The first is that there exists a powerful, spiritual intelligencia, whose Pawns infuse traditional Christian doctrine with subtle compromises, rendering it a blend of many religions.

It is the second view of the Black Internationale that is the most controversial. To the extent that we can see a deviation from traditional views of Christianity, we can document the changes. However, when dealing with specific denominations such as Lutherans, Baptists, Methodists, or Catholics — one must "walk on eggs." Because of the vast number of researchers and historians who subscribe to this theory, I feel that I would be remiss if I did not share this view with you. This view of the Bishop or Princes of the Black Internationale includes, not Catholicism or the Pope, but rather, the office of the papacy of the Roman Catholic Church. I make this distinction because I do not want anyone to have the perception that this view of the Black Internationale is anti-Catholic — it is not. It expresses, rather, a fear of the vast money and power at the control and disposal of the office of the papacy (should that office be occupied by a man of evil, or even misguided, benevolent intent).

Further, I must tell you that I do not necessarily endorse this view of the Black Internationale; although, I do believe that the office of the papacy can, and may very well, act as one of the primary players, as we approach the end of *The Game of Princes.*

It is with this in mind that I will attempt, in a dispassionate and purely clinical way, to present this argument, as if it were my own, which is recorded by Malachi Martin. This former Jesuit and Vatican insider, in *The Keys of This Blood,* refers to the office of the papacy as the Black

34

Internationale. There are, of course, many problems in even including the office of the papacy to this unholy trinity; not the least of which are some of the doctrines of the Catholic church.

Perhaps the first doctrine that gives rise to suspicion of the office of the papacy, for many, is the doctrine of papal infallibility. There are many, even within Catholicism, who question this doctrine. I will not attempt to debate this from a theological standpoint. However, the case can be made from history alone, that infallibility is, at the very least, questionable. The doctrine of infallibility was declared by the Vatican Council, which met in Rome in 1870, as follows:

> ... We teach and define that it is a dogma divinely revealed that the Roman Pontiff, when he speaks *ex cathedra,* that is, when in discharge of the office of pastor and doctor of all Christians, by virtue of his supreme Apostolic authority, he defines a doctrine regarding faith and morals to be held by the universal Church, by the divine assistance promised him in blessed Peter, is possessed of the infallibility with which the divine Redeemer willed that His Church should be endowed for defining doctrines regarding faith and morals, and that therefore such definitions of the Roman Pontiff of themselves — and not by virtue of the consent of the Church — are irreformable.

It seems odd that this doctrine was not declared prior to 1870. Edward J. Tanis, in his booklet, *What Rome Teaches,* wrote:

> *Ireneus,* who was a disciple of Polycarp (a disciple of John the apostle), died about the year 200. He knew what the early church believed and taught, and he wrote many books against heresies of various kinds, but Ireneus never taught that Christ intended any bishop to be the infallible head of the church.
>
> *Tertullian* was the greatest theologian of the early church before Augustine, the learned scholar who developed the doctrine of the Trinity, emphasizing the equality of the Father, Son and Holy Spirit. He died in the year 220. If any man knew what Christ and the apostles taught, Tertullian knew it. But Tertullian never heard of an infallible head of the church.
>
> One of the ablest scholars in the early church was *Jerome,* who died in 420. He provided the church with a new and better translation of the Scriptures, and until this day his Latin [Vulgate]

35

translation of the Bible has been in use in the Roman Catholic Church, evidence that this scholar is held in high esteem among Roman Catholics. But even so great a scholar did not teach that the church had an infallible head.

Gregory the Great was one of the most powerful and influential popes, bishop of the congregation in Rome from 590 to 604. He made a large contribution to the improvement of the preaching and music of the church and was an ardent defender of the Catholic traditions, but Gregory never taught that he was the infallible head of the whole church. Foakes-Jackson, the scholarly historian, quotes Gregory the Great as saying that the title of pope as "Ecumenical Bishop" (bishop of the whole church) was "proud and foolish" and "an imitation of the devil."[18]

Loraine Boettner, in her book, *Roman Catholicism,* goes on to say:

The clear teaching of history is that the office of pope was a gradual development. The early bishops in Rome knew nothing of it. They neither claimed the title nor exercised the power. But as time went on, particularly after the fall of the Roman empire, more and more power, political as well as ecclesiastical, fell into the hands of the bishop of Rome, and so the papacy developed.

... That the popes have not always been considered infallible is made clear by a review of events in the late 14th and early 15th centuries.[19]

A glaring example of the fallacy of papal infallibility, and perhaps one of the darkest hours in history, is the Inquisition. While the Bible states grounds for the death penalty, I have yet to find within the writ of Scripture, the process by which a man should be tortured mercilessly on instruments of slow death (such as the rack). Nor are there Biblical grounds for taking property from one's heirs for the supposed sins of the fathers. These practices would be in direct contradiction to the Scriptures.

There is a weakness in Martin's argument that the office of the papacy could, acting on its own, be the sole inhabitant of the forces of the Black Internationale. I find it difficult to believe that all of Christendom, or the other world religions, would willingly acquiesce to global Catholicism.

Further, Christianity and Catholicism have been in direct opposition to some within the Red Internationale. These Princes (such men as Albert

Pike, who controlled the inner circle of the inner circle of Free Masonry and others who were direct spiritual descendants of Adam Weishaupt, a defrocked Jesuit priest) believe that Satan is the god of light and that Yahweh, the god of the Bible is, in fact, evil. According to these "dark prophets," Eve's eating of the forbidden fruit in the Garden of Eden brought knowledge and enlightenment into the world, which was blessed by the true god of this world, Lucifer (Angel of Light), and punished mercilessly and unjustly by the god of darkness, Yahweh. Herein we see a major spiritual rub between a New World Order based solely upon the office of the papacy and the New World Order proposed by the Red and Golden Internationales.

An argument could be made that Adam Weishaupt and others were Jesuit-trained, disinformation officers. It was their job, their unholy calling, to appear to be anti-Christian or anti-Catholic, as a part of an elaborate scheme to confuse the people; almost every doctrine and belief would then be open to interpretation. However, because of Weishaupt's historical break with Catholicism, the strongest argument is that he became the spiritual heart-and-soul of the Red Internationale.

Again, I would remind you that those within the inner circles of all three of these groups flow back and forth, with one central theme of com-monality, and that is — *a one-world government.* All of them believe that world government and power should be in the hands of a few wise men, namely themselves, who can direct adequately, fairly, and justly the affairs of men.

There is a major point of divergence between the three internationales; specifically, who should be in charge of this governing body, moving the pieces, and calling the shots. Each Prince believes that he and/or his Internationale should be at the head of the New World Order.

Martin states that this struggle for dominance in the New World Order will be a "no-holds-barred, three-way global competition." And he acknowledged that once a victor has emerged in this titanic struggle for dominance of the New World Order, every aspect of our lives will be affected.

According to Martin, our way of life (as both private citizens and citizens of a country), even our family life, jobs, education, political sys-tems, money, business life, industry, even national identities and cultures, will be "radically altered forever." Like Martin, I believe that the competi-tion will be a three-way affair, inasmuch as there are only three rivals with enough money, power, and resources to establish this New World Order. However, unlike Martin, who believes that the competition will be between the United States, the [former] Soviet Union, and the Catholic Church, I believe that the three-way competition will be between the three Internationales described above.

One thing is clear: *there can eventually be only one victor.* And as we all know — "to the victor go the spoils." But long before the final dye is cast, it would seem inevitable that this competition for global hegemony will result in protracted and violent confrontation.

That the office of the papacy, and specifically that of Pope John Paul II, will be involved in the struggle for control of the New World Order is, at least in Martin's estimation, very clear. In fact, Martin goes on to say,

> "...the **chosen** [emphasis mine] purpose of John Paul's pontificate —
> the engine that drives his papal grand policy and that determines his
> day-to-day, year-to-year strategies — **is to be the victor of the
> competition now well under way.**" [emphasis mine][20]

This does not necessarily mean that Pope John Paul II is a man driven by blind or personal ambition. Nor is it my position, at this point in time, to determine for you, the reader, or for anyone else, the intent of the Pope. Rather, my intent is to point out the history of such framers and schemers, who would set up a New World Order.

As the Golden and Red Internationales bring about the rise and fall of nations and economies, it will inevitably lead people to a sense of frustration and despair. During these times of uncertainty, people will look for spiritual meaning in their lives. Unfortunately for both the Golden and Red Internationales, what they have to offer has very little in the way of comfort to "lost sheep." However, a world-wide religion can, and I believe will, give comfort to many. I believe that this blend of religions, probably a pseudo-christian pantheism, will be packaged and sold as the missing ingredient capable of filling the vacuum which will be created by global despair. And the argument can be made that no one is in a better position than the office of the papacy to fill the role of head of this spiritual hegemony.

Because of the respect for the office of the papacy, even among Moslem, Hindu, and other religious states, the office of the papacy is perhaps uniquely positioned to bring an end to factionalism and perhaps even create homogeny, with most religious systems. Additionally, while the Golden Internationale and the Red Internationale may have placed key members in positions of power in governments and diplomatic chambers throughout the world, only the office of the papacy has its own diplomatic representatives in every major, and in most minor, countries world-wide, including a representative in the United Nations.

Under the leadership of the office of the papacy, the glaring tragedies of the United Nations (the oppression, overthrow and enslavement of free peoples to totalitarian, socialist, or communist regimes) could be esponged as mistakes made by an altruistic, but misguided, organization. Who then could question the beneficent intent of a man or organization that would unite the world in a commonality and tolerance of all religions? All of us would then be asked to become global citizens with delegated responsibilities to feed the poor, house the homeless, etc.

Should, in fact, Pope John Paul II arise as the leader of this New World Order, there would be yet one more obvious advantage for him. The millions of people who have lived under the oppression of communism have fully accepted the pope as one of them, inasmuch as he too, supposedly, lived under the tyranny of communist rule in Poland.

It is Martin's contention that the office of the papacy (with its call to return to a moral base) would, in all likelihood, seem a positive and regenerative hope for the world. This would be particularly true in the former communist countries, where for decades life has been reduced to nothing more than a plodding, gray repression, filled with lack, bondage, and despair. According to Martin, Pope John Paul II's vision is:

> When John Paul started into the millennium endgame —
> **when he initiated it** [emphasis mine] — all of his moves were tied
> to his clear but decidedly long-range vision that he could supersede
> the plans of both East and West; and, further, that he could leaven
> and finally supplant those superpower plans with some system that
> would tie the condition of the whole world no longer to the success
> barometers in Moscow and Washington but to the legitimate and
> absolute needs of the whole of mankind.[21]

As we continue to look at the contenders in this global chess game, **the most probable victor will be a world-wide religious system, which can bring homogeny and eventually hegemony in the area of world religion.** This is, in all probability, the glue which will hold the New World Order together ... at least in its beginning stages.

Further, while I agree with Martin that there will be a winner in the battle of the Princes, it is my opinion that all of the Internationales will experience highs and lows as the process continues. Finally, even as a victor appears to emerge, it will continue to be a tenuous victory, marked with ongoing power struggles, the rise of fiefdoms, and a continuing battle for superiority. In other words, this is, and will continue to be, a global game to determine the *"King of the Hill."*

Are there plans afoot for a New World Order? The answer to this question is undeniably ... *Yes.* It is already developing and unfolding ... even as you are reading this book. So ...

we will look for the plan
and
meet the Princes who've made the moves to date in...

The Game of Princes.

SECTION II

THE ADVERSARY

Chapter 1

The Order

At times life seems both strange and mysterious. As I review my remembrances as a child ... life was good. Yet, as we review the remembrances of Yorel Legov ... life is decidedly bad. A study of history shows us that every event is involved in a *cause and effect* relationship. Life was either good or bad because someone or something made them that way. As good decisions were made, life was good. Conversely, as bad decisions were made, life was bad.

As is the case with history, the future is bound by the same law of cause and effect. Our future will be determined by the decisions we make. If those decisions are good, the future will follow suit. If our decisions are bad, so will be the future.

I believe that those who would set up the New World Order are making decisions that will ultimately lead us to destruction. Therefore, I view them as the *Adversary*.

The ideas that they put forward are not new and have, in fact, existed in a diabolically organized form since before the birth of this nation in 1776. However, it was in that fateful year that two completely different governments and philosophies of government were born. These are competing in the same time and space, on the global chess board in *The Game of Princes*.

One philosophy of government established a nationalistic, constitutional republic. It was based on the principles of individual liberty and unalienable rights, granted by the Creator, and among these were "Life, Liberty, and the pursuit of Happiness." These foundational principles are rooted in what has come to be known as *Judeo-Christian values*. The founding principles of this government will be discussed later.

The founding philosophy of the second government, born on May 1, 1776, laid the basis for a global, socialistic democracy. The vision of such a government has been seen by countless tyrants throughout the history of the

43

world. However, this new government was different in one very important aspect. It did not rely on the brute force of armies, which at some point in time, always meet a superior Adversary. From the warring states in China; to the Egyptian Empire; to the empires of Greece and Rome; and all others, their failing had been the same: they relied upon the strong arm of force, rather than upon the cunning and subterfuge of manipulation.

It is much easier to conquer a people and, for that matter, a world, when they do not know that they have been conquered. Thus, it is with skill, cunning, and diabolical verve that the birth of the second government, described by George Bush as the New World Order, has slithered into position. It has conquered nations and armies (all of this with the stroke of a pen), has transferred gold from one pocket to another, and transferred zeros from one computer to another.

George Bush's credentials as a spokesman for the New World Order include membership in the elite fraternity called, The Order of Skull and Bones; a secret, if not occultic organization for the would-be privileged in this country. They have been working toward a New World Order as long, or longer than, probably any other organization we might study.

Research done by Antony Sutton, in his book, *America's Secret Establishment: An Introduction to the Order of Skull & Bones,* reveals that many prominent members of the Council on Foreign Relations (CFR) have been members of The Order. W. Averell Harriman, William P. Bundy, McGeorge Bundy, Henry L. Stimson, J. Richardson Dilworth, Henry Luce, Henry P. Davison, George Bush, and Winston Lord are just a few of the students listed on their members roster.

Larry Abraham, a noted author, has stated: "The founders, partners, and directors of some of this country's most powerful financial institutions, both past and present, appear far too frequently in both The Order and the CFR to be mere coincidence."[22]

Some believe that The Order had its origin in the days of Demosthenes, in Greece in 322 B.C. Sutton believes that there is some validity to this thesis because The Order's records are dated by adding 322 to the current year. He uses the example of the records for the year 1950: dated Anno - Demostheni 2272.[23]

The Order of Skull and Bones has also been linked to The Illuminati using this dating method. Membership catalogs are headed at the top of each page by the letters "P" and "D"; an example being the year 1833 would be listed as "Period 2 Decade 3." The Period remains constant at "2" while the Decade increases by one each ten years. Therefore, when the first Yale University group was designated "P.231-D31, the organization started in the U.S. was in the third decade of the second period. This would place the organization of The Order of Skull and Bones within the time frame of the ordered disbanding of the Illuminati by the Bavarian government circa 1796.[24]

The Order has been known for more than 150 years as Chapter 322 of a German secret society, whose members are sworn to silence. Initiates are no longer referred to by their proper names, but are designated as *Knights*. Older Knights are called *Patriarchs;* and the outsiders are called *Gentiles* and *Vandals*. Most members deny membership in The Order.

It was incorporated as The Russell Trust in 1856, and it was also once known as the "Brotherhood of Death." The American chapter was formed in 1833 at Yale University by two men. The first, General William Huntington Russell, brought a charter to the U.S. from his student days in Germany and later went on to become a member of the Connecticut State Legislature in 1846-47. He was also the founder of the Collegiate and Commercial Institute in New Haven, Connecticut.

The second, Alphonso Taft, was the father of our former President, William Howard Taft. He served as the U.S. Secretary of War in 1876, and became the U.S. Attorney General in 1886-87; U.S. Minister to Austria in 1882-84; and finally, the U.S. Ambassador to Russia in 1884-85.

The Order takes in only fifteen initiates per year. There were thirteen names listed on the original membership, and two names were left blank. Sutton believes these were the names of the German connections.

George Lord and his father, Daniel, who established the New York law firm of Lord, Day and Lord, were initiated in 1854, and their law firm is the legal representatives for *The New York Times* and the Rubin Foundation, one of the benefactors for the Institute for Policy Studies (yet another "think tank") in Washington, D.C. Of this same family, Charles Edwin Lord was acting comptroller of the U.S. currency in 1981; and Winston Lord was Chairman of the CFR in 1983.

The Order was responsible for creating, in the 1880s, both the American Historical Association and the American Economic Association. Andrew Dickson White, a member of The Order, was the first President of the American Historical Association. Is it any wonder what view of history is being taught in the schools, when they control those who are rewriting it?

Pierre Jay, an initiate of 1892, became a Vice President of Manhattan Bank and the first Chairman of the New York Federal Reserve.[25]

In 1920, Theodore Marburg became the founder and President of the American Society for the Judicial Settlement of International Disputes. The first Chairman was former President William Taft. This society was the predecessor of the League to Enforce the Peace, which later developed into the League of Nations and finally into the United Nations.[26]

Up through 1983, a group of twenty to thirty families seemed to dominate the order. Some of these families are: Whitney, Lord, Phelps, Wadsworth, Allen, Bundy, Adams, Harriman, Rockefeller, Payne, and Davison.

In the communications fields some of the membership includes Henry Luce of *Time-Life;* William Buckley (1957) of *National Review;* Alfred Cowles (1913) of Cowles Communications, the *Des Moines Register* and *Minneapolis Star;* Emmert Bates (1932) of Litton Educational Systems; Richard Ely Danielson (1907) of *Atlantic Monthly;* Russell Wheeler Davenport (1923) of *Fortune;* and John Chipman Farrar (1918) of Ferrar, Straus, the publishers.

In oil companies, The Order's membership includes: Percy Rockefeller, the Paynes, and the Pratts. Shell Oil, Creole Petroleum, and Socony Vacuum are also connected.

Lumber company connections tie in the Weyerhaeuser family, who are also in the Trilateral Commission.

Sutton claims:

> The Order has either set up or penetrated just about every significant research, policy, and opinion-making organization in the United States, in addition to the Church, business, law, government and politics. Not all at the same time, but persistently and consistently enough to dominate the direction of American society. The evolution of American society is not, and has not been for a century, a voluntary development reflecting individual opinion, ideas and decisions at the grass roots. On the contrary, the broad direction has been created artificially and stimulated by The Order.

"Not all organizations know they have been penetrated or used for another purpose."[27]

Chapter 2

The Illuminati

The Protocols of the Meetings of the Learned Elders of Zion (The Protocols) are the founding principles of the secret society that has come to be called the *Illuminati.* They have been translated and retranslated numerous times. In one particular version, translated from Russian by Victor E. Marsden, Russian Correspondent of *The Morning Post,* the Illuminati is presented as a "Jewish conspiracy." But as you have already begun to see in the previous pages, and as you will continue to see in subsequent pages, this is erroneous and, in fact, is most probably part of the coverup of the true intent.

While some of the Princes are Jewish, the majority are also comprised of several other nationalities, religious groups, and nonreligious individuals. So why would the Princes want to have the world blaming the Jews for *The Protocols?* That's easy. If the blame can be laid at the feet of the Jews, then we will look no further for the real Princes.

Although most believe that the Illuminati was formed in 1776 in Bavaria, its history predates this. It has been "tied directly through Masonry to the sun and Isis cults of ancient Egypt."[28]

However, many historians believe that the Egyptian mystery religions date back to the period after the flood, when Noah's grandson, Nimrod (son of Cush), became the wicked and powerful King of Babylon. He was so wicked that he actually married his own mother, Semiramis. He was later killed by his uncle, Shem (another of Noah's sons), because of his vile ways.

After his death, Semiramis declared Nimrod to be the sun god, Baal. Two of the many other names he was given were Sol and Tammuz. Manley P. Hall, a 33rd degree Mason, wrote in *The Secret Teachings of All Ages* that "Sun worship played an important part in nearly all the early pagan Mysteries.... The Solar Deity ... was slain ... and brought back to life and became the savior of His people."[29]

Semiramis became the goddess of the mystic religion of the Chaldeans and was called Ishtar (the goddess of love and fertility) and Rhea (the great mother of the gods). This occultic religion was carried over from the Chaldean (Babylonian) culture into the Egyptian culture as Isis, goddess of fertility; the Caananite culture as Ashtoreth, goddess of fertility; the Phoenician culture as Astarte, goddess of love and fertility; the Roman culture as Venus, Queen of Heaven; the Greek culture as Aphrodite, goddess of love and beauty and also Cythe*rea*; the Teutonics culture as Eostra, goddess of Spring; and finally, in Western culture, as Easter, the goddess of fertility.[30]

In the year 1090, Hassan Sabath, a member of the Ishmaelian sect of Islam, formed the "Order of Assassins." They were known to have used hashish and murder in their search for *illumination.*

There have been other authors who have stated that Joachim of Floris founded another group of *Illumined Ones,* in the eleventh century. This group taught a doctrine of "poverty and equality," but later became quite violent and began stealing from the wealthy.

Illuminati was used in 1492 by Menendez Pelayo relating to the Alumbrados of Spain. They were condemned by the Catholic Church in 1623.

In 1786 in Bavaria, a prominent attorney named Von Zwack (code name "Cato"), provided the evidence for the existence of an international order known as *The Illuminati.* It is important that this evidence was not provided voluntarily, but was seized by authorities, acting on a tip, in a raid on Von Zwack's home. The members of this secret society fled to all parts of Europe and elsewhere and the organization continued their plans. In 1798, George Washington, in a letter addressed to Rev. G. W. Schneider, said:

> I have heard much of the nefarious and dangerous plan and doctrines of the Illuminati, but never saw the book until you were pleased to send it to me. It was not my intention to doubt that the doctrine of the Illuminati had not spread in the United States. On the contrary, no one is more satisfied of this fact than I am....[31]

Whether or not the ideas of later "fellow travelers," such as John Ruskin or of future collaborators such as Rhodes, Milner, Rothschild, Morgan, Rockefeller, House and others, were influenced directly by Weishaupt (code name "Spartacus") is unclear. However, the indirect influence on these men and their enterprises, methodologies, and ideas is quite clear, as we shall see.

But for now, we need to look at the core doctrine, strategy, and tactics of the Illuminati's plan for world domination.

Adam Weishaupt was a Jesuit priest and professor of Canon Law, at Ingolstadt University in Bavaria (which today is a part of Germany). His pervasive use of occultic symbols and practices in his secret order strongly suggests that he had extensive contact with, if not involvement in, other secret societies or occult organizations.

Rev. Clarence Kelly, a noted author on the Illuminati and Free Masonry believes that Weishaupt most likely had contact with Lodge Theodore of the Masons, an occultic group within Free Masonry as early as 1774 (three years before he became a Mason), because Lodge Theodore appears in the correspondence of the Illuminati. There are several references made to an inner ring under "the secret chapter of the Lodge of St. Theodore."

Weishaupt's thesis, as summed up in *The Protocols,* was the antithesis of the traditional theology and philosophy taught by the church and the educational system and closely resembled the philosophy of Lodge Theodore. Author Ralph Epperson, in his book, *The Unseen Hand,* says:

> There is reason to believe that Weishaupt's contempt of religion started on July 21, 1773, when Pope Clement XIV "forever annulled and extinguished the Jesuit order."
>
> The Pope's action was in response to pressure from France, Spain, and Portugal, which independently had come to the conclusion that the Jesuits were meddling in the affairs of the state and were therefore enemies of the government.
>
> The response of one ruler, King Joseph of Portugal, was typical. He "hastened to sign a decree by which the Jesuits were denounced as traitors, rebels and enemies to the realm..."
>
> So the three nations presented "the categorical request that he (the Pope) should suppress the Jesuit order throughout the world."
>
> The Pope agreed and banned the order.[32]

Whether or not the banning of the order was the cause of Weishaupt's contempt for the church and religion is questionable. It is more likely that the banning was a result of the activities undertaken by the Jesuits, developed out of an already existing anarchistic, anti-church, and anti-Christian opinion.

However, it is clear that many, even in America, viewed this Society as evil. When the Order was restored by Pope Pius VII in August of 1814 to their former "rights and privileges," former president John Adams wrote to

Thomas Jefferson, "I do not like the re-appearance of the Jesuits. If there was ever a body of men who merited eternal damnation on earth ... it is this Society...."[33]

It is probably fair to assume that as a former Jesuit priest, Weishaupt, who in all likelihood already hated the church, was concerned by the actions of the Pope. Quite possibly he harbored a desire to create an organization strong enough to "protect" himself and the other Jesuits, and perhaps even ultimately overthrow the institution of the Catholic Church (which for all practical purposes, represented the embodiment of Christianity in the mind of Weishaupt).

To this day, one of the aims of the Princes is to eliminate Christianity. The reasons for this specifically anti-Christian sentiment are plethora and will be discussed later. But in simplest form, Christianity represents a Sovereignty above the sovereignty of the State and as such represents the sword of Damocles hanging over the head of any "would-be" world, dictatorial power.

The "theology" of Weishaupt was a compilation of the ideas of philosophers such as Jean Jacques Rousseau and the anti-Christian doctrines of the Manicheans. Additionally, it is believed he was indoctrinated in Egyptian occultism in 1771 by a dubious, traveling merchant named Kolmer, who was reported to have traveled Europe in search of converts. For the next five years, this Jesuit priest, born in Germany on February 6, 1748, formulated a plan under which all occult systems and secret societies could be reduced to a singular, all-powerful, and all-encompassing organization.

Modern recorded history has typically given the Illuminati only brief mention, if they have mentioned it at all. *The Encyclopedia Britannica,* (15th ed, F.N. "Illuminati") describes the Order of the Illuminati as follows: "A short-lived movement ... founded as a secret society in 1776 in Bavaria by Adam Weishaupt, professor of cannon law at the University of Ingolstadt and a former Jesuit. Its aim was to replace Christianity by a religion of reason. It was banned by the Bavarian government in 1785."

At best, this cursory explanation is misleading; at worst, it is absolute fraud. It neither chronicles the depth of the madness of Weishaupt, nor the depth and expanse of his secret society which was embraced by many intellectuals and men of power of his day. Further, is it passes lightly and matter-of-factly over a key statement which says, "Its aim was to replace Christianity by a religion of reason." This statement becomes extremely important, as later we discover that *The Protocols* became the founding principles of the *Communist Manifesto.*

Weishaupt believed, "When at last reason becomes the religion of man, so will the problem be solved."[34]

He also taught, according to Epperson, that "there was a need for world government to replace what used to be the national governments. This entity was in turn to be ruled by members of the Illuminati: 'The pupils (of the Illuminati) are convinced that the order will rule the world. Every member therefore becomes a ruler.' "[35]

While Weishaupt believed in world domination and ownership, controlled by himself and his *illumined ones,* (a phrase used by many New Age disciples today), he adopted, at least for public dissemination, one part of Rousseau's theology, which stated:

> The first man who bethought himself of saying, "This is mine," and found people simple enough to believe him, was the real founder of civil society. What crimes, what wars, what murders, what miseries and horrors would he have spared the human race [if someone would have warned;]...Beware of listening to this imposter; you are lost if you forget that the fruits of the earth belong to all and the earth to no one.[36]

This is, in fact, the basis for world communism. That property, and the possession of the same, is the ultimate evil. It follows then that ownership is the substance of war, murder, stealing, and all other evils under the sun. Again, this is the antithesis of the heretofore universally taught doctrines of Christianity that existed in Europe. Rousseau, and subsequently Weishaupt, taught that ownership went against the natural order of things.

Nesta Webster, a noted historian, sights nature itself as a refutation of the concept of Rousseau:

> Ownership of property ... is not peculiar to the human race. The bird has its nest, the dog has its bone that it will savagely defend.... if everything were divided up today all would be unequal again tomorrow. One man would fritter away his share, another would double it by turning it to good account, the practical and energetic would soon be more prosperous than the idler or the wastrel. The parable of the ten talents perfectly illustrates the different capacity of men to deal with money.[37]

Weishaupt believed that the concept of ownership of property was

51

resultant of mankind's abandonment of his "noble" nomadic life, in deference to a sedentary life of fixed residence. And, as later espoused by the creed of communism, man should disavow any individual ownership in property: "To each according to his need, from each according to his ability." Again, while this was his espoused position, there is no historical record of Weishaupt ever taking this "noble" action himself. In contrast, his goal of world domination of government, with himself and the other illumined ones sitting on the seat of power, would directly contradict this philosophy. Like all good, megalomaniac pragmatists, he believed that the "end justified the means."

What Weishaupt and his current disciples really want is for each of us to give up all that we have to the beneficent and benign control of the Princes, leaving everyone without any ownership of personal liberty — except, of course, the beneficent Princes, to whom each of us bow in allegiance.

The Protocols involve twenty-four general and sweeping postulates, which outline the belief system of Weishaupt and the "illumined" ones. This plan for world-wide subversion will be discussed in greater detail later in this Section, but in essence, they can be categorized into five principles. These five points were and still are the cornerstone of Weishaupt's, and subsequently his ideological descendants, vision of the New World Order.

1. Abolition of all ordered governments including monarchies and republics, and the establishment of democracy; which devolves quickly into false freedom and mob rule.

2. Abolition of a sense of patriotism and nationalistic intent.

3. Abolition of inheritance and any sense of ownership in private property through societal collectivism.

4. Abolition of the family, family life, the institution of marriage, collective ownership and communal education of children.

5. Abolition of all religion - specifically Christianity, which was to be replaced with humanism - the worship of reason.

Upon examination of these principles, one quickly finds that the teachings of Weishaupt are diametrically opposed to the basis of western thought and the Judeo-Christian values, recorded in the Bible, upon which this country was established. Exemplary of this would be the concept of *democracy*.

Remember that this country was established upon the basis of a constitutional Republic, not upon the premise of democracy. Our Founding Fathers warned repeatedly of the evils of democracy, because democracy is the ability of the majority, or for that matter, a vocal minority, to steal the unalienable rights from all others in society by a majority vote. That then is *mob rule.* The basis then for governance changes from that of eternal absolutes of right and wrong to "mob psychology."

As history is quick to point out, mob rule is always the quickest road to anarchy and its subsequent reign of terror. This is always followed by the knee-jerk reaction of the people demanding that law and order be restored. On almost every occasion, this has led to absolute, totalitarian or dictatorial rule. This, of course, fits in with the grand design of the Order of the Illuminati and the New World Order proponents of today.

Interestingly then, when we look at the correlation between the modern father of the New World Order in Weishaupt, and further down the road to the enlightened thinker, Ruskin, and his disciples, Rhodes, Milner, Rothschild, Baruch, Morgan, and the rest of the "boys club," we see a commonality in two ways.

First, we see commonality in the design of their secret societies. All insist on secrecy and deal in subterfuge.

Secondly, we see a commonality in ideology. That is, in all, we see the same five points as the guiding philosophy of these men. In some cases, as in the case of Weishaupt, and to some extent Ruskin, and Rhodes, we see these taking written form. However, in all cases, we see the actual belief in these points, although not always in written form, very clearly demonstrated in the practical outplaying of their one-world government scenarios.

They camouflage their actions through the actions of others, constantly hiding behind people or institutions of purportedly good intent.

Chapter 3

Free Masonry

In 1777, Weishaupt was initiated into the Masonic Order, the Lodge of Good Council, in Munich, Germany. His purpose was not to become part of this benevolent order, but to infiltrate it and to control it altogether.

In fact, the Masons held an International Congress at Wilhemsbad in July, 1782, and "Illuminism" was injected into Freemasonry by indoctrinating the Masonic leaders....[38]

At the acceptance of the Order of Illuminati into Free Masonry, we see an intermingling and, at the same time, a divergence of the forces that would create, institute, and dominate a New World Order, under the auspices of the Red Internationale. There is, yet, a second leg of this unholy alliance, which has gathered itself under Free Masonry, the New World Order capitalists. While many of the players shift back and forth between the Red and Golden Internationales, there is a barely perceptible, yet very important, battling of the forces of the New World Order. Some of the New World Order capitalists have been readily defined and will be further defined in the rest of Section II. However, it is incumbent upon us, now, to begin looking at the role of these members of Free Masonry in the institution of one-world government.

In the game plan of the Red Internationale (or specifically, Free Masons), the United States was a strategic piece to be captured enroute to a universal democracy — a "New Atlantis." In the early 1600s, this plan fit neatly, if not perfectly, into a tradition passed down for thousands of years and kept safe, in what was, at the time, the greatest commonwealth the world had ever known, the British Empire.

Masons in England believed that North America was, in fact, the continent, from which the New Atlantis would spring. Many believe the

55

legend of Atlantis is beyond myth and is pure silliness, but famed, Masonic writer, Manley P. Hall, claimed that the legend of Atlantis was central to the teachings and philosophies of all secret societies. To that extent he might be right. Hall claimed that Free Masonry is "... a shadow of the great Atlantean Mystery School, which stood with all its splendor in the ancient City of the Golden Gates, where now the turbulent Atlantic rolls in unbroken sweep."[39]

Hall and other illumined Free Masons describe the destruction of Atlantis as a tragedy; however, many researchers believe that the destruction of Atlantis parallels the Biblical account of the flood. We are told in Genesis that the destruction of the earth, and with it, Atlantis, was necessary because the pre-flood world had become so vile, violent, and corrupt.

> And God looked upon the earth, and, behold, it was corrupt; for all flesh had corrupted his way upon the earth.
>
> And God said unto Noah, The end of all flesh is come before me; for the earth is filled with violence through them; and, behold, I will destroy them with the earth.
>
> And, behold, I, even I, do bring a flood of waters upon the earth, to destroy all flesh, wherein is the breath of life, from under heaven; and every thing that is in the earth shall die.[40]

Author and supposed Atlantian authority, Ignatius Donnelly, in 1882, wrote that the uncanny similarities between the Atlantian destruction and the Great Flood of Genesis proved that they were, in fact, the same event. He states:

> "The deluge plainly refers to the destruction of Atlantis and that it agrees in many particulars with the account given by Plato. The people destroyed were, in both instances, the ancient race that had created civilization; they had formerly been in a happy and sinless condition; they had become great and wicked; they were destroyed for their sins - they were destroyed by water."[41]

I find it remarkably quizzical that this corrupt society, which in Plato's version was the destruction of Atlantis, and in the Biblical account was the pre-flood society of Noah, is identical to the New World Order society, which the Princes are trying to reinstate upon the current population of the world. It is also interesting that the very Christianity, that both of these utopian societies have decried and would abolish, predicts the coming of such a society, in Matthew 24:37-39 which says, "For the coming of the Son of Man will be just like the days of Noah. For in those days, which were before the flood, they were eating and drinking, they were marrying and giving in marriage, until the day that Noah entered the ark."

Plato wrote about Atlantis around the year 400 B.C. in his dialogue, the *Critias*. His writings were taken from an account originating with the Greek philosopher, Solon, who is credited as being the father of Greek democracy.

Critias is said to be the oldest recorded legend of Atlantis, but according to author, William Still, in his book, *New World Order: The Ancient Plan of Secret Societies* says, "... information about Atlantis is still possessed by the highest initiates of the secret societies."[42] Manley P. Hall details in his book, *The Secret Destiny of America,* how Solon obtained his information.

In summary, he says that Solon, while studying with the priests, in the temple of Isis in Sais, Egypt, was told the story of Atlantis around 595 B.C. Solon was taken by the priests underground to secret caves. The Nile River flowed through these chambers and here the priests and Solon boarded a boat and were taken to an island.

On the island he saw columns which he was told were placed there by a "lost people" which had the laws of the Atlantians inscribed upon them. These laws were left inscribed as a guide for mankind until the Atlantian civilization would once again prosper.

They stated that Atlantis had been destroyed when the father of all gods, Zeus, became angry at the sixty million inhabitants' transgression of the laws. His anger was so great that it caused the entire island to sink beneath the sea, taking with it all of the people and culture of Atlantis. Hall believed that "the philosophical empire [Atlantis] would come again, as a democracy of wise men." In the record of almost every civilization, for which ancient legends exist, the one thing that they all uphold in common is a flood tradition in the distant past.

In a letter written by Albert Pike on July 14, 1889, to the 23 Supreme Councils of the world, he said:

> That which we must say to the crowd is we worship a God, but it is the God that one adores without superstition.
>
> You may repeat it to the 32nd, 31st and 30th degrees -- The Masonic religion should be, by all of us initiates of the high degrees, maintained in the purity of the Luciferian doctrine.
>
> If Lucifer were not God, would Adonay and his priests calumniate him?[43]

Manley P. Hall wrote in *The Lost Keys of Freemasonry:*

> When the Mason learns the key to the warrior on the block is the proper application of the dynamo of the living power, he has learned the mystery of the Craft.
>
> The seething energies of Lucifer are in his hands and before he may step onward and upward, he must prove his ability to properly apply energy.[44]

That the base philosophy of the illumined Masons, and subsequently, the Red Internationale is this Luciferian society of Atlantis, or the Atlantian Covenant, is well documented. However, it is important again that I remind the reader that because there is subterfuge, corruption, and maniacal intent within an inner circle of Free Masonry, do not presume that all Masons are evil, maniacal men. On the contrary, evil men, throughout history, have deceitfully used, as Pawns, those who knew nothing of their scurrilous plans. But, at its core, at its inner circle, the enlightened initiates ...

those in charge, have a philosophy identical to the philosophical bent of Weishaupt and others. It is Luciferian.

Chapter 4

The First Move

The world is governed by very different personages from what is imagined by those who are not behind the scenes.

Benjamin Disraeli

The truth frequently seems unreasonable; the truth frequently is depressing; the truth sometimes seems to be evil; but it has the eternal advantage, it is the truth, and what is built thereon neither brings nor yields to confusion.

Henry Ford I

Most people sometime in their lives, stumble across the truth. Most jump up, brush themselves off, and hurry on about their business as if nothing had happened.

Winston Churchill

As the madness continued, none but the most naive thought that life would ever be the same again. The forces of anarchy were well-organized and well-financed. The body politic had disintegrated to a state of paralysis, in large part due to the indecisiveness and lethargy common to a government and a people, who have abandoned their core values, which act as a rudder for the ship of state and society at large.

Now a state of siege existed throughout the land. Political figures were being taken captive by the roving bands of citizen gangs. The blood ran in the streets. The innocent were being brutally murdered, and the butchers called these executions. Over seventy thousand Christians had been slaughtered for their intolerance and heresy to the world's religion. During the riots, stores were being looted, arms stolen, and no one was safe — even in their own home.

The revolution which had started, supposedly as a political statement

59

against repression of the people, had devolved into a bloodbath. The three Internationales had come together in a frighteningly powerful, unholy alliance.

The Golden Internationale had affected disruptions in the shipping of food and other necessities to the riot ravaged cities and ports. As a result, the people in frustration, anger, and confusion had completely lost confidence in the government's ability to alleviate the problem.

The financial system of the Nation had been treasonably undermined by the powerful global bankers. The national debt had increased five-fold in the last decade. Inflation was running rampant. Financial chaos was the order of the day.

Within the government the Red Internationale had done its job well. They had managed, in just a decade, to place people in important policy making positions throughout the government. As the head of state called endless conferences, summits, and other gatherings of the brain trust, little did he know, that with every mindless meeting, the demise of the nation drew ever closer. With every meeting, there was more confusion and more indecisiveness as the saboteurs contrived endless debate and conflicting advice. Ever more paralyzing, mixed signals were sent to a government already plagued by a lack of direction and a clear plan of action. The result was not just a lack of right actions. It was a complete lack of any action. Even incorrect actions may have accidently worked. But there was no action. To the people, this translated to a "let them eat cake" attitude by the government.

But perhaps most devastating was the work of the Black Internationale. Their maniacal brand of *theolotics* (the theology of politics) had left the people and the heads of state with no core principles upon which they could rely. Anyone who relied on the anachronistic principles of God and country was seen as the enemy. This was a new order, and this new order had no time for such nonsense as Biblical Christianity. Christianity was, in fact, the antithesis of the new order. The power of all spiritual guidance and decisions rested, not in some outdated book, but rather, in the representative of "god" in the flesh. Only the foolhardy dared question the voice of *Reason*. To do so would probably cost you your life.

In the national assembly the final dye was cast. For some time the members of that body had become more and more corrupt. Instead of leading the people in virtue, they in many cases led the charge to perversity, but this was the ultimate. Now for all the world to see, they had touched and had been touched by the madness of the land. In a grotesque display of decadence, a scantily clad stripper had been ceremoniously placed in the front of the national assembly. And as she was slowly stripped naked by lecherous assistants, she was crowned the "goddess of Reason."

Christianity and worship of a deity were banned by the government. This was the Age of Reason. This was the culmination of the new order. God was dead — long live Reason. And still the madness raged. The cities were riot-torn war zones. Only the dead knew peace — and in the madness peace had come to many.

What you have just read is not a futuristic story of someday in the New World Order. This is history. This is the story of the French Revolution. The events, while loosely depicted, and written with a certain amount of literary license, actually took place. A prostitute/stripper was brought before the national assembly and crowned the goddess of Reason. Christianity and deity worship was banned in the new French Republic for more than three years.

The three Internationales did come together in an unholy alliance in the French revolution. In fact, over 70,000 Christians were martyred in the madness. Pope Gregory XIII, gleeful over the slaughter of these "heretics," gave that the messenger who had brought him the news of the French Revolution 1,000 crowns (gold coins). A parade then commenced to the Church of St. Louis where a special mass was performed.

Bastille Day is still celebrated in France on July 14th, in support of the myth that the people of France overthrew the oppressive King Louis XVI and Marie Antoinette, beginning with the storming of the Bastille prison. The storming of the Bastille was supposedly to free the political prisoners. However, this does not square with history. According to Nesta Webster, "A plan of attack on the Bastille had already been drawn up, it only remained now to set the people in motion."[45]

It would appear that the real plan of attack was to storm the Bastille, not to release political prisoners (supposedly hundreds of them were imprisoned there) but rather, to capture the much needed weaponry to start the revolution. In fact, when the mob, which was made up of some angry Frenchmen but lead by mercenaries from the south of France, Italy, and Germany, reached the Bastille, they found only seven prisoners. This raid, supposedly to free oppressed political prisoners from the "political torture chamber," contained four forgers, two lunatics, and the Comte de Solages, who had been imprisoned for "monstrous crimes against society," at the request of his family. This torturous, dark dungeon had fallen into virtual disuse since 1776.

61

Like the later Communist or Bolshevik Revolutions, a common myth also sprang up that the French Revolution was a massive uprising of the people. This is simply a myth of history. "Out of 800,000 people living in Paris only approximately 1,000 took any part in the siege of the Bastille...."[46]

According to Webster, another observer of the French Revolution was Lord Acton, whom she quotes as saying, "The appalling thing in the French Revolution is not the tumult but the design. Through all the fire and smoke, we perceive the evidence of a calculating organization. The managers remain studiously concealed and masked; but there is no doubt about their presence from the first."[47]

So, one might reasonably ask, what does this have to do with how far the Princes of the New World Order have come? The answer must be given in two parts. First, we see the convergence of the three Internationales collaborating to float a "trial balloon," which was to become the established pattern for the New World Order. Secondly, we see the underlying strategy, which has been, and is still being, employed in the establishment of the New World Order.

Professor John Robison, A.M., Professor of Natural Philosophy, and Secretary to The Royal Society of Edinburgh, in studying the effects of the Illuminati and Free Masonry on the French Revolution, in 1798 stated: "I have seen that the most active leaders in the French Revolution were members of this Association, and conducted their first movements according to its principles, and by means of its instructions and assistance...."[48]

Whether one examines *The Protocols,* the *Communist Manifesto,* or any other of the related works written on the overthrow of governments, these same strategies and tactics are employed.

We will first look separately at their plans and then see how they merge collectively to usher in the advent of the New World Order. I think it is important to remember that while each of the Internationales is competitive with the other two, all three are bent upon the same end result. Therefore, while competing among themselves, they will never get to a point of dissolving their globalist plan for the New World Order; so, while at times competitive, it is also important to remember that the Princes flow effortlessly in and out of each others ranks, with quiet comfort and grace.

Remember, also, that throughout history, entire generations of globalists and internationalists have given their life's work over to the dream, the goal, and the vision of creating the New World Order.

It is also important to remember that this is not some high-minded utopian, spiritual dream. This is a real, live, flesh-and-blood, sinew-and-bones plan and has been in existence, in modern history, since the days of the Illuminati, and prior to that, with their founders and their mentors.

So it is, in this section, that we will examine a number of specific types and examples that will lead us to the formation of the New World Order. They fall primarily into three categories; and yet, each one overlaps and invades the space of the other. The three prime categories would be the economic, political, and spiritual aspects of the New World Order. It is important to see that each of these three major components has literally hundreds and hundreds of minor components. And, in fact, it is these minor components which have been individual keys to the success of the Princes.

There have been those who have seen the foreshadowing and impending onslaught of the New World Order. Unfortunately, all too often those who have caught a glimpse of the New World Order have seen only tiny pieces of the leviathan. As such, they saw issues or symptoms of the New World Order and have mistakenly thought that the issue or symptom displayed was the enemy. Consequently, all too often, they have found themselves like Don Quixote, tilting at windmills.

The war against the New World Order has been fought on an issue-by-issue basis, as opposed to a category-by-category basis. That is to say, that many good-hearted, well-meaning, and honorable people have been fighting to their last breath, hundreds and hundreds of issues that were either insignificant to the plan, or, in fact, smoke screens to draw attention away from the plan. They have, thereby, wasted their time, money, and in some cases, their entire lives.

With the vast power and financial capabilities of the proponents of the New World Order, to fight them on an issue-by-issue basis is bound to bring defeat. It would be like putting out one small brush fire in the middle of a raging forest fire; while the intentions are good, they are of little effect, and all are consumed in the inferno.

It is important that we begin to establish the broad or general outlines of the working plan followed by each of the three Internationales as they go maniacally along their way to the New World Order. We will examine their points of commonality and their points of conflict, but in general we will discover that while each has its own master plan, they are frighteningly similar in structure, methodology, and intent. The three Internationales will eventually create a shared system called the New World Order.

Those who would establish the New World Order are at the bottom line pragmatic. They are not citizens of a specific nation; they are *globalist*. If it means that they have to destroy a system which they have built, which we call communism, and replace it by the same system using another name with a slightly different look, they will do it. If they have to destroy the economy of the United States to bring about their world hegemony, they will do it. To them, as pragmatists, **the end does justify the means.** If, in fact, it means the destruction of tens of thousands of people in Somalia, Croatia, China, the former Soviet Union, Germany, or wherever, the end ultimately, in their minds, justifies the means. The end, of course, is to establish a New World Order, which concentrates economic, political and "religious" hegemony and control of that hegemony in their hands.

Meanwhile *The Game of Princes* plays on. **America, Europe and the entire world are being duped into believing that it is the complexity of life and the random forces of history that are shaping world events.** They systematically ridicule and destroy the credibility of anyone who would oppose their globalist attempt. But wise and prudent men throughout history, from George Washington to Winston Churchill; from Abraham Lincoln to John F. Kennedy; right up through today's modern leaders, including Margaret Thatcher, Ronald Reagan, and others, have understood the globalist intent of these Princes. They have begun to see the "Unseen Hand," described so aptly by Ralph Epperson in his monumental work by that title.

In his book, *When the World Will Be As One,* Tal Brooke makes an interesting observation:

> If it takes communism to get the Eastern bloc and Asia in line, fine. Or if it takes some varied socialism for modern Europe, fine. If America needs a New Age bromide, no problem. The meshing of the net of steel to capture the world has been a quiet conspiracy out of public view. Its big events, as we shall see, have taken place at quiet meetings where an elite few move enormous amounts of capital. The superrich and the superbrilliant have teamed up while the masses watch television and eat at McDonald's. Their small, dull, prosaic worlds never embrace the truly colossal perspective around them. And should one of the masses look up for a second, there is always an army of experts, intellectuals, and skeptics to ridicule any suspicions. It is the "complexity of life" argument tied in with the "random forces of history" argument that sages of today use to numb a public deeply preoccupied with their own immediate problems.[49]

And so it is, that the major works of history, the plans to consolidate the planet under a New World Order, go unnoticed. The warnings of our Founding Fathers go unheeded and The Princes maniacal vision remains unseen. Meanwhile, we the masses, like sheep, are dramatically preoccupied with Monday Night Football. Should we, or should we not, purchase that new house, new car, or other material opiates which have enslaved us to a system of indebtedness, lethargy, moral nonchalance, and the selling of our national soul, our heritage, history, and even our constitutional/Biblical values, upon which we built two hundred years of almost unbroken and certainly unprecedented, scientific, economic, moral, political and cultural prosperity.

However, the same cannot be said of the shadowy figures who have moved according to a master plan, behind the dark curtain of history. We find ourselves now in a world scarred with misery, suffering, and lack, balanced on the other side by the moving of the *Unseen Hand* of greed, avarice, and power. We must begin looking at the master plan, which guides these unseen forces, which are aptly summed up in *The Protocols*. Written by Adam Weishaupt and his Illuminati friends, *The Protocols,* for all intents and purposes, were not original thoughts. They were, in fact, mere plagiarists of Plato's *Republic.* However, they were brilliant, in the respect that they were both pragmatic and expansionistic upon those simple economic, political, and spiritual concepts of the early form of what we know as communism. They and their ideological descendants have been fiendishly clever in the public relations approach they have taken, in the packaging, and selling of the New World Order.

For instance, one of President Clinton's former financial advisors is Derek Shearer, an avowed New World Order Socialist. In a speech and later in his book, *Economic Democracy,* he stated: "In the U.S. we can't use the "S" word (*socialism*) too effectively.... we have found that in the greatest tradition in American advertising the word 'economic democracy' sells. You can take it door to door like Fuller Brushes, and the door will not be slammed in your face."[50]

Hence, in the Clinton-Gore campaign we heard the new term for socialism - *economic democracy.* Take a tired, failed, and destructive concept, wrap it in pretty paper, tie it about with a nice pink ribbon, and *voila!* What you couldn't give away to the American people, they will now pay good money for.

It is to our chagrin, that we, in the last forty years, have been so preoccupied with the labels of communism, socialism, and other titles that we have missed the grandest target — the New World Order. Soviet communism, in and of itself, was not and is not a threat to the United States or the world. It is, rather, a symptom created by, expanded upon, and exploited by the New World Order establishment. If, in fact, the plan of the New World Order, based upon *The Protocols,* were not so evil, and its implementation so treacherous and murderous, the New World Order establishment would indeed deserve our applause for their insight, their dedication, and their brilliance.

Unfortunately, in light of their dramatic achievements toward world enslavement, we must not only *not* applaud their efforts, we must expose and stop them, while there is still time. We will not discuss the step-by-step detailed plan for stopping the Princes of the New World Order dead in their tracks in this country here, but I can tell you, that it is all I can do to finish this section, so that I can move on to finally give you the blue print for victory. However, before we can stop the New World Order ...

we must fully understand the plan and view it in light of both historical context and current world events.

Chapter 5

The Game Plan

In *The Protocols,* we see the entire game plan for the establishment of the New World Order. We will attempt to arrange these in topical order. As you recall, we talked about the five fold attack of those who would create the New World Order. Listed in order they are:

1. Abolition of all ordered governments including monarchies and republics, and the establishment of democracy; which devolves quickly into false freedom and mob rule.

2. Abolition of a sense of patriotism and nationalistic intent.

3. Abolition of inheritance and any sense of ownership in private property through societal collectivism.

4. Abolition of the family, family life, the institution of marriage, and the substitution of collective ownership and communal education of children.

5. Abolition of all religion - specifically Christianity, which was to be replaced with humanism - the worship of reason.

Because *The Protocols* predate many of the other documents discussed, we will use these as the basis, or the foundational belief system, operational plan, and strategy for establishing the New World Order. We will see how these five basic steps in the strategic plan have been employed in the undoing of America. We will mix with these five basic strategies both the ten planks of the *Communist Manifesto,* as well as other documents which are nothing more than expository additions to the foundation of *The Protocols.* To repeat an earlier statement: were it not so maniacal and evil, one would have to sit back and admire the brilliance of the plan to establish the New World Order.

Most historians agree that in the growth and decline of civilizations, there are three phases which occur. The first is a period of expansion. The second is a period of conflict, within and without a civilization. And finally, there is a process of decay. Each is marked by distinct characteristics. However, the transition from one phase to another is sometimes blurry. Also, there may well be significant periods of overlap.

In most cases, there are events, to which one can point, that are, if not catalysts, at least symptomatic of catalytic events. That is to say, the shifting from one phase to another always has a direct cause; however, the events which mark the transitions may not be the direct cause of the shifting of phases, but rather, may be symptomatic of a long process or series of causes, which precede the moving from one phase to another. This transition process will become more clear as we begin to examine certain historic events in these United States.

While identifying by a specific date in history, the event that caused the shifting from one phase to another in the progression of a civilization, or in this case, these United States, may be difficult; we can at least mark those points in history where the pressure of change found a weak point, in the make up of society, and burst forth in an historic event. As an example, while we may not know exactly when the tiny little cracks began to form in a dam, it is very easy to mark the time and date when the dam actually broke.

However, if we are to learn from the example of the breaking of the dam, we must seek to understand what caused it to break. Such is the study of civilization. The exact date of the beginning of a period of decay in a civilization is not always easy to pinpoint. Nor is any phase in the three phase process irreversible. A nation in decline is not necessarily a nation that is irretrievably destined to fall. There can be significant periods of decline in a nation, and then, for whatever reason, that nation can begin again to undergo a period of expansion ... starting the cycle over again.

If the course of a nation is to be changed for good or for bad, it is important to understand what it is that makes nations or civilizations rise or fall. Understanding these forces allows the course of history in a civilization to be altered. While tactics for changing a nation can indeed be complex, the strategy is really rather simple. All one needs to do is find out what core values the nation or civilization held at its inception or its apex (which one generally finds to include the same core values), then identify the foundational source for its core values. Then one can begin to undermine that foundation and its related belief system.

That is exactly the plan followed by the Internationales or Princes who are working to submerge this nation into the New World Order. Even as you are reading this book, and wondering if all of this could possibly be true ... they are working.

Protocol Number 1

Political freedom is an idea but not a fact. This idea one must know how to apply whenever it appears necessary with this bait of an idea to attract the masses of the people to one's party for the purpose of crushing another who is in authority. This task is rendered easier if the opponent has himself been infected with the idea of freedom, so-called liberalism, and, for the sake of an idea, is willing to yield some of his power.

Our right lies in force. The word "right" is an abstract thought and proved nothing. The word means no more than: — Give me what I want in order that thereby I may have a proof that I am stronger than you.

In any state in which there is a bad organization of authority, an impersonality of laws and of the rulers who have lost their personality amid the flood of rights ever multiplying out of **liberalism,** I find a new **right** — to attack by the **right** of the strong, and to scatter to the winds all existing forces of order and regulation, to reconstruct all institutions and to become the sovereign lord of those who have left to us the **rights** of their power by laying them down voluntarily in their **liberalism** [emphasis mine].

So then the question must be asked, how does one create chaos in the midst of order? Chaos always leads to fear and confusion and the clamor of the people for someone to lead them.

Chaos is the first cousin and precursor to totalitarian rule. Indeed, it was chaos that brought Napoleon to power in France. In the chaos and resultant fear of that period of France's history, the people found the blind leading the blind. When the blind lead the blind the result is inevitably that they fall into a pit ... the pit of confusion, fear, and panic. Fearful people perceive, mistakenly, that anything is better than what they have. Panic then leads to the acceptance of anybody who will lead. In France at that time, that "anybody," was Napoleon.

The rise to power of Adolph Hitler and the Nazi Party in pre-World War II Germany was a result of chaos. The Treaty of Versailles signed at the end of World War I, virtually assured World War II and the rise of a Hitlerian type. The demanded "reparations" assured political, spiritual, and economic chaos in post World War I Germany. It is interesting to note that the negotiators of that treaty were John Maynard Keynes (British economist), Paul Warburg (Chairman, Federal Reserve Bank), Max Warburg (head of German banking firm M.M. Warburg & Co. and brother of Paul Warburg), Lord Curzon (British Foreign Secretary), John Foster Dulles (a founder of the CFR), and Allen Dulles (later Director of the CIA). All of these men were advocates, and more, champions of the New World Order.

Those who would create a New World Order have perfected chaos and subtly directed it to produce desired results. It is the direction of the forces of chaos in specific areas and at specific targets that we shall now examine.

Without the effects of "liberalism," it is impossible to tear down a society. It is this liberalism which is the catalyst for chaos, in the body politic and in society in general. Liberalism is not, as some may think, purely a political or social phenomenon. Rather, it is, according to *The Protocols,* a new *liberalism* of the core values, or an eroding of the moral or Biblical Law (Law-Word) foundation, which can redirect a nation.

Historians agree that the basis for any successful society has been a law system, based on a moral code, which has always used as its foundation "religion." Therefore, liberalism in America, because of our Christian or Judeo-Christian foundation, had to attack the principles of Biblical Law if the other four stratagems of *The Protocols* mentioned earlier were to be successful.

Let us then move forward in that maniacal plan for a New World Order, as it first embraces and then crushes the life out of our unalienable rights of "Life, Liberty and the pursuit of Happiness." Remember that the basis for success in all areas of the five general categories outlined earlier is the successful undermining of the moral/religious heritage of this Nation. Remember also, according to the Founding Fathers, the origins of our free constitutions and the principles of liberty were, in fact, built on a foundation of "Biblical Christianity." Thus, an attack, or more precisely, a twisting of the meaning of the Constitution and Bill of Rights, was, and is, an attack on the founding principles of the Nation. In the case of the Church Of The Holy Trinity v. United States, 143 U.S. 471, the Supreme Court in 1892,

70

after mentioning various circumstances, stated: "... These, and many other matters which might be noticed, add a volume of unofficial declarations to the mass of organic utterances that this is a Christian nation."[51]

Today as we examine society in America, we see attacks on the traditional understanding of rights. This has led to the invention of some of the most ridiculous "rights" ever imagined. Animal rights is a good place to start. How do animals get rights under the Constitution of the United States? Since when is it the unalienable right of an animal to the "pursuit of Happiness?" Just exactly how does an animal pursue happiness? I realize that there are millions of pet owners out there who love their pets and want to take care of them and provide them with a good home. However, this is the pursuit of happiness for the owner — and not the pet. I have never yet met a dog who aspired to the Presidency of the United States. While I have been in the "dog house" for things I have done, and while I have heard of "cat houses" (a few of them legally operated in Nevada or Texas), I have never met a cat who aspired to build a four bedroom, three bath home, in the "burbs," complete with a three car garage, into which it could not fit the two feline family cars, for lack of space. Further, the Batmobile is not owned by a bat family from Hackensack, New Jersey.

I believe that human beings have an obligation to treat all of the creation, including animals, with decency. But, to go from this position to the plague of animal rights laws (now pervasive all over this country), is to move from the sublime to the ridiculous. Some animal advocates will literally attack, both verbally and physically, those poor, unenlightened souls who have the brutish gall to wear a fur coat while passing through an airport. There are many reported cases of such fur-bearing humans being sprayed with paint, showered with blood, and even physically assaulted, when they were unfortunate enough to cross the path of these rabid sympaticos of animal rights.

Interestingly, Hitler's New World Order (Nazi Germany) was marked by a preoccupation with animal rights. In their book, *Understanding Nazi Animal Protection and the Holocaust,* authors Arnold Arluke and Boria Sax, describe how Hitler's Third Reich passed numerous animal protection laws. They believed even shoeing a horse was being abusive.

German laws were enacted that ended animal experimentation and dissection for research, while at the same time, experiments were conducted on humans, usually without anesthesia, on the most efficient surgical means of castrating Jews. The Nazis justified these actions in their belief that it

71

was possible to:

> ... increase the moral standing of animals and decrease the moral standing of people, thus integrating human characteristics to animals.... Animals were to be protected for their own sakes, rather than their relationship to man ... "returning to the animal nature within man, communing with nature, and elevating animal life to the level of cult worship, as alternatives to modernity, technology, and urbanization ... would lead to the spiritual and ideological changes necessary ... for a new national self-identity."
>
> Around 1935, the Nazis shifted their concentration on protection of farm animals and pets to include wildlife. They talked of "establishing conservation and breeding programs," and passed laws governing hunting.[52]

Sound familiar? In this country we have more environmental and animal protection laws than can be read, yet, both abortion and euthanasia are on the rise. Like Hitler, we somehow disparage human life, while passionately protecting animal "rights."

We all know of welfare rights, gay rights, rights of "free speech" — which has devolved into the right to obscenity, vulgarity, and pornography. Supposedly, we have human rights, ecology rights, minority rights, women's rights, handicapped rights, and with all of these rights — the average American citizen has no rights. Because the unalienable rights, upon which this country was founded, have been thrown out to make room for all of these other supposed rights, America has come to a point where the Bill of Rights of the Constitution of the United States has been so perverted that only the perverted are protected.

The forces of the New World Order have brought about a condition of chaos, just as they said they would, amid the flood of rights, ever multiplying out of liberalism. Recent surveys indicate, whether it is the past administration of George Bush or the successor administration of Bill Clinton, that Americans feel that America is on the wrong track. People instinctively feel that something is drastically wrong. Most analysts believe that the election of Bill Clinton was not so much a support of his ideology and world view, but rather, a sense of foreboding about the direction that the country was heading.

How then does this relate to the five-fold strategy of the Internationales to dissolve this country into the New World Order? Actually, the question

72

has already been answered. In the attachment of so many parasitic **rights,** the life blood of the unalienable rights has been sucked off by the vampire forces of **liberalism,** which are the fangs of the New World Order. In the next several chapters we will discuss in detail the step by step plan of the Internationales to implement their plan for a New World Order. Keep in mind, however, that this is not a new concept.

The idea of a New World Order in America is as old as America.

Chapter 6

Sweet Democracy

1. **Abolition of all ordered governments including monarchies and republics, and the establishment of "democracy;" which devolves quickly into false freedom and mob rule.**

This is a time of frustration and confusion for most Americans. The uncertainty about our economy, banks, and industry, even our spiritual and moral values, is at an all time high, according to numerous national polls. Even our future and our past seem uncertain in the minds of many. That empty nagging feeling of "impending disaster" hangs like a dull gray shroud over the heads of Americans. The professional doom and gloomers of television, radio, newspapers, state and national legislatures, and even the pulpits have finally convinced America that all is not well. Unfortunately, most of the doomsday rhetoric they espouse is the potentially fatal consequence of our present course of action, should we continue on that course.

Our economy is in a mess. Our banks, savings and loans, pension funds, insurance companies, and stock market are hanging by a financial thread. Crime is at an all time high; citizens, and especially women, are no longer safe in their own homes, let alone out in public and unprotected. Nationally, we are bankrupt with a $4 trillion plus national debt, which is growing at a pace of over $1 billion a day. Many Americans are only one or two paychecks away from homelessness; and personal and business bankruptcies are at an all time high.

Industrially, we are behind and quickly falling further behind the economic powers of Europe and Japan, as our economy has for three decades been shifting to a "service economy." Our trade deficits with foreign nations are soaring, and there seem to be no viable solutions being offered by either major political party.

Even the supposed "death" of communism, once a cause for rejoicing, has revealed a dark side. As White House-led Congressional budget cutting in defense continues unabated, hundreds of thousands of defense, military, and military-related jobs are disappearing. What was supposed to produce a "peace dividend" has, in fact, produced massive unemployment and an economic stumbling block.

Unfortunately, in addition to the economic problems that our massive disarmament has caused, we have left ourselves in a vulnerable military position. On October 1, 1992, only six Senators voted against the Strategic Arms Reduction Treaty (START). This treaty requires:

> ... radical changes in U.S. strategic nuclear forces in ways that will reduce their robustness, survivability and perhaps even their deterrent value.... Under its terms, the former Soviet Union can retain a vast first-strike potential and the capacity to break out from or cheat on START's limitations that give nightmares to hard-headed strategic planners.
>
> ... START verification provisions permit Russians to have eight hours' notice of U.S. missile inspections. During that period, warheads that exceed START limits could be removed from missiles to conform to treaty limits....[53]

According to Howard Phillips, Chairman of the Conservative Caucus: "Cheney and Bush closed down a key element of SDI [Strategic Defense Initiative], thus making it impossible for us to have a strategic defense until the year 2002, at the earliest."[54]

And yet, according to most reliable sources, Russia, and several members of the Commonwealth of Independent States (the former Soviet Union), still have all of their nuclear weapons and — guess what — they are still aimed at the United States. Now for the bad news. According to Pentagon sources, as much as 80 percent of Russia's Gross National Product (GNP) is now being expended on weapons production.

Even as communism "disappears," the world is becoming an ever-more dangerous place. Wars and rumors of wars persist. Famine, pestilence, disease, earthquakes, and other disasters seem to capture the headlines daily. Worse, there are no apparent answers in sight.

In the midst of all of this, the two institutions upon which, historically, we were able to depend — the family and the church — seem to be in a state of decay. AIDS, pornography, drug abuse, homosexual activism, abortion, environmental problems, and the new rise of racial and class tensions, occupy much of our elected representative's time. It seems strange, that with all of the collective wisdom of the leaders in state capitals and in Washington, D.C., that none of these collective brain trusts are seemingly able to solve even one of these problems.

America is scared, uncertain, and ready for a change. Perhaps, this is best evidenced by the Perot phenomenon of the 1992 elections. Even with Mr. Perot's entrance into the presidential sweepstakes, the candidate of preference for most Americans was not on the ballot: none of the above.

In a speech made at the first national convention of the U.S. Taxpayers Party in New Orleans, Louisiana in September of 1992, Jack Gargan of THRO (Throw The Hypocritical Rascals Out) said:

> Just about that time [after the Korean War], a cartoon made its first appearance in the papers; it was called "Peanuts." From the beginning, Lucy would tee up the ball at the start of the football season, and she'd say, "Come on Charlie Brown, kick the ball."
>
> At first he'd come running and at the last second, she'd snatch the ball out of the way and he'd end up on his tail. Every year you figured, "Come on, Charlie Brown, you're going to wise up one of these days."
>
> But every year, Lucy conned Charlie Brown. She'd say, "Charlie, I promise you, *this time* I won't pull the ball away."
>
> Now here it is, football season, and Lucy is going to tee up the ball and say to Charlie Brown, "Come on, Charlie, kick this ball."
>
> So help me, he's going to do it again. Sadly, that's the story of American politics.[55]

While Jack Gargan is in no way affiliated with the U.S. Taxpayers Party, and there are many issues upon which I am in firm disagreement with him; on this one issue, I am in complete agreement. This portion of his speech reminded me of a television commercial I saw several years ago. The ad, which was for margarine, depicted a French chef, who refused to use the margarine. However, when pressured, he finally tasted the product and exuberantly declared, "There is no *difference!*" It is unfortunate, but true, that the same can be said of the Republicans and Democrats of today's monopoly parties.

I am sure that right now there are several "dyed in the wool" Republicans and Democrats who are chafing at this statement. However, if one is interested in truth, it is important that we begin examining the evidence to see if this statement can be supported. To do so perhaps a short historical perspective is in order.

In 1776, these United States were instituted as a complex republic. The election of representatives was significantly different from the system which we have today. For instance, before the seventeenth amendment to the Constitution, the state legislatures chose those who would serve in the Senate of the United States. The net effect was two-fold. First, elected officials, who were responsible to a small group of people from their home area, would choose for the people, the individual who was to serve as their Senatorial Representative, in Washington D.C. This caused them to be, in many cases, more prudent in their choice. First, they had to face the folks back home for careless or imprudent decisions; and secondly, it made those Senators responsible to a small and usually better-informed group of political accountants, namely their State Legislature.

The changing of the vote from a small informed group (the State Legislature) to a larger group (the entire population of the state), changed America to a simple republic, which is nothing more than a democracy. Such democracy is, in reality, nothing more than the rule of the "proletariat," which according to Karl Marx, in the *Communist Manifesto,* is the first step toward communism.

This fundamental change is important because it gave rise to changes in the foundational system of this nation. It removed, for all practical purposes, the ability of the less than affluent to represent the people of the state in Washington. The reason for this is simple. No longer was an individual able to meet with a few hundred people and clearly express to them how he would represent the people of his state in Washington. Instead, now he would have to be a man of means, or at least one to whom means were available, because to win office under the seventeenth amendment, one had to run state-wide campaigns. This, of course, was the beginning of the end for our republican form of government. Because of the requisite money needed for influence in the media, for state-wide travel in campaigns, and for campaign finances in general, one had to be willing — in order to have his back scratched — to promise to scratch a few others when the time arose.

As the process for electing Senators was changed from the "few in the state capital" to the "voice of the people," in reality, the people lost *any* voice they once had. The process was now in the hands of the rich and powerful. As one might expect, with no accountability to a small, select group of well-informed examiners, these Senators, now the new barons of power and influence, needed only tell the people what they wanted to hear and all would be well. For who could examine what they had actually done? Being so far away, and with "such a complex business as the federal government" they were, for the most part, insulated from those to whom they were supposed to have accountability.

In addition to the selection process of Senators, the number of members of the U.S. House of Representatives was frozen at 435. The Constitution originally stated that the states were to have one representative for each thirty thousand people, and that no state should have less than one. This was later changed to reflect proportionately the population growth, with a maximum seating of 435. Ostensibly, this had the same effect as the change in the election of senators, which would come later, inasmuch as the number of people represented by an individual in the House of Representatives was greatly enlarged, making the Representative less accountable to a smaller, more homogeneous group of the citizenry. As such, the government of the United States began to take on a "way off in Washington" mentality. This would not have been so bad if the House of Representatives was limited in its power as the Constitution had insisted.

As a result, a number of concepts, which were previously thought unconstitutional, were introduced by the Congress. Most of these were cloaked in "general welfare" rhetoric and served not, as was supposed by the masses, for the good of the people, but rather, for those who were bent on mass centralization of power for the federal government. This is a very important concept as expressed in the following Protocol.

Protocol Number 5

> ... We shall create an intensified centralization of government in order to grip in our hands all the forces of the community.... These laws will withdraw one by one all the indulgences and liberties which have been permitted ... to wipe out any unenlightened who oppose us by deed or word.

As we view America today, only the most naive or traitorous would suggest that government is more effective than in the past. With every new regulation, we lose more and more of our freedoms. When one considers that this was the intent of the Princes, one can only say that they have been remarkably successful.

Perhaps one reading this chapter would say, "This is America, we are the most powerful, wealthiest, and freest nation on the face of the earth." To that person, I would issue this challenge: Think of one thing that you can do that is not controlled by the government, or one of its agencies. In my lectures I often pose this challenge to my audiences, and then they attempt to come up with one thing that we can do that is not regulated by the government. The list usually includes:

I can take a walk. Wrong. The minute that your feet hit the sidewalk or "public" street you are regulated by city, county, state, or national regulatory groups. And if you stay on your own property, your walk is still being restricted because you are imprisoned in your walking to that which is yours and yours alone, not to mention the zoning placed on your property by some government agency, which in some cases (wetland areas), even restricts where one can walk on his own property.

I can go for a ride in my car. Wrong. The "government" owns the streets upon which you must drive. They have taken for themselves the power to grant licensure for you to drive your car; they have dictated that the car must be built under the power of the Federal Trade Commission (FTC), and they have determined how much fuel will be available to an area, and to a large extent, how much that fuel will cost, by the amount of taxes and environmental regulations they place on the sale of a gallon of it.

Finally, after naming about ten, fifteen, or twenty things that audiences erroneously believed they still had control over in their life, someone will say, **"I can pray."** But even this has come under severe restriction. If you pray in your church, you can only pray privately if that prayer contains certain political topics. Because under the IRS regulations, restricting the activities of churches under the provisions of their 501(c)(3) status, all but the most general political prayers are restricted. Further, one is not allowed to pray in schools, public buildings, or for that matter, in public, unless you do it silently. Otherwise, you might inadvertently offend someone else. And, if you are forced to pray silently, then the form of your prayer is even dictated by the state.

So the challenge remains to think of one thing that you can do that the state is not in some way acting in a regulatory capacity; from building your house to repairing your house; to when and how often you can mow or water your lawn; to opening and running a business; to making out a business plan to comply with the standards set by OSHA, EPA, EEOC, IRS, and hundreds of other regulatory bodies. The centralization of power in mega-government is nearing completion, which we shall examine in still more detail shortly.

While former President George Bush ran on a Republican Party platform of "less government" involvement in the lives of the citizens, the proliferation of federal regulations increased more dramatically during his term of office than in any previous presidential administration.

Since the goal of the New World Order Princes is centralized power, they had the right man in George Bush. Not only is he a member of The Order (Skull and Bones) and the CFR, but he is also the son of Prescott Sheldon Bush (now deceased Senator from Connecticut), who, in the 1930s, was on the Board of Directors of Union Banking Corporation of New York. This bank, along with Guarantee Trust of New York (Morgan Family), was one of the heaviest financiers of the Nazi Regime.

Union Banking Corporation had the following Directors: E. Roland Harriman, Director and Vice President and a member of the Skull and Bones Society; H.J. Kouwenhoven, Director and Nazi Banker who was Managing Director of the Bank Voor Handel; J.G. Groeningen, Director and Nazi Party member of the Steel Cartel; C. Lievense, Director and President of Union Banking Corporation of New York; E.S. James, Director and Partner of W.A. Harriman and Company, that also financed the Soviet Union for years.

Prescott Bush was also a partner in the private, international banking firm of Brown Brothers, Harriman for over forty years. This banking firm is said to have also financed the Soviet Union. Prescott Bush had knowledge and participation in the financing of both Hitler and the Soviet Union.[56] Carrying on the family tradition, President Bush spent billions of your hard-earned tax dollars to continue financing the Soviet Union.

During the 1992 Presidential debates, Presidential candidate Bill Clinton revealed that Prescott Bush opposed Joseph McCarthy during the Senate hearings on Un-American Activities. Considering the folks he was involved with, is it any wonder?

George married Barbara Pierce of the Pierces of Rye, New York. Her father, Marvin Pierce, in 1954, was the president of McCall Corp., of *McCall's Magazine* fame.[57] Her brother, Scott Pierce, formerly the president of E.F. Hutton, was, in May of 1985, charged with over 2,000 counts of check kiting, which according to Jack Anderson of the *Washington Post,* cost the United States taxpayers "billions of dollars." He plead guilty to check kiting (mail fraud), but was never sentenced for these charges. In this

81

multi-billion dollar debacle *no one* went to prison. *Now that's what I call a kinder, gentler America!*

George Bush will probably be best remembered for two things: one was his now famous Presidential campaign promise in 1988, "Read my lips — no new taxes," which upon his election was followed by one of the largest tax increases in the history of this country; and, secondly, for his popularization of the term "the New World Order." While much mention was made of this New World Order by those in the media, they all feigned ignorance as to its meaning or implications.

Perhaps, even more interesting, is the fact that during the Presidential election of 1992, all three candidates for that position, the highest office in the land, were members of, or had ties to the CFR. Lest anyone think that I am just out to crucify Mr. Bush, I should also tell you that President Bill Clinton, a Democrat, is also is a member of the CFR and the Trilateral Commission.

The "Independent" candidate, H. Ross Perot, while not listed as a member of the CFR, is apparently tied to the organization. In fact, the seconding letter for Perot's entrance into the CFR was written by none other than Bush himself. Whether Perot's invitation to that organization was later rejected by the CFR, or by Perot, or whether he is just an unpublished member of that organization, as is widely speculated, we don't know.

We do know that John P. White (his chief campaign issues coordinator) served in the Carter Administration. Another advisor, Felix Rohatyn played an important role in both launching and advising the Perot movement during his on-again and off-again Presidential campaign. Both are members of the CFR.[58]

What a strange race Mr. Perot ran. Why would he, at the height of his popularity, suddenly and without any credible explanation, drop out of the campaign, only to re-enter the race when Bush was beginning to make strides in the polls? Does it not also strike you as strange that a man like Bill Clinton should receive such overwhelming support from the media with his obvious shortcomings, womanizing, and at least the appearance of discrimination in employment practices?

If one didn't know better, one would almost believe that it was a ... well we can't say the "C" word ... everybody knows that only "Kooks" believe in "Konspiracy." (Notice I didn't say the "C" word). To further allay any fears we might have, the "church" has for the last twenty years also told us that only Kooks believe in Konspiracies. And most have sworn to protect the sheep from "Konspiratorial Nuts" and "Kommie Chasers."

It is, therefore, reasonably safe to assume, because all three candidates associate with the CFR, that they all espouse a similar view of the New World Order. After all, if one is a member of a bridge club, one assumes that such an individual knows how to play bridge and enjoys playing the game. Likewise, membership in an exclusive organization like the CFR would indicate that its members accept and adhere to those philosophies which are part and parcel of the CFR.

No matter how you slice it, all three of these candidates were members or in ideological harmony with the powerful Council on Foreign Relations. They have a lot of company. Most of the movers and shakers throughout the United States and around the world are members of either CFR, Trilateral Commission, or one of its sister organizations. It is interesting to note that while Bush, Clinton, and Perot all professed different plans and used different music in their "wooing" ... they all wanted the same thing: to dance us into the New World Order.

A vast amount of research has gone into uncovering the goals, purpose, the secrets of the CFR. While we have yet to specifically define this New World Order, we can at least begin to sketch an outline of the CFR's version of the New World Order.

The CFR is one of the major power brokers in U.S. and world-wide politics. Before we can proceed to look at the specifics of the CFR's version of the New World Order, we need to look at the founders and the foundations. As a wise man, a gardener with limited English once told me, "So goes the root, so goes the tree."

So what is the origin or belief system of this mysterious Council on Foreign Relations (CFR)? From what dark origin did it spring? What is its purpose and how did it rise to such a position of preeminence and power? Perhaps we can begin tracing both its intent and origin by studying what those who know it best have written and said.

Antony Sutton states that within the CFR there are a group of individuals who belong to a secret society, the Order of Skull and Bones, who are sworn to secrecy, and who, more or less, control the CFR. The meetings are used for their own purposes to promote their ideas and to "weigh up people who might be useful, to use meetings as a forum for discussion."[59]

For some time it has been rumored that the CFR and Trilateral Commission are the shadow government of the United States. Through their members, alliances, power, and control of financial systems, they may secretly run the world. However, when asked about this, CFR President Winston Lord assured us, "The Trilateral Commission doesn't secretly run the world. The Council on Foreign Relations does that."[60]

Incidently, Winston Lord is also a member of The Order (Skull and Bones). Maybe he wasn't joking when he made the claim that the CFR runs the world. While his remark was possibly made "tongue-in-cheek," I believe there is much truth both in hidden and revealed humor. His remarks are further solidified in the words of Dr. Carroll Quigley:

> ... there is an inner core of intimate associates who unquestionably knew that they were members of a group devoted to a common purpose and an outer circle of a larger number on whom the inner circle acted by personal persuasion, patronage distribution and social pressure. It is probable that most members of the outer circle were not conscious that they were being used by a secret society.[61]

The public relations department of the CFR says that they are a policy study group. Their publication says that they are not connected with the government, nor do they do any government contracting, etc. However, it is difficult to know exactly what goes on behind the CFR's closed doors at the Harold Pratt House, 58 East 68th Street, New York, N.Y. or at its Washington address, located at 2400 N Street, N.W., Washington, D.C. As stated in the By-Laws, reconfirmed by resolution of the Board of Directors on September 11, 1973:

> ... no Council meeting shall be made generally open to the public or media except upon action by the Council's Board of Directors.
>
> Notwithstanding the above Rule, the Board of Directors may, from time to time, prescribe rules governing the subsequent release of any Council records.
>
> ... the reformulation would make it legitimate for a U.S. governmental official to report by memo to his colleagues and superiors what he learned at a Council meeting. Similarly, the reformulation recognizes that a lawyer may give such a memo to his partners, or a corporate officer to other corporate officers. It would not be in compliance with the reformulated Rule, however, for any meeting participant (i) to publish a speaker's statement in attributed form in a newspaper; (ii) to repeat it on television or radio, or on a

speaker's platform, or in a classroom; or (iii) to go beyond a memo of limited circulation, by distributing the attributed statement in a company or government agency newsletter. The language of the Rule also goes out of its way to make it clear that a meeting participant is forbidden knowingly to transmit the attributed statement to a newspaper reporter or other such person who is likely to publish it in a public medium. The essence of Rule as reformulated is simple enough: participants in Council meetings should not pass along an attributed statement in circumstances where there is substantial risk that it will promptly be widely circulated or published.[62]

The CFR, as one can see from the above By-Laws, is a semi-secret organization whose membership is published, but the minutes of its meetings are not. Why all the secrecy when their stated purpose according to the 1992 Annual Report is:

> ...a nonprofit and nonpartisan membership organization dedicated to improving understanding of American foreign policy and international affairs through the free exchange of ideas....
>
> As a leader in the expanding community of institutions concerned with American foreign policy, the Council recognizes its responsibility to contribute to the public dialogue on significant international issues.[63]

Although we don't see the words *New World Order,* the concept of a one-world government or global, central planning organization of some sort, is implied, particularly, if one goes beyond their annual report and reads their banner publication, *Foreign Affairs.*

Admiral Chester Ward, the former Judge Advocate General of the U.S. Navy and a former member of the CFR for over twenty years, stated that the CFR was formed for "the purpose of promoting disarmament and submergence of U.S. sovereignty and national independence into an all-powerful one-world government.... They are the ones who carry on the traditions of the founders.... This lust to surrender the sovereignty and independence of the United States is pervasive throughout most of the membership...."[64]

They state, on page 6 of the above mentioned Annual Report, "The Council on Foreign Relations has no affiliation with, receives no funding from, and does no contract research for the U.S. government or any other government. Its budget is funded through members dues, income from publications, subscriptions to its Corporate Program, endowment income, foundation grants, and voluntary gifts."

However, an examination of this club of the American elite reveals it has played a major role in shaping the thinking and/or ideology of its members and U.S. policy. James Perloff, in *Shadows of Power,* observed that:

> ... through early 1988, fourteen secretaries of state, fourteen treasury secretaries, eleven defense secretaries, and scores of other federal department heads, have been CFR members.... According to the CFR itself, as of June 1987, 318 of its members were current U.S. government officials.[65]

It is a fact that since the 1940s, better than 80 percent of all of the heads of the Executive Branch of the federal government have come from the ranks of the CFR and the Trilateral Commission. That is an extraordinary percentage when one considers that in 1992, the CFR listed only 2,905 members (by invitation only), and the Trilateral Commission far fewer! Former Trilaterals in Public Service include: George Bush, Richard C. Darman, Lawrence S. Eagleburger, Alan Greenspan, Carla A. Hills, Lowell Murray, Donald B. Rice, Brent Scowcroft, and William C. Winegard. (See Appendix A for 1992 List of CFR and Trilaterals.)

Can you imagine the hue and cry if even one President filled 80 percent of his cabinet positions with members of a particular religious denomination? For example, imagine if even one President filled 80 percent of his cabinet positions with constituents of the several million-member Southern Baptist Convention. The media, Congress, feminists, the homosexual community, and hundreds of special interest groups would be in an uproar. There would be so many demands for an investigation of the Presidents' actions that the noise would be deafening.

Yet the media, Congress, and special interest groups say nothing when over 80 percent of all the positions within the Executive Branch of the United States government, for over fifty years, have been filled by members of the CFR. Seems a bit odd, doesn't it?

A CFR position paper entitled *Study No. 7, Basic Aims of U.S. Foreign Policy* (1959) proposed that the United States seek to "build an international order." Some of the steps sighted as essential to this process were:

1. Search for an international order in which the freedom of nations is recognized as interdependent and in which many policies are jointly

undertaken by free world states with differing political, economic and social systems, and including states labeling themselves as "socialist."

2. Safeguard U.S. security through preserving a system of bilateral agreements and regional arrangements.

3. Maintain and gradually increase the authority of the U.N.

4. Make more effective use of the International Court of Justice, jurisdiction of which should be increased by withdrawal of reservations by member nations on matters judged to be "domestic."

Admiral Ward, after he left the CFR, had the following to say:

> Once the ruling members of the CFR have decided that the U.S. Government should adopt a particular policy, the very substantial research facilities of CFR are put to work to develop arguments, intellectual and emotional, to support the new policy, and to confound and discredit, intellectually and politically, any opposition.[66]

That the CFR is one of the most powerful organizations in the United States can hardly be questioned. Just a list of its membership clearly defines it as the preeminent "club" for the rich and powerful. The CFR's membership reads like the *Who's Who in America.* It includes most of the top names in the media, business, religion, charitable foundations, and politics.

As further evidence, consider the following of President Clinton's appointees: **Foreign Affairs:** Secretary of State, Warren M. Christopher (CFR Director 1982-91 and still member & TC); Secretary of Defense, Leslie Aspin, Jr. (CFR & IPS); National Security Advisor, W. Anthony (Tony) Lake (CFR & IPS); Director Central Intelligence Agency (C.I.A.), R. James Woolsey, Jr. (CFR); U.N. Ambassador, Madeline K. Albright (CFR); Deputy Secretary of State, Clifton R. Wharton, Jr. (CFR, Director 1983 - present); Under Secretary of State for International Security of Affairs, Peter Tarnoff (President 1986 - Present, CFR & TC); Deputy National Security Advisor, Samuel (Sandy) R. Berger (CFR); Chairman, Foreign Intelligence Advisory Board, William J. Crowe, Jr. (CFR Director 1990 - Present); **Monetary Policy:** Secretary of Treasury, Lloyd K. Bentsen (guest at 1992 Bilderburger conference); Director, Office of Management and Budget, Leon E. Panetta; Deputy OMB, Alice M. Rivlin (CFR Director 1989-1992 & TC); Deputy

Secretary of Treasury, Roger C. Altman (CFR); Chairman Council of Economic Advisors, Laura D'Andrea Tyson (CFR); Secretary of Labor, Robert B. Reich; Secretary of Labor, Robert B. Reich, (Rhodes scholar); Secretary of Commerce, Ronald H. Brown, (former law partner of Robert Strauss who is CFR & TC); U.S. Trade Representative, Mickey Kantor (LA attorney); Chairman, National Economic Council, Robert E. Rubin (Co-Chairman Investment banking firm Goldman, Sachs & Co.); Secretary of Health and Human Services, Donna E. Shalala (CFR Director 1992 & TC); Secretary of Housing and Urban Development, Henry G. Cisneros (CFR & TC); Secretary of Interior, Bruce Babbitt (CFR & TC); Economics & International Trade, Franklin D. Raines (CFR); **Domestic Council:** Agriculture, Mike Espy; Transportation, Federico Pena; Energy, Hazel O'Leary; Education, Arts, Labor & Humanities, Johnnetta Cole (CFR); and Natural Resources/Environment, Energy & Agriculture, James Gustave (Gus) Speth (CFR).[67]

Looks to me like President Clinton better not schedule any cabinet meetings at the White House on the same day as the Washington D.C. chapter meetings of the CFR or Trilateral Commission — or there won't be anybody left to attend *his* meeting.

For the position of Attorney General, Janet Reno was finally approved after Zoe Baird and Kimba Wood were "disqualified" on the grounds of employment of "illegal aliens." Reno's appointment was opposed by Florida attorney Jack Thompson. He testified to Strom Thurmond, former ranking Republican member of the U.S. Senate Judiciary Committee, that Reno had violated Chapter 800 of the Florida State Code, which states, "whoever commits any unnatural and lascivious acts with another person, shall be guilty of a misdemeanor of the second degree." He asserted that Reno is a closet lesbian, who has used call girls for sex and has harassed her office employees.

Thompson further claimed that Reno had worked with Donna Shalala, the new HHS Secretary, to "generate a fraudulent Florida Bar grievance against me because of my now proven-correct concerns about the University of Wisconsin's illegal sale of pro-homosexual audio tapes to the Dade County School system."

Additionally, Thompson stated, that in 1981, Reno was arrested for shoplifting at Jordan Marsh on Biscayne Boulevard in Miami, Florida; that she has a severe alcoholic abuse problem; and that he (Thompson) had "been told by an impeccable individual known and respected by every single Senator on the Judiciary Committee that the Florida Bar and the Florida Judicial

Qualifications Commission have never nominated Reno to a federal judgeship because of certain disqualifying characteristics."[68] Yet, even with all of this information, both the Republican and the Democratic members of the Senate voted unanimously for her confirmation as Attorney General. **There is no difference between the two "major" political parties.**

Heading the CFR is Honorary Chairman David Rockefeller, who is also the North American Chairman of the Trilateral Commission. The other Officers and Directors of the CFR as of September 1992, are as follows:

Officers: Peter J. Peterson, Chairman of the Board; B.R. Inman, Vice Chairman; Peter Tarnoff, President; John Temple Swing, Executive Vice President; Alton Frye, Vice President, Washington; John A. Millington, Vice President, Planning and Development; Margaret Osmer-McQuade, Vice President, Meetings; Nicholas X. Rizopoulos, Vice President, Studies; David Woodbridge, Treasurer; Ana Figueras, Assistant Treasurer; and Judith Gustafson, Secretary.

Directors: John E. Bryson, James E. Burke, John L. Clendenin, William S. Cohen, William J. Crowe, Jr., Kenneth W. Dam, Thomas R. Donahue, Robert F. Erburu, Thomas S. Foley, Maurice R. Greenberg, Richard C. Holbrooke, Robert D. Hormats, Karon N. Horn, James R. Houghton, Karon Elliott House, Charlayne Hunter-Gault, B.R. Inman, Jeane J. Kirkpatrick, Joshua Lederberg, Donald F. McHenry, Peter G. Peterson, Donna E. Shalala, Strobe Talbott, Paul A. Volcker, and Clifton R. Wharton, Jr. Other Honorary Officers and Directors Emeriti are Douglas Dillon, George S. Franklin, Caryl P. Haskins, Grayson Kirk, Charles MacMathias, Jr., James A. Perkins, Robert A. Scalapino, Cyrus R. Vance, and Glenn E. Watts.

Most Americans believe that the workings of our foreign policy and the decisions that are made fall under the direction of the President of the United States. However, such would not seem to be the case.

Even the CIA may well be co-opted in this movement toward global government. I offer the following from Larry Abraham, as just another thread which is binding down Gulliver. However, instead of the Lilliputians, who were the silly little men who bound Gulliver on a mythical island, *these men are very real.* They are not silly, nor are they little. They are playing a serious game. They are playing for *Cheque † Mate.*

> The full Central Intelligence Agency involvement in Watergate may never fully be known. According to former White House aide Charles Colson, Nixon thought the Agency was in on the plot "up to their eyeballs." Ask yourself this one very important

89

question: If the President of the United States doesn't control the C.I.A., and if it can work to unseat him, who *does* control it? One clue may lie in the fact that every CIA director, from its founder Allen Dulles, right up to this very moment, has been (and was before his appointment) a long-time member of the CFR, and that includes George Bush.[69]

Senator Jesse Helms recognized the CFR's involvement within the Establishment and made the following statement before the Senate in December 1987:

> The viewpoint of the Establishment today is called globalism. Not so long ago, this viewpoint was called the "one-world" view by its critics. The phrase is no longer fashionable among sophisticates; yet, the phrase "one-world" is still apt because nothing has changed in the minds and actions of those promoting policies consistent with its fundamental tenets.
>
> Mr. President, in the globalist point of view, nation-states and national boundaries do not count for anything. Political philosophies and political principles seem to become simply relative. Indeed, even Constitutions are irrelevant to the exercise of power....
>
> In this point of view, the activities of international financial and industrial forces should be oriented to bringing this one-world design — with a convergence of the Soviet and American systems as its centerpiece — into being.[70]

Founded in 1921, The Council On Foreign Relations has been accused of being the Princes' chief link to the U.S. Government. Arthur Schlesinger, Jr., a 1992 CFR member, has called the CFR a "front organization" for "the heart of the American Establishment."[71]

While the CFR came into existence on July 29, 1921, its history considerably predates that. To get a true picture of the ideology and founding of the CFR we need to journey back in history. Fear not, dear reader. I am not going to give you a boring history lesson with the dreaded pop quiz when I am finished. Rather, I am going to spare you the details and take you to the high points (or low points — depending on your point of view) of the CFR's history, and of its founders. Or as the Sundance Kid said to Butch Cassidy, "Who are these guys?"

Author Carroll Quigley states emphatically that there is a plan for a

New World Order. As "one of the boys," Dr. Quigley traces the beginnings of the CFR back to 1870, with the coming of John Ruskin to Oxford. Quigley relates:

> Until 1870 there was no professorship of fine arts at Oxford, but in that year, thanks to the Slade bequest, John Ruskin was named to such a chair. He hit Oxford like an earthquake, not so much because he talked about fine arts, but because he talked also about the empire and England's downtrodden masses, and above all because he talked about all three of these things as moral issues.[72]

So, who is this John Ruskin and what influence did he have on the world and, specifically, the course of America's history and the New World Order.

John Ruskin (1819-1900) was the London-born son of a wealthy wine merchant. He inherited position, fortune, and an Oxford education in art, literature, architecture, mathematics, as well as Latin and Greek. This much-traveled Oxford graduate became the Slade professor of Art at his educational home in 1870. However, it appears that art was really a secondary interest to him. He was a "social progressive" whose students participated in such diverse community experiments as road building.

According to W. Cleon Skousen in *The Naked Capitalist*, Ruskin "established the 'St. George's Guild' which was designed to set up a model industrial and social movement, to buy lands, mills and factories, and to start model industries or cooperatives on socialist lines." The Guild failed, but as Dr. Quigley points out, the ideas of Ruskin were planted in the fertile minds of his students who were the scions of the British aristocracy.[73] Ruskin believed that the state must take control of the means of production and distribution, and organize them for the good of the community as a whole; but he was prepared to place the control of the state in the hands of a single man. Ruskin said: "My continual aim has been to show the eternal superiority of some men to others, sometimes even of one man to all others...."

Skousen remarked concerning Ruskin's above statement:

> No doubt Ruskin underrated the corruptibility of man and the coarseness inherent in all forms of government. He would have been horrified by the exploits of Hitler and Stalin. In spite of its materialist philosophy, he would, I think, have approved of Communism; the peasant communes in China, in particular, are exactly on his model.[74]

If this type of statement sounds familiar to you, it should. This is, in effect, the foundational treatise of Marxist Socialism. According to Kenneth Clark, author of *Ruskin Today,* Ruskin "could not imagine a worse disease than the capitalist society of the nineteenth century." Reportedly, Ruskin was an avid, daily reader of Plato's *Republic,* which is, in the words of Clark, "... the source book of all dictatorships."[75] Plato advocated the following:

1. Ruling class with powerful army keeping society subordinate to authority of rulers.
2. Take over by whatever force necessary to eliminate existing government.
3. Use of force to eliminate existing social structures.
4. Elimination of marriage and the family. All women belong to all men and all men belong to all women.
5. Children to be raised by the State.
6. Women to be equal with men - to fight in wars and perform same labor.
7. Selective breeding under government control to produce children.
8. Inferior children to be destroyed.
9. Three classes of society: ruling, military, and workers. Classes would be determined by the rulers for all others.
10. All above to be taught as a "religious" principle.[76]

This same vision of the "ideal society" held by Ruskin was ex-pressed in the writings of Karl Marx, an obscure writer, whose name was not even attached to his work until twenty years after its publication. These writings teach citizens to "give up" their rights for the sake of the common good, but it always ends in a police state. This is called *preventive justice.* Control is the key concept. Read carefully these points from the *Communist Manifesto:*

1. Abolition of private property.
2. Heavy progressive income tax.
3. Abolition of all rights of inheritance.
4. Confiscation of property of all emigrants and rebels.
5. Central bank.
6. Government control of communications and transportation.
7. Government ownership of factories and agriculture.
8. Government control of labor.
9. Corporate farms, regional planning.
10. Government control of education.[77]

Ruskin spoke to the Oxford undergraduates as members of the privileged, ruling class. He told them that they were the possessors of a magnificent tradition of education, beauty, rule of law, freedom, decency, and self-discipline but that this tradition could not be saved, and did not deserve to be saved, unless it could be extended to the lower classes in England itself and to the non-English masses through the **world** [emphasis mine]. If this precious tradition were not extended to these two great majorities, the minority of upper-class Englishmen would ultimately be submerged by these majorities and the tradition lost. To prevent this, the tradition must be extended to the masses and to the empire.[78]

This, the opening address of Ruskin, had such a profound effect on a young disciple named Cecil Rhodes, that he copied it down by hand and carried it with him for the next thirty years. Ruskin's philosophical bent took root in the fertile mind of Rhodes. Coupling his ruling class philosophy with remarkable business acumen and financial support, which he received from Lord Rothschild and Alfred Beit, he was able to exploit and control the gold and diamond wealth of South Africa, with DeBeers Consolidated Mines and Consolidated Gold Fields. He attained the position of Prime Minister of Cape Colony from 1890 until 1896. According to Quigley:

> In the middle 1890s Rhodes had a personal income of at least a million pounds sterling a year (then about five million dollars) which was spent so freely for his mysterious purposes that he was usually overdrawn on his account. These purposes centered on his desire to federate the English-speaking peoples and to bring all the habitable portions of the world under their control. For this purpose Rhodes left part of his great fortune to found the Rhodes Scholarships at Oxford in order to spread the English ruling class tradition through the English-speaking world as Ruskin had wanted.[79]

Continuing on, Quigley says,

> Among Ruskin's most devoted disciples at Oxford were a group of intimate friends including Arnold Toynbee, Alfred (later Lord) Milner, Arthur Glazebrook, George (later Sir George) Parkin, Philip Lyttleton Gell, and Henry (later Sir Henry) Birchenough. These were so moved by Ruskin that they devoted the rest of their lives to carrying out his ideas. A similar group of Cambridge men including

Reginald Baliol Brett (Lord Esher), Sir John B. Seeley, Albert (Lord) Grey, and Edmund Garrett were also aroused by Ruskin's message and devoted their lives to the extension of the British Empire and uplift of England's urban masses as two parts of one project which they called "extension of the English-speaking idea." They were remarkably successful in these aims because England's most sensational journalist William T. Stead, (1849-1912), an ardent social reformer and imperialist, brought them into association with Rhodes. This association was formally established on February 5, 1891, when Rhodes and Stead organized a secret society of which Rhodes had been dreaming for sixteen years.[80]

Now the stage is set for the formation of Cecil Rhodes "secret society." To summarize Quigley, the major players were Rhodes (as the leader), Stead, Brett (Lord Esher), and Milner comprising the executive committee, and finally, Arthur (Lord Balfour), Sir Harry Johnston, Lord Rothschild, Albert (Lord) Grey, and others as members of a "Circle of Initiates," while there was to be an outer circle known as the "Association of Helpers," later organized by Milner as the Round Table organization.[81]

I realize that I have taken you down memory lane a century or so, but it was important that we establish the basis for what was about to emerge as the Council on Foreign Relations. With that in mind, let's go back to Dr. Quigley's *Tragedy and Hope.*

As governor-general and high commissioner of South Africa in the period 1897-1905, Milner recruited a group of young men, chiefly from Oxford and from Toynbee Hall, to assist him in organizing his administration. Through his influence these men were able to win influential posts in government and international finance and became the dominant influence in British imperial and foreign affairs up to 1939. Under Milner in South Africa, they were known as Milner's Kindergarten until 1910. In 1909-1913 they organized semi-secret groups, known as Round Table Groups, in the chief British dependencies and the United States. They still function in eight countries. They kept in touch with each other by personal correspondence and frequent visits, and through an influential quarterly magazine, *The Round Table,* founded in 1910 and largely supported by Sir Abe Bailey's money. In 1919 they founded the Royal Institute of International Affairs (Chatham House) for which the chief financial supporters were Sir Abe Bailey and the Astor family (owners of *The Times*).[82]

While in Paris, France for the Paris Peace Conference on May 30, 1919, at a dinner at the Majestic Hotel, Colonel Edward Mandel House, President Wilson's chief advisor, along with members of the Inquiry (a group of one hundred men from New York assembled by House), other U.S. internationalists (including such notables as Paul Warburg and Bernard Baruch), and some members of the British delegation to the Conference, met and resolved that an "Institute of International Affairs" would be formed. It would have two branches — one in the United States, the Council on Foreign Relations (CFR), and the other in England, which came to be known as the Royal Institute of International Affairs (RIIA). Do you see a common thread once again in the web? Again, quoting from Quigley:

> After 1925 a somewhat similar structure of organizations, known as the Institute of Pacific Relations, was set up in twelve countries holding territory in the Pacific area, the units in each British dominion existing on an interlocking basis with the Round Table Group and the Royal Institute of International Affairs in the same country.[83]
>
> There does exist, and has existed for a generation, an international Anglophile network which operates, to some extent, in the way the radical Right believes the Communists act. In fact, this network, which we may identify as the Round Table Groups, has no aversion to cooperating with the Communists, or any other groups, and frequently does so. I know of the operations of this network because I have studied it for twenty years and was permitted for two years, in the early 1960s, to examine its papers and secret records. I have no aversion to it or to most of its aims and have, for much of my life, been close to it and to many of its instruments. I have objected, both in the past and recently, to a few of its policies (notably to its belief that England was an Atlantic rather than a European Power and must be allied, or even federated, with the United States and must remain isolated from Europe), but in general my chief difference of opinion is that it wishes to remain unknown, and I believe its role in history is significant enough to be known....[84]

Please remember, this is the same Dr. Carroll Quigley that President Bill Clinton, in his acceptance speech for the Democratic Presidential nomination, named as his mentor, along with President John F. Kennedy. That would mean that Clinton is an ideological disciple of Dr. Quigley.[85]

> ... the American branch of this organization (sometimes called the "Eastern Establishment") has played a very significant role in the history of the United States in the last generation....[86]
> This front organization, called the Royal Institute of International Affairs, had as its nucleus in each area the existing submerged Round Table Group. In New York it was known as the Council on Foreign Relations, and was a front for J.P. Morgan and Company in association with the very small American Round Table Group.[87]

This cadre of secret world government proponents began making remarkable penetration into the power structures of the American press. They were able to accomplish this through their influence over five American newspapers. These papers included *The New York Times, New York Herald Tribune, Christian Science Monitor, The Washington Post* and the *Boston Evening Transcript.*

Because they used their money and influence to their shrewd advantage, the shadowy members of this secret society have been hiding behind their front organizations such as the Council on Foreign Relations and have for some time dictated American foreign and economic policies, and many aspects of life in America. As we will see shortly, their influence, if not outright control, has extended from the Ivy League to media (including the national television networks); from the governors' mansions of many states to the halls of Congress; and even to 1600 Pennsylvania Avenue. But more on that later. We need now to begin looking into this group's goals for world government, (with themselves, of course, in control), and the methods that they have used to bring about "change." This quote from Dr. Quigley speaks volumes concerning the plan of the Princes.

> The chief aims of the elaborate, semi-secret organization were largely commendable: to coordinate the international activities and outlooks of the English-speaking world into one (which would largely, it is true, be that of the London group); to work to maintain the peace; to help backward, colonial, and underdeveloped areas to advance toward stability, law and order, and prosperity along lines somewhat similar to those taught at Oxford and the University of

London (especially the School of Economics and the Schools of African and Oriental studies.)[88]

Why was it so important that these "nations" be taught along the lines taught at Oxford, the University of London, etc.? These were decidedly socialist. In fact, one could comfortably say that they endorse *global socialism* as the last best chance for the world. It would seem odd indeed that these men who were considered the ultimate capitalists would want to promote a system of socialism.

Perhaps it has something to do with the fact that under the form of government, such as we had before we strayed into socialism, Americans were fiercely independent, which independence was backed by a Constitution guaranteeing them the right to that independence. Whenever this is the case, the citizenry is almost impossible to control.

However, this is not the case under socialism. In a socialistic society rights no longer come as the Declaration of Independence says from a *Creator.* Rather, they are a privilege granted by the *State,* and therefore revokable by that State.

This concept is paramount to understanding the goals that this secret society has for the future of America and the world — specifically as it relates to this, as yet, "fuzzy" New World Order — fuzzy because the information given previously is still subject to interpretation.

Quigley, who is the ultimate apologist for these Insiders (or the Princes as I have called them in this book), contends that these are men of conscience whose ideology simply conflicts with the founding principles of America. But because he feels that their stated goals for some sort of world government (which will be defined in greater detail later) are for the most part benign, they are the ultimate act of good will and are the only hope of salvation for the world. Let us therefore proceed with what Quigley sees as benign intervention ... but which I define as

the conspiracy of the New World Order.

97

INTERLOCKED ILLUMINATI FRONTS

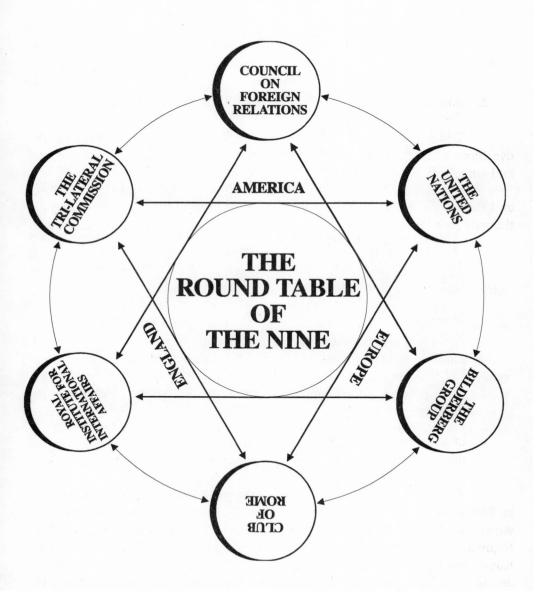

Chapter 7

Hug-A-Tree For Me

2. Abolition of a sense of patriotism and nationalistic intent.

Today, as we view the global crisis, we see the prospect of an evermore malignant environment in which we must exist, raise our children, and somehow safeguard for our grandchildren.

When individuals involved with the CFR, the Trilateral Commission, and the Order of the Illuminati are in control, it necessitates exploration of the past as a key to understanding their form of "governance" for the future.

> The time was passed for yet another polished-up version of the ancient empire of Rome, in which all of the world was forced to be Roman.
>
> Rather, the new globalist mind envisioned an interdependence that would somehow accommodate the fact of the world as a shrinking place,...
>
> Some means was energetically sought by a few, was desired by many, and came to be expected by all, through which every national and cultural entity would actively share in and contribute to the material development of all. Everyone would have to be on board, for inter-dependence required an absence of strife. And an absence of strife required that there be no have-nots, or "outsiders" among the nation.[89]

There are two ways of achieving the goals stated by Malachi Martin in *The Keys of This Blood.* You can simply exterminate the have-nots — which has been tried in the past, unsuccessfully, under the regimes of the Inquisition, Hitler, Lenin, Trotsky, Stalin, and today's communist leaders in Russia and China. The second, and most saleable choice, is to offer a utopian dream of wealth redistribution throughout the world, "to each according to his need, from each according to his ability."

Obviously, if you are going to maintain this distribution, it will have to be an active, ongoing process. If you took all of the wealth of the world and redistributed it, by tomorrow there would again be the haves and have-nots. But, faced with the threat of war throughout the world; faced with starvation of vast numbers of people; faced with environmental crisis, caused, in large part, by members of the Golden Internationale, we see the people, the masses, clamoring for someone who can take charge and make sense out of the chaos.

Perhaps the most devastating weapon in the New World Order government's arsenal is the environmental juggernaut. This is a frighteningly powerful tool, and under the thousands of pages of unconstitutional environmental laws - there's no one - and I mean — NO ONE — who is safe.

Before I begin a discussion of this problem, I want to go on record as being concerned about the environment. I believe, as I have stated before, that human beings have an obligation to treat all of the creation, including animals, with decency. Now, having said that, let's examine the effects of some of this heavy-handed, environmental legislation.

We are told that those who will be effected most by these "Green" laws will be the giant American corporations. If these are truly *American* companies, why would anyone in America want to pass such draconian laws? Does anyone wish to leave American companies crippled and unable to continue to compete in a meaningful way? Of course not — but don't worry — these are not *American* companies being "hurt," but large multinational corporations, which have secretly, from behind the scenes, been supportive, if not the originators of, many of these environmental laws. Their goal is to centralize power.

Steven Schmidheiny (enviromaniac, socialist, and wealthy elitist), in an article entitled "Business, Banking, and Sustainable Development" stated that he was startled, surprised, and elated that big companies — whom he hadn't expected to join (because of their environmental problems) — all joined up with Maurice Strong's front group, the Business Council for Sustainable Development. Can you imagine that companies like Dow, DuPont, Shell, Chevron, Nippon Steel, Ciba-Geigy, Alcoa, Volkswagen, and Nissan would join in?

He then goes on to mention that one major sector from which they had received no cooperation was banking. But now, they too are buying tickets to board the fast moving Green train.

The pattern is so familiar. First they oppose — then they "relent" and get on board. Naturally, we admire them so much for biting the bullet and doing the right thing. Well, it's not the right thing that they are doing. It is only the right thing for them. These draconian, environmental laws being passed under the auspices of the Rio Earth Summit, a United Nations function, and specifically sponsored in this country by the Environmental Protection Agency, are not putting Dow Chemical out of business. They are putting the mom and pop filling stations and dry cleaning businesses out of business. They aren't closing down the *Rockefellers* — they are closing down the *Little-fellers*.

A clear example, The Clean Air Act (CAA), which Bush signed November 15, 1990, will add to the current $32 billion cost of "clean air" in the United States, an additional $50 billion. The main costs, which will be borne by businesses, will inevitably result in higher prices to consumers, further exacerbating an already anemic economy.

Some experts believe that the total job loss, as a result of the CAA, will be 3.8 million. But this may well be only the tip of the iceberg. The CAA creates a Chemical Safety Board whose decisions and findings may not be reviewed by courts or the administration. Non-compliance may result in any person being assessed stiff fines and possible jail time. Pittsburgh now has clean air, but no steel mills.

Pollution control costs have gone ballistic; from $50 million in 1972, to $115 billion in 1989; and projections are that costs will rise to the neighborhood of $200 billion by the end of the decade. That's an expensive neighborhood! Economists (Alan Manne of Stanford University and Richard Rickels of the Electric Power Institute) have estimated that U.S. companies will have to spend $800 billion to $3.6 trillion in coming years, to cut carbon dioxide emissions to levels now demanded by environmentalists.[90]

Real dollars are probably much higher. But even by conservative estimates, because of the relationship of the cost of doing business and the availability of jobs, this translates to 4 million fewer jobs. Foreign companies do not have to operate under such Orwellian environmental laws, and so it is becoming increasingly more difficult for American companies to compete.

Estimates are that 150,000 businesses may have to secure individual EPA permits to do business; which could subject company executives with up to 450-year prison sentences and fines of $25,000 per day for non-compliance.

According to *Forbes* magazine, in 1990, the dollar cost for EPA regulation compliance was $1.4 trillion. Additionally, the EPA is offering "snitch" fees to disgruntled employees or competitors of up to $10,000 each.

The unconstitutional EPA, which was created by President Richard Nixon's Executive Order in 1970, began with 3,860 people and a budget of $303 million; today the EPA has a staff of 18,000 environmental terrorists with an annual budget of $4.5 billion. EPA admits that compliance with its regulations costs Americans $130 billion annually — or, $1,000 per family. The actual costs are probably twice that high. With this kind of a budget, they have been able to create a very convincing public relations lie.

Current EPA laws define as much as 70 percent of U.S. land as wetlands. The EPA and the U.S. Army Corps of Engineers have decided that wetlands don't even have to be wet; the presence of water 18 inches below the surface for just seven days a year, gives them just cause for declaring that area a wetland.

Richard McGown, a farmer in Missouri, faced prosecution because he restored 150 acres of brushland to corn production (which yielded an incredible 150 bushels per acre). Why? Because the U.S. Army Corps of Engineers had his land declared a wetland — simply because there were cattails on his property. Cattails! For crying out loud! By the way, these cattails later turned out to be wheat sorghum.

John Pozsgai, a self-employed truck mechanic, received three years in prison, five years probation, and $202,000 in fines for placing topsoil and clean fill dirt on his own property after removing 7,000 old tires from the former dump site. Pozsgai, a Hungarian refugee with no criminal record, was ordered to restore his property, not to what it was, but to a wetland condition according to plans drawn up by the U.S. Army Corps of Engineers. This is just one of a growing mass of similar cases. His crime was cleaning up his own land.

The Indianapolis Star on January 28, 1991, reported a senior citizen and his son who were ordered to serve twenty-one months in federal prison for putting nineteen loads of clean building sand on a ¼ acre lot on which he planned to build his retirement home.

On December 11, 1990, Chicago's Sierra Club "Swamp Squad"(an environmental, terrorist, spy mob), received a $50,000 grant to spy on developers and private land owners, who might potentially "violate" wetlands.

The EPA guidelines as amended in March 1989, under section 404 of the 1972 Clean Water Act, gives the EPA control over at least half of the farmland in America, and requires the land owners to obtain federal permits for usage.

Real estate has suffered tremendously as government legally steals land under EPA laws. This has caused wild fluctuations in land prices. Land dumping by the federal government has further hurt an already shaky market. Couple this with laws that require a contractor to clear his property usage with the U.S. Army Corp of Engineers and the EPA or face jail, and the recipe for disaster is on the books.

The Endangered Species Act is allowing several government agencies to grab and restrict land; as a result, "private land is quickly becoming a thing of the past."

Since 1965, the National Park Service has spent $4.66 billion to acquire 5,391,885 acres of private land for parks and open space. The federal government now owns more than one-third of the land in the United States. More than 91 million acres, one-eighth of the land, is now off limits to public access.

The U.S. Constitution says that the only land that can be owned by the federal government is for forts, magazines, arsenals, dock yards, and other needful buildings (such as federal court houses, national capitals, and etc). It makes one wonder, what is really going on behind the Green Door?

It appears, today, to be the Anglo-Saxon tradition vs. the public trust doctrine of the Justinian Code (an earlier version of what could be described as the god-State, of the super regulatory, and now demised Roman Empire). The Justinian Code maintains that in all private property, there is a broad-based and loosely defined (nebulously and, therefore, tyrannically applicable) public ownership interest. Therefore, land and resource grabs are a protection *for* the public interest and *from* private interests (and any potential damages which may be contemplated by the other owner, the private citizen).

This principle was used in the 8.5 million acre logging prohibition on federal land in the Pacific Northwest, where a habitat was created to protect the northern spotted owl. This resulted in the loss of 150,000 jobs in Washington, Oregon, and California.

This taking or killing of listed species extends to private property as well. Resultantly, seventy-acre "owl circles" now dot private land throughout western Oregon. The number of these circles is growing exponentially, as more and more of these "rare and endangered" species are found everywhere.

> Question: If they are so stinking rare, how is it that so many of them are being found?

Answer: It only stands to reason, at least to me, that if they are finding that many of them — they AIN'T that rare.

Question: What are many people doing when they find a spotted owl on their property?

Answer: Killing it and burning it so there will be no trace that this fine feathered fetter ever came near their property.

Al Gore has been leading the charge for protection of the spotted owl. He said:

> I helped lead the successful fight to prevent the overturning of protections for the spotted owl. In the spirited Senate debate, it became clear that the issue was not just the spotted owl but the "old growth" forest itself. The spotted owl is a so-called keystone species, whose disappearance would mark the loss of an entire ecosystem and the many other species dependent upon it. Ironically, if those wishing to continue the logging had won, their jobs would have been lost anyway as soon as the remaining 10% of the forest was cut.[91]

This is not a quote from some left wing, socialist, New World Order Nut — a nobody. These are the words of the left wing, socialist New World Order Nut that we elected Vice President of the United States! Does he not know that trees are being planted by the thousands, everyday, all over the country, to replenish the timber supply?

By the way, the spotted owl is only one of 570 varieties of animals, birds, fish, plants, and insects, currently on the endangered or threatened list. The Oregon Silverspotted Butter-fly's presence stopped construction of a golf course. The runs of wild salmon are affecting river traffic, irrigation, forestry, and hydroelectric power generation along hundreds of miles of the Columbia River and tributaries.

Another 274 million acres, including farms, ranches, industrial sites, even whole cities, are now officially "waters of the U.S.".

Similarly, even cattle herds are being effected. One rancher has been ordered to fence off a creek on his land, for which he owns the water rights, so that his cattle cannot drink from it. The argument is that the cattle may damage the habitat of the Laughton Cutthroat Trout, which has been declared endangered. Deprived of the use of his own water, this rancher will be forced to reduce the size of his herd by 25 percent from 8,000 to 6,000, with no compensation for his losses.

In Oregon's Klamath County, crops were drying in the fields and the wells were going dry. Spring rains did not come again, making it the seventh year in a row. Water was available from a local reservoir, but it couldn't be touched. The reservoir has become the "habitat" for two subspecies of suckerfish, which are protected by the Federal Endangered Species Act.

The gold mining industry had been clobbered with ridiculous fines, as much as $250,000, for accidentally killing four (that's 4!) common birds, which has led to the closing of fifty-four mines in the past two years.

And now, for the bad news, there are yet another 3,000 nominees on this elite, endangered, or threatened list. At the rate they are going, they can leave all of the "critters" off of the list and replace them with just one new one ... MAN!

In Swain County North Carolina there is a cemetery which cannot be regularly visited. This one-time farming area is now off limits to former residents. The area has been declared a federal wilderness area — to be "untrampled by man." The former residents are now allowed in only once a year to visit their family's graves. The people are hauled in on a cattle trailer by the park service.

After forming the EPA, Nixon gave it vast "legal" authority. It has since promulgated tens of thousands of regulations. Many of these carry criminal penalties for violation and are strangling private industry and private property ownership.

Historically, courts had ruled that government regulations that reduced the value of private property was "taking" private property and awarded the owner just compensation. EPA head William K. Reilly, described the courts' concern with constitutionally protected property rights as "anachronistic." Reilly appears to believe: It's ours, ain't it — we stole it.

These laws steal freedom and make our unalienable rights alienable. Our Founding Fathers believed these rights were granted by the Creator, but now the EPA says our freedoms are alienable, revocable gifts granted by the State. These laws are dangerous and as a result, many ordinary, law-abiding Americans are being given stiff financial penalties and/or imprisonment.

In 1990 the Justice Department returned 134 federal indictments for "environmental crimes" — a 33 percent increase over 1989. More than 50 percent were convicted and 84 percent of them are serving time in prison.

If we do not soon reassert our "unalienable" rights, we will have none. The god-State, which deems itself deity, will have decided that they are societal Creators and withdraw our rights.

105

This is not a close facsimile, but an exact copy, of the Stalinist system still operating in the CIS (former Soviet Union). The CIS requires permits for every minuscule economic move. Left unchecked, EPA laws could well force our stores shelves to look just like those in the CIS — empty!

In the last Presidential debacles, or debates, it was clear that all three candidates wanted the EPA to have global status. This is, in reality, nothing more than a division of Global Eco-dictatorship, Inc., aka, The New World Order.

Free speech is also threatened by the federal land grab gestapo. In 1992, Mike Hayden (a Bush official) declared that rights to freedom of speech don't apply on federal land. This is the case where the Park Service shut down the Everglade's Institute for publishing information which was not in agreement with the Service's positions. If that is, in fact, the case and Federal Land is by definition, whatever the federal government owns — does that then also apply to courts, the Halls of Congress, the White House, and other government buildings? If free speech isn't allowed on public land (and all land under the Justinian doctrine of the public trust is public), where does that allow for the freedom of speech? If this right can be done away with, what about all of the others?

If their goal is tyranny — they are succeeding.

Chapter 8

My Horse Surrendered

In the movie, *The Outlaw Josey Wales,* in a conversation between Josey Wales and the Indian, the Indian made a statement that is both funny and tragic. In speaking of his people's surrender he said, "I never surrendered ... my horse surrendered." The inference was, when his horse surrendered, it caused his capture, inasmuch as he was on the horse and the horse was his vehicle of war. The difference between his surrender and the surrender of his horse, which caused his capture and apparent surrender, is a fine distinction — especially since he had control of his horse. However, it is a difference worth noting, in light of the onward marching of the Princes to establish the New World Order.

In this country, we haven't surrendered, but our politicians have, and subsequently, it has led to our capture. However, like the Indian, we have supposedly had control over the leaders of the three branches of our government. Again, it is a fine line between our surrender and our horse's (that is those who exercise representation for us in the three branches of government). Nonetheless, it is a difference worth noting.

Similarly, since they have surrendered that which they had no right to surrender — that is, *our rights* — it is then our prerogative to *unsurrender them.* Later, we will discuss, in detail, how this surrender can be undone. But for now, we must see just how many of our rights have been surrendered and how this process came about.

As you have just read, one of the most powerful tools at the disposal of the Princes is the environmental movement. Now let's consider if and how our unalienable rights, and the subsequent enumeration of those rights, listed in the Bill of Rights, have been attacked, neutralized, or done away with all together.

We hold these truths to be self evident, that all men are created equal, that they are endowed by their Creator with certain unalienable Rights, that among these are Life, Liberty and the pursuit of Happiness. That to secure these rights, Governments are instituted among Men, deriving their just powers from the consent of the governed.

Unanimous Declaration of 1776

If indeed these rights are unalienable, it would stand to reason that government, no matter what laws and regulations they pass, cannot alienate these rights from us. The safeguards to these rights were so important to our Founding Fathers that they listed them separately from the Constitution in the Bill of Rights, which was ratified in December of 1792. In the preamble to the Bill of Rights we find these words:

The conventions of a number of States having at the time of their adopting the Constitution, expressed a desire, in order to prevent misconstruction or abuse of its powers, that further declaratory and restrictive clauses should be added: And as extending the ground of public confidence in the Government, will best insure the beneficent ends of its institution.

Thus the Bill of Rights was given to protect the people's rights from government. In so doing, the Founding Fathers chained down government, which throughout history has had a tendency to become the master of the people, instead of its servant. So it was that the Bill of Rights was written to further restrict government.

Still, the question remains, are these rights, while still possessed by the people, enjoyed by the people? Sadly, in the case of Article I of the Bill of Rights, the answer is a resounding, No!

Article I

Congress shall make no law respecting an establishment of religion, or prohibiting the free exercise thereof; or abridging the freedom of speech, or of the press; or the right of the people peaceably to assemble, and to petition the Government for a redress of grievances.

We will discuss later in greater detail from their own writings, what the Founding Fathers said that this clause meant. However, for now, we need to discover which, if any, of these freedoms we still enjoy.

Is there freedom of religion? In only the very narrowest sense do we still enjoy religious freedom; for in every state of the Union, there are laws which govern churches and their operation at the federal level. There are whole sections of the Internal Revenue Code which dictate the conduct of churches. Unfortunately, almost every church in America has taken on corporate status, and accepted from the government chartering under section 501(c)(3) of the IRS code. In so doing they have made themselves a creation of the State.

First, in accepting the status of 501(c)(3), churches have acknowledged the federal government's power and authority over them and their activities. As such they both technically and actually named the State (the Federal Government) as head of the church. This change in the positional authority of the church, from that of the historically held view that "God" not the "State" was the head of the church, came about in a most cunning and devious way.

In 1913, the Congress of the United States illegally adopted the 16th Amendment to the Constitution of the United States, which created the Progressive Income Tax. The Office of the Solicitor of the Department of State sent to Philander Knox, then the Secretary of State, a Memorandum on February 15, 1913, stating:

> In the certified copies of the resolutions passed by the legislatures of the several states ratifying the proposed 16th amendment, it appears that only four of these resolutions (those submitted by Arizona, North Dakota, Tennessee and New Mexico) have quoted absolutely accurately and correctly the 16th amendment as proposed by Congress. The other thirty-three resolutions all contain errors either of punctuation, capitalization, or wording. Minnesota, it is to be remembered, did not transmit to the Department a copy of the resolution passed by the legislature of that state. The resolutions passed by twenty-two states contain errors only of capitalization or punctuation, or both, while those of eleven states contain errors in the wording....[92]

Philander Knox disregarded this information and erroneously informed both the Executive and Legislative branches of government that the 16th Amendment had been properly ratified. It had not. In order for an Amendment to become law, it must first be accepted by resolution in the exact form as was proposed. As you can plainly see, this only occured in four states.

This was a skillful lie, perpetrated upon America by the Princes-controlled print media and the Princes-controlled President of the United States. Although Wilson was elected to the Presidency, the most powerful man in the White House, and therefore the "Shadow President," was Colonel Edward Mandel House, whom Wilson described as his "alter ego." By this time the Princes also controlled the leadership within the Congress of the United States.

Under this law that never was, citizens and businesses were to be taxed, but in their generosity, these benevolent leaders wanted to excuse the churches from taxation. This was all a smoke screen; because by excusing churches from taxation, the Princes accomplished two important objectives. First, by excusing the churches, they did not incur the collective wrath of the church in America. Secondly, to be eligible for the exemption, churches had to accept the status, terms, and conditions of the federal government, thus putting themselves under the auspices of the government.

The very first **prohibition** of the Congress of the United States was to "make no laws respecting an establishment of religion." This was instantly rendered null and void, through this cunning maneuver. Not only was the Congress making laws respecting the establishment of religion; they now controlled all "religion" in the United States.

Now, further regulations have been added to the IRS code restricting churches from naming corrupt politicians, endorsing those with whom they agree, or speaking out on moral or social issues such as homosexuality or abortion. All over the United States, ministers are being fined tens of thousands of dollars; having their churches stripped of their status as a 501(c)(3); and in the most draconian of cases, under the tyranny of the corrupt, judicial system in America, being given prison sentences — as much as twenty and thirty years!

This was seen most recently in the high-profile case of Jerry Falwell and his *Old-Time Gospel Hour*. Falwell was fined $50,000 by the IRS and lost his tax-exempt filing status, due to "involvement of religious groups in politics."[93]

So much for Article I of the Bill of Rights — Freedom of Religion. In this one act, a major goal of the Princes, namely the destruction of all religion — especially Christianity — has been, if not achieved, advanced mightily.

Article II

A well regulated Militia, being necessary to the security of a free State, the right of the people to keep and bear Arms, shall not be infringed.

Article III

No Soldier shall, in time of peace be quartered in any house, without the consent of the Owner, nor in time of war, but in a manner to be prescribed by law.

In the majority of these United States, the state Constitution defines the term *Militia*. Most states use language which in effect says, the militia is *every able bodied citizen of the state*. It is not the Army of the United States, it is every able bodied citizen of the several states of the United States. The distinction is important, inasmuch as the Founding Fathers supposed that there was to be no standing army. This is made clear by Alexander Hamilton's *Federalist Paper Number 29:*

> By thus circumscribing the plan, it will be possible to have an excellent body of well-trained militia ready to take the field whenever the defence of the State shall require it. This will not only lessen the call for military establishments, but if circum-stances should at any time oblige the government to form an army of any magnitude, that army can never be formidable to the liberties of the people while there is a large body of citizens, little, if at all, inferior to them in discipline and the use of arms, who stand ready to defend their own rights and those of their fellow citizens. This appears to me the only substitute that can be devised for a standing army, and the best possible security against it, if it should exist.[94]

In light of this, the right of the people, who are the militia, of which an army would be comprised in a time of war or threat of war, cannot have their right to keep and bear arms abridged. If one looks up the definition of *abridge* in *Webster's Desk Edition Dictionary* these words would be found: "Abridge - To shorten, lessen, or curtail."

Proponents of "gun control" — which is *not* gun control at all but "people control" as it relates to the purchase of weapons — would have us believe that by restricting the flow of weapons to the people, that the people are actually safer. However, the statistics do not bear this out. In fact, since the beginning of gun legislation, abridging the right of the people to keep and bear arms, the use of such weapons in the commission of crimes has dramatically increased.

This isn't too hard to understand. Imagine, if you will, an armed robber going into a convenience store or bank, telling the customers to lay on the floor; then telling the clerk or teller to hand over the money. Usually today, the people involved obey the robber because they aren't armed and have no way to defend themselves or their property.

However, imagine the same scenario, but this time with several of the citizens armed. As the would be robber pulls his gun and declares that this is a stick up, the citizenry, also armed, replies, "No this is a screw up on your part" as they, in unison, pull their weapons and relieve this now ridiculous looking, would-be thief of his weapon, defusing a potentially harmful situation.

But this is really a side issue. The purpose of the well armed citizenry was not just for protection from other citizens. It was first and foremost a protection of the citizens, of the several states from a potentially intrusive, oppressive, or dictatorial federal government. The weaponry was to remain in the hands of the people, not in the hands of the state. Thus the right to keep and bear arms was a right guaranteed the people to protect them against the abuses of power already suffered by the Founding Fathers, at the hands of the king of England.

However, the right of the people to keep and bear arms has been violently abridged. One state, Florida, has even gone so far as to amend their Constitution to prescribe a mandatory waiting period for the purchase of a weapon. Further, Federal law now prohibits the sale of certain types of automatic and semi-automatic weapons, thus rendering the weaponry of the citizenry — that is the militia — far inferior to that of the unconstitutionally formed, standing, national army. So much for Article II of the Bill of Rights, and so much too for one of the safeguards to our unalienable right to life, should the government decide to turn the army on the people, which has happened several times, even recently in America.

In fact, the President, by Executive Order (which is nothing more than legislation created by the Executive, and therefore, an abuse of the separation of powers in the Constitution) can declare a federal emergency (or at least the perception of an emergency in the eyes of the President) and use the unconstitutional army for whatever purposes he chooses, even if that purpose is the "justifiable" taking of American lives, property, or depriving individuals of liberty.

112

Article IV

The right of the people to be secure in their persons, houses, papers, and effects against unreasonable searches and seizures, shall not be violated, and no Warrants shall issue, but upon probable cause, supported by Oath or affirmation, and particularly describing the place to be searched, and the persons or things to be seized.

For all of you TV buffs, who have watched the fiction created by the media, where criminals are set free because the evidence uncovered was obtained without a warrant, I have a surprise for you. This actually happens. However, it is much less common than we have been led to believe.

In most cases, these laws work for the professional criminals and their lawyers (who are, for the most part, professional criminals themselves). In many more cases, this unalienable right to liberty and security in our persons, papers, and effects is denied. In fact, with the web of laws that no one can possibly keep track of (including judges), we now accept, as a right of law enforcement, what heretofore would have been considered an unconscionable breach of Article IV of the Bill of Rights.

Article IV's prohibition was against general searches, which the colonists had suffered under the hands of the kings and their representatives. General searches of people's homes, shops, papers, and persons were common. Too often the colonists had to pass through "check points" or had their homes or businesses ransacked, with nothing more than an anonymous tip that they were involved in something illegal.

Today, this abominable practice is a common tool of law enforcement and government agencies. There are so many examples of this behavior that it would be far too lengthy to begin to list them all. However, for the purposes of a good example of a bad example, let's look at an agency that exists now in every state. While it operates under many different names (Child Welfare Division, Health and Rehabilitative Services, Children's Protective Services or any other of the dozens of euphemisms for these agencies and their "storm troopers"), the function and result of their operation is, to varying degrees, a plague on the land.

Examine carefully what is happening. In many cases, warrants are received by child welfare workers based upon nothing more than an anonymous phone call. There is no sworn oath or affirmation, thus rendering the entire search and subsequent kidnapping by the state unconstitutional.

Further, Article VI of the Bill of Rights guarantees citizens a trial by jury and the right to face his accusers. However, in these cases the accuser is anonymous, and there is no way for an individual to face their accuser. Further, since the state already has their children, the parents must prove themselves innocent before their "legally" kidnapped children will be returned to them. Additionally, in most states these types of cases are heard in unconstitutional Juvenile Courts, which almost uniformly deny a right to a jury trial.

Most of us would agree that if an individual is, in fact, guilty of a infamous crime, such as child abuse, that they should be punished. However, remember that in the case of these child-snatching welfare workers, the suspected abusing parent is not arrested. They instead, arrest the children and put them into what is arguably an even more dangerous situation - the care of the state or state sponsored foster care. It should be noted that there are thousands of loving, caring, and conscientious foster parents. However, there are also many perverts, sadists, and profiteers who receive, in some cases, up to a thousand dollars a month per child; as even the several states own records, which are sealed from the public, will indicate.

Interestingly, between 70 and 90 percent of the allegations against parents turn out to be false. Yet, in many cases, the lives and reputations of even the falsely accused are ruined forever. In thousands of cases across the United States, families have been bankrupted by endless court battles with the state. These often result in the loss of parents' jobs, which happens as a result of the thousands of hours needed to comply with the terms and conditions of the Child Welfare Division's edicts, if parents ever want to see their children again.

Article V

No person shall be held to answer for a capital, or otherwise infamous crime, unless on a presentment or indictment of a Grand Jury, except in cases arising in the land or naval forces, or in the Militia, when in actual service in time of War or public danger; nor shall any person be subject for the same offence to be twice put in jeopardy of life or limb; nor shall be compelled in any criminal case to be a witness against himself, nor be deprived of life, liberty, or property, without due process of law; nor shall private property be taken for public use without just compensation.

Article VI

> *In all criminal prosecutions, the accused shall enjoy the right to a speedy and public trial, by an impartial jury of the State and district wherein the crime shall have been committed, which district shall have been previously ascertained by law, and to be informed of the nature and cause of the accusation; to be confronted with the witnesses against him; to have compulsory process for obtaining witnesses in his favor, and to have the assistance of Counsel for his defence.*

Everyday in the court rooms of America, Articles V and VI, are not just breached, they are completely shattered in what we sarcastically call, *courts of justice.* If you believe that you are going to get justice in a "court of law," it is only because you have not been in a real courtroom recently. It is routine in criminal cases for judges to move trials from one jurisdiction to another, violating Article VI of the Bill of Rights. This is supposedly done to protect the accused from receiving an unfair trial in the jurisdiction where the crime was committed. However, the very purpose of having the trial in the district wherein the crime was committed, was so that the character of the person would be well known and the jury would then be better able to judge the facts in the case, based upon the integrity of the witnesses and the actions and character of the accused.

Further, Article VII is almost uniformly violated in any trial where there is a "hung jury." Individuals are routinely retried with a new jury.

Article VII

> *In suits at common law, where the value in controversy shall exceed twenty dollars, the right of trial by jury shall be preserved, and no fact tried by a jury shall be otherwise re-examined in any Court of the United States, than according to the rules of the common law.*

When a jury is considered a "hung jury," that means that there is not a unanimous decision that can be reached among them, for either guilt or innocence. In other words, there cannot be reached a unanimous verdict of guilt. That being the case, there must be "reasonable doubt" in the minds of at least some of the jurors. If there is reasonable doubt, then the person is to

115

be considered innocent, because he or she has not been proven guilty. Article VII says "no fact tried by a jury shall be otherwise re-examined in any Court of the United States." Yet, in almost every court in the land, when there is a hung jury, the poor person is drug through the court system again, with all of the attendant trauma, expense, and non-flattering notoriety which goes with such trials.

To this point we have pretty well shot down Articles I through VII. Perhaps, we can still find solace in Article VIII of the Bill of Rights.

Article VIII

Excessive bail shall not be required nor excessive fines imposed, nor cruel and unusual punishment inflicted.

It is hard to say whether bail requirements today are excessive. It would seem to me that if bail were to be "not excessive" we would have to find out the financial capability of each individual. However, this is not done. For most crimes, bail is set by rules of tradition. $1,000 is the bail for this crime, $1,500 is the bail for that alleged offence, and so on. What is excessive? Probably, for a poor person, $1,000 is extremely excessive. For the working poor whose entire monthly income is only seven or eight hundred dollars, requiring a figure which approaches 10 percent of his or her annual salary for bail is excessive. But we live in a day of judicial formula, not justice. You see, justice is hard to pinpoint. Justice requires a fixed standard of law. That no longer exists in this country. Our laws change daily. In fact, while a judge is rendering a decision based upon today's law, the very law he used in rendering judgement is often being changed. His decision, based upon the new law which passed just that day, will overturn his decision or change the ruling in some way. Many times judgement will be withheld, pending the passage of a new law.

The result of such instability in law is quite evident. There is no longer a fixed anchor of right and wrong in society. When there is no such anchor, society wanders spiritually and morally. The result is predictable. The courts become overrun and there is a break down in "law and order."

Typically, the professional criminal learns the system and understands how to beat it. Justice is slapped in the face. The innocent, who don't know the system or can't afford to hire those who do, are punished under dubious, confusing, conflicting, and unjust laws. Again justice is slapped in the face.

Finally, no one has any confidence in the courts. The innocent are punished, the guilty go free, and the people begin "taking the law into their own hands." They suppose they can't possibly do any worse than the courts. As a result, we see the birth of the vigilante. There was a time when the word vigilante had a positive connotation. It meant someone who was vigilant. But, that was back in the days of this nation when we had citizen law enforcement, real justice, and courts which operated under the Constitution of the United States. A vigilante was simply one who stood vigil for his fellow citizens.

Those days are gone. Now, if one stands vigil for his fellow citizens, he will probably be charged with some sort of crime on behalf of the citizens whom he was attempting to protect. Having been charged with a crime, he will also probably be sued, by some liberal, peoples' group (such as the American Civil Liberties Union (ACLU). Subsequently, he will most likely be jailed, given excessive bail, and finally, bankrupted by his defense of the criminal and civil suits brought against him. And the rest of us will have learned the lessons that the system wanted us to learn.

First, we learned that "taking the law into your own hands is illegal." This, despite the fact, that the courts, who are to represent justice on our behalf, have been an abysmal failure and, in fact, are working — in many cases — against us.

Second, we have learned that if you get involved (between the system created by the Princes and their surrogates, groups such as the ACLU), you will be destroyed financially, in your reputation, and every other way possible.

Third, you will learn to "sit down, shut up, pay up, and stay out of what doesn't concern you." You will also learn that ...

no good deed goes unpunished.

Chapter 9

A Poor Move Before — A Poor Move Still

I remember, from my childhood, each of us being given, by our teachers, a can marked *U.N.I.C.E.F.* This fund was supposed to be for the starving and underprivileged children around the world. At Halloween, each of us was instructed to collect money for this "worthy" cause. And as the trusting, albeit naive children we were, each of us would dutifully knock on doors and greet the occupants with the words, "Trick or Treat for U.N.I.C.E.F."

In 1961, U.N.I.C.E.F. funds, earmarked for needy children, were — with U.N.I.C.E.F.'s knowledge and consent — temporarily diverted to help finance the slaughter of innocent children during the U.N.'s vicious war against the tiny, anti-Communist nation of Katanga (a breakaway nation from the communist-controlled Congo). Former U.S. Representative, H.R. Gross, a Republican from Iowa and a staunch Conservative critic of the U.N., discussed the sordid matter on the House floor on June 19, 1961. He reminded his colleagues that during hearings on the bill being debated, government witnesses had admitted that Secretary General U Thant had borrowed from the Children's Fund to help finance the Congo operation.

According to Congressman Gross, "After the committee adjourned, the witnesses provided a statement showing that U.N. officials got $12 million from the United Nations Special Fund and grabbed $10 million from the United Nations Children's Fund, U.N.I.C.E.F."

In 1960, the communist state of the Belgian Congo received independence and became known as Zaire. Katanga, one of its provinces, wanted no part of the "Red Revolution" and wanted to align itself with the West. The communist regime asked the United Nations to "put down rebellion and restore law and order in the Congo." This, of course, was just a ploy. Katanga already had law and order. Katanga was emerging as an anti-Communist nation, whose government was patterned after the now extinct constitutional republic given the United States by our Founding Fathers. But, therein lay the seeds of their demise.

The U.N., in violation of its own charter, then intervened in Katanga, supposedly to "help." Their real intention was to force an anti-communist state back under the control of the communist Congo regime, while publicly stating they were *protecting* Katanga from communism.

Katanga was not threatening anyone, nor was she involved in hostilities toward any of her neighbors of the former Congo. She was a nation that was well-educated, industrially advanced, and rich in minerals and natural resources. Her crime? She chose to secede from the Congo and remain independent and free from the anarchical, Marxist regime that had gained control in Zaire.

After receiving "permission" from Katanga's President Moise Tshombe, U.N. "peace-keeping" forces stationed themselves in Katanaga under the guise of offering protection from Communist advances toward this small nation. The U.N. forces began their assault.

The first attack came at 4:00 A.M. when the U.N. forces took over all communications centers, put a blockade around the foreign minister's residence, surrounded the barracks of the Katangese army, and arrested over four hundred European officers and noncoms. Simultaneously, it began arresting and expelling from the country hundreds of other European residents, who were suspected of being technicians or advisors.

There was no resistance, due to the fact that the Belgian officers, who were on loan to Katanga, were under orders not to fire on U.N. troops.

> Soldiers and civilians alike were taken from their families at bayonet point, rounded up into detention centers, and expelled from the country. There were no charges brought against them, no hearings, no habeas corpus, no right of appeal, no opportunity to put their personal affairs in order. It was a police state operation.[95] *Time* magazine described it this way: "The 11,600 black Katangese troops remained passive, possibly because U.N. soldiers staged furious public bayonet drills and small arms exercises in a pointed show of power." Remarked one senior ... U.N. officer: "We have these soldiers scared witless."[96]

U.N. forces struck again on September 13, 1961, when they began an attack on the post office. Ray Moloney, a UPI correspondent, made the following report: "United Nations troops were firing from the hospital ... I also saw U.N. troops fire on a Katangese ambulance as it tried to reach the twitching bodies of unarmed Katangese police who were ripped to pieces by U.N. machine-gun bullets after the cease fire sounded."[97]

G. Edward Griffin, in his detailed account of Katanga and of the U.N., *The Fearful Master,* goes on to describe the incident as follows:

> ... frustrated in its anticipation of an easy victory, the United Nations began to turn Operation Morthor [the Hindi word for Smash] into Operation Terror. Blue-helmeted soldiers displaying U.N. emblems of peace fired wantonly at civilians, ambulances, automobiles — anything that moved. A Roman Catholic priest was murdered on his way to collect the Holy Sacrament from St. Paul's Convent; the charred remains of his body were later found in the burned shell of his automobile which had been hit by a bazooka shot from a United Nations armored car.... A housewife was murdered while riding with her husband down a peaceful street to buy groceries.[98]

Almost every Article of the U.N. Convention was violated. If one were to account all of the incidents of horror perpetrated against this peaceful, previously prosperous nation of Katanga, it would take a book all by itself. Suffice it to say, that unlawful arrests, kidnappings, rapes, unspeakable tortures, dismemberments, and bombings of ambulances and hospitals (including the maternity wards) were all tools of these U.N. "peace-keeping" forces.

So brutal and common were these attacks against the civilians that a former Harvard fellow, then a professor of surgery at the University of Elisabethville, sent a telegram to the President of Harvard Faculty of Medicine urgently pleading for him to intervene.

> WE URGENTLY REQUEST YOUR INTERVEN-TION IN ORDER TO PUT A STOP TO THE KILLING OF CIVILIAN COLOURED AND EUROPEAN MEN AND WOMEN AND CHILDREN BY U.N. FORCES — WOM-EN HAVE BEEN SHOT AT AND WOUNDED IN THEIR HOMES, WORKERS IN THE STREETS — STOP — SO HAVE RED CROSS SERVANTS — STOP — DURING LAST TWO DAYS JET PLANES HAVE BEEN SHOOT-ING AT CIVILIAN CARS DOWNTOWN AND IN THE COUNTRY — STOP — MORTARS ARE SYSTEMATI-CALLY SHELLING RESIDENTIAL AREAS — STOP — FOR THE SECOND TIME PRINCE LEOPOLD GENERAL

AFRICAN HOSPITAL HAS BEEN SHELLED — STOP — PLEASE INFORM ACADEMIC AND MEDICAL WORLD AND PUBLIC OPINION AND INSIST ON U.N. GIVING UP SUCH REPULSIVE METHODS — STOP — IN THE NAME OF THE 46 CIVILIAN DOCTORS OF ELISABETHVILLE.[99]

Apparently U.N. Convention Article 3 which says, "Persons taking no active part in the hostilities shall be treated humanely; in particular, murder of all kinds are prohibited," — meant nothing to these blood-thirsty mercenaries.

All of this was summarily ignored by the U.N. In fact, according to a U.N. spokesman, Secretary General U Thant asked that his "congratulations" be given to Messrs. Smith and Urquhart and to U.N. military commander, General Raja, and to the troops themselves for the "mastery which they displayed!"[100]

Then on December 12, U Thant stated the goal of the U.N. operations in Katanga was merely to "regain and assure our freedom of movement to restore law and order, and to insure that, for the future, U.N. forces and officials in Katanga are not subject to attacks." However, when President Tshombe called for a cease-fire five days later, U Thant responded by saying, "For us to stop short of our objectives at the present stage would be a serious setback for the U.N."[101]

Article 27 of the U.N. Charter states: "Women shall be especially protected against an attack on their honor, in particular rape." Yet three European women were brutally raped, one on December 20th and the other two on Christmas Eve.

The 46 Civilian Doctors of Elisabethville, who published their entire report in *Forty-Six Angry Men,* sent the following telegram to President Kennedy, Pope John, and fourteen other world dignitaries imploring them:

SOS TO THE MORAL CONSCIENCE OF THE WORLD - STOP - IMPLORE YOU TO INTERVENE WITH ALL YOUR AUTHORITY TO STOP THE TERRORIST BOMBARDMENT OF HOSPITALS AND CIVILIAN POPULATIONS BY U.N.O. ... ON OUR HONOUR AS PHYSICIANS WE DECLARE AS LIES THE DENIALS OF U.N.O. SECRETARIAT-GENERAL -STOP - INSIST UPON INQUIRY HERE BY HIGH MAGISTRATES AND PRESIDENTS OF MEDICAL ORDERS OF ALL CIVILIZED

NATIONS - STOP - ONLY MEANS OF CONVINCING THE WORLD OF INCONCEIVABLE ACTIONS OF U.N.O. ALAS DISHONOURED - STOP - INSIST UPON CREATION INTERNATIONAL TRIBUNE COMPETENT JUDGE CRIMES AND MISDEEDS U.N.O. PERSONNEL WHO BENEFIT FROM IMMUNITY CONTRARY TO NATURAL LAW.[102]

Congressman Donald C. Bruce had entered into the Congressional Record on September 12, 1962, that at the height of the massacres in Elisabethville, President Tshombe personally appealed to the United States to help put an end to the destruction of the city. Adlai Stevenson, U.S. Ambassador to the U.N. responded saying, "the U.S. is very pleased with the plans of the Secretary-General to bring Katanga under control."

President Tshombe surrendered in January, 1963, and Katanga's independence, as Griffin so aptly puts it, "was ground into the mud by United Nations boots. The last flame of freedom in the Congo flickered and died."[103]

Now compare Katanga to the work going on in Somalia with specific reference to the U.N.'s demand that the people be disarmed before the U.N. will come in and relieve the U.S. in the relief effort. Isn't this the first step that they took in Katanga? They disarmed the military and the people.

What other commonality was there between Katanga and Somalia? Katanga was rich in mineral resources. In doing research for this book, I obtained access to information on Somalia, produced by the CIA for use of United States Government officials. It lists as one of Somalia's natural resources, uranium. Uranium is one of the key ingredients in the production of nuclear weapons.

Additionally, there was the following: "Note: strategic location on Horn of Africa along southern approaches to Bab el Mandeb and route through Red Sea and Suez Canal."

And we can't forget about the interests of the Princes. Somalia, a barren, nomadic, fly-infested, ugly, little piece of real estate is rich in oil reserves. Before its collapse, the nation of Somalia, through its leadership, had made contractual arrangements with the oil companies of the Princes for the exploitation of Somalia's oil reserves.

Next, let's examine in brief, a speech that was made by former President George Bush on September 21, 1992, to the General Assembly of the United Nations.

Across the globe we all look forward to a future free of war,

123

a world where we might raise our children in peace and freedom. And this institution, the United Nations, born amidst the ashes of war, embodied those hopes and dreams like no other.

... This is the first general assembly to seat you as truly independent and free nations (former Soviet Union states). And to you and the leaders of the other independent states, I say: Welcome home; we are now truly United Nations.

However, George Bush went far beyond this in speaking of the United States' role in the New World Order and its relationship to the United Nations when he said: "First, we face the political challenge of keeping today's peace and preventing tomorrow's wars." That being the case, a United Nations strong enough to enforce world peace is also one that has to be strong enough to go to war — which Bush spoke clearly of later in his speech.

Additionally, Bush laid out three challenges to the world for the growth of democracy. The third challenge of which he spoke was a common economic challenge: "... we face the common economic challenge of promoting prosperity for all, of strengthening an open, growth-oriented free market international economic order while safeguarding the environment."

If, in fact, we are to develop an international economic order, that means that we are going to have some organization which can create hegemony within the economic spheres of the world.

Meeting these challenges will require us to strengthen our collective engagement. It will require us to transform our collective institutions. And, above all, it will require that each of us look seriously at our own governments and how we conduct our international affairs. We, too, must change our institutions and our practices if we are to make a new world of the promise of today; if we're to secure a 21st century peace.

In the next few paragraphs of his speech Bush made some interesting observations.

Let me begin with peacekeeping. The United Nations has a long and distinguished history of peacekeeping and humanitarian relief.

But, as much as the United Nations has done, it can do much more. Peacekeepers are stretched to the limit while demands for their services increase by the day. The need for *monitoring and preventive* [emphasis mine] peacekeeping, putting people on the ground before the fighting starts, may become especially critical in volatile regions.

Obviously, what Bush is talking about is U.N. interdictive action, but that action has seldom, if ever, been truly peace-keeping. Rather, it has been, throughout its history, an enforcement of the global ideas of the U.N.. Again, I refer you back to the slaughter and carnage of the U.N. in the peaceful kingdom of Katanga. However, those who try to tell the truth about such an incident as Katanga, Somalia, and, of course, the coming destruction of South Africa and other nations on that continent, will be ridiculed as lunatics, branded as conspiratoralist, and isolated from the population by being ignored in the mainstream media.

In George Bush's New World Order, he saw hegemony in the realm of the economic, but especially in the realm of the political, falling under the auspices of the United Nations.

I welcome the Secretary General's call for a new agenda to strengthen the United Nations' ability to prevent, contain and resolve conflict across the globe...

Robust peacekeeping requires men and equipment that only member states can provide. Nations should develop and train military units for possible peacekeeping operations and humanitarian relief. And these forces must be available on short notice at the request of the Security Council....

If multinational units are to work together, they must train together. Many nations — for example, Fiji, Norway, Canada and Finland — have a long history of peacekeeping. And we can all tap into that experience as we train for expanded operations. Effective multinational action will also require coordinated command-and-control and interoperability of both equipment and communications. Multinational planning; training; field exercises will be needed. These efforts should link up with regional organizations....

We also need to provide adequate logistical support for peacekeeping and humanitarian operations. Member states should designate stockpiles of resources necessary to meet humanitarian emergencies, including famines, floods, *civil disturbances.* [emphasis mine]. And this will save valuable time in a crisis....

We will need to develop planning, crisis management, and

125

intelligence capabilities for peacekeeping and humanitarian operations....

We must ensure adequate, equitable financing for U.N. and associated *peacekeeping* [emphasis mine] efforts....

As I said, we must change our national institutions if we are to change our international relations. So let me assure you: The United States is ready to do its part to strengthen world peace by strengthening international peacekeeping.

So, in the examination of the words of former President Bush before the United Nations, we see some very important principles laid out. We first see that he adheres to the philosophy of political hegemony of the United Nations. If that hegemony is going to take place, that is, a process of command, control, and the ability to enforce its dictates, the United Nations must have more men, money, and machines. It's important again to remember that any organization strong enough to enforce peace is also strong enough to inflict war and damage, as was the case in Katanga.

Next, he said we need to begin helping the U.N. create the necessary ingredients, such as stockpiles of resources, which would be necessary to meet humanitarian emergencies, famines, or floods, but above all, we must be ready to send peacekeepers and supplies to any place where the people get "out of line." This could, and would, be (as proven by history), termed a *civil disturbance*, into which the U.N. must thrust its will.

But, how are you going to know if there is a civil disturbance any place in the world? Many times the civil disturbance is a result of the people rising above the tyranny of the dictatorship of a socialistic government. Well, naturally, you are going to have to have an intelligence system, which Bush also proposed when he spoke concerning developing a plan with crisis management and intelligence capabilities for peacekeeping. Naturally, we are going to have to throw more dollars toward these efforts if they are to become a reality.

The goal is to strengthen world peace by strengthening international peacekeeping. Perhaps the most salient point here is the definition of world peace. If world peace means that nobody is fighting with anybody anywhere about anything, then probably that means that all have accepted a common ideology. Otherwise, there is no way to avoid conflict of one sort or another. However, if we all accepted one ideology, then it is very simple to keep world peace.

A commonly quoted definition for peace coming out of the socialist state known as the Soviet Union, now dissolved into the CIS, is "no further opposition to communism." Could this same definition be applied to the goals and ideas of the U.N.? When there ceases to be resistance to the political, financial, and spiritual globalist agenda, as set forth by the U.N., then there will indeed be peace. Bush clearly saw the demand for increasing "peacekeeping" armies, and to meet this need he said:

> I have directed the United States Secretary of Defense to place a new emphasis on peacekeeping. Because of peacekeeping's growing importance as a mission for the United States military, we will emphasize training of combat, engineering and logistical units for the full range of peacekeeping and humanitarian activities.

It only follows, that working together with all this will be the United States' capabilities for transport, logistics, communications, and intelligence, which we now freely give to the U.N.. The question that arises in my mind is very simple. What if the U.N. doesn't like what the United States is doing? What if they have access to our military, engineering, logistics, lift, communications, and intelligence capabilities — can they, in fact, be used against us, if we don't fall into line? What if we have a point of disagreement with the hegemony being created by the U.N.?

Well, to make sure that the military of the United States does not support the will of the people for freedom, Bush said: "I have further directed the establishment of a permanent peacekeeping curriculum in U.S. military schools." This, indeed, is a dangerous trend! Our military schools are now to be used for New World Order training.

And, of course, Bush was willing to pledge your tax dollars to ensure that his dreams for the New World Order come into existence when he said: "And, finally, the United States will review how we fund peacekeeping and explore new ways to ensure adequate American financial support for the U.N. peacekeeping and U.N. humanitarian activities."

It is indeed a perilous time in which we live. Every attempt throughout history to create a "New World Order" has resulted in the mass slaughter of humanity; the enslavement of both the bodies and minds of the peoples involved; and finally, the totalitarian rule of the elite few.

New World Orders have always been monopolistic concerning control of economic, political, and spiritual values. In the realm of the military, in order to ensure that there is no competition, Bush said, "We believe the

127

Security Council should become a key forum for nonproliferation enforcement ... and sanction proliferators."

That is, anyone who would have the audacity to develop nuclear weapons to protect themselves against a neighbor with nuclear weapons would, of course, have to be sanctioned. Now, while I agree that proliferation of nuclear weapons is destructive, I would vehemently oppose a United Nations to whom has been entrusted the safeguarding and keeping of the nuclear forces of the world, inasmuch as these weapons will be at their disposal. I would oppose their right to inflict their will (which is reflective of their history, i.e. Katanga), on any nation.

Obviously, no New World Order would be complete without economic hegemony. According to Bush:

> I stated yesterday ... that the United States would be strongly engaged with its global partners in building a global economic, financial and trading structure for this new era ... I will propose creating a $1-billion growth fund ... to support U.S. businesses in providing expertise, goods and services desperately needed in countries undertaking economic restructuring ... None of us can afford insular policies.

To make sure that each of us is on a common footing, Bush would make sure that our technologies, our businesses, our expertise, our goods, and our services are transferred all over the world. Harken back now to the creed of communism: "To each according to his need, from each according to his ability."

I find it very difficult to believe that it is in the best interest of the citizens of the United States to begin to pour billions of dollars into the New World Order. It's one thing to conquer a people and enslave them; it's another thing, to use cunning language and picturesque rhetoric to trick them into paying for their own execution. This is, of course, what the United Nations is all about — the execution of the United States as a nation and dissolution into a New World Order — and with it, the dissolution of your "unalienable Rights, that among these are Life, Liberty and the pursuit of Happiness."

And finally, from Bush — his commitment to this goal:

"And let us pledge ourselves to fulfill the promise of a truly United Nations."

Chapter 10

It's Ours Ain't It - We Stole It

3. Abolition of inheritance and any sense of ownership in private property through societal collectivism.

How did the real power to bring these changes about accumulate in our country? It is, in brief, the Federal Reserve System (FED). It is this system, as most Americans know, that controls and regulates the money supply of the United States. What few Americans have known is that the FED, that organization from whom the United States Treasury takes its monetary directions and orders, is not an accountable agency of the United States government.

It is a pseudo-governmental agency that is privately owned by some of the richest and most powerful men in the world. It is the product of a conspiratorial effort that dates back to the early nineteen hundreds and finds its origins in what Congressman Charles Lindbergh, Sr. (father of famous aviator Charles Lindbergh, Jr.) called "the Money Trust." Congressman Lindbergh shocked many in 1913 with this statement:

> The Money Trust (the title popularly used at the time referred to the consortium of financial monopolists on Wall Street, which included, among others, Rockefeller, Morgan, Warburg, and Schiff), caused the 1907 panic, and thereby forced Congress to create a National Monetary Commission....

Heading the commission was Senator Nelson Aldrich, who often acted as spokesman and apologist for the international bankers. The commission spent two years studying the central banks of Europe and at a secret meeting at Jekyll Island, Georgia, developed the conspiracy which was to become the Federal Reserve Bank of the United States.

Twenty-five years later, Frank Vanderlip, President of the Rockefellers'

129

National City Bank wrote in the *Saturday Evening Post:*

> ... in 1910, ... I was as secretive, indeed as furtive, as any conspirator. I do not feel it is any exaggeration to speak of our secret expedition to Jekyll Island as the occasion of the actual conception of what eventually became the Federal Reserve System.
>
> We were told to leave our last names behind us. We were told further that we should avoid dining together on the night of our departure. We were instructed to come one at a time and as unobtrusively as possible to the terminal of the New Jersey littoral of the Hudson, where Senator Aldrich's private car would be in readiness, attached to the rear end of the train for the South.
>
> Once aboard the private car, we began to observe the taboo that had been fixed on last names.
>
> Discovery, we knew, simply must not happen, or else all our time and effort would be wasted.[104]

After the meeting on Jekyll Island, the conspirators, at the urging of Senator Aldrich, allowed him to present the Aldrich Bill — which failed — in large part because of the suspicion raised by Senator Aldrich's close connections to the "Money Trust."

However, using only slight changes, and a different name the FED became law in December 1913. It was passed under dubious circumstances and it granted control over interest rates and the size of the national money supply to private bankers. The public was propagandized into believing that the FED given these remarkable powers, could and would stabilize the national economy, preventing further panics and bank runs. This excuse has been proven a complete lie by the Great Depression, various recessions, bouts with inflation, deflation, and the federal debt, which now stands at over $4 trillion.

Perhaps better than anyone else, Congressman Lindbergh saw and forthrightly spoke about the FED when he said:

> This act establishes the most gigantic trust on earth.... When the President signs this act the invisible government by the money power, proven to exist by the Money Trust investigation, will be legalized....
>
> The money power overawes the legislative and executive forces of the Nation and of the States. I have seen these forces exerted during the different stages of this bill....
>
> This is the Aldrich bill in disguise....[105]

But, perhaps Congressman Lindbergh was over-reacting. It was hoped, that as time went on, the Federal Reserve would do exactly what it said it would do — that is — to be the servant of the people. Unfortunately, it did not. Congressman Louis McFadden, who chaired the House Committee on Banking and Currency from 1920 to 1931, said:

> When the Federal Reserve Act was passed, the people of these United States did not perceive that a world banking system was being set up here.
>
> A super-state controlled by international bankers and international industrialists acting together to enslave the world for their own pleasure.
>
> Every effort has been made by the Fed to conceal its powers but the truth is - the Fed has usurped the Government.
>
> It controls everything here and it controls all our foreign relations.
>
> It makes and breaks governments at will.[106]

Congressman McFadden, and countless others through the years, understood that the FED was one of the tools being used to set up what we now know as the New World Order. In fact, McFadden charged that the FED, the International Bankers, and others carefully contrived the stock market crash and the resultant Great Depression, and the looting of $80 billion from the Treasury of the United States of America.

But there is a price to be paid for being right and being able to prove it. There were two failed assassination attempts on his life. However, operating under the old motto, if at first you don't succeed ... they later poisoned him at a banquet and he subsequently died, and with him the charges and proof of the allegations of treason. But a valuable lesson had been learned — **don't go against the Money Trust.**

Having now silenced one of the few men brave enough to take on the Golden Internationale, the Princes moved with speed into their outlets in the Media. Here was unveiled the classic example of: *Thesis, Antithesis, Synthesis.* Here's how it works.

The *thesis* in America had always been that the free enterprize system worked and that the less government was involved the better off business would be. The *antithesis,* in this case, would be that the government should and must be involved in every aspect of business and banking because the "free enterprize" system had failed. That is how "gradualism" works. One presents the existing thesis, challenges with the antithesis, and accepts a *synthesis* or compromise. The plan is simple and effective. Let's call the number 10 the thesis; we will assign the number 0 to the antithesis. In this equation the synthesis could be represented by 5 or some other number in between 0 and 10.

That's how it works. You attack a value, no matter how tried and true, with an antithesis, and if you can lure your opponent into compromise — either through pressure or his own *nâiveté* — you win. You may not take him all the way to "0" but if you take him to 5, 6, or even 9, you have moved him from his position and the process begins again.

Such was the story during the depression of the 1930s. Despite ample evidence that the government, acting as a surrogate of the shadow government behind the FED, had caused the misery and suffering of the late 1920s and 30s, the Princes'-controlled media convinced America that government intervention was needed. Thus began the next major push away from a Republic to pure democracy which, while different in rhetorical terms, is nonetheless identical to communism. By definition, a Republican form of government elects representatives to protect "right," or "rights," for the benefit of the people, in a limited sphere of authority. The *antithesis democracy* is the supposed direct rule of the people (i.e., the rule of the proletariat) to determine what is to be "right" or "rights."

Under Roosevelt's New Deal democracy (socialism), the preferred form of government for the Princes really took hold in America. The recurrent theme was let those who have much, help those with little. In other words: "To each according to his need, from each according to his ability." Marx and Engels would have been proud of Roosevelt. Roosevelt and socialism was "prophesied" two decades earlier by "Colonel" Edward Mandel House in his book *Philip Dru, Administrator.* The revolution that he spoke of after the crash and depression did not happen, but it was not for lack of trying on the part of the Princes. However, remember that in the game of thesis, antithesis, synthesis, winning is not getting everything, it is getting anything. And they have gotten plenty. This process, of course, has been repeated so often that now we have the largest, socialist bureaucracy in the world.

As stated earlier, the federal government controls virtually every aspect of our lives. But, nowhere is this more clear than in the previously described theory of economic democracy, espoused by President Clinton during his campaign. One of his former economic advisors, Derek Shearer, developed this term in his book, *Economic Democracy.* Shearer is part of the Clinton "informal" economic advisory team. This informal team met Clinton in 1969 at Oxford. According to an article in the *San Francisco Examiner,*

July 17, 1992, Shearer "has been one of the architects of Clinton's Rebuild America Plan."

In *Economic Democracy,* written with Martin Carnoy, Shearer says corporations are too "impersonal and powerful" and that a strategy to achieve economic democracy "must start by dismantling or at least restricting the power of these corporations."

Shearer and Carnoy call for a "democratically" planned central economy — like that of the former Soviet Union — one centrally planned by government bureaucrats. Additionally, they would be in favor of complete government control of all capital markets.

> A strategy of reform must transfer capital from corporations to the public.... The logical vehicle for that process should be government.... The objective ... is to provide a vehicle for governmental takeovers of entire industries without the immediate financial and ideological burdens that large-scale nationalization efforts would entail.

As an alternative to nationalization, pervasive governmental control of virtually all business behavior would be recommended. What if an industry refuses to bargain with the government? Shearer says, "real sanctions must be levied.... These could include denial of tax advantages and other subsidies, denial of export licenses, threat of antitrust suits, and so on."

There you have a summation of the Clinton economic plan. Remember again that Mr. Clinton is the chosen bearer of light by the Princes. There are, of course, a number of reasons that the Princes would want society (in general) and business (in specific) controlled to such draconian extremes. First, if government controls business, and in effect, through its control can force business to "bargain," it can mean mega dollars for government — both through taxation and permit fees. Secondly, it redistributes (steals) the wealth of corporations, to gives it to those who "have need."

Finally, in stealing the wealth from corporations, it eliminates any competition that the multinational industrialists may be getting from the "unenlightened." Keep in mind that the progressive income tax was not created for redistributing wealth to the needy. That is only the public relations campaign. Its real purpose is to see that wealth is stolen from the most productive, which usually translates to the most successful ...

thereby allowing the Princes unchallenged economic superiority.
This follows perfectly their plan.

133

Protocol Number 6

We shall soon begin to establish huge monopolies, reservoirs of colossal riches, upon which even large fortunes of the unenlightened will depend to such an extent that they will go to the bottom together with the credit of the States on the day after the political smash....

In every possible way we must develop the significance of our Super-Government by representing it as the Protector and Benefactor of all those who voluntarily submit to us.

It is obvious, to those whose brain is still functioning, that America, as a nation, no longer has the ability to think and reason clearly. We crave "freedom" and demand "choice" in all things. But *freedom* is not the right to choose. Rather, it is the result of making right choices. Continuing on in Protocol Number 6 we read:

... as landed proprietors they (the unenlightened) can still be harmful to us from the fact that they are self-sufficing in the resources upon which they live. It is essential therefore for us at whatever cost to deprive them of land. The object will be best attained by increasing the burdens upon landed property — in loading lands with debt. These measures will check land-holding and keep it in a state of humble and unconditional submission.

During the depression of the 1930s, more than three-fourths of Americans owned their own land. They did not owe money on it; they did not rent from anyone. They owned land. In fact, one of the reasons that we were able to work out of the Great Depression was that so many of the people were self-sufficient. In the 1990s, less than ten percent of Americans own their own land. Even those who do are subject to constant real estate tax rate hikes, special levies, and all manner of "loading lands with debt." Every day, average men and women are losing their land to debt and taxation.

In a Presidential study commissioned under George Bush to examine the problem of farmland foreclosures, some very interesting conclusions were reached. This, I am sure, was considered a misfortune by Bush, inasmuch as these commissions typically spend a lot of time and money and come to very few exacting conclusions. However, in this instance, the commission decided that it would take its role seriously. In so doing, they have undoubtedly created a report that will be forever buried in Bush's Presidential papers.

In examining this confidential report of the *Project 1995* Task Force, we find that the Princes have plans to create a "central agency," through which all others would access. The "owners" of the Farm Credit System should be willing to transfer in 1995, to this new phase of business technology. These owners, who have been behind the scenes, pulling the strings, are, none other than members of the Trilateral Commission.

According to an interview we had with Supreme Court Justice William C. Goodloe (retired), one of the members of the Task Force, money is intentionally lent in an effort to steal the farmlands of America. The borrower is told that he can have a small amount of additional credit or consolidate his farm loans into one loan. However, there is one catch. He can't collateralize part of his farm. He must pledge the entire farm for the loan. Then, as soon as he misses a payment — or needs an extension — they've got him. By denying loans for seed, etc., they can legally bankrupt him and take over the farm.

This process has been repeated so often and so blatantly that the aforementioned investigation was triggered. The final result was a shelving of that report. However, Judge Goodloe has reported to me that several states have asked to have the investigation continued. Hearings are to be scheduled in those states over the objections of many powerful forces.

I challenge anyone to find, specifically in the Constitution, the authority for any branch of government to have the power to redistribute the wealth of the nation, or of any of its citizens. There are, of course, those who would say, that power is given under the "General Welfare" clause of the Constitution. However, we will through the statements of James Madison, the chief architect of the Constitution, explore the exact meaning or intentions of the Founding Fathers, concerning the General Welfare clause later in this book. Wait until you read what Madison said.

Article IX

The enumeration in the Constitution, of certain rights, shall not be construed to deny or disparage others retained by the people.

Article X

The powers not delegated to the United States by the Constitution, nor prohibited by it to the States, are reserved to the States respectively, or to the people.

135

With the advent of the super state at the federal level, we have created such entities as the Federal Department of Education, Federal Department of Transportation, Federal Department of Labor, Federal Communications Commission, Federal Trade Commission, National Endowment for the Arts, and the list goes on and on. Yet, please show me specific authorization for any of these agencies in the Constitution of the United States, as demanded by Articles IX and X of the Bill of Rights. So, there goes the last remaining Articles of the Bill of Rights. This battle for the soul of America is being lost and with it our rights and freedoms as Americans. We now have only "limited" rights, "controlled" freedom. So much for the Constitution and Bill of Rights.[107]

Welcome to the New U.S.S.A. — an economic democracy. Socialism at its best!

Chapter 11

All In The Family

4. Abolition of the family, family life, the institution of marriage, and the substitution of collective ownership and communal education of children.

Protocol 16

In order to effect the destruction of all collective forces except ours we shall emasculate the first state of collectivism — the universities, by re-educating them in a new direction. Their officials and professors will be prepared for their business by detailed secret programmes of action from which they will not with immunity diverge, not by one iota. They will be appointed with especial precaution, and will be so placed as to be wholly dependent upon the Government.

We shall exclude from the course of instruction State Law as also all that concerns the political question. These subjects will be taught to a few dozens of persons chosen for their pre-eminent capacities from among the number of the initiated. The universities must no longer send out from their halls milksops concocting plans for a Constitution, like a comedy or a tragedy, busying themselves with questions of policy in which even their own fathers never had any power of thought.

... We must introduce into their education all those principles which have so brilliantly broken up their order. But when we are in power we shall remove every kind of disturbing subject from the course of education and shall make out of the youth obedient children of authority, loving him who rules as the support and hope of peace and quiet.

Classicism, as also any form of study of ancient history, in which there are more bad than good examples, we shall replace with the study of the programme of the future. We shall erase from the memory of men all facts of previous centuries which are undesirable to us, and leave only those which depict all the errors of the governments of the unenlightened. The study of practical life, of the obligations of order, of the relations of people one to another, ... will stand in the forefront of the teaching programme....

... You know yourselves in what all this has ended for the unenlightened who allowed this crying absurdity.

We shall abolish every kind of freedom of instruction. Learners of all ages will have the right to assemble together with parents in the educational establishments as it were in a club: during these assemblies, on holydays, teachers will read what will pass as free lectures on questions of human relations, of the laws of examples, of the limitations which are born of unconscious relations, and finally, of the philosophy of new theories not yet declared to the world. These theories will be raised by us to the stage of dogma of faith as a transitional stage towards our faith. On the completion of this exposition or our programme of action in the present and the future I will read you the principles of these theories.

In a word, knowing by the experience of many centuries that people live and are guided by ideas, that these ideas are imbibed by people only by the aid of education provided with equal success for all ages of growth, but of course by varying methods, we shall swallow up and confiscate to our own use the last scintilla of independence of thought, which we have for long past been directing towards subjects and ideas useful for us. The system of bridling thought is already at work in the so-called system of teaching by object lessons, the purpose of which is to turn the unenlightened into unthinking submissive brutes waiting for things to be presented before their eyes in order to form an idea of them....

According to authors Marshall Foster and Mary-Elaine Swanson in *The American Covenant*, on September 12, 1905, the first meeting of the Intercollegiate Socialist Society was held. The meeting was not attended by thousands, hundreds, or even dozens of people. In fact, the sum total of the attenders was five. But they were quite a quintet.

Included at the meeting, held in a loft above Peck's restaurant at 140 Fulton Street in Lower Manhattan, were Upton Sinclair, writer and socialist; Jack London, author; Thomas Wentworth Higginson, Unitarian minister; J.G. Phelps Stokes, husband of a socialist leader; and finally, Clarence Darrow, a lawyer. The men were gathered with the common goal of overthrowing the predominantly Christian world-view which still pervaded these United States of America. Officially, their purpose was to "promote an intelligent interest in socialism among college men and women."

To their credit, these young intellectuals chose a proven method of attack, now known as gradualism (thesis, antithesis, synthesis), the theory which historians credit to Roman General Quintus Fabius Maximus. Over the next seven years, these men and their fellow travelers painstakingly established chapters on forty-four other college campuses and in public schools around the country. A short five years later, there were sixty-one chapters, including twelve graduate schools.

In 1921, the organization underwent a name change to League for Industrial Democracy and entered the mainstream of the educational elite in America. In only a decade and a half, they had established one hundred twenty-five chapters of student study groups. By this time, John Dewey, recognized as the leader of the progressive education movement, had risen to the vice presidency of the League, and later in 1941, he had ascended to the presidency, and the well-known, liberal, socialist theologian, Reinhold Niebuhr, was the treasurer.

General Douglas McArthur said, "In war nothing is impossible as long as you use audacity." *Audacity* is exactly what these visionaries had. While only a small minority, they dared to first embrace and then to proselytize their liberal views of society and education. Obviously, in conservative, "Christian" America this was a daring and controversial movement. However, their persistence paid off to the extent that now these once radical and formerly abhorrent views permeate, even dominate, the cultural and educational spheres of America.

This was, in fact, the beginning of the second American Revolution. The moves made by these men (the Pawns of the Princes) in what we now recognize as a global chess game, were as brilliant as they were maniacal. There are a couple of lessons that should be learned from this second American Revolution. First, we see the power of those who are willing to enter wholeheartedly into the arena of ideas. Remember that they were only a tiny minority when they began their war on America!

The second lesson that we must learn is the lesson of their legacy. We have, since the early 1940s, and with fervor since the early 60s, embraced the philosophies of these revolutionaries. The results have been stunning and invasive in all aspects of life in America.

From the start, the Princes have taken a deep and abiding interest in their activities. They and their philosophical disciples in education have received vast sums of funding and ideological support from all of the major foundations of the Princes, including the Carnegie, Ford, and Rockefeller Foundations. As a general rule, if these foundations endorse such movements, be very wary of them. When these foundations add money to their endorsements, you can rest assured that whatever the movement, it is going to work to their advantage in establishing The New World Order.

Obviously, this dogma from Protocol Number 16 has not only been implemented, but done so masterfully. "We shall abolish every kind of freedom of instruction."

In the early 1960s, there were two important Supreme Court decisions that would forever change the course and direction of education and life in general in the United States. As you begin to see the depth and scope of these decisions, I believe that you will, perhaps for the first time, understand the relationship between those who would set up their New World Order and their subtle moves on the global, and in particular, the American chess game now well underway.

One of the exciting aspects of history is the ability to look back and examine relationships between events, their effects on a culture, and resultantly, on the people and institutions of that culture. Since the mid 1960s, we have seen a dramatic reversal in what was once the most efficient, and arguably the best, public education system in the world. Today, our educational system ranks among the worst in the industrialized nations of the world. Even the self-admitted liberals in the network media are making much of the decline of education in America. There are very few Americans who are not saddened, shocked, alarmed, and outraged at the "product" the educational system is turning out.

American children attend one of the most expensive school systems in the world. It becomes more expensive every year, yet the results seem to get worse. Since the mid 60s, SAT (Standard Achievement Test) scores have fallen 100 points. Illiteracy has increased approximately 500 percent in both the black and white sectors of society. The dropout rate has climbed exponentially. Many states now report dropout rates before high school graduation of almost 50 percent.

Educationally, America can no longer compete with the rest of the industrialized world. In fact, there is an entire generation which history will record as the lost generation. But, what is more damaging is the fact that we are well on our way to a second lost generation. If we allow this trend to continue, we will have back-to-back lost generations.

Yet, even with the much-discussed, failing educational system, the "experts" are demanding that the current trends in non-education be continued and, in fact, accelerated. The failed policies of the "enlightened" educational monopolists, embodied by the New World Order elite within the National Education Association (NEA), have amassed tremendous power, having placed their surrogates into the ranks of the Federal Department of Education. Together, the NEA and the Department of Education have made recommendations that would steal children from parents earlier and earlier and place them in State run schools.

What is truly alarming is the type of education that these "experts" want to give our children. Instead of the history of America, our children are being given multiculturalism; in place of geography, the rich interplay of nations; and in place of the basis for culture and its effects on the history of people, they are being taught globalism and cultural blending. *Values Clarification* (which is being taught nationally) is, in the final analysis, a valueless system of socialization — as opposed to the "antiquated" notion of right and wrong. Children are now taught what to think, instead of how to think. All of this leads to a world of gray. There is no room for black or white. Nothing is an absolute. There is nothing to stand for or against. All is blended into a surreal state of blandness, void of passionate dreams; and the vision that made America what it was, has been lost.

Why would a nation, built on the principles of private property, individual achievement, and the free enterprise system — a nation whose very economic future depends upon transferring these values to the next generation — create an educational system which poisons the lifeblood and directly undermines the foundation of its future?

Protocol Number 9

In order not to annihilate the institutions of the unenlightened before it is time we have touched them with craft and delicacy, and have taken hold of the ends of the springs which move their mechanism. These springs lay in a strict but just sense of order; we

141

have replaced them by the chaotic license of liberalism. We have got our hands into the administration of the law, into the conduct of elections, into the press, into liberty of the person, but principally into education and training as being the corner-stones of a free existence.

We have fooled, bemused and corrupted the youth of the unenlightened by rearing them in principles and theories which are known to us to be false although it is by us that they have been inculcated.

In the reading of this Protocol, it is easy to see the plan — and the horrible beauty of the plan. It can be summed up as the dumbing of America.

Lest we give too much credit for the destruction of the heritage of America, and the despoiling of our future to the New World, elitist leaders of the National Education Association, we must remember two contributing factors. The first of these is us. We have allowed it to happen. We have blindly followed the cunning plan of the Princes, and in so doing, have been a part of our own destruction. But there is a way, to both undo the damage already done, and to change our future, which we will discuss in Sections III and IV. It's us against them, and the sooner we realize that, the sooner we can begin laying the axe to the tree of corruption they have planted, nurtured, and groomed for generation after generation.

While it is tragic that as few as five of the surrogates of the Princes could completely take control of, and plant the seeds of destruction for, an entire nation, it is also encouraging to know that each of us has the power to undo the work of generations of the Princes and their surrogates, given the right tools (which we will discuss later).

The second thing that we must remember is that the socialist educators were not alone. They had powerful friends in the media; and together, they have completely monopolized the time, and as a result, the thinking processes of our children.

There are several aspects of media, perhaps we should begin by discussing individual medium. It is interesting how Hollywood has been willing to sacrifice audience as well as profits to churn out thousands of movies which made no money. One might say, "Well, they didn't know at the time that it wasn't going to make money or they wouldn't have made it." Or similarly, "We give the public what they demand, and if that means, sex, violence, and perversion ... so be it." That would be a logical conclusion.

However, it simply isn't supported by the facts. In his book, *Hollywood vs. America,* author Michael Medved reveals startling, if not shocking, facts. He says in the chapter "Motivations for Madness:"

> If nothing else, an honest account of the entertainment industry's tortured path to its present predicament should shatter, once and for all, and beyond any question, one of the most enduring myths about the movies: the peculiarly persistent notion that Hollywood gives us sex and violence only because we demand it.
>
> Recent history shows conclusively that whatever motivations pushed the motion picture business to its current obsessions, financial self interest was not among them. How could an industry that radically changed its focus and thereby permanently sacrificed nearly two-thirds of its audience be described, in any serious sense, as "following the money?"[108]

In presenting the bleak and bloody visions that trouble so many of our fellow citizens, the popular culture isn't responding to some primitive blood lust of the American people; it is, rather, following its own warped conceptions of artistic integrity, driven by some dark compulsion beyond simple greed.

In summarizing, Medved goes on to say that "universally accepted assumption" that the purveyors of pornography, violence, and stupidity in Hollywood grind out so many "R" rated films because they make money cannot be supported in any sense by the facts. Only one "R" film from the 1980's, *Beverly Hills Cops,* made it to *Variety's* top ten list, even though "R" rated films "accounted for more than 60 percent of all titles released in this period." Conversely, "PG" rated films absorbed 60 percent of *Variety's* top ten list, while accounting for only 25 percent of the total releases. Medved goes on to say,

> During this period, all "G" films earned a median box office gross of $17.3 million, while "PG" titles earned a median figure of $13.0 million. For "PG13" releases, the numbers dipped sharply to $9.3 million, while "R" pictures returned even more pathetic median gross of $8.3 million....
>
> ... Taken together; the numbers since 1980 show that a given "G" or "PG" film is nearly five times more likely to place among the year's box-office leaders than an "R" film.[109]

Why then would Hollywood's movie industry continue making "R" rated films that have an 80 percent less chance of real success than their family-oriented counterparts? Is it because America wants these movies? If box office results are any criteria, the answer is a resounding, NO.

Consider, for example, a survey of the movies-going-public quoted by Medved indicates:

> Whenever they are asked their opinion by pollsters (as they were in a comprehensive Associated Press survey in 1989), overwhelming majorities indicate that they want less violence in movies (82 percent), less sexual content (72 percent), and less foul language (80%). Their recent box office behavior indicates that when they express such opinions, the members of the mass audience might actually mean what they say.[110]

If the continuation of the attack by Hollywood on the traditional values of family, religion, and, in fact, all of the "things" that America was built on, are not making money and are not what the people want, what then is the motivation "behind the scenes?" Perhaps Medved's following conversation with an agent might give us a clue:

> I recently spent an hour arguing with a powerful agent over the surprisingly hostile attitude in recent films and television programs toward the institution of marriage. While acknowledging the trend, he insisted that it reflected current realities and expressed the American public's overwhelming desire to "move beyond" the limitations of the nuclear family. When I trotted out a wealth of census figures and survey data suggesting that most Americans remain deeply and stubbornly attached to the old mores and family ideals, my friend deftly changed the basis for his defense. "Maybe we are a little bit ahead of the curve on this one," he acknowledged. "But sometimes that's what you've got to do. You've got to take special risks to help that audience evolve to the next level of consciousness."[111]

Finally, we see what this all about. It is to help us evolve to the next level of consciousness. The same motivation can be seen in the television industry, where we are now being systematically taught that it is "ok" to abandon the tenants of our morality.

Society and especially our children are being preached to from the pulpit of the classroom that they must accept all lifestyles, including

144

homosexuality, lesbianism, and other perversions. They are handed a condom and graphically told how to use it in "safe sex" classes.

Doctors wear face guards, two surgical gowns, two pair of gloves, cover all parts of their bodies, and surgical coverings over their shoes, when working with AIDS patients. Dr. Lorraine Day, a trauma orthopedic surgeon, who for fifteen years was on the faculty of the University of California, San Francisco, School of Medicine as Associate Professor and Vice Chairman of the Department of Orthopedics, and was also Chief of Orthopedic Surgery at San Francisco General Hospital, redesigned a "space suit" to wear when performing surgery on her patients.

Yet, our children are told that sex is safe as long as they wear a condom — even though they are taking off all of their clothes, kissing passionately, sweating, etc. The January 13, 1989 issue of the *Journal of the American Medical Association* detailed that an examination of saliva after deep passionate kissing revealed that 91% of saliva specimens contained red blood cells. It is a fact that blood is one of the methods of transference of the HIV virus (AIDS). Spread of the disease by kissing was reported by the *Lancet,* a British medical publication, as early as December 22, 1984.

The Center for Disease Control drafted regulations which stated: "Each person ... would have to be told ... that they cannot engage in sexual intercourse, kiss someone, or seek medical or dental care without exposing their partner or health care provider to this possibly deadly virus."[112]

Condoms have not been proven safe. According to Jane Chastain, author of *I'd Speak Out On The Issues If Only I Knew What To Say:*

> ... if used perfectly, under laboratory conditions, [a condom] has a 3 percent failure rate; in general use it is up to 33 percent. That means you can get pregnant one-third of the time, or catch AIDS one-third of the time. That's not good enough. That's sexual roulette. Until now, the big back-up for Planned Parenthood programs has been abortion. There is no abortion for AIDS.[113]

In the House of Commons Third Report from the Social Services Committee, Session 1986-87, "Problems Associated With Aids," London, Dr. John Seale of the Royal Society of Medicine stated:

> The AIDS virus persists in an infectious state (ie as cell-free virions) in blood and semen at levels up to 25,000 virions per millilitre, according to the only published paper giving this critically important information. Cell-free virions detected easily in saliva over two years

ago, but quantitive studies have still not been published.

... research effort into infectivity of bodily fluids indicates that saliva is more infectious than genital secretions, but that blood and serum is vastly more infectious than either. Consequently the idea that condoms can have any significant effect on the spread of AIDS in a nation is utterly preposterous.

Governments all over the world are spending millions of pounds advising their citizens to prevent AIDS by using condoms on the basis of manifestly fraudulent misrepresentation of scientific evidence presented by scientists themselves.[114]

These ideas of "safe sex" have been reinforced through evangelists like Norman Lear and others, not to mention the great teacher ... the TV. This isn't about what America wants. This is about helping us take that next step in the "evolution of society." Perhaps that next step is embracing the militant homosexual movement; blaming the Jews for everything that's wrong; or maybe we should turn the hatred of society toward those bigoted Christians, who still want to live life by a set of antiquated rules, such as "Thou shalt not commit adultery" or "Thou shalt not murder."

But don't forget that while these steps are being taken in the evolutionary process that the list of qualified good citizens for the New World Order is growing ever shorter. Soon it may not include anyone who does not embrace the eco-dictatorship proposed by Vice President Al Gore or the proposed homosexual army of Bill Clinton. And, of course, excluded will be Hillary Clinton's list of those who commit crimes against the global community by having too many children, thus using up more than their fair share of the world's resources, including air, water, food, and other renewable resources. After all — if the world is to be as one — there has to be homogeneity of thought and purpose. The problem is, it's always someone else's thoughts and purposes. Nonetheless, the obvious purpose for all of this is to begin building a consensus of opinion among us, the "unenlightened."

In his book *Saturday Morning Mind Control,* author Phil Phillips sums up the relationship between TV and your children.

Recognize that TV is not a playmate or an entertainer nearly so much as it is a teacher for your child. Your child can't tell the difference between make-believe and fantasy on The Box. The messages that come over a TV set are reinforced because they are repeated and repeated. They spawn mental rehearsal; repetition substitutes for feedback. As such, the messages of television become ingrained in a child's memory patterns through a process of attention getting, modeling, and repetition. The program, the characters, and the story lines are all repeated and repeated.

Repetition is the key to learning. Repetition is the key to brainwashing [emphasis mine].

The critical questions are these: What messages are being repeated? Is your child hearing messages that you want to have reinforced?[115]

According to Phillips there are 250,000 TV sets made in America everyday and about 250,000 children born everyday. Ninety-eight percent of all U.S. homes have TV sets and the children in those homes will watch on average 27.3 hours of TV every week. In other words, by the time a child reaches the age of twenty he will have watched seven years of television, which is longer than it would have taken him to earn a masters degree. But the important question is, what is your child learning by a constant process of repeated messages? Phillips says:

> Today's cartoons are filled with religious propaganda. That may not bother you if you are a follower of Eastern thought, Hinduism, new-age philosophy, Zen, or a participant in occult practices. Unless, of course, you are a strong adherent, and then you should be leery of the place given to competing viewpoints.
>
> If you are an atheist, you should be concerned. Your child is being fed a steady diet of religious symbols.
>
> If you are a Christian or an orthodox Jew, take heed. Your child is being taught something that is the opposite of what you believe!
>
> Much of religion has to do with the issue of power — what it is, who has it, how one gets it, and how it works.
>
> Your child's perception of power is tangible. "Mine," says a child. "Yours," he may have to ultimately admit.
>
> The perception of power on today's cartoons is quite different. The power has a spiritual source: a supreme power, a force, an entity beyond the person who or which causes that person to have power or not to have power. The power is absolute. It possesses. It controls.
>
> Virtually all Eastern religions claim that spiritual power lies

within. It is the force that compels one toward some type of self-realization or self-actualization.[116]

Obviously, these views would be quite the opposite of the traditional Judeo-Christian view of spiritual power, in which power rests with God and not inside man waiting for "actualization."

Secondly, the typical Judeo-Christian understanding provides for a free will acceptance or rejection of "God" and his power in the life of an individual. This is not the case in the occult, eastern mysticism, Hinduism, or a plethora of other religions that are being taught to children on Saturday morning (and Monday through Friday before and after school — or all day long in the case of younger children).

Author Phillips points out that a character named *She-Ra, Princess of Power,* gets her name from "Ra," or Isis of Egypt, Queen of Heaven (Semiramis). She gets her power by reciting an incantation, "For the honor of Greyskull." She is part of the Great Rebellion Freedom Fighters (the good guys). She-Ra and the other characters have "familiars," that is familiar spirits or spirit guides. Further, She-Ra often consults her medium or wizard, Light Hope, for advice. Her shaman is called the Sorceress, who appears in the crystal stone of She-Ra's sword.

The message here is pantheistic. There are elements of the occult, Hinduism, eastern mysticism, new age, and about everything else, everything, of course, except any reference to Judeo-Christian religious traditions.

These basically pagan or occult messages are repeated in virtually every popular cartoon series. *He-Man Master of the Universe* follows the same practices. *The Real Ghostbusters* abounds with occultic blasts, portrays spiritism as "good science" and in some episodes, for instance *The Revenge of Murray the Mantis*, contains several derogatory comments about kids, according to Phillips on page 121 of *Saturday Morning Mind Control.*

Then there are the loveable *Care Bears.* How could one find fault with bears whose message is care for one another? Well, according to author Phillips: "When they are animated, they weave a subtle message filled with magic, humanism, the practice of transactional analysis, Bahai beliefs, and the notion of spirit guides. The bears are cute, but new age nonetheless."[117]

Probably only the most naive fail to see through the *Teenage Mutant Ninja Turtles.* Both the movies and the cartoon series are filled with occultic practices, such as Splinter in his often repeated classic lotus position with a large yin/yang symbol behind him. Commonly depicted are mind control, hypnosis, mental telepathy, meditation, psychic ability, and other pagan practices. Again, this is fine for New Agers or pantheists, but, for the rest of us, this is a direct conflict with traditional Judeo-Christian values held in America.

Unfortunately this is just the tip of the iceberg. From the *Smurfs* which is filled with "white magic" to *Archie Comedy Hour* (with Sabrina the Teenage Witch), *Black Star, Defenders of the Universe,* and literally dozens of others, the theme is obviously occultic.

This naturally takes us to the next step in the process of *societal evolution* — the teaching of the new religion. Remember, as stated earlier, one of the goals of the New World Order to be established is the destruction of any competitive religious system, especially Christianity. In fact, any religion, other than Christianity, which is practiced, except on a fanatical basis, is fine because most teach an acceptance of all religions. In the classic sense, it is the "all roads lead to Rome" type of thinking. It doesn't matter what you believe, so long as you are sincere about it. However, Christianity is exclusive. Christianity says there is only one way — and it is that exclusivity which makes it dangerous to the Princes and their goals for the New World Order.

Protocol Number 14

When we come into our kingdom it will be undesirable for us that there should exist any other religion but ours of the "One God" with whom our destiny is bound up by our position as the Chosen People and through whom our same destiny is united with the destinies of the world. We must therefore sweep away all other forms of belief. If this gives birth to the atheists whom we see today, it will not, being only a transitional stage, interfere with our views, but will serve as a warning for those generations which will hearken to our preaching....

Protocol Number 4

But even freedom might be harmless and have its place in the State economy without injury to the well-being of the peoples if it rested upon the foundations of faith in God, upon the brotherhood of humanity, unconnected with the **conception of equality** [emphasis mine] which is negatived by the very laws of creation, for they have established subordination. With such a faith as this a people might

149

be governed by a wardship of parishes, and would walk contentedly and humbly under the guiding hand of its spiritual pastor submitting to the suppositions of God upon earth. This is the reason why it is indispensable for us to undermine all faith, to tear of minds out of the unenlightened the very principle of Godhead and the spirit, and to put in its place arithmetical calculations and material needs.

In future chapters we will discover exactly what religion these Illumined ones are preaching. The Princes are promoting through their own surrogates, Hollywood and the television networks, their religious and philosophical beliefs.

Cleverly, the Princes have advanced their "evangelism" effort on two fronts — children and adults. They are attempting to retrain adults with movies and sitcoms, and our children with *Saturday Morning Mind Control.*

However, that is only one manifestation of their power. Organizations such as the American Council of Churches and its global counterpart, the World Council of Churches, speak for the "church," at least in the public and media sense.

It is important that we begin to see this effort not as splintered or random attempts at a globalist, Luciferian religion. It is a well-organized plan of attack against the one religion that historically has been a foil to them. This has led to what a former associate of mine has termed "abandonment theology". It is the process whereby the Christian church in America has abandoned the historical and Biblical beliefs and accepted a *liaise-faire* attitude toward traditional Christian faith, which is the corner stone of the founding of America. We will discuss the historical significance of this in the next section. However, a society without foundational beliefs is a society in trouble. There is an old saying, "If you stand for nothing, you will fall for anything." And that is the plan. Lest we forget our friends in the news media:

Protocol Number 2

In the hands of the States of today there is a great force that creates the movement of thought in the people, and that is the Press. The part played by the Press is to keep pointing out requirements supposed to be indispensable, to give voice to the complaints of the people, to express and create discontent. It is in the Press that the Triumph of freedom of speech finds its incarnation. But the unenlightened states have not known how to make use of this force; and it has fallen into our hands. Through the Press we have gained the power to influence....

Protocol Number 3

... To this end we have stirred up every form of enterprise, we have armed all parties, we have set up authority as a target for every ambition. Of States we have made gladiatorial arenas where a host of confused issues contend ... A little more, and discords and bankruptcy will be universal ...

Babblers inexhaustible have turned into oratorical contests the sittings of Parliament and Administrative Boards. Bold journalists and unscrupulous pamphleteers daily fall upon executive officials.

Protocol Number 5

We shall assume to ourselves the liberal physiognomy of all parties, of all directions, and we shall give that physiognomy a voice in orators who will speak so much that they will exhaust the patience of their hearers and produce an abhorrence of oratory.

In order to put public opinion into our hands we must bring it into a state of bewilderment by giving expression from all sides to so many contradictory opinions and for such length of time as will suffice to make the unenlightened lose their heads in the labyrinth and come to see that the best thing is to have no opinion of any kind of matters political, which is not given to the public to understand, because they are understood only by him who guides the public. This is the first secret.

The second secret requisite for the success of our government is comprised in the following: To multiply to such an extent national failings, habits, passions, conditions of civil life, that it will be impossible for anyone to know where he is in the resulting chaos, so that the people in consequence will fail to understand one another.

In a recent conversation with a friend, the statement was made: "I hear so much on the news, from so many different sides, that I really don't know what to believe any more."

Congratulations are in order for the Princes. They have fulfilled one of their primary objectives. The networks and their "talking heads" on the evening news broadcasts have mastered the art of double speak. They have carefully staged the issues and presented them to us using two methods of deception. First, they use the technique described earlier: thesis, antithesis, synthesis. Secondly, they take the traditional values held by America and Americans and apply them in a "worst case scenario" and then give an endless stream of other seemingly enlightened solutions to the problem.

The result of this technique is predictable and beneficial to the Princes. Let's take an example of the news in the not-too-distant past. A young boy, who had less than a perfect home, wanted to divorce his parents and live with his foster parents. Here's the plan. The ACLU (another Pawn of the Princes) takes this boy's case in his effort to divorce his parents. The national media picks up the story and makes it the lead headline for better than a week. The upshot is, that the traditional American view of children being a ward, and further, a possession of the parent, is overturned in one — this one — instance. **However, it is important to remember that tough cases make bad law**.

But rather than acknowledge that this is an isolated incident, a "worse case scenario," the media plays it up as a symptom of society and all of its ills. In fact, the presentation of this type of case in this light is one of the causes of the societal ills.

Following this exposé, we are greeted with the babblers who have more inane solutions to this and other ills of society than one can possibly assimilate. For them to be successful in undermining the foundations of our belief and cultural system, they must first present no answers that will really work. This is key. **Every option, but that which is appropriate and workable, is given for our consideration.** But, when one considers that this is just another step in promotion of the "Children's Bill of Rights," a humanistic concept created by the Princes' globalist world parliament, the United Nations, one begins to see the logic of this type of insanity. There is, if you will, "a method to their madness."

One can rest assured that this is a well-conceived plan of attack. The same treatment is given to almost every topic; from animal rights, where the case of unsanitary and cruel conditions are exposed in "puppy mills," to AIDS, where the lingering death of a young boy with AIDS was dragged before us night-after-night. The important aspect of all of this, is that one will never be given a viable solution to the problem by the media. There is a solution to the problem of AIDS. It is chronicled in several books written on the subject including Gene Antonio's *The AIDS Cover-up?* This particular subject and its solution will be dealt with later. I believe that neither the problem nor the solution is any great mystery. However, the national media, in their "wisdom," has given answers as ridiculous as giving the disease political status, to spending billions and billions of dollars on fruitless research. The result has been ... "To multiply to such an extent national failings, habits, passions, conditions of civil life, that it will be impossible for anyone to know where he is in the resulting chaos...."

Accordidng to author, George Grant, one of the most noted scholars of revisionist history and chaos at the turn of this century was Henry Cabot Lodge. In the introduction to Grant's book, *The Last Crusader: The Untold Story of Christopher Columbus*, Grant quotes Lodge's thoughts on American history: "Nearly all historical work worth doing at the present moment in the English language is the work of shoveling off heaps of rubbish inherited from the immediate past."[118] This trend toward historical revisionism has continued unabated for decades and has remarkably increased recently.

During the nation's recent "celebration" of the quincentennial of Admiral Christopher Columbus' discovery of America, the most curious tales began to appear. Stories were told of this exquisite and brilliant man of the sea that would have us believe that he was all but a mad, blood-thirsty, incompetent, sexual pervert, with delusions of grandeur. In fact, Admiral Columbus was a brilliant sailor, whose purpose for his explorations were both to (1) spread Christianity, and (2) help free the Holy Lands by first generating profits from his explorations and by finding an alternate back route to sneak up on the "Moslem hoard."

The conclusion, that he was a man of deep faith and conviction, is borne out by letters written by Columbus during that period. Columbus wrote in his diary on December 26, 1492:

> I hope to God that when I come back here from Castille, which I intend on doing, that I will find a barrel of gold, for which these people I am leaving will have traded, and that they will have found the gold mine, and the spices, and in such quantities that within three years the Sovereigns will prepare for and undertake the reconquest of the Holy Land. I have already petitioned Your Highnesses to see that all the profits of this, my enterprise, should be spent on the conquest of Jerusalem, and Your Highnesses smiled and said that the idea pleased them, and that even without the expedition they had the inclination to do it.[119]

153

And as for his being a blood-thirsty sex fiend who brutally butchered people, without cause, just to fulfill his own sick desires, he wrote concerning his initial encounters with the Indians:

> I gave to all I approached whatever articles I had about me, such as cloth and many other things, taking nothing of theirs in return.... They also give objects of great value for trifles, and content themselves with very little or nothing in return. I, however, forbade that these trifles and articles of no value (such as pieces of dishes, plates, and glass, keys, and leather straps) should be given to them,... as being unjust, and myself gave them many beautiful and acceptable articles which I had brought with me, taking nothing from them in return. I did this in order that I might the more easily conciliate them, that they might be led to become Christians....[120]

Grant goes on to say, "That kind of gentle evangelistic concern was actually typical of Columbus — and leavened his relations with all men everywhere. It would ultimately prove to be the manner of both his doing and his undoing."[121]

The same type of character assassination of personages from American history has been, and continues to be, at a much more cunning and accelerated pace. This is all part and parcel of the destruction of our sense of patriotism and nationalism, which falls right in line with the plan as outlined in the following Protocol:

Protocol Number 5

> The second secret requisite for the success of our government is comprised in the following: To multiply to such an extent national failings, habits, passions, conditions of civil life, that it will be impossible for anyone to know where he is in the resulting chaos, so that the people in consequence will fail to understand one another.

While "New Dealer" Franklin Roosevelt is given sainthood status, George Washington is being "trashed" as an incompetent military leader and immoral demagogue by revisionist historians. Woodrow Wilson, the modern father of globalism in America, and puppet of the Princes, is knighted, and Thomas Jefferson, who while in his twenties, could write music, survey a plot of land, cauterize an artery, and speak several languages, is sardonically cast as a "deist." While other great men of history, such as Madison, the

154

chief architect of the Constitution of the United States, is either ignored or written off as a narrow minded "constructionist," constitutional heretics, are praised for their anti-family, plantation politics. Lyndon Johnson's "Great Society," for instance, was heralded as a bright and shining accomplishment in American political history.

In all, we have failed to understand one another, just as the Princes planned because the basis for our common heritage, history, culture, and morality have been replaced with fables. The common values for which we fought and upon which we built these United States, have been replaced by pious sounding doctrines of destruction. The dominant media culture has taught that taking from the successful and productive and giving to the needy by force of law is honorable; that fostering anarchy in the name of dubious "rights" is liberty; and that the deeds of evil men, whether sitting in the halls of Congress, or at 1600 Pennsylvania Avenue, are reflective somehow of the historical values of America.

As a result, we are told that the values once held near and dear by Americans are wrong and destructive, and unfortunately, all too often, the blind mob of society is willing to accept the lie. This for them is reason enough to abandon the pearls of American culture, love of God, family responsibility, love of country, and old fashioned patriotism, and accept in their place the swill of societal collectivism and the enshrining of counter productive doctrines that have the ring of "fairness." Still, the monotonous drone of the Princes and their high priests of globalism continue to mesmerize the masses, while we, the "unenlightened," sit glazed over in apathy, embarrassed by the glories that were America.

We fail to see ourselves being enslaved, chained, and sold as chattel by the Princes of the New World Order.

Chapter 12

Your Guess Is As Good As Mine

Protocol Number 4

In order to give the unenlightened no time to think and take note, their minds must be diverted towards industry and trade. Thus, all the nations will be swallowed up in the pursuit of gain and in the race for it will not take note of their common foe. But again in order that freedom may once for all disintegrate and ruin the communities of the unenlightened, we must put industry on a speculative basis: the result of this will be that what is withdrawn from the land by industry will slip through the hands and pass into speculation, that is, to our classes.

At the writing of this book, the European Economic Community (EEC) has come into existence. The North American Free Trade Agreement (NAFTA) has been signed by former President George Bush. The basis of both is trade, industry, and commerce. And yet, with all the machinations of government to create "trade and industry," there is truly no basis for a prosperous future. We have become so distracted by the prospect of being able to produce our way out of the world's economic slump, that we have lost sight of the values upon which the prosperity of the past was built. We have been so emersed in the process of industry that there has been no time for renewing those ideals which naturally lead to productivity.

Yet, underlying all of this is the second tenet of Protocol Number 4: "We must put industry on a speculative basis." The stock market, banks, savings and loans, insurance policies, while being cloaked in terms of protectionism, are speculative. We have been encouraged to let money work for us or, even better, someone else's money, rather than earning by real work. We have been encouraged to take any real estate equity and utilize it in speculative ventures. The destruction, thus speculative, has been enhanced as the FED has contrived disastrously low earnings on CD's paid by banks. This, coupled with the fear created by the recent collapse of both banks and S&L's, has forced billions of small investors' and retirees' dollars into the stock market.

Even while professional investors representing mega-institutions, insurance companies, pension plans, etc., are fleeing the market, an unsuspecting American public is being enticed into the speculation of industry. Unfortunately, for many who cannot afford it, their money will "slip through their hands and pass into speculation, that is, to our classes [the Princes]."

Protocol Number 6

To complete the ruin of the industry of the unenlightened we shall bring to assistance of speculation the luxury which we have developed among the unenlightened, that greedy demand for luxury which is swallowing up everything. We shall raise the rate of wages which, however, will not bring any advantage to the workers, for at the same time, we shall produce a rise in prices of the first necessities of life, alleging that it arises from the decline of agriculture and cattle-breeding: we shall further undermine artfully and deeply sources of production, by accustoming the workers to anarchy and to drunkenness and side by side therewith taking all measure to extirpate from the face of the earth all the educated forces of the unenlightened.

In order that the true meaning of things may not strike the unenlightened before the proper time we shall mask it under an alleged ardent desire to serve the working classes and the great principles of political economy about which our economic theories are carrying on an energetic propaganda.

The ruination of industry in America, and further of society, is proposed in this section of Protocol Number 6 through the very concept of luxury. The trick, as stated, is to make people think that the lobbying for higher wages on the part of their union, Congress, or social reformers, is going to bring them a higher standard of living. However, it is with chagrin that I must tell you, that since the early 1960s (even though wages have increased dramatically), the standard of living has not only *not* increased, but has, in fact, declined. Again, we see a correlation with the decline in American society in yet another component — the standard of living — at that same mysterious date in the early 60s, when those two famous Supreme

158

Court decisions were handed down which banned prayer and bible reading from the schools.

Still, in all, the social reformers in government — and for that matter — outside government, continue unabated in their "... ardent desire to serve the working classes and the great principles of political economy...." However, it is the blind leading the blind, as we read the last half of this Protocol which says, "... about which our economic theories are carrying on an energetic **propaganda.**" But, the schemers and utopian dreamers never learn the lessons of history, and subsequently, are doomed to repeat the mistakes.

Protocol Number 13

The part played by liberals, utopian dreamers, will be finally played out when our government is acknowledged. Till such time they will continue to do us good service. Therefore we shall continue to direct their minds to all sorts of vain conceptions of fantastic theories, new and apparently progressive: for have we not with complete success turned the brainless heads of the unenlightened with progress, till there is not among the unenlightened one mind able to perceive that under this work lies a departure from truth in all cases where it is not a question of material inventions, for truth is one, and in it there is no place for progress. Progress, like a fallacious idea, serves to obscure truth so that none may know it except us, the chosen....

When we come into our kingdom our orators will expound great problems which have turned humanity upside down in order to bring it under our beneficent rule.

Who will ever suspect then that all these peoples were stage-managed by us according to political plan which no one has so much as guessed at in the course of many centuries?

What is perhaps more aggravating than anything else is that we have fallen for the entire plan. We obscure truth and accept in its place the lie, that is even now leading us to the brink of disaster. How can one improve on the truth? Truth is truth and there is no room for improvement, and still "liberals and utopian dreamers" try.

I find it interesting that the Princes describe their rule as "beneficent." Look at their own words in the following Protocols:

Protocol Number 9

> ... Super-Government subsists in extra-legal conditions which are described in the accepted terminology by the energetic and forcible word — Dictatorship.

Protocol Number 20

> ... The rich must be aware that it is their duty to place a part of their superfluities at the disposal of the State since the State guarantees them security of possession of the rest of their property and the right of honest gains. I say honest, for the control over property will do away with robbery on a legal basis.

What has been more damaging than the monopolistic control of our economy, is the destruction of our sense of private property by the accomplishment of these goals? Believe it or not, there are actually "Welfare Rights" organizations all across America. They are those who believe that sponging off of society (the producers within society), is a *right*.

What is even sadder is that there are actually people of means who believe that it is both their duty and honor to pay unconstitutional, illegally authorized, and dramatically destructive income taxes, which are destroying the very core of our society. In a recent conversation with a very successful business man, I was told, "I like paying my taxes ... the freedom that this country gives us is what has given me the ability to acquire what I have today." But the very freedom which this man has enjoyed is being stolen from him every time he pays taxes. The proof of this statement is two-fold. First, we can examine the process of the building of wealth in this nation, since the inception of this plank of the *Communist Manifesto,* known as the progressive income tax; and second, the Princes' own words which tell the real purpose for this devilish doctrine.

Protocol Number 20

> This social reform must come from above, for the time is ripe for it — it is indispensable as a pledge of peace.
>
> The tax upon the poor man is a seed of revolution and works to the detriment of the state which in hunting after the trifling is missing the big. Quite apart from this, a tax on capitalists diminishes the growth of wealth in private hands in which we have in these days

concentrated it as a counterpoise to the government strength of the unenlightened — their State finances.

The taxation that the United States government has imposed on all America has two purposes. First, on the poor, this type of tax is, as the Princes tell us, the "seed of revolution and works to the detriment of the state." It causes the oppression of the "little guy" till he gets to a point that he, with Jack Gargan says, "I'm mad as hell and I'm not going to take it any more!" In his efforts to not "take it anymore," he has no one but his fellow unenlightened to turn to; and often in blind rage he rebels and lashes out. But, in his blind fury, he hits the wrong target; he destroys in many cases that which should have been clung to and chooses instead to cling to that which got him in the mess in the first place.

It would be impossible for me to tell you the number of times that I have heard even supposed conservatives say, "I do think that the tax system in this country is unfair. It's time that the rich paid their fair share." What an insane statement. Yet, those poor deceived souls that would "soak the rich" through the Progressive Income Tax somehow have not perceived that the reason for their condition, in many cases, is the Progressive Income Tax.

It has stolen Americans' jobs by crushing business and robbing the citizens of income. According to the General Accounting Office (the official "watchdog" agency of the Congress of the United States), the average American now pays 48 percent of everything he or she makes in one form of taxation or another.

During the Dark Ages the average serf lost 25 percent of every thing he made to taxation. History books are replete with dismal reports of the oppression of the serfs. Yet, we are told, almost on a daily basis by the elected thieves in Washington, D.C. and in state capitals around the country, that the problem is: "We need to expand revenue if we are to care for the needs of the people."

Let me translate that statement for you. Since the only real power that the Congress has is to tax and spend, they want to expand their power base by "revenue enhancements" (investments), which are euphemisms for *more taxes*. Meanwhile, the oppression of taxation continues to expand at a pace never before matched in the history of a free nation.

Which brings us to the second effect of the insidious income tax; namely, the protection of the monopoly of mega-wealth held by the Princes. By stealing the income of Americans through the Progressive Income Tax,

161

the Princes have eliminated the possibility of anyone ever again approaching their wealthy status — unless, they have ordained it.

At this point one might well suppose that it is too late to turn America around. The Princes have virtually accomplished every one of their goals. They have effectively abolished our constitutional republic and replaced it with democracy which has, even as they predicted, devolved into false freedom and little more than mob rule. Still utopian dreamers and liberals, who either knowingly or unknowingly are the stooges of the Princes, continue to push us further toward democracy, which, as we read earlier, is nothing more than an euphemism for the type of government described in Marx's *Communist Manifesto.*

A sense of patriotism and nationalistic intent has been lost to America through the rewriting of history and the ill treatment of the Founding Fathers of this Nation; coupled with the wars of the Princes, that is the wars planned, staged, and scripted by them — including the Vietnam War — which gutted America financially, politically, and morally.

We no longer, as a people, believe in the rightness of our destiny. We have lost the vision of the Founding Fathers that planted this great land.

The abolition of inheritance and any sense of ownership in private property, are all but *fait-accompli* with the Progressive Income Tax, Inheritance Tax, and a plethora of other illegal and oppressive taxes. In addition to all of these, the perilous condition of inheritance and private property are exasperated by zoning laws, use laws, EPA's ever-growing "Eco-dictatorship," and the mind-boggling jumble of laws which are hemorrhaging from Washington D.C. and our state capitals.

The final stage of the overthrow of private property and inheritance is the re-education of society toward "societal collectivism." Under this teaching, each of us has some sort of "Carmic" or "Cosmic" collective responsibility to "society" at large — to help evolve mankind (the species) to the next step in "evolutionary enlightenment." Of course, this is all hogwash, or as the Princes describe it, "crying absurdity." But, to the *pseudo enlightened,* it makes all kinds of sense. Meanwhile, private property and the rights of inheritance have gone the way of the Model T. The one difference is that the Model T was supposedly replaced with something better — which is not the case here, unless of course you are looking forward to the "dictatorship," as the Princes describe it, of the New World Order.

There are those who would tell us that the goal of the "welfare state" is to help strengthen families. Obviously, those who would support the welfare state towards that end fall into one of three categories. The first of these categories is the innocently stupid, who are ignorant of the real goals of the Princes, and who are somehow unable to look over their shoulder and objectively view the history of the last thirty years, under the theolotics of the "Great Society." The second category consists of liberals or utopian dreamers, whose egotistic view of their own "enlightenment" (read foolish and destructive belief system), will not allow them to see the truth of their own folly, or the fact that they are the Pawns of the Princes. Finally, the truly "enlightened," who are a part of this centuries-old conspiracy to institute their "beneficent Dictatorship," vainly imagine themselves Princes, unknowingly are part of a deeper conspiracy — and they themselves dance on the strings controlled by the *Unseen Hand.*

As you have seen throughout this section, there is never one piece of the conspiracy that does not have an effect in all areas of the five general goals of the Princes. One can see the destruction of the family due to the vast amounts of income stolen from families through taxation and the craving of luxury. A huge bill is now facing these United States for the maintenance of the welfare state, which leads us back to the enslaving tax burden born by Americans.

Gone are the days of the *traditional* family. In many families both parents are absent from the home, leaving generations of *latch-key* children who are being raised by the evangelists of the New World Order. These include many unaware teachers in the public school system, The New Age, New World Order, and occultic prophets and prophetesses, whose writings are the trash through which our children are being indoctrinated by these surrogate parents. Most tragically, even our own misguided churches, either knowingly or unknowingly, have fallen prey to — and passed along — the "theology of abandonment," enhancing and reinforcing the alienation of parents and their children.

Protocol Number 13

In order that the masses themselves may not guess what they are about we further distract them with amusements, games, pastimes, passions, people's palaces.... Soon we shall begin through the press to propose competitions in art, in sport of all kinds: these interests will finally distract their minds from questions in which we should find ourselves compelled to oppose them.

163

When the family is not being distracted by financial demands, keeping up with the Joneses, or trying to figure what went wrong with their marriage, there is the ever pervasive distraction of "busy-ness." Today Americans are so busy that they hardly have time to be families. Children are involved in little league, soccer, band, clubs, extra curricular activities at school, and so many other all-absorbing activities, that there simply isn't time for family.

But just in case there is a little time left on the weekends, there are televised sports: baseball, football, basketball, hockey, and countless other distractions. What time is left for family, marriage, and the spiritual somehow gets eaten up.

The final and fifth goal is really the foundation for the Princes' success in all other areas: the abolition of all religion, especially Christianity, which is to be replaced with humanism — the worship of reason. In this area, the Princes of the New World Order have been most successful. America is probably one of the most religious nations on the face of the earth. However, the "faith of the fathers" from which we obtained "Life, Liberty and the pursuit of Happiness," has been subtly changed. In the process, the foundation of what our Founding Fathers called Biblical Christianity has been severely weakened, if not destroyed.

Again, as discussed earlier, the institution of the 501(c)(3) status (required by the State if an organization, such as a church, is going to be recognized as a tax exempt entity) has placed the State squarely at the head of the church. As a result ...

the "God of our fathers" has been replaced by the "god-State."

Chapter 13

The Founding Fathers' Legacy

5. Abolition of religion, especially Christianity, which was to be replaced with humanism — the worship of Reason.

> Our laws and our institutions must necessarily be based upon and embody the teachings of the Redeemer of mankind. It is impossible that it should be otherwise; and in this sense and to this extent our civilization and our institutions are emphatically Christian.... This is a religious people. This is historically true. From the discovery of this continent to the present hour, there is a single voice making this affirmation.... We find everywhere the clear recognition of the same truth.... These, and many other matters which might be noticed, add a volume of unofficial declarations to the mass of organic utterances that this is a Christian nation.
>
> Supreme Court Decision, 1892
> Church of the Holy Trinity v. United States

In light of the dominant media culture, with words like "democracy," phrases like, "Separation of Church and State," and other well-known, but equally false and destructive ideas running rampant in society, it is difficult for us, as modern-day Americans, to envision just exactly what it was that our Founding Fathers gave us. We imagine, somehow, that this was a nation that went to war against a foreign government, which was tyrannizing the land, stealing the wealth of our people, through undue taxation, and regulating their lives to the extent that freedom had disappeared.

This was not the case. There were tyrannical laws — of that there is no doubt. There was oppression of the people. But, the whole perspective changes when you realize under what form of government they operated. It was not under a foreign government, but under their own government in England. They were English people in an English territory. They fought

165

not against a foreign tyrant. Rather, they resisted their government for a number of reasons, not the least of which were "Life, Liberty, and the pursuit of Happiness."

At the beginning of this chapter we quoted the Supreme Court decision of 1892. The Supreme Court declared this to be a "Christian" nation. This was not done lightly, nor was it done as a result of a "theistic" court. Rather, it was based upon a "volume of unofficial declarations" which were added to "masses of organic utterances." This was a Christian nation. Our Founding Fathers said that they gave us a Christian nation. Yet, somehow we find that so hard to believe in this era of the "separation clause."

Why is it so difficult for us to imagine this being a Christian nation? We have no problem imagining the state of Israel being a Jewish nation. We have no problem acknowledging Saudi Arabia as a Moslem nation. And yet, somehow, we think it perverse that this should be a Christian nation. But, that is what our Founding Fathers said it was; and it has not just been the Founding Fathers asserting this. Throughout the history of this nation, America has been developed on the principles of Christianity. Those principles, according to the popular media culture, are anachronistic, heavy-handed, anti-sex, anti-women, anti-people decrees which came down from a legalistic, Puritan background and must be purged, if the land is to progress into the enlightenment of what will be — the New World Order.

Across America we are voting special rights for homosexuals. Cities, towns, and organizations are being sued for putting up nativity scenes during the Christmas season. This is, indeed, an interesting turn of events.

As we judge a government or an institution, we must examine it carefully to first find out what it once was, whether or not it worked, and then finally, what it has become. Let's compare the early complex republic, known as these United States that was given us by the Founding Fathers, with the simple republic or democracy into which this country has changed, and its resultant failures or successes.

According to Daniel Webster, "our ancestors established their system of government on morality and religious sentiment. Moral habits, they believed, could not safely be trusted on any other foundation than religious principle, nor any government be secure which was not supported by moral habits."[122]

They gathered together to write the Constitution in Philadelphia. After many weeks of struggle and little progress, the wise old gentleman, Benjamin Franklin, rose to address the assembly on June 28, 1787.

166

... In the beginning of the contest with Britain, when we were sensible of danger, we had daily prayers in this room for Divine protection. Our prayers, Sir, were heard and they were graciously answered. All of us who were engaged in the struggle must have observed frequent instances of a super intending Providence in our favor.... Have we now forgotten this powerful Friend? Or do we imagine we no longer need His assistance?

I have lived, Sir, a long time, and the longer I live, the more convincing proofs I see of this truth: that God governs in the affairs of man. And if a sparrow cannot fall to the ground without His notice, is it probable that an empire can rise without His aid? We have been assured, Sir, in the Sacred Writings that except the Lord build the house, they labor in vain that build it. I firmly believe this....

I therefore beg leave to move that, henceforth, prayers imploring the assistance of Heaven and its blessing on our deliberation be held in this assembly every morning.[123]

I think it is obvious from the words of the Supreme Court, Benjamin Franklin, and a "volume" of other evidences, that our Founding Fathers gave us, in fact, a Christian nation. However, even before this nation was a separate nation, back in the 1600s, the very purpose of the Pilgrims was to establish a government based upon the Bible.

William Bradford in his writings of the Pilgrims, describes their first official act as, "being thus arrived in a good harbor and brought safe to land, they fell upon their knees and blessed the God of heaven, who had brought them over the fast and furious ocean, and delivered them from all the perils and miseries therin to set their feete on the firme and stable earth, their proper elemente."

In 1683, the early founders of this nation gave us the Rhode Island Charter which says, "We submit our persons, lives, and estates unto our Lord Jesus Christ, the King of kings and Lord of lords and to all those perfect and most absolute laws of His given us in His Holy Word."[124]

According to historical revisionists; according to the liberal media; even according to many "church leaders," these Laws of Scripture were much too oppressive and tyrannical for a nation to bear for long. After all, there were over six hundred laws given to mankind by their Creator.

Yet today, Americans suffer from a plague of laws. State Houses consider every year thousands upon thousands of new laws. At the federal level there are so many laws being passed, that there are laws passed about laws — even laws which contradict each other. In fact, there are hundreds of thousands of pages of regulations concerning laws, which are so complex, wordy, dubious, and often inane, that no one fully understands the law.

It is easy, at the slightest examination, to find that even judges do not know the law. It has become too complex for any one man or any one system to handle. Lawyers constantly present briefs based upon court cases, based upon past interpretation of law, based upon new interpretation of law, and based upon new law. In most cases of any complexity, the judge has to retire to chambers to consider all of the law being presented. However, it would be impossible to consider *all* of the law!

Our "elected officials," lawyers, the A.L.C.U., the dominant media culture, and others, insist that Biblical law is a system that represses the people. They claim it is too tyrannical, complex, and inflexible. How much more their own argument would decry the system they have created — where now there are so many laws that no one can judge by the law! Even while a case is being adjudicated, new laws are being passed which would contradict past adjudications.

In the early days of this country, it was said, "Ignorance of the law is no excuse." Then each man had a copy of the law. The Scriptures were very prevalent in this nation. In fact, during the war for independence from England, one of the first official acts of the Congress of the United States was to order the printing of Bibles that each man might have one, and thereby, know the founding principles of this nation. The rights to life, liberty and property were not plucked from thin air. They were based on a "religious code" that our Founding Fathers sought and found in Scripture. The right to life, based upon the Commandment, "Thou shalt not murder." The right to liberty based upon the second half of the law which dealt with man's relationship to man, and the unalienable right to the pursuit of happiness were found in a code of regulation known as scriptural law, which regulated man's conduct in relationship to the Creator and his fellow man.

One of George Washington's early official acts was to proclaim a day of Thanksgiving to "acknowledge the providence of Almighty God, to obey His will, to be grateful for His benefits, and humbly implore His protection and favor."

Alexis DeTocqueville, a nineteenth century French philosopher, visited America and upon his return to France he said America was a land "aflame with righteousness" and "America is great because America is good; and if America ever ceases to be good, America will cease to be great."

Abraham Lincoln said, "It is the duty of nations, as well as of men, to owe their dependence upon the overruling power of God and to recognize the sublime truth announced in the Holy Scriptures and proven by all history, that those nations only are blessed whose God is the Lord."

Noah Webster, speaking of the foundations of this great land said, "The religion which has introduced civil liberty is the religion of Christ and His apostles.... To this we owe our free Constitutions of government." He also said: "The moral principles and precepts contained in the Scriptures ought to form the basis of all our civil Constitutions and laws. All the miseries and evils which men suffer from vice, crime, ambition, injustice, oppression, slavery, and war, proceed from their despising or neglecting the precepts contained in the Bible."

John Quincy Adams said: "The first and almost the only Book deserving of universal attention is the Bible."

Andrew Jackson is said to have remarked: "Go to the Scriptures.... The joyful promises it contains will be a balsam to your troubles."

"The foundations of our society and our government rest so much on the teachings of the Bible that it would be difficult to support them if faith in these teachings would cease to be practically universal in our country," exclaimed Calvin Coolidge.

And finally, Abraham Lincoln expounded, "All the good from the Savior of the world is communicated through this Book; but for the Book we could not know right from wrong. All the things desirable to man are contained in it."[125]

As we view the breakdown of society today (with the dramatic increases in crime, drug abuse, alcohol abuse, and every form of evil under the sun which now pervade America), we can trace it to the fact that no longer do we understand the difference between right and wrong.

In the 1700s, William Blackstone, an English professor of law, wrote commentaries which served as the basis for applying law in the first century of the fledgling American republic. His entire theory of law was based on the Judeo-Christian principles of absolutism. Those absolutes, Blackstone said, were revealed in the Law of God, contained in the Bible.

Like Blackstone, the Founding Fathers had a Biblical concept of the Law, rights, and freedoms. They believed rights and freedoms were derived from just, absolute, unchanging law. Therefore, in the Declaration of

Independence that our Founding Fathers expounded, based upon eternal Law, two important and fundamental principles.

The first of these was that they believed in a Creator who was sovereign in the affairs of governments and men, who had established absolute standards to which all men and governments were accountable.

Secondly, they understood that man, in his own wisdom could not be his own law and judge. If man were, in fact, lawgiver and judge, both law and judgment would be based on the varying opinions of men. It was, therefore, totally unacceptable as a constant, ongoing, and eternal standard.

As stated earlier in this book, there is no room for progressivism within truth. Truth is truth. It cannot be changed. It cannot progress or evolve into something else. It is already, thoroughly absolute and completely set. It needs no evolutionary process. Law then, seen as truth providing justice, was in the minds of the Founding Fathers, set by scripture; and as such, it was absolute, unchanging, and uncompromising.

Perhaps as a point of reference, we might ask then, historically, which system worked best? Historical revisionists have stated that life under "Biblical law" was oppressive, repressive, and tyrannical. It dishonored women, eschewed sex, and gave us a code of morality to which no one could attain.

Yet, all three of these statements are found to be unprovable and unfounded. Man did have, under Biblical law, a moral code of high standing. But it was a moral code with absolutes to which everyone could, if not attain, at least aspire. Those basic tenets are foundational to all people, all men, all civilizations everywhere: "Thou shalt not murder" and "Thou shalt not steal."

As far as Scriptures eschewing sex, nothing could be further from the truth. Rather, it eschewed immorality and condemned adultery and fornication, which has become the basis for the broken family and of a preponderance of social diseases. It has, in fact, become the foundation for the plague of AIDS now sweeping America and the world. AIDS is slow, certain, and painful death. In condoning a violations of ordinances against fornication, adultery, and murder, we have developed a system of genocide, which rather than curing the problem of fornication, adultery, and murder, merely hides them beneath the cloak of a "right to privacy."

In all, since 1973, when Roe v. Wade was enacted judicially and unconstitutionally as the law of the land, we have slaughtered thirty million American people. We now have lost thirty million people who will never enter the work force to support the elderly on what we now know as social security. Thirty million people who will never become a productive part of society. Depending upon the system of prognostication, one to three percent of those thirty million people would have been geniuses; that one to three percent, who may have been brilliant scientists, statesmen, architects, designers, or engineers, will never — ever — contribute to making this once great nation, great again.

Was this a Christian nation? From perhaps the earliest document of the Americas, the *Mayflower Compact,* we find these words by William Bradford:

> In the name of God, Amen. We whose names are under-written, the loyall subjects of our dread soveraigne Lord, King James, by the grace of God, of Great Britaine, Franc, and Ireland king, defender of the faith, etc., haveing undertaken, for the glorie of God, and advancemente of the Christian faith, and honour of our king and these presents solemnly and mutualy in the presence of God, and one of another covenant and combine our selves together into a civill body politick, for our better ordering an preservation and furtherance of the ends aforesaid; and by vertue heard to enacte, constitute, and frame such just and equall lawes, ordinances, acts, Constitutions, and offices, from time to time, as shall be thought most meete and convenient for the generall good of the Colonie, unto which we promise all due submission and obedience. In witnes whereof we have hereunder subscribed our names at Cap-Codd the 11. of November, in the year of the raigne of our soveraigne lord, King James, of England, France, and Ireland the eighteenth, and of Scotland the fiftie fourth. An Dom. 1620.

Throughout early American history, law, economy, politics, and social relationships were governed by the "immutable law of Scripture." But, as reported earlier, this began to change with the formation of a new set of ideas, principles, and morals upon which certain "enlightened individuals" thought society should be shaped and bound.

And so it was that Madeline O'Hare (an avowed atheist), John Dewey (who through his teachings and ideological descendants, still rules the educational system of America from the grave), and other humanits, began the work that would culminate in 1962 and 1963, when the Supreme Court — in two landmark decisions — changed the course of America, and thus, changed almost two hundred years of progress, prosperity, and liberty.

Inscribed above the head of the Chief Justice of the Supreme Court of the United States, are some interesting symbols and language. Overshadowing the written words are an American eagle, protecting the Ten Commandments found in the Bible. At the beginning of each session of that court, the same cry is heard, "God save the United States and the honorable Court."

It is, then, incredible that these jurists, who see every day above their heads the Ten Commandments and hear the prayer "God save the ... honorable Court," could have rendered decisions banning prayer and Bible reading in the public schools in 1962 and 1963. This, I believe, caused the rapid downturn of American society, education, politics, and the beginning of the disintegration of the family and the moral system of law and order.

Using a perversion of the "Separation Clause," the Court ruled that requiring the reading of the Bible violated the Separation Clause. Further, even a cursory examination of the educational history in America reveals that our once great educational institutions were founded by Christians — upon Christian principles.

In 1636, the Puritans of the Massachusetts Bay Colony saw the necessity of founding an institution of higher education. The following is from the 1643 *"Description of Harvard College,"* which can be found in the historical records of Harvard University.

> It please God to stir up the heart of one Mr. Harvard (a
> godly Gentleman, and a lover of Learning, there living amongst us)
> to give the one halfe of his Estate (it being in all about 1700.1.)
> towards the erecting of a Colledge, and all his Library;...

Harvard's first President and faculty believed true knowledge rested solely on a personal relationship with their Savior. As proof of their deep and abiding Christian convictions, we need only examine the rules and precepts they adopted.

> 2. Let every Student be plainly instructed, and earnestly pressed to
> consider well, the maine end of his life and studies is, to *know
> God and Jesus Christ which is eternall life,* Joh. 17.3. and therefore
> to lay *Christ* in the bottome, as the only foundation of all sound
> knowledge and Learning.
> And seeing the Lord only giveth wisedome, Let every

one seriously set himselfe by prayer in secret to seeke it of him *Prov.* 2.3.

3. Every one shall so exercise himselfe in the Scriptures twice a day, that he shall be ready to give such an account of his proficiency therein, both in *Theoretticall* observations of the Language, and *Logick,* and in *Practicall* and spirituall truths, as his Tutor shall require, according to his ability; *seeing the entrance of the word giveth light, it giveth understanding to the simple,* Psalm 119. 130.

4. That they eshewing all profanation of Gods Name, Attributes, Word, Ordinances and times of Worship, doe studie with good conscience, carefully to retaine God, and the love of his truth in their mindes, else let them know, that (notwithstanding their Learning) God may give them up *to strong delusions, and in the end to a reprobate minde,* 2 Thes. 2. 11, 12. Rom. I. 28.

8. If any Schollar shall be found to transgresse any of the Lawes of God, or the Schoole, after twice Admonition, he shall be lyable, if not *adultus,* to correction, if *adultus,* his name shall be given up to the Overseers of the Colledge, that he may bee admonished at the publick monethly Act.

Section 3. *The times and order of their Studies we read:*
The fift(h) day reads Hebrew, and the Easterne Tongues...
Afternoone.
The first yeare practice in the Bible at the 2d. houre.
The 2d. in Ezra and Dan(i)el at the 3d. houre.
The 3d. at the 4th. houre in Trostius New Testament.

... Every Schollar, that on proofe is found able to read the Originalls of the *Old* and *New Testament* into the Latine tongue, and to resolve them *Logically;* withall being of godly life and conversation; And at any publick Act hath the Approbation of the Overseers and Master of the Colledge, is fit to be dignified with his first Degree.

Every Schollar that giveth up in writing a *System,* or *Synopsis,* or summe of Logick, Naturall and Morall *Phylosophy, Arithmetick, Geometry* and *Astronomy:* and is ready to defend his *Theses* or positions: withall skilled in the Originalls as abovesaid: and of godly life & conversation: and so approved by the Overseers and Master of the Colledge, at any publique *Act,* is fit to be dignified with his 2d. Degree."[126]

And so it was in the 17th century, that over fifty percent of Harvard's graduates entered the Christian ministry. As the new century of the 1700s dawned, many Christians in Connecticut believed that Harvard was too expensive and too far away, and so they started Yale College as an institution of higher learning and an alternative to Harvard. Likewise, Princeton (originally called the College of New Jersey) in 1746, was chartered as a result of the evangelical fervor of the first "Great Awakening."

Princeton managed to retain its spiritual impetus longer than any of the other Ivy League schools and was, in fact, directed by Presidents of evangelical intent, until at least the early 1900s.

In 1754, evangelist George Whitfield secured a charter for Dartmouth College from King George III of England. The charter specified the school's intent was to reach the Indian tribes and educate and Christianize English youth. The school had a strong missionary thrust and was launched in the state of New Hampshire under the royal charter.

Likewise, Columbia University, originally known as the King's College, had as its first President, a missionary to America. The college of William and Mary was started by the Church of England. Rutgers University, originally known as Queen's College, was founded by Dutch Reformed Revivalists. The Baptist churches that were scattered up and down the Atlantic, founded Brown University. With but one exception (the University of Pennsylvania), every college founded in the colonies prior to the American Revolution was established by Christian churches and missionaries and men of Christian intent.

While they eventually abandoned their original Judeo-Christian roots, these Ivy League universities and colleges produced some of the greatest theologians and Christian thinkers of the time. With these great Christian minds and leaders in society, politics, education, and religion — the country grew and prospered.

Later, the traditions of Christianity, which were the basis of wisdom and education, were slowly abandoned by the Ivy League schools, though Chrisitianity remained implanted in the minds of the people. In fact, almost every school district opened its school days with Bible reading and prayer. Many states had mandatory curriculums for Bible readings for students. This was, indeed, a Christian nation, but this changed in 1962 and 1963. In one of the most audacious and far-reaching decisions the Court had ever made, the Judeo-Christian principles of morality and governance were banned from the educational curriculum of students. The Court thus rejected those things upon which this nation was founded.

The first reason given for their decision was the non-existent doctrine of "Separation of Church and State," supposedly, drawn from Article I of the Bill of Rights. As we will discover later, the first Article of the Bill of Rights was to protect the church from the state — *not the state from the church.*

Secondly, they reasoned that the Ten Commandments might be harmful to students if anyone happened to read them as they passed through the halls (where they were often posted).

As discussed earlier, the consequences of such a fatal flaw, have become remarkably clear over the past thirty years. This is well documented by the graphs on this and the following pages.

Over the last thirty years, we the American public, through our elected

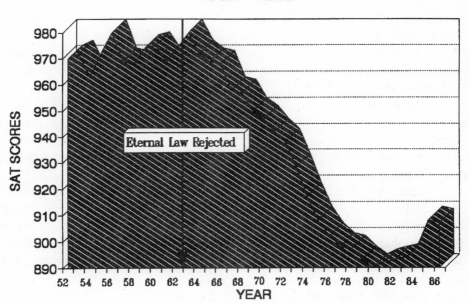

SAT Total Scores
1952 - 1986

175

Includes: Gonorrhea Syphillis Chancroid Inguinale Lymphogranuloma Venereum AIDS

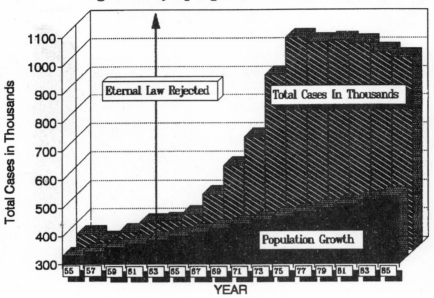

Divorce Rates
Divorces Per 1, 000 Total Population

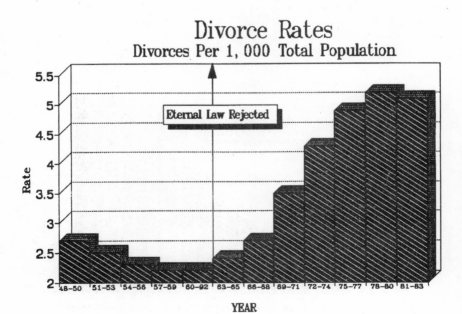

Births Per 1,000 Unwed Women

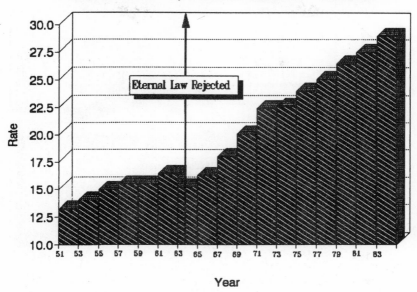

Year

Violent Crime:
Number Of Offenses

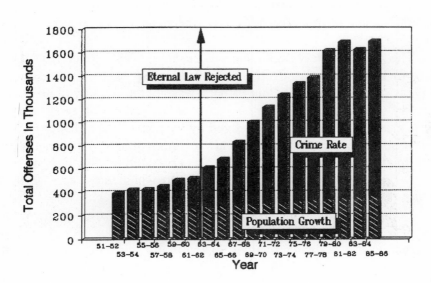

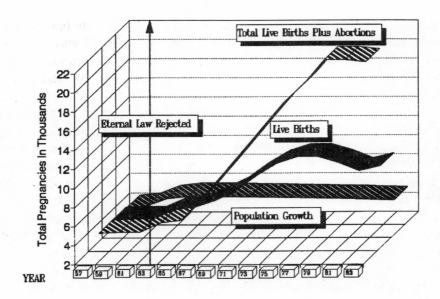

officials, have spent enough money on welfare to have purchased all of the assets of all of the Fortune 500 Companies in America and nearly all of the farm land in America. Still poverty, since the 1960s and the beginning of Lyndon Johnson's Great Society, has doubled from 8 percent to 16 percent in this nation. If our poverty programs were created to foster poverty, they have worked remarkably well. However, if our poverty programs were designed to alleviate poverty, they have been an embarrassing, shameful failure.

The Great Society was meant to ensure for each American a basic standard of living, ending poverty, and fostering equality for all. However, equality, as stated by the Founding Fathers, was not the equality of all persons. Rather, it was the equality of all persons under Law; that each would be treated honestly and justly, being judged by the same Law. However, as the Law was perverted and became the law of humankind, or humanism, law became relative. There were no longer clear absolutes — black or white. Rather, we had huge masses of gray area into which most cases fell, and "situation ethics" became the order of the day.

No longer were all men equal under Law. Adjudication of law became nothing more than a humanistic intent at situational justice. Therefore, with the destruction of the absolute values that had built this nation to the greatest nation on the face of the earth (perhaps the greatest nation in the history of

178

the world), the foundation for success in society, that is absolute law, became irrelevant. Absolute law, which said, "Thou shalt not covet," was forgotten and cast aside. For it was covetousness, the desire to take from one to give to another, that became law. And with the advent of the welfare state, came the intrusion of government into every aspect of our lives.

No longer was a wage paid to an employee, under a contractual arrangement between employer and employee. No longer was the employer able to structure his employment policy, based upon the lines of adherence to the code of ethics of the employer. In the Great Society, an employer could no longer make hiring decisions based on whether a job applicant did or did not represent the employer's moral, ethical, or business code.

Today, under humanistic law, an employer is forced to employ those who may or may not represent his ideas or ideals. Further, the wealth of producing citizens is stolen and redistributed to non-producing citizens within society.

In the selling of this idea to America, we were told that it was our duty, collectively, to care for those who had less than we, who were less fortunate than ourselves. We had created, through the warped educational processes of Dewey and others, a societal moré that each of us was entitled to a certain minimum amount of prosperity. Even prosperity was redefined. We harken back, to the "two chickens in every pot" mentality, which has become pervasive in America. If we again go back to *The Protocols,* we see the direct intent of creating a false definition of prosperity, based upon greed and envy, which was destined to destroy the moral fabric of America.

This same concept later expressed itself in the all too familiar words of the proponents of communism with the idea "to each according to his need, from each according to his ability." This was a far different system than envisioned by the Founding Fathers.

In a debate on the floor of the House of Representatives, James Madison (of Virginia) debated John Laurance (of New York) in February of 1792. The point of the debate was the controversy surrounding the "general welfare clause" found in Article I, Section 8.

Mr. Laurance contended, "The general welfare is inseparably connected with any object or pursuit which in its effects adds to the riches of the country."

Madison successfully argued:

> I, sir, have always conceived — I believe those who proposed
> the Constitution conceived, and it is still more fully known, and more

179

material to observe that those who ratified the Constitution conceived — that this is not an indefinite government, deriving its powers from the general terms prefixed to the specified powers, but a limited government, tied down to the specified powers which explain and define the general terms. The gentlemen who contend for contrary doctrine are surely not aware of the consequences which flow from it, in which they must either admit or give up their doctrine.

It will follow, in the first place, that if the terms be taken in the broad sense they maintain, the particular powers afterwards so carefully and distinctly enumerated would be without any meaning, and must go for nothing. It would be absurd to say, first, that Congress might do what they please, and then that they may do this or that particular thing. After giving Congress power to raise money and apply it to all purposes which it may pronounce necessary to the general welfare, it would be absurd, to say the least, to superadd a power to raise armies, to provide fleets, etc. In fact, the meaning of the general terms in question must either be sought in the subsequent enumeration which limits and details them, or they convert the government from one limited, as hitherto supposed, to the enumerated powers, into a government without any limits at all.

... There are consequences, sir, still more extensive, which, as they follow clearly from the doctrine combated, must either be admitted, or the doctrine must be given up. If Congress can apply more money indefinitely to the general welfare, and are the sole and supreme judges of the general welfare, they may take the care of religion into their own hands; they may establish teachers in every state, county, and parish, and pay them out of the public treasury; they may take into their own hands the education of children, establishing in like manner schools throughout the union; they may undertake the regulation of all roads, other than post roads. In short, everything, from the highest object of state legislation down to the most minute of police, would be thrown under the power of Congress; for every object I have mentioned would admit the application of money, and might be called, if Congress pleased, provisions for the general welfare.[127]

Madison made it clear that he conceived, and those who proposed and signed the Constitution believed, that this was a government of limited power, deriving its power **not** from the "general welfare" of Article 1, Section

8, but rather, from the specified powers, which they were allowed to undertake. But, they were limited and tied down only to those specific powers. This same concept is repeated inthe following Articles of the Bill of Rights, which state:

Article IX

> *The enumeration in the Constitution of certain rights, shall not be construed to deny or discourage others retained **by the people.**" [Emphasis mine].*

Article X

> *The powers **not delegated** [emphasis mine] to the United States by the Constitution, nor prohibited by it to the States, are preserved to the States respectively, or to the people.*

This, in the minds of the Founding Fathers, was an important concept. It was based on the Judeo-Christian principle that men should govern themselves by a code of morals prescribed by Biblical Law, which should not have superimposed over it, the edict of government.

It's interesting that Madison warned that unlimited government could take to itself the care of religion, which is precisely as we discussed earlier, what it has done under the tenets of the IRS code 501(c)3. Government has, in fact, by that act taken the care of religion in their hands, and determined what religion may or may not do in the United States.

Secondly, in what now appears to be prophetic utterance, Madison said that if this doctrine was allowed to proceed as a general welfare unrestrained, that the government could establish schools in every state, county, and parish, and appoint teachers for the educating of our children; paying the educators out of the public treasury. Madison understood, as did all the Founding Fathers, that if government controlled education, our schools could, and likely would, be changed from educational institutions to propaganda houses.

In fact, Madison said government would even go so far as to take upon themselves the regulation of all roads (which is forbidden by the Constitution), other than post roads, and would take control of every object of state legislation, down to the most minute things — even the police. This, of course, the government has done through federal mandates and various other methods of controlling states via federal funding.

The enumerated powers of which Madison spoke are found in Article 1, Section 8 of the Constitution. Listed in order, they are:

1. To borrow Money on the credit of the United States;
2. To regulate Commerce with foreign Nations, and among the several States, and with the Indian Tribes;
3. To establish an uniform "Rule of Naturalization," and uniform capital Laws on the subject of Bankruptcies throughout the United States;
4. To coin Money, regulate the capital Value thereof, and of foreign Coin, and fix the Standard of Weights and Measures;
5. To provide for the Punishment of counterfeiting the Securities and current Coin of the United States;
6. To establish Post Offices and Post Roads;
7. To promote the Progress of Science and useful Arts, by securing for limited Times to Authors and Inventors the exclusive Right to their respective Writings and Discoveries;
8. To constitute Tribunals inferior to the Supreme Court;
9. To define and punish Piracies and Felonies committed on the high Seas, and Offenses against the Laws of Nations;
10. To declare War, grant Letters of Marque and Reprisal, and to make Rules concerning Captures on Land and Water;
11. To raise and support Armies, but no Appropriation of Money to that Use shall be for a longer Term than two Years;
12. To provide and maintain a Navy;
13. To make Rules for the Government & Regulation of the land and naval Forces;
14. To provide for calling forth the Militia to execute the Laws of the Union, suppress insurrections and repel Invasions;
15. To provide for organizing, arming, and disciplining, the Militia, and for governing such Part of them as may be employed in the Service of the United States, reserving to the States respectively, the Appointment of the Officers, and the Authority of training the Militia according to the discipline prescribed by Congress;
16. To exercise exclusive Legislation in all Cases whatsoever, over such District (not exceeding ten Miles square) as may, by Cession of particular States, and the Acceptance of Congress, become the Seat of the Government of the United States, and to exercise like Authority over all Places purchased by the Consent of the Legislature of the State in which the Same shall be, for the Erection of Forts, Magazines, Arsenals, dock-Yards, and other needful Buildings; — And
17. To make all Laws which shall be necessary and proper for carrying into

Execution the foregoing Powers, and all other Powers vested by this Constitution in the Government of the United States, or in any Department or Office thereof.

That's it! That is all the power that is granted to the government of the United States. Those who pervert the Constitution with massive spending and welfare programs do so illegally, and have indeed, as Madison said, "superadd"[ed] to the Constitution their own beliefs, which are not contained in the Constitution, and in fact, which were opposed strenuously by the Founding Fathers.

In examining even these items listed in Article I, Section 8 of the Constitution, George Washington, had much to say on the borrowing of money by the government, regulating commerce with foreign nations and among the several States and the Indian Tribes. Washington also addressed these in his Farewell Address.

Obviously, there are many duties charged to the federal government. However, in examining the seventeen powers enumerated to the Congress of the United States, where do you see the authorization for a Department of Education; the authorization for a Department of Energy; the authorization for the Federal Department of Transportation; the authorization for OSHA; or, the plethora of other agencies created by Congress? That power does not exist.

Those who contend for a limited government, limited in both its expanse and invasion into our private lives, are considered by many to be radicals. However, nothing could be further from the truth. Those who would superadd powers to the Constitution, which the Constitution specifically forbids them from doing, are indeed the radicals — the revolutionaries — who are trying to overthrow the Constitution of the United States. In fact, as a result of Supreme Court cases, we now see that the Amendment process of the Constitution has been taken from the hands of the people and put into the hands of the Congress and the Supreme Court (neither of which has the constitutional authority to take upon themselves that responsibility).

In the devolving of the American Constitution; in the devolving of American society; in the devolving of the body politic; in the devolving of the system of law, justice, and order in America, we see one common root: the destruction of the Judeo-Christian values upon which this nation was built — eternal, immutable Law — Biblical Law.

For more than three decades, we have attempted to buy our way out of poverty and the scourge of other social ills, which have been fostered by collapsing America's foundation. Empirically, the data would suggest that the methods we have chosen have been a failure. It is the folly and fate of fools to continue in failed policies. The answer for the social and economic ills of America is not bigger, more pervasive government; such government has been the root cause of our deepening problems. The attempt to place government in the position of God is the cancer that is killing us. **It will never be the cure which saves us, since God alone can provide for our needs.**

There was a time when this nation understood that it was "Divine Providence" which supplied the needs of mankind: his physical needs, his emotional needs, and his spiritual needs. However, that day has passed, and I fear that if we do not retrace our steps, we will have no future.

Before the end of this century, probably much sooner than that, America, our government, will be so indebted that it will take every penney raised in personal income taxes just to pay the interest on the national debt. If, in fact, taxation now consumes 48 percent of everything the average American earns (as the General Accounting office claims), what will the tax rate be then? Are we to be reduced to mere wage slaves of a federal bureaucracy? Noah Webster said:

> I deduce this definition of the most perfect practicable system of government; a government where the right of making laws is vested in the greatest number of individuals, and the power of executing them in the smallest number.

> ... The legislators of the American states are neither swayed by a blind veneration for an independent clergy nor awed by the frowns of a tyrant. Their civil policy is or ought to be the result of the collected wisdom of all nations, and their religion, that of the Savior of mankind. If they do not establish and perpetuate the best systems of government on earth, it will be their own fault, for nature has given them every advantage they could desire.

> Every stride of Tyranny in the best governments in Europe has been effected by breaking over some constitutional barriers. But where a Constitution is formed by the people and unchangeable but by their authority, the progress of corruption must be extremely slow, and perhaps tyranny can never be established in such government, except upon a general habit of indolence and vice.[128]

James Madison said in a letter to George Mason on July 14, 1826:

> ... it is proper to take alarm at the first experiment on our liberties. We hold this prudent jealousy to be the first duty of citizens and one of the noblest characteristics of the late Revolution. The freemen of America did not wait till usurped power had strengthened itself by exercise and entangled the question in precedents. They saw all the consequences in the principle, and they avoided the consequences by denying the principle. We revere this lesson too much, soon to forget it.[129]

There has, for some time, been a push by both the Executive Branch and Congress of the United States, to grant certain nations most favored nation status. This status is one afforded to those with whom we have supposedly good, fair, and equitable trading status. These are nations with whom we enjoy a common morality — or sense of societal view. There are, of course, problems with this.

In the first place, it drags us into entangling alliances, which is never good for a nation which intend to be self-sufficient. We must not entangle ourselves in the alliances that lead to trade wars and economic battles throughout the world. We need not be a part of the United Nations organizations dealing with trade and global trade treaties, such as the General Agreement on Tariffs and Trade (GATT).

Secondly, there is the problem of taxation. Every time we grant the most favored status to a particular nation state, we put ourselves in a position of lowering that state's tariffs, imposts, and import fees on those imported items. If the tax base from trade is decreased, personal income taxes must be increased to make up the difference. In other words, we give countries like China — to whom we have now granted most favored nation status — a free ride at the expense of the American people. Meanwhile, we have millions of unemployed American workers.

China, as you will recall, heavily uses prison laborers (slave prison laborers). Most prisoners there are political prisoners who had the misfortune of not being smiled upon by the communist state. These prison slave labor forces (because they cost practically nothing) are able to produce goods for sale abroad — and particularly in the United States — at very low costs. The Chinese have long been recognized as a nation which will readily dump goods all over the world (but particularly in this country) at bargain basement prices and driving our markets out of existence. Meanwhile, the Chinese government is lining its pockets off the sweat of slaves.

The entire concept of most favored nation status is not one that the Founding Fathers embraced. George Washington, in particular, had stern words against the concept of most favored nations. For many years in this nation, we honored the words and wisdom of Washington; and resultantly, we saw America grow and prosper. We saw this nation become the foremost international trading power.

Washington, in his Farewell Address to the Congress at the end of his second term as President, said these words concerning most favored nations:

> In the execution of such a plan nothing is more essential than that permanent, inveterate antipathies against particular nations and passionate attachments for others should be excluded, and that in place of them just and amicable feelings toward all should be cultivated. The nation which indulges toward another an habitual hatred or an habitual fondness is in some degree a slave. It is a slave to its animosity or to its affection, either of which is sufficient to lead it astray from its duty and its interest. Antipathy in one nation against another disposes each more readily to offer insult and injury, to lay hold of slight causes of umbrage, and to be haughty and intractable when accidental or trifling occasions of dispute occur....[130]

He is speaking of the ills of pronounced animosity or affection (most favored or most unfavored nations) and how such entangling alliances and political animosities lead to the enslavement of this country. But he goes on to say:

> So, likewise, a passionate attachment of one nation for another produces a variety of evils. Sympathy for the favorite nation, facilitating the illusion of an imaginary common interest in cases where no real common interest exists, and infusing into one the enmities of the other, betrays the former into a participation in the quarrels and wars of the latter without adequate inducement or justification. It leads also to concessions to the favorite nation of privileges denied to others, which is apt doubly to injure the nation making the concessions by unnecessarily parting with what ought to have been retained, and by exciting jealousy, ill will, and a disposition to retaliate in the parties from whom equal privileges are withheld; and it gives to ambitious, corrupted, or deluded citizens (who devote

themselves to the favorite nation) facility to betray or sacrifice the interests of their own country without odium, sometimes even with popularity....[131]

Washington, in this section of his speech, speaks specifically about facilitating the illusion of an *imaginary common interest.* To the degree that we, the United States, share a common interest with a favored nation, or with all nations on an imaginary basis, we again build the foundation for the New World Order. It is this very principle of imaginary common interests that is facilitating the "global society," into which George Bush, Bill Clinton, Al Gore, and apparently the Congress of the United States, would slam dunk this nation.

Washington also discussed the dangers posed to elected officials, or to citizens in general, that might be deluded into betraying or sacrificing the interests of this nation, in deference to that of a "favored nation."

> Against the insidious wiles of foreign influence (I conjure you to believe me, fellow-citizens) the jealousy of a free people ought to be *constantly* awake, since history and experience prove that foreign influence is one of the most baneful foes of republican government. But that jealousy, to be useful, must be impartial, else it becomes the instrument of the very influence to be avoided, instead of a defense against it. Excessive partiality for one foreign nation and excessive dislike of another cause those whom they actuate to see danger only on one side, and serve to veil and even second the acts of influence on the other....[132]

Washington makes several salient points. He reminds us, implores us, to listen to him: free people need to be constantly awake. History is replete with examples of the dangers to a republican government from foreign influence. It is important for you to notice that **he calls this government a republican government — not a democracy. They are not synonymous.**

Had we heeded Washington's words, World War I and World War II would have been unnecessary. In paraphrasing Winston Churchill: Had the United States stayed out of World War I — kept out of business that was none of ours — it (World War I) would have ended as another skirmish on the European continent and would have been placated, by the parties involved, in very short order. However, our entrance into World War I, as explained earlier, had nothing to do with protecting the rights of anyone; rather, it was the basis for tremendous financial profits for the Princes. World War I also laid a foundation for world governance by the Princes through the League of Nations and later the United Nations. Again, quoting Washington:

> Our detached and distant situation invites and enables us to pursue a difference course. If we remain one people, under an efficient government, the period is not far off when we may defy material injury from external annoyance; when we may take such an attitude as will cause the neutrality we may at any time resolve upon to be scrupulously respected; when belligerent nations, under the impossibility of making acquisitions upon us, will not lightly hazard the giving us provocation; when we may choose peace or war, as our interest, guided by justice, shall counsel.
>
> Why forego the advantages of so peculiar a situation? Why quit our own to stand upon foreign ground? Why, by interweaving our destiny with that of any part of Europe, entangle our peace and prosperity in the toils of European ambition, rivalry, interest, humor, or caprice?
>
> It is our true policy to steer clear of permanent alliances with any portion of the foreign world, so far, I mean, as we are now at liberty to do it; for let me not be understood as capable of patronizing infidelity to existing engagements. I hold the maxim no less applicable to public than to private affairs that honesty is always the best policy. I repeat, therefore, let those engagements be observed in their genuine sense. But in my opinion it is unnecessary and would be unwise to extend them.
>
> Taking care always to keep ourselves by suitable establishments on a respectable defensive posture, we may safely trust to temporary alliances for extraordinary emergencies.[133]

Obviously, George Washington and the Founding Fathers envisioned a nation that was not involved throughout the world. They did not envision NATO and SEATO and every other cockamamie organization that our politicos have dreamed up. Washington, being an honorable man, encouraged this nation to keep those agreements that had already been made. However, he implored his fellows not to expand upon, and certainly not to avail themselves of, the opportunity to make new and yet more entangling alliances.

Those elected to office and serving in Washington, D.C. have robbed America. They have betrayed America and Americans through their oppressive taxations and economic restrictions (as a result of trade treaties and alliances all over the world). And, in cheating America and Americans out of those dollars (which should have come from import fees, trade tariffs, etc.), they have forced upon us excessive taxation at home — to the point now that it is very difficult for American businesses to compete world-wide.

Our problem with world trade is not — and never has been — England, Germany, Japan, or China. Our problem is that the Congress of the United States is stealing 48 percent of everything we earn. Was this a simple mistake? Having read to this point, I doubt that you will come to that conclusion. It is — rather — of particular design. Those who would metamorphize these United States into The United Nations or some global system, which will eventually become The World Government (singular), have carefully laid the plan for bankrupting America. The Princes plan depends on entangling trade, creating economic and military alliances, and bankrupting morality. In speaking of morality, which Washington inexorably tied to religious principle, we find these words:

> It is substantially true that virtue or morality is a necessary spring of popular government.
>
> Promote, then, as an object of primary importance, institutions for the general diffusion of knowledge. In proportion as the structure of a government gives force to public opinion, it is essential that public opinion should be enlightened.[134]

Washington understood the concept of this government. This republican government would not work unless there was a religious and a moral people, who through self-restraint, would prohibit the evils that have destroyed every other nation.

During the 1992 elections, much was made of the fact that there was a third political party — *the Perot movement* — entering this Presidential debacle. Much was made by the news commentators of the destructive nature of such forces, saying that America has a long history and tradition of the two party system. Well, first of all, that is historically inaccurate. There have been dozens and dozens of parties across America. Many times there were several parties represented in the Congress of the United States.

The Democratic Party, while the oldest, has not, until the last forty years, taken complete control of the government. Prior to that, there were many separate parties holding seats within the Congress. There was a new party formed in the mid 1850s, the Republican Party, which won its first

Presidential election with its candidate, Abraham Lincoln. But what of political parties? Washington had comments on this as well.

> All obstructions to the execution of the laws, all combinations and associations, under whatever plausible character, with the real design to direct, control, counteract, or awe the regular deliberation and action of the constituted authorities, are destructive of this fundamental principle and of fatal tendency. They serve to ... put in the place of the delegate will of the nation the will of a party, often a small but artful and enterprising minority of the community, and according to the alternate triumphs of different parties, to make the public administration the mirror of the ill-concerted and incongruous projects of faction rather than the organ of consistent and wholesome plans, digested by common counsels and modified by mutual interests.[135]

When the will of the party or their parochial desires (either to further their own ends or to foil the plans of another party — all for the sake of the party) in any way convolute that which is generally good for the nation — they are wrong! That is the exact scenario that we face today.

In all, most of what is being done by the generally reprobate, and self-serving political parties is destroying America. But our vastly overpaid, disingenuous representatives in Washington could care less. Their only concern is power — both gaining and keeping it. Again, Washington warned us, but we simply haven't heeded his advice.

We have taken the gold of constitutional principle and traded it for the dung of corrupt, political party contrivance.

Chapter 14

It Could Never Happen Here

Most Americans are completely unaware of what happened in Katanga, and don't fully understand the "goings on" in Somalia. But, let me assure you that we have not seen the last of the U.N. peace keeping forces. The U.N. army will be used more and more to bring its peculiar brand of peace to the world.

As a matter of fact, they have had some test runs here in the United States. *Operation Longhorn* involved an estimated 115,000 Army and Air Force personnel, in and around the Fort Hood area, during the period March 25 - April 15, 1952. In April, 1952, in the little town of Lampasas, Texas, *Operation Long Horn* was launched. The activities were reported in their local press, the *Lampasas Dispatch,* in an article printed on April 3, 1952, by Wilbur Martin entitled, "Lampasans Under Heel of Aggressor Liberation," wherein Martin stated:

> Lampasas "lost democracy" Thursday in a make-believe incident that was very real.
>
> Hundreds gaped silently as big, green-clad Aggressor troops took over this little ranching town of 5,000 persons, closed churches ... and set up concentration camps.
>
> In cold, gloomy weather and intermittent showers the troops arrested businessmen, loaded citizens into barbed wire concentration camps, conducted brief one-sided trials....
>
> Clyde Northington, President of the school board, was sentenced to "death" for carrying a pistol and being out after dark. He received an offer of life imprisonment if he would get the school board to back the Aggressor form of teaching.
>
> Sound trucks blared propaganda throughout the day telling the people they were "liberated" and had a "new, humane government of the Centralist party."

During the 1992 Presidential election, I was asked, along with my Co-Chairman of the U.S. Taxpayers Party of Florida, William "Bruce" Bendt, to debate Andre Marrou, the Libertarian Presidential candidate, and supporters from the Bo Gritz campaign at the *Taxpayer Action Day Picnic,* an annual event sponsored by Citizens Against Government Waste. Following the debate, I met Chuck Noel, one of the Gritz campaign organizers. In a subsequent meeting, he supplied me with the following maps, which had been sent via facsimile from the Gritz campaign headquarters. (Bo Gritz, as you may recall, is a former U.S. Intelligence operative and Green Beret Congressional Medal of Honor recipient.)

While I have made repeated attempts to verify the information provided to me by the Gritz people through one of my U.S. Senators, I have had little or no cooperation from his office. Seems they are too busy to take time out of their hectic schedule of purloining our money and constitutional rights to be bothered with me. After all, I'm just a constituent who is concerned about the future of this nation. Besides, I'm sure that they checked their records and found out that I was not a major, or for that matter even a minor, contributor to the Senator's campaign.

Be that as it may, these maps purportedly detail areas of the United States that have been designated as "detention facilities" — authorized through the Federal Emergency Management Act (FEMA) and augmented by the Department Of Defense (DOD) Budget Amendment — which passed with the 1991 Fiscal Budget. Each site can detain between 32,000 to 44,000 people minimum. It is indicated that the Texas and Alaskan sites may be much larger and more heavily armed. For the area west of the Mississippi, Oklahoma City is the central processing point for detainees and can handle up to 100,000 people at a time. There are twenty-three FEMA authorized and stationed detention centers and twenty DOD Budget authorized and stationed centers for a total of forty-three detention centers.

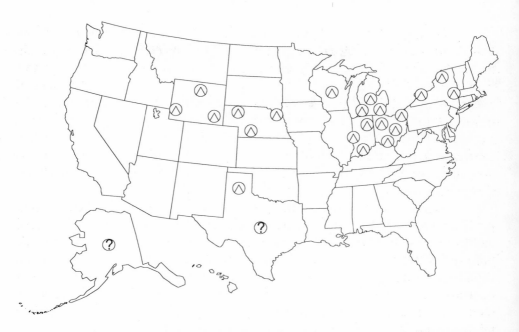

If these maps (and the information on them) are authentic, there are also United Nations Battle Groups whose entrance to the United States was passed under Presidential Executive Order signed 11 November 1990 by George Bush. There appear to be fifteen locations on this map.

FINCEN is the U.S. Treasury Department's Crime Enforcement Network. They use foreign military and secret police brought into the United States for deployment against U.S. Citizens. Most identified FINCEN units are at company strength (160 men plus). Some are as large as brigade strength (2,600 men plus). (See map below.) FINCEN's stated mission is:

    A. House to house search and seizure of property and arms
    B. Separation and categorization of men, women, and children as prisoners in large numbers
    C. Transfer to detention facilities of aforementioned prisoners

NOTE: All FINCEN uniforms, equipment, helicopters, etc. are black.

Again, according to the information we received from Gritz' headquarters, "The Multi-Jurisdictional Task Force (MJTF) is the Velvet Glove on the Iron Fist." This is the motto on the cover page of the MJTF police guidelines and authorizing legislation. This force is made up of:

    1. Military - Convert those National Guard Units that are not banned by the President into a National Police Force
    2. Convert all surviving local and state police to national police
    3. Convert street gangs into law enforcement units for house to house searches(L.A., Chicago, & New York are in the process now)

MJTF's mission is:

1. House to house search and seizure of property
2. Separation and categorization of men, women, and children: as prisoners in large numbers
3. Transfer to and the operation of detention camps (43+)

During our meeting with Noel on November 6, 1992, he also gave me a picture that he personally took of troops training in Charlotte County, Florida on October 23, 1992. He recapped the events for me as follows:

> I attended a weekly meeting of concerned persons on Thursday, October 22, 1992. We were discussing the location of U.N. Troops in the U.S.A. I had a map showing many confirmed locations. One of the members of the group spoke up and claimed to have seen some military-types training in a remote area of our county. He said they were dressed in black or dark uniforms, and were training with riot sticks!
>
> The next afternoon at 4:00 P.M. I went looking for these people. I looked all around the area and finally found them. They were marching and exercising with their sticks, just as I was told. Their uniforms were very dark brown, almost black. They wore a black helmet (full-size padded) with a full face shield. I couldn't see their faces through the shield. They carried a long riot stick. They each had a belt with several pouches.

They were training in a little-used park. I pulled in and looked at their cars. No one else was around. Their vehicles were either local or from the surrounding counties. I took my camera and began walking across the open field to where the men (all men) were training. As I approached them, I took 2 pictures. The man giving commands didn't see me take them, but I think the troops did. There was an individual who was in uniform, but not participating off to the side. I walked over to him. I will record our conversation to the best of my ability here:

Me: "Are these Police Academy recruits?"

He: "No, (hesitation) they are detention center assistance."

Me: "Oh, you mean they are going to work out at the prison?"

He: "No, they are trained to be on call to all the detention centers in south Florida."

Me: "So, they're prison guards. Are we expecting a prison break?"

He: "They aren't prison guards. They are hand-picked. Some are Sheriff's deputies, some are police officers, some are correctional officers. They are mostly ex-military."

Me: "What will they be used for?"

He: "They are all certified agents. They will be on call for the Sheriff, the local Police Chief, and the County Emergency System. We'll be glad to have these men in our county [Charlotte] in the future!"

Me: "Well, how much can you handle with 15-20 guys?"

He: "This isn't all of them. We have 4 platoons; 2 riot platoons, like this one, and 2 shotgun platoons."

Me: "That should slow 'em down! These guys look pretty good! How long have they been training?"

He: "Only two weeks! Can you believe it?"

Me: "You must be pushing them hard."

He: "We are going to central Florida this weekend for a big conference. There's going to be some competition with about 8 other areas, and we want to look good."

At this point, I raised up my camera (which I had been holding at my side, out of sight) and took this picture (on facing page). Then I quickly walked away. No one said anything or tried to stop me.

Since then, at least 6 other trips have been made to this area to see these troops and confirm my story. No one has seen them again as of October 31, 1992.

NOTE: The uniforms had a patch (round) which I couldn't read.[136]

Chuck Noel, photographer.

If these maps are true and troops are in training for detention centers, this is a far cry from the dreams, goals, and vision set down by our Founding Fathers! They did not envision a New World Order. They envisioned a people, a nation, free, united by the bonds of equality before law and free within the law to pursue happiness. Interestingly enough, those concepts have been radically changed.

The "right to life" is being denied regularly in this nation. Equality under law with a corrupt judicial system is a myth, not a practice. And even the word "equality" has been reconfigured to mean equality of status — economic status, political status, social status — when the Founding Fathers never intended any such thing. And, of course, the right to "pursue Happiness" has been changed to pursuing the right to happiness. Happiness is not a right. Pursuing happiness is. I am not responsible for making you happy; nor are you responsible for making me happy. Collectively, as a society, we are not responsible for making any individual happy.

Having clouded the meanings, then, even of the Constitution, the Princes have thoroughly alienated us from our unalienable rights and emasculated all ten of the original Bill of Rights. They have done it so thoroughly that most Americans don't even recognize what the Constitution said or what the Bill of Rights was about. We have lost — not by a military struggle — but by a surrender of our principals. **Such surrender has always**

197

led to the destruction of nations and is a key principal for building the New World Order.

America has been dumbed, dulled, and tranquilized into a state of semi-conscious existence. We have become the "Stepford" Nation. We look without seeing. We listen without hearing. We experience without feeling. To paraphrase a recent commercial of the past - *"I've fallen and I don't want to get up."*

It is difficult to recover from a serious ailment or accident when the will to live has left an individual. Most doctors, when judging the potential for recovery of a patient from a life threatening incident, take into consideration the patient's "will to live." Is it possible that the will to live is no longer among the attributes of America? Is it possible that too many of us have been pushed down so long, misled so many times, and have been lost so long that we no longer have the desire to find our way back? Has it become easier for America to simply lay down and die in the wilderness, than to muster the strength to pick ourselves up, find again our trail, and force ourselves to begin retracing our steps back to greatness?

If you will begin the quest, you will find that the elitists of the New World Order have some fatal flaws, which if exploited, can stop their progress here in this country within just months. We can bring these New World Order Princes to their knees if — **you're willing to learn the truth — which is the only weapon that can stop them in their tracks.**

But I must warn you that if you turn the page and go on to Sections III & IV, you are taking a risk. You will learn step-by-step how to stop the Princes. If you're not willing to win — if you haven't the courage to be free — if you don't want the responsibility of protecting your family's finances in the financial crash (that most experts agree is eminent or already underway) — then don't go on any further. I'll close this section with this verse.

The Dunciad
Religion blushing veils her sacred fires,
And unawares Morality expires.
Nor public flame, nor private, dares to shine;
Nor human spark is left, nor glimpse divine!
Lo! thy dread empire Chaos! is restored:
Light dies before thy uncreating world;
Thy hand great Anarch! lets the curtain fall,
And universal darkness buries all.
Alexander Pope 1688-1744

198

SECTION III

THE NEXT MOVE

Chapter 1

The Making of Revelation

> Then I saw another beast, coming out of the earth. He had two horns like a lamb, but he spoke like a dragon. He exercised all the authority of the first beast on his behalf and made the earth and its inhabitants worship the first beast, whose fatal wound had been healed. And he performed great and miraculous signs, even causing fire to come down from heaven to earth in full view of men. Because of the signs he was given power to do on behalf of the first beast, he deceived the inhabitants of the earth. He ordered them to set up an image in honor of the beast who was wounded by the sword and yet lived. He was given power to give breath to the image of the first beast, so that it could speak and cause all who refused to worship the image to be killed. He also forced everyone, small and great, rich and poor, free and slave, to receive a mark on his right hand or on his forehead, so that no one could buy or sell unless he had the mark, which is the name of the beast or the number of his name. This calls for wisdom. If anyone has insight, let him calculate the number of the beast, for it is man's number. His number is 666.
>
> Revelation 13:11-18

There is ample historical evidence of a conspiracy for world-wide domination. We have seen the involvement of the Princes, who believe that they are the ones who rule and reign over this earth. They have been setting in motion their political, economic, and spiritual hegemony.

What the Princes don't realize is that the plan is much more elaborate than they imagined. It is a conspiracy that began at the beginning of human history. It is a conspiracy that throughout the ages of man, throughout the almost six thousand years of human history, has been slowly, like a great chess game, unfolding.

201

It is then, as we view this passage of Revelation, that we see the conspiracy that will come to fruition throughout the world. The question that begs answering is, "Just exactly what will this system be?"

There are, of course, those who are looking for "The Anti-Christ." In the famous writings of Nostradamus, he too predicted the rise of an Anti-Christ. He said the man of lawlessness would come dressed in a blue turban. Interestingly enough, the United Nations helmets and berets, are, in fact, blue.

Is it possible that the United Nations is that beast which is spoken of in Revelation? Is it possible that the conspiracy that has been unfolding for these many, many centuries is to culminate in the united world power of the United Nations?

Frankly, yes! It is possible that the United Nations could, in fact, be that entity or beast. Revelation speaks of a beast with two heads; one was wounded by the sword, wounded unto death — and yet, it came back to life. This might reference the League of Nations and its untimely death. The sword which caused the wound could have been the United States' refusal to endorse that early League of Nations, and yet, it was given life again under the new name of the United Nations.

There is ample evidence, as we have seen in Katanga (and as we are seeing, and will continue to see, in places such as Somalia, South Africa, and many other nations around the world), of the brutal power of such a world organization.

The United Nations is proposing, and may eventually be successful in enforcing, world-wide taxation for the maintenance of global "peace keeping" forces. The United Nations is growing daily in strength, power, and prestige, and is also demanding global ecological treaties so draconian in nature as to practically bankrupt every industrialized nation on the face of the earth.

Under the auspices of the United Nations, there has been developed a Children's Defense Fund and a Children's Bill of Rights, which strip parents of their God-given rights and responsibilities to raise their children according to the mandates of Scripture. The United Nations has taken over every facet of child development: from education, to socialization, to religion. It dictates to parents the "proper" upbringing of children as to what they should watch on television; what they should be taught in the public schools; and what forms of discipline are and are not appropriate.

Much has been made in the United Nations of establishing a world-wide currency as one means of sanctioning those nations who will not comply with their United Nations version of arms treaties, economic treaties, environmental treaties, human rights treaties, etc. Under the auspices of the United Nations and the globalist thinkers, we have established the World Bank and a global economic system. All of these things would lead many to believe that the United Nations is, in fact, the culmination of the New World Order conspiracy.

However, I believe, it is important to remember that the "Anti-Christ," mentioned in the epistles of John, would describe many world leaders. It would aptly describe Stalin, Hitler, Mussolini, Idi Amin, and many greater and lesser dictators throughout the ages.

I believe what is more important than a particular Anti-Christ is the system or spirit of Anti-Christ. It is the spirit or system of Anti-Christ that is, in the opinion of this writer, that upon which we must focus and against which we must fight.

There are, perhaps, a couple of points that we must keep in mind. First, the definition of the word *anti*. Anti might mean to oppose. For example, I am anti-pornography. That means I am against pornography. But *anti* might also have another meaning.

In Italian restaurants it is common to see on the menu antipasto. *Anti*pasto is not a dish that opposes pasta, but rather, it is a substitute for pasta. Likewise, the "Anti" in Anti-Christ might mean *someone* or a *system,* that while it might oppose, it really acts more like a substitute Christ.

As such, it may well be a system of law and governance that cleverly opposes, while substituting for, a system of eternal Law. The Anti-Christ system might well be a system of world law which subverts the eternal Law given to man. It would govern one's family, personal life, dealings with others, dealings in the governance of peoples, the church, education, finance, and every other aspect of human existence with humanistic law. Humanistic law is that which seeks to elevate to deity the god-State.

Over the years, much has been made of the mystery of the number 666. Revelation says that it is a mystery, but that the wise will figure it out. Well, after years of puzzling over this dark statement, I believe that I have found the answer.

Remember first that the 666 is said to be the number of a man. I believe that the 666 is actually a combination of three sets of sixes. The first 6 represents man's political system. The second 6 represents the economic system of man, and finally, the third 6 represents the religious system of man. They are together represented by the three internationales and their three areas of expertise. It is in combining the three 6's that we see the one combined number of 666, and it is also in this combination of numbers that we see one number representative of one system — that of the Anti-Christ, or ...

the system of 666, in which the attempt will be to create a one-world system of political, economic, and spiritual hegemony.

Chapter 2

I Fought The Law

Every nation or every government is maintained by a set of laws. Those laws reflect both the moral intent of the people and their source of worship. Law then tells much about a society. Law addresses the specific issues of the governance of the public and private lives of individuals. Law, and specifically the source of that law, is then, the god of whatever nation it guides.

Law, in its most basic form, reveals the religious life and religious system of the governed. Both secular history and the Bible record that Hebrew society was governed by a Law system. That Law system was founded on, and governed by, the "Law of God (Yahweh)." It was this Law of Yahweh that directed their lives and their behavior in terms of family, church, society, government, and economics. Even the sphere of education was governed by the Law of Yahweh.

The Founding Fathers, while not all "Christian" (although primarily Christian), saw themselves Biblically as the New Israel, or Christendom. As such, they adopted as their own the "Law of God," and saw themselves no less than Israel and as being subject to that Law, in the governance of every aspect of their lives.

The New Haven Colony Fundamental Agreement of March 2, 1641, established that the Law of God was their fundamental agreement.

> And according to the fundamental agreement, made and published by full and general consent, when the plantation began and government was settled, that judicial Law of God given by Moses and expounded in other parts of Scripture, ... hath an everlasting equity in it, and should be the rule of their proceedings.

Later, in 1644, that same theme was continued:

> It was ordered that the judicial laws of God, as they were
> delivered by Moses ... be a rule to all the courts in this jurisdiction in
> their proceedings against offenders....

As we have just seen, the laws in the early governance of this nation were derived from Mosaic Law, delivered to the Hebrew people, and adopted by the Founding Fathers as the Law of the land. This Law was both absolute and unchangeable.

The Founding Fathers, whether in the body politic or in matters of ecclesiastical purview, saw the Law of God as indispensable to the protection of freedom and liberty within the nation. The words of Thomas Jefferson are inscribed on his memorial on the south banks of Washington's Tidal Basin. Even today Jefferson still speaks.

> God who gave us life and gave us liberty. Can the liberties
> of a nation be secured when we have removed a conviction that these
> liberties are the gift of God? Indeed I tremble for my country when
> I reflect that God is just, and that his justice cannot sleep for ever.

It is a common heresy within the institution of the "church," that the Law of Yahweh was done away with at the resurrection of Jesus, the Messiah. The Founding Fathers did not hold to that view. They believed that there were, in fact, only two systems of law on the face of the earth — the Law of Yahweh (singular) and the laws of man (plural).

Whittaker Chambers is quoted as saying, "Humanism is not new. It is, in fact, man's second oldest faith. Its promise was whispered in the first days of the Creation under the Tree of the Knowledge of Good and Evil: 'Ye shall be as gods.'"[137]

For a couple of decades sociologists, scientists, doctors, philosophers, psychiatrists, psychologists, even the clergy, have deemed it their prerogative to rename what the Founding Fathers called sin. Our modern leaders camouflage every evil under the sun with clever catch phrases and "buzz" words.

What our Founding Fathers referred to as drunkenness because of their Christian heritage, we now call it *alcoholism* and deem it a social disease, rather than a sin. What the Law-Word called sodomy, we now call an *alternate life style,* giving this vile, degrading perversion a political identity

206

and the unassuming name of *gay rights* and *sexual orientation.*

Pornography is a perversion that brings death to a nation, and yet we call it *adult entertainment.* What our Founding Fathers called immorality, we now call the *new morality;* what the Law called adultery or fornication, we now call *stepping out* or *fooling around;* and what the Law called abhorrent social behavior (like stealing or filthy language), we now call *abnormal social development* or *anti-social behavior.* Instead of personal responsibility and accountability for our actions, sociologists would have us believe that everything can be traced back to the faults of our parents, who have led us into lives of codependency.

Codependency is yet another buzz phrase for a theology of the humanistic religion that is now pervading this country. Many Americans are buying into this lie. Codependency rarely teaches that one makes choices in life and one then must be responsible for those choices. Instead, it puts the blame on other persons or situations in our past thus making us "addicts" or "codependents" in various mannerisms or "habits."

The government of the United States stealthily, secretly, insidiously, and maliciously claims to be honoring a separation clause. However, they are creating a mystery religion that is now taught in the classrooms of our public schools, expounded upon in courts, and reflected by the law of the land. This mystery religion our government has created has ordained "evangelists" in our public schools and in public news broadcasting. It is the same religion spoken of by Whittaker — humanism.

Humanism is the combination of eastern mysticism, Hinduism, Muslim beliefs, and New Age philosophies, theologies, and theolotics. It is a combination of the worship of man, reason, the ecology, animism, and pantheism all rolled-up into one neat package — *the god-State.*

The religious belief of a society dictates: its laws, its social, familiar, governmental, economic, and educational behavior. It is, therefore, incumbent upon us to uncover the theology created by the god-State.

As such, we will begin looking specifically at the issues facing America and the theology of government in dealing with the goal of collapsing the economic, political, and spiritual system of the United States enroute to the New World Order. At its fruition, we will find the final result to be the enslavement of all peoples to a political, spiritual, and economic hegemony under the system of the god-State, or lawlessness, controlled by what the Scriptures call, *the spirit of Anti-Christ,* whose number is the number of a man — 666.

So sacred was the concept of religious (Christian) freedom to the Founding Fathers, that they sealed the protection of that right in the very first Article of the Bill of Rights. Today that right has been twisted, perverted, and used now by groups like the ACLU and others, as the tool for censorship against eternal Law.

The end consequence is that the Law, which was once a Law of both life and death, becomes only a law of death. Eternal Law, which sentences a murderer to death, protects the life of the innocent, because another innocent person cannot be murdered by the individual who was executed for his crime. But, where morality and law become humanistic, situational, or relative, there is nothing that protects good from evil. The murderer is allowed to live and to murder again.

History has shown that evil, left unchecked, is stronger than good, because it will stoop to any level, take any action, trample any rights, even end the lives of any who would oppose it. As evil becomes dominant in society, evil men rule and reign.

However, in a system already deluged with humanistic thought, philosophy, and theolitics, how does one approach the issues and overcome the obstacles to return America to our foundational principles? In examining any specific philosophy we must look at the logical conclusion.

Does the end justify the means?

Chapter 3

Sex And All That Jazz

There are those in society who would tell us that, to decriminalize prostitution, homosexuality, and all other forms of pornography, is the key to undoing the illicit power they have over society. Humanist sociologists also tell us that in countries where all pornography has been legalized, pornographic crime has all but disappeared. They cite as examples certain Scandinavian and other European countries. How stupid do they think we are? Obviously, the reporting of sex crimes disappears when those acts are no longer criminal.

Pornography is an interesting subject. In Biblical Law, *pornography* (from the Greek word *pornea, pornos,* or *exporneo),* means to indulge in fornication, a fornicator; metaphorically it means an idolater, anyone who sets up anything against, or in place of, the Law Word of Yahweh; and additionally, implying excessive indulgence, that is, a *libertine.* In other words, it is to be sexually or spiritually unchaste.

As you recall, one of the principles found within *The Protocols* is the introduction of pornography as a destructive influence in society. The liberalization of laws concerning pornography has had far-reaching and devastating effects on America. As a result, we have seen the degradation of women, children, and men. The practice of pornography is founded in the theory of evolution which says man is nothing more than an evolved animal, and as such, should be free to seek his own animalistic "pleasures."

In her book, *Soft Porn Plays Hardball,* Dr. Judith Reisman makes the following observations:

> The choice of love over hate is supported by Judeo-Christian values. Belief in love is the foundation for the biblical call to chastity, fidelity, delayed sexuality, and monogamy. Scripture condemns fornication, adultery, sodomy, and bestiality because of a belief in man-woman, spiritual-physical love. The underpinnings of these

209

morés could be called "unselfish love." Despite the well-known extremes ... and Victorian sexual standards, those societies produced strong nations and vigorous people economically, educationally, genetically, artistically, and governmentally.[138]

And so it is, that pornography is a broad category which may include, or may be included in the categories of adultery, fornication, and even homosexuality; all of which have somehow been sanctioned by the State.

The introduction by Hugh Hefner of *Playboy Magazine* opened the doors of acceptance for pornography. Through this door came many other ideas shared by Hefner and his fellow travelers. One of the most damaging of these is homosexuality.

Homosexuality is both a religious and political movement. In the political arena, homosexuality seeks to have a protected political identity. Homosexuals have ideologically sodomized both the courts and many politicians in their zeal or lust for protection as a "minority."

President Bill Clinton wants to force homosexuals onto the military of the United States. He has bought the lie that homosexuality is just another alternative life style. But is it? In addition to the obvious questions of sexuality, sexual behavior, and privacy, there is yet another aspect of sodomizing the U.S. military, that is, the loss of men of integrity from the military forces, who patently refuse to serve in an army that would allow such degradation as a part of its national policy.

Of course, the loss of such individuals will create a void. When a void is created, something will rush in to fill it. In this particular case, the most likely scenario is that the void will be filled, if not with homosexuals, with those sympathetic to the homosexual movement, thus creating an army lacking in integrity or morality.

However, this does create an army that fits in well with the charter of the United Nations and the world government into which many, including Bill Clinton and Al Gore, would submerge the sovereignty of the United States.

AIDS, which is, by-and-large, a result of homosexuality, is the first disease to ever have a political constituency. Unlike other communicable diseases, it is not contact traced, isolated, and segmented off from other parts of the population. Rather, it has been given a *social status* of mandatory inclusion.

Through careful words and craftsmanship, homosexuals, pornographers, and the like, have elevated AIDS to the status of *The Red*

210

Badge of Courage. It is spoken of with empathetic, sympathetic, and pathetic tones of sorrow for its victims. The network TV cameras often focus in on children, heart recipients, and athletes with AIDS, making them pitiful sights, which, most assuredly, they are. However, it has been the societal acceptance of pornography, adultery, fornication, and especially homosexuality, that has led to the spread of this disease among both the innocent and the guilty.

Homosexuality is a lifestyle. Statistically, it can include literally thousands of partners during the homosexual's lifetime. It frequently involves the abuse of alcohol, drugs, and sexual acts which (morality aside) can only be described as unsanitary. Any one of these activities is extremely detrimental to one's physical health. But, one (anal intercourse), in conjunction with other aspects of the *homosexual lifestyle*, has been medically proven to be devastating to the human body.

The homosexual lifestyle is a breeding ground and carrier for disease. As a result of the AIDS virus and other sexually transmitted diseases (as well as non-sexually transmitted diseases, generally present with the HIV virus), an epidemic threatens the medical and governmental systems of the United States. Additionally, because of the unique characteristics of the HIV virus, the body of a homosexual may well become an incubator for other diseases, including new and virulent strains of tuberculosis, now reaching epidemic proportions in New York and other areas of the country.

As we, society, tolerate what is evil, the results and judgments of that evil, come upon us all, "innocent" and guilty alike; because, in a society where tolerance is the rule of the day, there are few innocent. The innocent truly are they who stand up against such abominable ideologies. Therefore, the acceptance and tolerance of homosexuality is a decree of guilty upon the society which permits it.

Yes, one might say, but almost half of the United States still have laws on the books governing and declaring sodomy (thereby homosexuality), illegal. Yet, under the current social mores, prosecution based on such charges is practically, if not completely, impossible.

The results of homosexual behavior are very clear. A male homosexual who does not contract AIDS has an average life expectancy of 41 years. The life expectancy of a male homosexual with AIDS is reduced to about 33-35 years, according to studies done in California on a nation-wide test group.

And now, as homosexuality becomes socially "acceptable" in the world of politics, and as homosexuals fight to enter the military under the blessing of President Bill Clinton, they will find new and renewed strength in corrupting and deteriorating a once vibrant society.

The harm that will be done morally and punitively, as a result of this movement, cannot be calculated. Samuel Adams, one of the signers of the Declaration of Independence, warned: "A general dissolution of principles and manners will more surely overthrow the liberties of America than the whole force of the common enemy. While the people are virtuous they cannot be subdued; but when once they lose their virtue they will be ready to surrender the liberties to the first external or internal invader."[139]

The obvious retort by the pro-homosexual segment of society is that we should "just leave them alone. If we don't bother them, they won't bother us."

But that would be akin to saying that an infection in your foot should go untreated since it is not infecting the rest of your body. If left untreated that infection will spread and become gangrene and will eventually destroy the entire body. Such is true of the allowance of perversions such as homosexuality. What is diseased in the body must be eliminated. What is diseased and evil in society must be discouraged, not encouraged. If not, the societal body will die from the infection of homosexuality. This is born out by both history, and more importantly, by an eternal Law — the Law of Yahweh.

Interestingly, in Hebrew society, where the Law was first written, this particular sin, homosexuality, was viewed with particular disgust and disdain. Many reasons could be given for this, but perhaps the most practical is that at the time of the creation, man was created to have sexual relations with woman, not man. In allowing homosexuality, the command for procreation, the plan given to man to be "fruitful, multiply, and have dominion over the earth," was corrupted at its very root.

In Hebrew society, homosexuals were not even considered people. The Hebrew word often used to describe a homosexual was *dog*. A prostitute, while not considered a "citizen," was at least considered a human being. However, a homosexual was considered a dog — a subspecies — not even to be categorized as human.

In the book of Deuteronomy, the Hebrew people are told, "There shall be no whore of the daughters of Israel, not a Sodomite of the sons of Israel." Isaiah, writing to the Hebrew people said that they were going to be led into captivity because of their "sins" (breaking of eternal Law). One of those sins listed in the King James was, "women rule over you." The word *women* there is probably a bad translation. Many scholars believe it actually means *effeminate ones,* that is homosexuals, as they had taken their place in government. The land, and society in general, had been polluted to the point where the land itself was going to "vomit" the people out and they would be led into captivity.

There are those who would claim that homosexuality or legalized prostitution is between consenting adults, and therefore, "no harm — no foul." However, a proper understanding of the Law, which our Founding Fathers had, indicates that while a particular crime may be against a person, ultimately, it is against the One who gave the Law. Therefore, transgression of the Law is not just against another human being or property, but foremost against the Law and the Lawgiver. In simple English, this means the transgression of the Law is a transgression against Yahweh and, therefore, the judgments and punishments set aside by the Law were to be exercised fully and completely. However, lest anyone think that this applies only to homosexuals, we need to continue our discussion with the subjects of adultery and fornication.

Both adultery and fornication also fit into the general category of pornography. The penalty for homosexuality was death. Likewise, the penalty for adultery and fornication were the same. Again, it is important to remember that a society that tolerates any sexual sin is a society that is allowing disease to strike at its very heart. The penalty of death for these three transgressions was the same as the penalty for murder. While many people can see that the death penalty is necessary for murderers, they hardly see fornication, adultery, or homosexuality on the same plane. However, apparently in the eyes of the Creator, all four are equally destructive.

In Paul's epistle to the Romans he describes the Law of Sin and Death and the Law of Life. The murderer is put to death under the Law of Sin and Death, but it is the Law of Life to the rest, as society is protected from that murderer. The question as to whether this is a deterrent in society is really a moot point. That execution will discourage that individual who has committed such a crime from ever perpetrating it on society again is clear.

Because this Law has not been applied, we have seen in America the dramatic rise in crime, and especially in crimes against women. But, it has become equally devastating to the family.

**Any society that has no set code of morality or law
is a society that is subject to anarchy.**

Chapter 4

There's Nothin' Like A Good Woman

The most popular books on the shelves of book stores today seem to be about dysfunctional individuals and families. When society loses its rudder, both individuals and families go astray. The Founding Fathers believed that the family was the basic unit upon which all society was built.

Historical revisionists would have us believe that our Founding Fathers were male chauvinists who despised women and treated them as chattel. Such is not the case. The Constitution which gave the right of the vote to the male did it based upon a Biblical model. Ours was a representative government (republic) and the representation of the family rested with the husband, as the head of the household.

Along this line of thinking, the humanists of today also tell us that the Bible is demeaning to women, considering them to be second class citizens. Nothing could be further from the truth. Often we hear quoted from I Peter 3:7: "likewise, ye husbands, dwell with them according to knowledge, giving honor unto the wife, as the weaker vessel...."

The word *weaker* may be more appropriately translated *finer* vessel. The illustration drawn here is the difference between a clay pot and a Ming vase. One does not take a Ming vase to a professional wrestling match and swill beer from it. Rather, it is given a place of honor in the home. Likewise, that position of honor is to be afforded the wife. She is not to be considered as "weak and feeble-minded." Rather, as a vessel of honor.

In fact, it was in the beginning that the Lord gave woman to man as his helper. She was to assist her husband, whose command was: to be fruitful, multiply, and take dominion over the earth. Therefore, respectively, she is second in command in dominion over the earth! To say that this is a position of inferiority would be to say that being Vice President of the United States is a position of disgrace because it is not the Presidency.

Obviously, this would be ludicrous! Being second in command in

215

dominion over the entire earth is hardly a position of disgrace. Rather, it is a position of importance, respect, and honor. That then is the basis for the command in I Peter — husbands *honor* your wife.

I can already hear the feminists out there telling me that I would again reduce women to being "barefoot, pregnant, and in the kitchen." This, I assure you, is not the case. My wife and I are the parents of four wonderful children. We have two grandchildren. My wife has served as homemaker. She has been barefoot, pregnant, and in the kitchen. But, she has also been in the office — with me; in business — with me; truly a partner relationship. She is my helper, my companion, my friend, and my assistant in having dominion over the things that are around me and in the areas of responsibility that I have.

But, even if what the feminists are even now murmuring as they read these lines were true (that I would have her barefoot, pregnant, and in the kitchen) ... is it better that she be barefoot, pregnant, and in the kitchen, than the *slave* of the feminist movement? Let's examine just a few of the results of feminism in America.

In general, the status of women, despite the feminist's rhetoric to the contrary, has declined steadily over the last thirty years. Rape and sexual crimes against women is up five-fold since the changing of the role of women from that of the *finer vessel* to that of *equal.* The rate of divorce, leaving women to raise children alone, has dramatically increased. The fastest growing element within society of the working poor is single women with children. Further, the incidence of domestic violence and abuse in the home against women has dramatically and radically escalated.

The status of the average working woman (which implies that women who raise families and assist their husbands in businesses, etc. are not working women) is absolutely abominable! The woman, enslaved to the notion that she must work outside the home, labors under two false assumptions. The first false assumption is that her *identity,* and therefore her *self-worth,* is wrapped up in the *position* she holds.

Secondly, is the peculiarity within American society that in order to "get ahead" both husband and wife must work, if they are to "keep up with the Joneses." However, studies and common logic would indicate that if a woman is working for $1,000 a month, by the time the government takes out the taxes, the increased expense of additional transportation, insurance, wardrobe, makeup, parking, lunches, child care, and other expenses necessary for employment (union dues, etc.), her hourly wage may well be reduced to between $1-$2 per hour.

You talk about slave wages?! I made that kind of money twenty-five years ago at the age of thirteen as a baby sitter, and I did not have to please cranky, overaggressive bosses, who made sexual advances in the workplace. While babysitting for the same $1.00 per hour, my employer — the parent — was always gone. I had the run of the house, very little pressure, and plenty of time to pursue other activities, such as homework, etc.

Does that then mean that a woman cannot contribute to the economic interests of her family? No. In fact, quite the opposite is true. Proverbs describes a "good woman" as follows:

Who can find a virtuous woman? for her price *is* far above rubies.

The heart of her husband doth safely trust in her, so that he shall have no need of spoil.

She will do him good and not evil all the days of her life.

She seeketh wool, and flax, and worketh willingly with her hands.

She is like the merchants' ships; she bringeth her food from afar.

She riseth also while it is yet night, and giveth meat to her household, and a portion to her maidens.

She considereth a field, and buyeth it: with the fruit of her hands she planteth a vineyard.

She girdeth her loins with strength, and strengtheneth her arms.

She perceiveth that her merchandise *is* good: her candle goeth not out by night.

She layeth her hands to the spindle, and her hands hold the distaff.

She stretcheth out her hand to the poor; yea, she reacheth forth her hands to the needy.

She is not afraid of the snow for her household: for all her household *are* clothed with scarlet.

She maketh herself coverings of tapestry; her clothing *is* silk and purple.

Her husband is known in the gates, when he sitteth among the elders of the land.

She maketh fine linen, and selleth *it;* and delivereth girdles unto the merchant.

Strength and honor *are* her clothing; and she shall rejoice in time to come.

She openeth her mouth with wisdom; and in her tongue *is* the law of kindness.

She looketh well to the ways of her household, and eateth not the bread of idleness.

Her children arise up, and call her blessed; her husband *also,* and he praiseth her.

Many daughters have done virtuously, but thou excellest them all.

Favour *is* deceitful, and beauty *is* vain: *but* a woman *that* feareth the LORD, she shall be praised.

Give her of the fruit of her hands; and let her own works praise her in the gates.[140]

What I find interesting about this example of the virtuous woman is that in these few verses, we find a basis for the proper approach to:

1. Marriage
2. The role of wives
3. Husbands honoring wives
4. Econoic independence for the family
5. Power economics of a truly liberated woman
6. Raising children
7. Care for the poor
8. Care for employees
9. International business plan, and
10. Functional family life.

Now remember, all of this is being accomplished by a woman whom feminists have called "antiquated" and a *slave.* You tell me — which truly is degrading to women? This example from Proverbs, gives a woman virtue, honor, and glory for what she does. In following the Biblical pattern for conduct within her own life, her family, and even her economic contribution to the family as a homemaker, are blessed. Her children rise up and praise her.

Compare the above woman to the feminist model of a woman, who goes out, puts up with abusive bosses, and ends up languishing in a job that after expenses pays $1-$2 per hour. Her children don't call her blessed, oftentimes they don't even know her.

I realize that many women have been extremely successful in the workplace and I am not discounting their contributions. However, what has been the cost to the individual, the family, and to the nation? We have now three, going on four, generations of children who have been raised by individuals other than their own parents. And we wonder what is wrong with kids today? Who has been there for them to set the values in their lives?

To me, it seems that feminism is the *enslavement* of women. The Biblical model is the *freedom* of women. It breaks the chains that bind women to a humanistic philosophy of the degradation of their sex.

America is at a crossroad today and must choose, as Paul says in Romans: the Law of Sin and Death — or — the Law of Life. You see, there is a way that seemeth right unto man, but the end thereof is the way of death. The United States is on a collision course with destruction. Our families are breaking down. Our women are being violated, degraded, and dehumanized. Men are devolving into lascivious animals. In the city where I live there are dozens of nude dance clubs. The advertising that they do outside is lewd, suggestive, and degrading of all humanity.

Unfortunately, there are now very few places where one can go to learn the Law upon which these United States were founded. It is unfortunate, but true, that even the institution of the Church has abandoned its historical understanding of Law and Righteousness and has adopted, instead, an antinomian stance. The word *antinomian* comes from the Greek word which means — against law or a false law.

It is this false law that the Church has chosen to adopt and teach. This false law, based upon the evolution of law, fits in perfectly with the humanist definition of society. It is, in fact, the way that seemeth right to a man, but the end thereof is of destruction. If America is to set her foot on the road to recovery, we must make some decisions. I believe that our future, both as a nation and as individuals, hinges on these two questions:

What is the standard by which we should judge our lives?
and
Is it important that we alter our pattern of behavior?

Chapter 5

The Big Ten

It has been jokingly said that if God had to take the Ten Commandments to our hostile Congress, he would probably come out with four or five
suggestions, with the other five or six being eliminated all together. The
entire bill would be reduced to a standard of general or vague guidelines.
But frankly, this would be a dramatic step up from where we are in America
today.

In Abington vs. Schempp in 1963, Bible reading and "The Ten
Commandments" were removed from the public schools.

Recently, John Peloza, a biology teacher at Capistrano Valley High
School (California), received a reprimand because he objected to teaching
evolution as "fact" in his classroom. His classes are now being monitored to
insure that he does not present the Biblical account of creation after the
State Board of Education recently passed new guidelines, prohibiting such
an account to be presented to the students.

The Virginia Supreme Court has ruled that Jerry Falwell's Liberty
University cannot issue a $60 million tax-exempt bond because the school
requires attendance in chapel services by students and faculty and requires
that they subscribe to a statement of faith.[141]

In 1963, the Supreme Court committed theft and high treason when
they removed the Bible and the Ten Commandments from the schools of
this land. The Court is guilty of theft because they stole the heritage and
future of this nation. The Court committed treason when they abandoned
those principles upon which the Constitution of these United States was
founded.

Since these Ten Commandments have been abandoned, society has
devolved into *polytheism*. Plainly stated, polytheism is a philosophy which
says, it doesn't matter what you believe — so long as you believe it strongly
enough. But, like all of the tenets of humanism, it elevates *reason,* that

221

which man thinks, to the position of god.

The First Commandment
>And God spake all these words, saying,
>I *am* The LORD thy GOD, which have brought thee out of the land
>of Egypt, out of the house of bondage.
>Thou shalt have no other gods before me.[142]

In America, the land which was built upon the principles of the Ten Commandments, we have chosen many other gods above Yahweh, the God of the Bible. Whether it be the "god of immorality" to the pleasing of our flesh with adultery, fornication, homosexuality, or pornography; whether it be the chasing down of the "god of money"; or whatever other god we have chosen, we have not chosen the God of the Bible. Yahweh identifies himself as **self-existent and the absolute One. His law is immutable and unchangeable.**

He reminds both Israel and us that our relationship with and to Him is one of grace, that is, His undeserved love and kindness. And yet, as we make government "god" and as government assumes that role, we find the tragic consequences that we see today in the "god-State" and welfare state that exist within this country.

For Israel, and now for the new Israel, Yahweh's people were to understand that their source and provisions were not to come from the hand of man, but from the hand of Almighty Divine Providence. Yet in today's society, we see people dependent upon the government for the provision of their needs. We pray to the "god-State" that we have created through marches, letters, and lobbying.

Genesis tells us that man was created in the image of Yahweh. Because we have abandoned Him and become corrupt, the god we have created — the State — is in our own corrupt image. Whether we subscribe to the Truth or not, there is still only one Truth, one Yahweh, and one Law.

There is one Law that governs the universe. There are not laws that govern the universe. We don't live in a multiverse — we live in a universe. In the denial of the Law of Yahweh as the supreme Law of the land, we have changed Law from *absolute* to *imperialistic*. The only law then that exists is one that is inflicted upon people as a coercive force. Imperialistic law is one "stronger" man's opinion over another man's opinion, thus relegating each man to creating his own law system.

Yahweh's Law forbids man's self-law. "You shall not do ... every

222

man whatsoever is right in his own eyes."[143]   But obviously, with the Ten Commandments removed from future generations and stricken down as a thing of scorn and potentially harmful, how will future generations know unchangeable and immutable Law?   The answer is simple ... they won't. Instead they will wander in darkness wondering what has happened to this nation.

In simple terms, we must acknowledge that there is one Yahweh and one Law and that to conform to Yahweh's Law is not an abstract idea.   In order to keep pace with current cultural events, men dress in different and sometimes uncomfortable garb.   They wear white shirts with tight collars and strung about their necks are tight-fighting, choking ties.   We have no problem conforming to the social morés of dress, even though they may be ridiculous.   And yet, conforming to the Law of Yahweh seems abhorrent to us.

If we, as parents, grandparents, teachers, and citizens don't teach our children the Constitution, its founding principles, and the Law of Yahweh, how will they know?   We have shirked this responsibility, and therfore our children don't know from whence they have come.   In not knowing, they do not know where they are going in the future.

Unfortunately, the presumption is that man can test Yahweh by testing His Law.   Quite the opposite is true.   Yahweh tests the hearts of men with the Law.   His Law is not on trial ... it is we, mankind, that are on trial.   The decisions that we make concerning this First Commandment, "Thou shalt have no other gods before me," will be what determines the rise and fall of this nation.   Upon this Commandment rests all of the ten.   It is important that you understand that the ten together combine to make one Law.

The Second Commandment

Thou shalt not make unto thee any graven image,
or any likeness *of any thing* that *is* in heaven above,
or that is in the earth beneath,
or that is in the water under the earth:
Thou shalt not bow down thyself to them, nor serve them:
for I the LORD thy God am a jealous God,
visiting the iniquity of the fathers upon the children
unto the third and fourth *generation* of them that hate me;
and shewing mercy to thousands of them that love me,
and keep my commandments.[144]

223

Obviously, in analyzing this Commandment, we see that our first obligation is not to use graven images or idols in worship. But it goes far beyond this. Anytime anything is esteemed above Yahweh, be it: government, houses, cars, or the ever-popular "prosperity" teachings of many television evangelists (which reduces Yahweh to a genie in a lamp; when we rub the magic lamp and say a few magic words, Yahweh gives us cadillacs and condos), it has become idolatry. But even in our religious institutions, as we pray to statues, holy instruments, saints, or whatever it might be, we have taken on the form of idolatry. This leads us away from the Yahweh's blessings and puts us under the curse of humanism.

The current state of law in America is exemplary of the idolatry that has been committed in this once great land. The foundations of this nation are found in the old Law, Yahweh's Law. But, that Law today is neither understood or obeyed. Consequently, Yahweh's Law is not enforced. Under the hundreds of thousands of laws and regulations across this country, lawmakers have caused law to devolve into each man doing what seems right in his own eyes.

When we are encouraged to glean from Law, as opposed to accepting it as a sealed unit, its abuse is inevitable. If I can pick out only a small part of the Law, I can use it against those for whom it was intended for good. The classic example of this is the stealing of phrases from unrelated Scripture. A good example would be: "And Judas went out and hanged himself," and several chapters later we read, "Go and do thou likewise." If we put the two together they read, "and Judas went out and hanged himself, go and do thou likewise." The two are unrelated. Law, taken out of context and pulled apart from a sealed unit, no longer represents Law or justice — but tyranny.

The laws of society will not raise or lower that society above the level of belief in and adherence to Yahweh's Law that the people display in that society. We must understand that **every law order is at war against every other law order.** Therefore, when those who would protest pornography or abortion are arrested under the "law of the State," it is a law system that is idolatrous and wars against the Law system or Law-Word of the eternal Yahweh.

I realize that even as I write these words that there are those who are going to be militantly agitated. But — TRUTH is TRUTH — and the acceptance or tolerance of a law system which is in conflict with the Law system of Yahweh is, in fact, idolatry. You can't have it both ways.

There are those who would tell us, "Let your conscience be your guide." Conscience can be seared. It can be directed by humanistic education. The book of Isaiah states: "What is evil they will call good and what is good they will call evil." This is the perfect definition of *humanistic society*.

However, the Law of Yahweh contained in His Word, the Bible, is unchangeable, remains steadfast, and leads to the success and prosperity of a nation. History teaches us that in this nation His Law was evidenced for almost two centuries.

The Princes would have us believe and we are constantly told through the media, and even by some pastors, that we must live lives of tolerance. Those who are seeking peace at the tolerance of alien law systems are, in fact, making a pact with evil. They are not seeking the peace that they profess — but slavery. Unfortunately, the only peace they will ever find is in the death of this nation and of themselves. We will then be relegated to the archives of history, along with the failures of past civilizations, to join them in the tombs of other fallen societies.

The death of a nation always begins with *liberalization*. The problem of conflict between liberalization, which is in reality humanism, and Biblical Law, cannot be solved peaceably or amicably. One system will be in charge and the other will be reduced to ashes. Under the laws of liberalism, every perspective religion, philosophy, and theology is made legitimate. Again, that creates each man a law system unto himself. In every system where liberalism or license (from where we get the word *licentiousness*) is permitted, anarchy develops.

Anarchy always results in the people begging for law and order, and the only entity powerful enough in a humanistic state to restore law and order is the "god-State." What follows is a legalistic, totalitarian, repressive regime which *always* takes power. To repress lawlessness, they use force. If force is not successful, all will rule. When all prevail, anarchy will again reign.

The Third Commandment

> Thou shalt not take the name of the LORD thy God in vain;
> for the LORD will not hold him guiltless
> that taketh his name in vain.[145]

To many in modern society, the Law of Yahweh seems oppressive and tyrannical. Often we hear the same prattle when it comes to Biblical Law, "It's so negative. Thou shalt not ... Thou shalt not." To that extent, they have rightly judged that Biblical Law is for the most part negative.

225

However, in its effect they have misjudged the nature and character of law. *Negativistic law* controls evil. *Positivistic law* controls people. Let me explain.

The concept of *negativistic law* has two major benefits. The first of these benefits is its practicality. Negativistic law seeks not to control a wide area or even influence a wide area of activity. It confines itself to a particular evil. Thou shalt not steal confines itself to the act of stealing. Thou shalt not murder confines itself to the act of murder. Thou shalt not bear false witness confines itself to speaking falsely.

As such, negativistic law has a limited scope and consequently, a very modest effect. Hence, the State, whose job it is to enforce law, has by the nature of negativistic law to deal only with a specific issue. The State has a very limited role in the lives of people inasmuch as its scope is limited to dealing with evil, not the controlling of people's lives.

Secondly, the negativistic nature of Biblical Law insures *liberty* because only evil is controlled. The rest of man's life is lived out from under the law. This concept of negativistic law chains down enforcers to enforcing prohibitions against evil, but forces the enforcer to be indifferent to the rest of man's life. As an example of this, Rousas J. Rushdoony points out:

> But, if the law is positive in its function, and if the health of the people is the highest law, then the state has total jurisdiction to compel the total health of people. The immediate consequence is a double penalty on the people. *First,* an omnicompetent state is posited, and a totalitarian state results. Everything becomes a part of the state's jurisdiction, because everything can potentially contribute to the health or destruction of the people. *Because the law is unlimited, the state is unlimited. It becomes the business of the state, not to control evil, but to control all men.* Basic to every totalitarian regime is a positive concept of the function of law.
>
> This means, *second,* that no area of liberty can exist for man; there is then no area of things indifferent, of actions, concerns, and thoughts which the state cannot govern in the name of public health. To credit the state with ability to minister to the general welfare, to govern for the general and total health of the people, is to assume an omnicompetent people. The state then becomes a nursemaid to a citizenry whose basic character is childish and immature. The theory that law must have a positive function assumes thus that the people are essentially childish.

At this point some might comment that Biblical faith, with its doctrines of the fall and of total depravity, holds to a similar view of man. Nothing could be further from the truth. Evolutionary faith, by foisting long ages of development for man, holds on the one hand that man's being is still governed by ancient, primitive drives and impulses, and on the other, that man today is still a child in relationship to future evolutionary growth.

Biblical faith, on the contrary, holds to the original creation of a mature and good man. The human problem is not a primitive nature, not childishness, but irresponsibility, a rebellion against maturity and responsibility. Man is a rebel, and his course is not childishness but sin, not ignorance but wilful folly.

Essentially, a fool cannot be protected, because a fool's problem is not other people but himself. The book of Proverbs gives considerable attention to the fool.[146]

In looking at the laws, ordinances, and statutes which govern the United States of America today, we see *positivistic law*. As such, control over the lives of people, as opposed to control over evil, is being accelerated exponentially with the multiplicity of laws being passed at local, county, state, and federal levels.

As an example of positivistic law, we see the laws governing the ways in which public businesses do business. They are regulated by fire codes, health codes, parking codes, sanitary facility codes, building codes, electrical codes, and many other codes. The purpose or goal is to "protect the public."

Assuming that the protection of the public is the function of law, law then takes on a positive sense. However, that same law does not assume the liability that it creates. Rather, those shopping at a grocery store are absolved of responsibility, and the business firms or property owners have foisted upon them total liability. Thus, the evildoer and the fool are both protected, while the business owner assumes total liability, penalizing responsible men.

Responsibility and liability are inescapable facts: if denied in one area, they are not abolished but rather simply transferred to another area. If alcoholics and criminals are not responsible people but merely sick, then someone is guilty of making them sick. Thus, Dr. Richard R. Korn, professor at the University of California School of Criminology at Berkely, has said that prostitutes should not be arrested and imprisoned, because they are "alienated poor children looking for a better way of life." ("New Approach to S.F. Vice," Oakland, Calif., *Tribune* [Friday, August 16, 1968], p. 10), If these prostitutes are simply "alienated poor children looking for a better way of life," then someone is responsible for their plight other than themselves, because their intentions were good ones. More than a few are ready to name the responsible party: *society*. But the prostitutes, their pimps, and the criminal underworld are all a part of our society in the general sense, and it is obvious that they are not being blamed. It is clear also that by guilty society the responsible and successful people are meant. Under communism, this means the total liability of the Christians and capitalists as guilty of all of societies' ills. As totally liable, they must be liquidated.

Responsibility and liability cannot be avoided: if a Biblical doctrine of responsibility be denied, a pagan doctrine takes over. And if the Biblical negativism is replaced with a law having a positive function, a revolution against Christianity and freedom has taken place. A negative concept of law is not only a safeguard to liberty but to life as well.[147]

Interestingly, Rushdoony connects rejection of negativistic law, which forbids swearing, to revolution. Ashley Montagu, an anthropologist, in defense of swearing did an informative study which gives us a frank statement of the meaning of swearing:

Swearing serves clearly definable social as well as personal purposes. A social purpose? But has not swearing always been socially condemned and proscribed? It has. That is precisely the point. Because the early forms of swearing were often of a nature regarded as subversive of social and religious institutions, as when the names of gods were profanely invoked, their use in such a manner was strictly forbidden.[148]

An important point is made here, false swearing is linked with subversion of eternal Law, and resultantly, society.

... blasphemy is more than taking the name of God profanely. It is defamatory, wicked, and rebellious language directed against God (Ps. 74:10-18; Isa. 5:5; Rev. 16:9, 11, 21). It was punishable by death (Lev. 24:16). Naboth was falsely accused of blasphemy (I Kings

32:10-13), as was Stephen (Acts 6:11), and Jesus Christ (Matt. 9:3; 26:65,66; John 10:36). Blasphemy against the Holy Ghost consisted in attributing the miracles of Christ, which were wrought by the Spirit of God, to Satanic power (Matt. xii. 22-32; Mark iii. 22-30). [Davis, *Dictionary of the Bible,* p. 98].[149]

Montagu points out that, according to the law, "In England, and in every one of the United States, it is still a legal offense to swear." Such laws are rarely enforced now. In recent years, women, once not normally associated with profanity, have become increasingly addicted to it.

The conclusion drawn by Rushdoony in considering Montagu's study, is that the direction of the language of a society is a telltale barometer of the health of that society. Therefore, language which is based in sexual acts and excremental words reflects the downgrading of the culture. It is also then reflected (that is, the downgrading of culture) in the profane use of Yahweh's name and the dishonoring by false swearing of an individual's own name.

> Even while protesting the "Puritanism" of Biblical morality, the ungodly reveal that to them sex and excrement are linked together as powers of the "underworld" of the unconscious, the primitive, and the vital.
>
> The direction of profanity is thus progressively downward. After the middle of the 20th century, a new profane word gained popularity, apparently "an American Negro invention," whose blunt fact was mother-incest. The term actually gained some "honorific" senses. Since then, other profane words having reference to homosexuality have become more popularly used. The references to other perversions have also increased. In brief, the direction of profanity is progressively downward. When the religion of the triune God is denied, the religion of revolution, the cults of chaos, take over. Vitality, power, and force are seen as coming from below; profane language seeks to be forceful, and the forceful is that which is below.
>
> ... as is already apparent, there is a religious progression in profanity: it moves from a defiance of God to an invocation of excrement and sex, and then perverted forms of sex. This religious progression is social as well as verbal. The profane society invokes, not God, but the world of the illicit, the obscene, and the perverted ... As the verbal profanity delves downward, so does society in its actions.[150]

Obviously, be it in the media, the workplace, or in the home, vulgarity and profanity are on the increase and that relates closely to the second part of The Third Commandment, which says, "Thou shalt not take the name of the LORD thy God in vain: for the LORD will not hold him guiltless that taketh his name in vain."[151]

In the earlier days of this nation, the Presidential Oath of Office was seen as falling directly and succinctly under the Third Commandment, inasmuch as by the taking of the Oath, the man elected President of the United States agreed to keep his obligations to this nation under the Constitution and under Yahweh, even as Yahweh was faithful to keep His word. The breaking of his Oath of office was, in fact, the invoking of divine judgment and the curse of the entire Law upon himself.

Today, in our courts of law, we see oaths taken frivolously because there are no longer any absolutes. We have denied the absoluteness of the Law and, therefore, the absoluteness of Yahweh in providing that law. As such, there is no fear of Yahweh or the judgment that will come, even for those things which men may not see. It only follows that the sanctity of oaths and vows disintegrates and eventually disappears. Truth, instead of being absolute, becomes relativistic. Truth then does not relate to an eternal Yahweh. Rather, truth relates to what is best for "me" in this situation.

It is, therefore, an act of disloyalty, perhaps even treason, to begin to dissolve our reliance upon eternal Truth and our governance by eternal law. Again, from George Washington's Farewell Speech, we find these words:

> Of all the dispositions and habits which lead to political prosperity, religion and morality are indispensable supports. In vain would that man claim the tribute of patriotism, who should labor to subvert these great pillars of human happiness, the firmest props of the duties of men and citizens. The mere politician, equally with the pious man, ought to respect and cherish them. A volume could not trace all of their connections with private and public felicity. Let it simply be asked, where is the security for property, for reputation, for life, if the sense of religious obligation desert the oaths, which are the instruments of investigation in courts of justice? And let us with caution indulge the supposition, that morality can be maintained without religion. Whatever may be conceded to the influence of refined education on minds of peculiar structure, reason and experience both forbid us to expect that national morality can prevail in exclusion of religious principle.[152]

Washington realized that the concept of oaths relied upon eternal Truth. He understood that without the sanctity of the Third Commandment, both in its narrowest and broadest sense, taking the name of the Lord in vain (being defined in both terms of vulgar speech and dishonoring of the eternal Creator and His divine Law (by swearing false oaths) would forever cut the cord for protection of "private property and public felicity." Additionally, false swearing would cease the ability of the courts to render justice.

Rushdoony points out that a false oath is much more serious than the act of stealing or murder, inasmuch as theft is an act against a single person or a group of individuals. Murder takes the life of a single person or group of individuals. However, a false oath "is an assault on the life of an entire society."

And so it is today in most of the courts across this land, that God has been removed from those oaths. Thereby, our cursory and less than honest use of oaths is both a Declaration of Independence from Yahweh and a Declaration of War against Him, His eternal Truth, and His Law-Word. That then breaks down law to nothing more than humanistic pragmatism, which states: whatever works for me, here and now, in this situation.

When law is reduced to relative nonexistence, only lawless anarchy is left. And it is in the throws of anarchy that we find revolution. The revolution's attack is not only upon the eternal Law of Yahweh, but against every man and his neighbor. When there is a breakdown of Law and Yahweh's soverignty is denied, a two-pronged conflict for control of the sovereignty once afforded the Almighty takes place. Rushdoony points out that there are two forms of totalitarianism that results: one the *totalitarian state;* and the other the *totalitarian individual.* Both the state and the individual want to rule with absolute impunity.

When the Law is no longer absolute, crime is undefinable. Treason is undefinable. The criminal is protected by law because the law recognizes no criminal. It has no absolutes and therefore, justice is impossible to render.

In such a lawless society, it is society that is responsible. Humanists would have us believe that we are responsible for the ills of the world; only man through *evolution* can somehow, someday, and someway, become *enlightened* enough to restore justice. But, without any absolutes, it is difficult to define justice — good or evil. It is rendered difficult to protect good and impossible to limit evil.

When the relativists (humanists) call for an "open society," their wish may be the cause that is our undoing. *An open society is a society that is*

231

open to all evil, but no good.

Therefore, as stated previously, the denying of the absolute Law of Yahweh is a violation of the Third Commandment, taking the name of the LORD in vain.

Some might ask the question, "If this country was founded on Biblical principles, why then did we have slavery and the evils of slavery?"

The answer to this is simple. We disobeyed the Law of Yahweh. The result of this disobedience is obvious. The Law, the eternal Law of Yahweh, prohibited the stealing, selling, or buying of an individual: "and he that stealeth a man and selleth him, or if he be found in his hand, he shall surely be put to death."[153] However, this eternal Law was violated. As a result, we in America have had racial tensions since that time and, as a consequence, one of the contributing factors to the Civil War was the battle over slavery.

The social ills created by the violation of this Law of theft can easily be seen. Still, society continues to blaspheme the name of Yahweh by ignoring His Law, and everything around us decays. Again, remember, the Law is a sealed unit. If one violates one point of Law, he violates the entire Law.

No where is this decay more evident than in the breakdown of the family. Children today are often disrespectful and disobedient. They don't honor their father and mother as the Fifth Commandment teaches. In fact, under Biblical Law, "he that curseth his father, or mother, shall surely be put to death."[154]

This violation of cursing and oath taking was considered every bit as serious as murder. This Law was enacted into early Massachusetts law and while no record exists of the death penalty being exercised, we do have record of severe whippings adjudicated by the courts on rebellious sons who struck their parents. In this sense, both the oath and the curse are an appeal to Yahweh to stand with us against tyranny or evil.

Remembering the negative aspect of Biblical Law, we must balance our activities in how we wage war against evil. Evil is to be reviled. It is to be stopped. However, because the Law-Word is negativistic and attacks a specific evil under that section of Law, only that evil can be attacked. This is not a general warrant, general search, or a "witch hunt" against a vague or perceived evil; rather, a clearly and specifically defined evil.

With the destruction of society through humanistic values (which have no value and contain no eternal or abiding Truth), society desperately begins seeking something to fill the void that has been created.

Remember, in *The Protocols* the Princes said they would introduce the idea of the pursuit of luxury and wealth as a tenet of society. How often have you heard a "self-made man" say, "I deserve what I got. I worked like a dog, sixteen hours a day, seven days a week, and I have finally arrived." The question is, arrived at what? While hard work and diligence are enjoined in the Scriptures, man was not necessarily defined by his ability to work, but rather, by his ability to rest. Which leads us to the Fourth Commandment.

The Fourth Commandment

Remember the sabbath day, to keep it holy.
Six days shalt thou labour, and do all thy work:
But the seventh day *is* the sabbath of the LORD thy God:
in it thou shalt not do any work, thou, nor thou son,
nor thy daughter, thy manservant, nor thy maid-servant,
nor thy cattle, nor thy stranger that *is* within thy
gates; For *in* six days the LORD made heaven an earth, the sea, and
all that in them *is,* and rested the seventh day: wherefore the LORD
blessed the sabbath day, and
hallowed it.[155]

The *sabbath,* known as the seventh day, was patterned after the sabbath of Yahweh in his creation rest. Isaiah says that "the wicked are like the troubled sea, when it cannot rest, whose waters cast up mire and dirt. There is no peace, with my God, to the wicked."[156]

America spends more on recreation, pleasure, consumable goods, and luxury than any other nation on the face of the earth. Over the last thirty years Americans have pursued with tireless vigor - rest. But like the stormy sea, they have no rest. In attempting to fill the void (the removal of Yahweh from our lives through humanism), we have been on the quest for rest — inexhaustibly and unfruitfully.

Because of the removal of Yahweh from society and the lives of individuals, there is now no ability to rely upon Yahweh, who says He will be our provider. We, mankind, have taken it upon ourselves to provide for ourselves. Therefore, we find no rest. However, Scripture tells us that when Israel failed to observe the weekly sabbath rests, the sabbath years (seventh year rest), and the Year of Jubilee (every fiftieth year rest), that the natural consequence of actions of failing to honor the sabbath was their captivity by a foreign nation. Likewise, in this nation, because we have dishonored the

233

sabbath, replied upon our own ingenuity and our own provision for our needs, we too have been led into captivity.

For instance, many fear old age. One recent television commercial stated, "There's only one thing worse than dying, that's outliving your money." It is a fear that many have, as government becomes more positivistic in its law and more materialistic in its intent towards society, to protect "the good of all the people." Rates of taxation go ever higher. Control over our lives, our businesses, and our abilities to prosper becomes increasingly heavy handed and tyrannical. As such, the possibility of our retiring on adequate funds becomes less and less probable. America has become enslaved to the fear of old-age poverty.

America has also become enslaved to the fear of job insecurity. As government takes on more positivistic law, it creates an evermore intrusive welfare state — to the detriment of the business community, our savings, and our estates. When all the above factors come together, it typically leads to business contraction: what economists call a *recession,* or a *depression.* We are reminded painfully of this fact night after night, as one of the major news networks hammers home a segment called, *The Money Crunch.*

As a further result of our chasing the almighty dollar and our inability to rest, both the husband and wife work long hours, and many times, to the abandonment of their families. Children are being raised in government-sponsored schools and in latch key programs with surrogate parents. The violation of the law of the sabbath has been one of the key elements in the destruction of the family.

The basic dishonoring of this, the Lord's day, has led to avoidance of setting time aside for rest; for teaching our families the Law of the Lord. Consequently, the breakdown within society, which began slowly, is now dramatically accelerating. In the first generation (perhaps thirty years ago) of humanistic society, America was still under the discipline of an earlier era. However, as that era gave way to humanistic thought, the second generation, raised under humanistic theology, saw no constraints upon itself. **Thus we see that good has devolved and evil has evolved within our society.**

The Fifth Commandment

Honour thy father and thy mother: that thy days may be
long upon the land which the LORD thy God giveth thee.[157]

The Founding Fathers realized that a republican form of government would only work to the extent that man would honor the eternal precepts of Yahweh. In today's headlines, we see the constant reminder of man's inability to control society — outside of force.

While social engineers may be happy with their experiment and think it only needs fine-tuning and tinkering to make it just right, evidence clearly points to the fact that just the opposite is true. Everything they have done has been wrong. The evidence is clear — look at the state of the American family.

Every day thousands, perhaps millions of lives are being destroyed by drugs. But drugs are only a symptom of the problem — *they are not the problem.* The problem is that which drives both children and their parents to drugs — the destruction of the family.

Parents have dishonored the Fifth Commandment and have taught their children, by their example, to do the same. In the dishonoring of eternal Law, children have not been taught to honor their parents and their grandparents. As a result, society is unraveling at the seams. In a society steeped in evolution, family is denied as the central core.

Whether it's Darwin or Freud, we see the unrelenting attack on the family. In Darwinism, the family is a primitive idea, which must fade and be replaced with a new *collectivism.* Freud teaches the evils of the family are the result of the primal hord, or primitive society, which was dominated by a violent primal father. The father, who because of jealousy and power plays, drove out the sons to proclaim exclusive sexual possession of the mother and daughters. Darwinian and Freudian psychology both conclude that family is evil, inasmuch as it is the propagation of these religious ideas that have stifled man. Therefore, the family must be destroyed if the Princes' goal to destroy religion is to be accomplished.

Further, Darwin & Freud see the right of private property stemming from the family. Naturally, if one is evolutionary, one must believe that property is a societal possession and not an individual or family possession. Again, the family must be eliminated and thus we see the constant unswerving attack on the family by psychologists, scientists, and, don't forget, the evolutionary clergymen. E. Adamson Hoebel, in his work, *Man in the Primitive World,* says,

> The essential nature of property is to be found in social relations rather than in any inherent attribute of the thing or object that we call property. Property, in other words, is not a thing, but a

235

network of social relations that governs the conduct of people with respect to the use and disposition of things.[158]

In other words, there is no inherent property right. Rather, property is a state of mind. This is a typical trick of the Princes. When something cannot be logically dealt with, it is simply redefined and explained away. Both religion and property are inherent to the central core of society — the family. Our Founding Fathers recognized this in guaranteeing the right to property when they denied Congress the power to make any law which religion (defined in their terms as Christianity) established. However, the attack to undermine the family can be seen in all aspects of society. The evolutionary theology of the end of the nuclear family and the doctrine of collective socialism is promulgated daily by the schools, media, and science. Of course, all of this is sponsored by the Princes.

Therefore, the dishonoring of the Fifth Commandment has only one logical conclusion. It leads to the destruction of religion and to the destruction of private property. Without the destruction of family, religion and private property, there is no hope for the New World Order. As each of us cherishes the right of inheritance and holds fast to ownership of private property, a right granted to us by our Creator and guaranteed by the Constitution, we will be unwilling to peaceably submit all that we have — our family, our freedom of religion, and the right to own private property — to the coming god-State.

Today's socialists (humanists) want to emancipate women from their enslaving role in American history: the Biblical origins of religion, responsibility, marriage, and property. (This emancipation then would supposedly lead women to be productive workers within society.) Socialist also want to emancipate children from the authority of their parents.

The generation that was educated under the Princes' evolutionary thoughts are now parents themselves. Unfortunately, they have no concept of what the responsibility of parenting is all about. They lack the knowledge of parental responsibility and of the inherent right of property to their children. They have willy-nilly let the State take possession and control of their children's lives and education.

Liberal social thinkers tell us that parents have no property rights in children, but someone *always* has property rights in children. If parents relinquish their property rights in their children, then that void will be filled. In today's society, the void has been filled by the State.

States now take possession of our children. This is evidenced by the fact that we have laws mandating how much, where, and how children should be educated. Every state in the United States has Child Welfare or Health and Human Services Divisions. Now, for any or no reason, the State may take your children away from you. Every year thousands and thousands of families are split apart by do-gooder child welfare workers. The basis of their philosophy is to destroy the family, reasoning that the State is a better parent. The further dishonoring of the Fifth Commandment has come in the dramatic rise of retirement homes. There was a time in this nation, when the elders in society were honored and revered for their wisdom, knowledge, experience, and for what they could teach future generations. In today's society, everyone is too busy chasing the dollar and in many cases, working two jobs. It is too inconvenient to care for our elderly. Instead, we pack them off to "old folks homes," where they live lives of quiet indignity, loneliness, and separation from all that they have known.

The Princes' social engineering has brought much of this about. We see it in education, science, the media, but most especially, in the tax laws of the United States. Government has been allowed, on our behalf and in our stead, to illegally and unconstitutionally assume the role of provider through the welfare state. Taxes have risen to the point where women are now forced to enter the work place in order to help the family financially survive. Meanwhile, there is no time, energy, or money to care for our elders.

This has been a major contributing factor in the destruction of the family. The State, not Yahweh, has become the center of the family, and we, its obedient disciples, toil tirelessly to serve our god-State.

The Sixth Commandment

Thou shalt not murder.[159]

In every society throughout history, there has been a prohibition against murder. The prohibition against such acts has always been clear, and the consequence of such an act has always been death.

However, in today's modern society, we are taught that violence begets violence; to punish a murderer, by putting him to death, begets more violence; and that life is cheapened by the death penalty. We are told that prison terms and rehabilitation are the answer. But, the data would suggest otherwise. Since capital punishment has fallen largely into disuse by society, the crime of murder has increased astronomically.

Let's think through this process logically. If, in fact, a murderer is

237

sentenced to jail for thirty years, then society is being told that the life of the victim is *only* equal to thirty years of the murderer's time in prison at the taxpayers' expense. This greatly diminishes the value of all human life.

Again, it is the Law of Sin and Death that declares the murderer guilty and demands the forfeiture of his life. The Law of Sin and Death is the Law of Life for the rest of society, who will be protected from the repeated violence of a murderer.

However, in today's society, your life now hangs in the balance because we have preferred the life of the murderer to the life of the rest of society. There is no protection of life — no sanctity of life, and as a result, violence within society is now unchecked and seemingly out of control.

When life is no longer an unalienable right, then life becomes cheap. This is evidenced in every aspect of society today. Murderers go unpunished. And those who are punished are given light prison sentences. To the shame of society, murderers often spend less time in prison than someone like television evangelist, Jim Bakker, whose real crime was that of over-booking a hotel.

This is not to be considered an excuse for Jim Bakker. He will be the first to tell you that he is in prison, not because of what the courts did or what the courts found, but rather, because he sinned against God and was placed in prison for dishonoring the sacred trust he had been given. This is not the point. The point is that the crime of murder is being treated more cavalierly than the crime of over-booking a hotel.

Murder in society today is so common that oftentimes we fail to notice when murders take place. Most of us are appalled and aghast at the crime of murder when it involves children or serial killers. Yet, in the case of the "common" murderer, who kills just one person in the heat of passion, we simply warehouse the murderer in a prison. In a few years, due to the overcrowded conditions of the prisions or for "humanitarian" reasons, we release the murderer once again upon society — often with fatal consequences.

Drugs are death — perhaps one of the most heinous forms of death invented by man. Unlike a knife or gun, which can bring death instantly, drugs murder a person and a society over a period of years. Drugs create violence and will bring certain death to our entire civilization.

How many cases of murder have been committed as a result of the quest for money to buy drugs? How many innocent bystanders have been murdered when drug deals went "bad"?

Every day thousands, perhaps hundreds of thousands of murders, go unheeded as drug lords and their retail arm, the drug pushers, destroy countless lives of citizens across the United States. They are murderering our children.

The United States government spends over two billion dollars a year for drug intervention along our southern borders. Obviously, this program of drug intervention has been an abysmal failure. The flow of drugs into this nation is not decreasing — but increasing. It is increasing because there are thousands upon thousands of distributors in the market place.

These pushers understand very clearly that selling drugs is extremely profitable. It is low risk, and even if caught, they are often given light prison sentences or are released. As a result, these murderers continue to stalk the streets, killing our children, destroying our families, and eroding society. There has been no disincentives against this crime of slow, debilitating murder. But murder is murder — whether it's done with an ax, a gun, a knife, or with drugs.

The same "enlightened" social engineers who tell us that to force a murderer to forfeit his life is wrong, also tell us that if we want to end the problem of drugs, we simply need to legalize them. This would be just one more case of the legalization of murder within society.

There is a way to deal with murderers among the population of America, and it falls under this Commandment: "Thou shalt not murder." It is, therefore, only logical that we return to the Biblical concept upon which this nation was built: that a murderer must forfeit his or her life in repayment for the life stolen. This elevates the value of a human life to its highest level — life for life. As these sources of distribution are taken away, America would find itself slowly being released from its enslavement to an illicit drug culture. But whether it's illicit drugs, crimes of passion, murder for hire, deliberate murder, etc., by removing the murderer from society, we would begin to see an end to the reign of terror and the shedding of innocent blood.

There will always be those who say, "Yes, but how many innocent people would be put to death under such "draconian" laws?" Obviously, the possibility always exists of innocent men being put to death in a corrupt system. However, even in these cases, historical precedence and Biblical law intervene. Biblically, the crime of murder was not punishable as a capital offense, except upon the establishment of two eye witnesses.

The next question would logically be, "Yes, but what if these two people lie about an innocent person committing a murder?"

Again, Biblical law provides justice. *Perjury* is false swearing or giving a false witness. It steals a person's rights, their unalienable rights, "to Life, Liberty and the pursuit of Happiness." Perjury constitutes the destruction of justice. Therefore, the penalty for bearing a false witness was set in stone: an eye for an eye, a tooth for a tooth, a life for a life.

How many times, in a court of law today, do we see individuals being prosecuted for perjury? Yet, in the early days of this country, Biblical Law was honored. One who committed perjury was subject to the Law. Biblical Law demands that the penalty for perjury be the same penalty that was going to be put upon the person falsely accused.

> If a false witness rise up against man to testify against him that which is wrong; then both the men, between whom the controversy is, shall stand before the LORD, before the priests, and the judges, which shall be in those days;
>
> And the judges shall make diligent inquisition; and, behold, if the witness be a false witness, and have testified falsely against his brother;
>
> Then ye shall do unto him, as he had thought to have done unto his brother: so shall thou put the evil away from among you.
>
> And those which remain shall hear, and fear, and shall henceforth commit no more any such evil among you.
>
> And thine eyes shall not pity; but life shall go for life, eye for eye, tooth for tooth, hand for hand, foot for foot.[160]

In light of Biblical Law, we must understand that the courts are inexorably, inescapably religious establishments. They are to administer the precepts of Law and morality. Humanistic courts, based upon laws, not Law, are going to continue the downward spiral toward complete denigration of Law. They involve themselves with building tricky and deceiving circumstantial cases, hiding certain facts, and allowing false statements.

However, in the proper understanding of Law, a violation of Law is a violation against Yahweh, as well as man. To believe otherwise is to put the concept of evil into the area of the abstract. Evil then becomes something separate from the individual committing the evil. If evil is held in the abstract, and neither the criminal nor the one who bears false witness is forced to pay for the evil that they have done, then the violation of the sovereignty of Yahweh continues in the compounding of the evil.

The church, in its abandonment theology, has taught, "Love the sinner — hate the sin," but in terms of the Scripture, this is impossible. Sin does not exist apart from the sinner, nor does evil exist apart from the evildoer. That is to say, murder does not exist without murderers and theft does not exist without thieves. It is, therefore, under the judgment of Law and the honest testimony of two individuals, that a person is condemned or convicted.

The application of this principle, in cases where a defendant's life is at stake, is that if a person gives a false witness, then he is to be executed. If the situation involves financial penalties, for example, that of $1,000, then the false witness has to pay the $1,000. This was the Law of the land throughout much of America's history.

> It is important to realize that this Biblical law was once a part of American law. It is still on the books in some cases.... "In Texas law, where perjury is committed on a trial of a capital felony, the punishment of the perjury shall be death." (See 32 Tex Jur 825, para 40;). In a California court, it was stated:

> "It is time that the citizens of this state (California) fully realize that the Biblical injunction: 'Thou shalt not bear false witness against thy neighbour,' has been incorporated into the law of this state, and that every person before any competent tribunal, officer, or person, in any of the cases in which such an oath may by law be administered, wilfully and contrary to such an oath, states as true any material matter which he knows to be false, is guilty of perjury, and is punishable by imprisonment in the state prison for not less than one nor more than fourteen years."[161]

But in all aspects of this command, it is important to remember that the command is a negative command: Thou shalt not bear false witness. We see in this command and in subsequent cases, Law within Scripture; the requirement that prosecution be brought against both false witnesses, liars, and slanderers.

The bearing of false witness also applies in the sense of banning a false prophet. In today's society, we think very little of the idea of a prophet. However, as the State sets itself up as the god-State, *Enroute to Global Occupation,* that is the New World Order, false prophets are a very important piece of equipment in their arsenal.

Scripture tells us that in the last days false prophets will arise and will represent the oracles of another god or power and another law. But, it says that their falsehood will be revealed by their predictions which do not come true.

We were told by the government that if we enacted a law concerning welfare that soon we would have the Great Society. We were told that poverty would cease to exist. We were told that the god-State could remedy the problems of the poor and the oppressed in this nation. Yet, their prophecies have been false and everything they have done has exacerbated the problem and not solved it.

If, in fact, this prophet of the State had been true, poverty would be on the decline, not on the incline. Crime among the poor would be going down, not up. If the social engineering planned by these *priests* (Legislators of the god-State) and the message delivered by their prophets were true, America would have been restored to what she was. Quite the opposite has happened. Never before in the history of this nation has crime, poverty, and injustice under laws (not Law) been more prevalent.

Throughout the Scriptures, we see false prophets crying, "Peace, peace ... when there is no peace." Today, we have similar false prophets who serve another god and proclaim another testament. And to their shame and to the destruction of this nation, ofttimes, the churches in America have gone along with this false teaching. Somehow, they consider it piety for the State to redistribute the wealth of individuals; taking care of other individuals. But in all, the poor have not been served — the poor have doubled in number; those without justice have not been served — injustice has now been spread to all people. America is hardly a land of peace, which these social engineers prophesied that it would be.

Again, one might be tempted to say, "But such laws were meant to do good." However, that is disputed by the ongoing efforts to create yet *more* of these laws, particularly in light of the thirty years of failure of such damnable ideas. No, the Princes knew exactly what they were doing. Both *The Protocols* and three decades of history in America show the falseness of their schemes.

I would point out that those who say Biblical/constitutional Law is narrow and constricting, are blind. I would ask the rhetorical question, "Which is more constricting? Ten points within a Law — or hundreds of thousands of laws, comprising millions of pages, that restrict every area of life in society?"

The Seventh Commandment
Thou shalt not commit adultery.[162]

For many years we have allowed certain destruction to come upon society with the abandonment of this Commandment. This Commandment is to protect the sanctity of marriage. It has been changed to read, in all practicality, "Love thy neighbor as thyself — just don't let thy neighbor's spouse find out."

Because marriage is historically and Biblically a type of our union with Yahweh, it serves in its connection with the family and family life, as a picture of our relationship to a divine Creator. Husband and wife were commanded to be one, even as we are to be one with our Creator, Yahweh.

The severe attack on this Commandment is all part of the plan of the Princes, who would impose upon us their New World Order. Remember, part of the Princes' plan expressed in *The Protocols* and in the tenets of communism, is the destruction of the family, which includes the destruction of marriage.

The institution of marriage has suffered tremendously over the past thirty years. It has been reduced to an earthly contract based upon feelings; rather than a divine contract based upon religious principles. As such, when those feelings change or *die* — often, so does the marriage. Even a marriage that is still legally intact, may not be a marriage, if the concept of mutual and moral submission to each other is missed or denied, in favor of *individualism* and *autonomy*.

Feminists would tell us, that for a woman to be in submission to her own husband, even as a husband is to be in submission to Christ, the head of the church, is to enslave women. But again, I would ask the more rhetorical question, "Which is *truly* slavery?" It is the dishonoring of this Commandment that is leading to broken homes, broken dreams, and broken bodies across this land. Currently over a hundred thousand people have died of AIDS. But this is just the tip of the iceberg. It will reach into the millions before it is finished. *Free love* (a term coined out of the 1960s), we are finding — is not free. The many emotional and physical scars that go with the dishonoring of this Commandment are deep and are, in fact, killing society.

Yet, anyone, who in a public forum stands up and says, "This is wrong," is said to be out of touch with the times. In my estimation, this accusation is, by-and-of-itself, a reason for holding this value. Perhaps it's time that Americans again prefer to be out of touch with the times, particuarly when those times are marked by sexually transmitted diseases, murder, and anarchy.

Still, the New World Order, humanistic educators would tell us that we cannot simply ask children to delay sexual activity as enjoined by this Commandment. So instead, we find ourselves in a society that passes out condoms to teenagers — instead of wisdom; and that grants abortion on demand — instead of demanding chastity. Our society sets up free clinics to treat the diseases that we spread among ourselves — as opposed to restoring spiritual clinics within the families to teach our children and ourselves right from wrong.

And thus as it has always been, a society that is no longer capable of distinguishing right from wrong — extinguishes itself. The assault on the family, as that basic core element of society, continues in the dishonoring of this Commandment.

The Eighth Commandment
Thou shalt not steal.[163]

Our Founding Fathers understood the concept of dominion. They believed that man was created in the image of God and therefore had certain unalienable rights to "Life, Liberty, and the pursuit of Happiness," which have among its characteristics, the right to property.

In Genesis we see that man was created to exercise dominion. Yahweh was to be the absolute, sovereign Lord and Creator, whose dominion knew no power or limits. Man was to be his vice regent and exercise dominion over the entire earth.

Ownership is an inherent part of dominion. In fact, Scripture says that a good man leaves an inheritance for his children and his childrens' children. Thus, the right of ownership and protection of private property, in the mind of the Founding Fathers, was not just a right — it was a command.

As our rights to private property have been stolen through *collectivism* or *governmentalism,* the right of dominion through the ownership of property transformed and became the privilege of the State. Society then took possession of private property and all property became *public*. As a result, all property is subject to violence, by both the State and individuals, within the collectivism of society. Remember, the government now owns almost one-third of all of the land in the United States.

To their discredit and to the destruction of this nation, even the church has participated in this lie. For too long, many churches have taught that the earth is Satan's realm, his footstool, and dominion. They have taught that private property is a burden of the flesh; rather than, an unalienable right

244

and a responsibility.

Therefore, if the dominion over property can be removed by the whim of government, then government sets itself up as god and assumes to itself the characteristic of sovereignty and the grantor — or remover — of all rights. Under such a system, we see either the boot of government stamping on the face of humanity, or anarchy (the rule of democracy), which always results in the bloody and tyrannical reign of the frenzied mob. Rushdoony describes three kinds of theft:

> Theft or stealing is taking another man's property by coercion, fraud, or without his consent. Cheating, harming property, or destroying its value is also theft. It is not necessary for the robbed to know of the theft for it to be a sin. Thus, to ride a train or bus without paying one's fare is theft, even though the transportation company is unaware of the act.
>
> Theft can be accomplished in a number of ways. *First,* in simple theft the thief robs the victim directly. *Second,* in complex but still direct theft, the thief robs the victim as part of a group of thieves. In such a case, a man may not be directly involved in the act of theft, but he is a party to it all the same as a knowing party in the corporate group of thieves. *Third,* theft can be accomplished by indirect and legal means, i.e., by passing a law which steals from the rich, the poor, or the middle-classes, for the benefit of a particular group. The state then becomes the agency whereby theft is accomplished, and a pseudo-moral cover is given by legal enactment.[164]

Therefore, it should be understood that theft — by any means — is still theft. Today, a double injustice is done to society under the current laws of the land. When an individual is caught, tried, and convicted of theft (either by direct or indirect theft), further violence is done to society when the thief is placed into a prison at the cost of $30,000-$40,000 a year at the taxpayers' expense. It's not bad enough that the thief stole the first time around — he now also deprives society of what is rightfully theirs, *forcing them to support him,* as he does nothing in prison.

There is a better way. It is the concept of *restitution.* Biblical Law requires restitution — not incarceration. While we may personally forgive the offender, the requirement of restitution and repentance remains. What the thief has taken must be restored to the person *from whom it was taken.*

245

The concept of restitution lessens society's burden and, in fact, restores to society that which was taken originally, while allowing the individual, the offender, to pay his debt in a way that is a blessing, as opposed to a curse.

A second problem that faces society in terms of theft is the problem associated with the protection of one's property against thieves. Interestingly, if a thief broke into a home, a barn, or a garage at night, when it was dark and he could not be identified, and his life was taken as a result of the attempted theft. Biblical Law considered this a reasonable response to the thief in the night.

However, the killing of a thief, except in self-defense during daylight hours, was forbidden because the thief could be identified and apprehended. The thief, upon apprehension, was to make restitution for his crime. If he could not make restitution, he was then made an indentured servant until such time as restitution was satisfied.

Additionally, Biblical Law also had requirements for the handling of a thief in instances where he was apprehended before he had a chance to dispose of the stolen goods. The minimum penalty would be to repay double the value of that which was stolen. For example, in today's society, if a car was stolen, the thief would be required to give back the car and an amount equal to the value of the car.

Laws concerning stealing also dealt with damage to another man's property, whether it was deliberate or accidental. There were also laws concerning responsibility for goods that were held in custody, rentals, or loans of property.

In fact, Biblical Law indicates that to steal a man's ability to earn a living is theft of his private property. Therefore, it can be logically assumed that when the government steals your livelihood, either through excessive taxation or odious zoning laws, they are stealing from you real and private property.

There was a time in this land when a man could produce a product and sell it for a living. In the 1990s, this is practically impossible. Recently, I knew of a family, the husband of which had been injured and suffered a permanent disability. The wife had recently lost her job. With house and car payments due and children to provide for, both the husband and wife felt the necessity of providing for themselves, without seeking the help of welfare programs. As a result, they determined they would go through neighborhoods and pick up discarded goods that could be repaired and sold, enabling them to meet their financial needs.

And yet, the laws of that city restricted them from selling these goods from their home. As it would happen, one of their "loving" neighbors called the city and complained. Immediately, an official from the city was dispatched to investigate the situation. Upon his investigation, this city official determined that this was, in fact, a violation of law, and that even if it meant the family losing their home and having nothing to eat, the law must be honored. They were ordered to cease and desist.

There was a time in this land, if a man was hungry, he could fish and his catch would feed his family. In most states, this is no longer true. The first thing you have to do is buy a fishing license. Then, if you catch any fish and have any left over after you have fed your family, you are not allowed to sell the excess fish on the open market. You have to be licensed to sell fish; you have to satisfy city, county, state and federal ordinances.

Under such laws, the rights to and use of private property, including the use of one's labor, which is also private property, is now forbidden. Only the sovereign State can now grant you the right to life, liberty, and property. The right of private property and self-determination has been stolen from us by the State through "legal" means. They have created laws which are no law.

In fact, under Biblical law, even seduction (which was an offense under the Seventh Commandment of adultery) was also a violation of the Eighth Commandment (pertaining to theft), because it robbed a girl of her virginity. In the case of a seduction, the seducer was required to pay money according to the amount of the dowry that was set for virgins. This is the concept of restitution.

The concept of reconciliation in Biblical Law is a concept of forgiveness, which is a judicial term. Since a court of Law demanded restitution under Biblical Law (to the offended party to establish reconciliation), it is basic to forgiveness, that is, to the re-establishment of the rights of citizenship. Therefore, forgiveness is always inexorably tied to reconciliation. And on a higher level, the concept of reconciliation is inseparable from the concept of salvation, because Yahweh's justice demands reconciliation and restitution. Jesus Christ, His Son, made that restitution on our behalf and reconciled us to Yahweh, the Judge and King, whose Law we had broken.

Therefore, the concept of theft is a broad concept. It includes not only the direct taking — but fraudulent taking, or even the liability of bystanders to a crime, as they do not involve themselves in preventing or stopping the crime. However, under today's laws, the "Good Samaritan" rule is very difficult to practice. Under the current perverse laws (which are not Law), a man may well be punished for trying to involve himself in the rescue, comfort, or aid of another.

Again, when laws work directly against Law, eternal Law, upon which this nation was founded, one must either assume: (a) that we have some very stupid and foolish people running the country, or (b) when it happens time and time again, that there is a treasonous plan to subvert the very foundations of our social institutions.

The most heinous example of theft by government occurs every day, as each and every twenty-four hour period, the government of the United States goes into debt over $1 billion. We have mortgaged the future of generations yet unborn. We have pledged these children to a debt they do not owe.

However, whether it is personal debt or national debt, in almost every case, it is because we have failed to honor yet another Commandment, the Tenth Commandment, which we will deal with shortly.

The Ninth Commandment

Thou shalt not bear false witness against thy neighbour.[165]

This Commandment has been, and continues to be, one of the most wildly perverted of the Ten Commandments. As Rushdoony points out on page 542 of *The Institutes of Biblical Law,* it is often interpreted, "Thou shalt at all times and under all circumstances tell the truth to all men who may ask anything of you."

Here again we see the contrast between positivistic and negativistic law. Negativistic law precludes a particular action, that is the bearing of false witness against one's neighbor. Positivistic law requires that we tell the truth in all circumstances, to anyone who would ask — even if it is damaging both to ourselves or to others; and even if the inquisition is made by those who would seek to do to us or someone else harm.

> It has been insisted by these critics (the moralists) that God will bless and deliver the person who tells the truth at all times. It must be added that these champions of truth-telling at all times have been notorious liars. They feel that they have a right to deny that they have made a statement unless the exact wording, to the last syllable, is exactly reproduced. Such pharisaic reasoning is characteristic of their thinking.

But does God require us to tell the truth at all times? Such a proposition is highly questionable. The commandment is very clear: we are not to bear false witness against our neighbor, but this does not mean that our neighbor or our enemy is ever entitled to the truth from us, or any word from us, about matters of no concern to them, or of private nature to us. No enemy or criminal has any right to knowledge from us that can be used to do us evil. Scripture does not condemn Abraham and Isaac for lying to avoid murder and rape (Gen. 12:11-13; 20:2; 26:6,7); on the contrary, both are richly blessed by God, and the men who placed them in such an unhappy position are condemned or judged (Gen. 12:15-20; 20:3-18; 26:10-16). Like examples abound in Scripture. No one who is seeking to do us evil, to violate the law in reference to us or to another, is entitled to the truth.[166]

Exemplary of this would be when a potential thief, rapist, or murderer inquires of you the whereabouts of land, objects, or persons that they mean to exploit. In fact, giving information in this instance, is, for all intents and purposes, involving yourself in the participation of a crime. The principle then of the Ninth Commandment does not require us to surrender our privacy or privileged information.

The Fifth Amendment of the Constitution of the United States protected that right when it said that no man *"shall be compelled, in any criminal case, to be a witness against himself."* When the State requires an individual to testify against another, under the "force of law," when that law is unjust or being used for evil, it violates of its own volition the Ninth Commandment and has set itself up as the god-State.

Likewise, during a situation of war, spying is legitimate — as are deceptive tactics. The art of deception is well-documented throughout the Scripture. Protection from usurpers requires both concealment and barriers. It is therefore incumbent that in light of the Ninth Commandment, we look once again at the First Amendment of the Bill of Rights:

> *Congress shall make no law respecting an establishment of religion, or prohibiting the free exercise thereof; or abridging the freedom of speech, or of the press; and to petition the Government for a redress of grievances.*

This grossly, misinterpreted Amendment to the Bill of Rights, was not written to give license to every lying, deceiving, and vile whisper of man, or to be turned into public proclamation. Rather, it was written for the pronouncement or speaking of truth. When the State uses the First Amendment to condone the proclamation of falsehood, lies, and those ideologies that would enslave men and the nation, they do violence to the Constitution, to the Law, and ultimately to the Lawgiver — Yahweh.

In the face of such lawless tyranny, the people under the siege of evil demand "law and order." In the recent past, we saw the riots in Los Angeles following the court's "not guilty" verdict in the Rodney King beating. The reign of terror was so pronounced that the people literally begged the government for martial law (totalitarian rule) in the situation. Naturally, the government willingly obliged the people.

It is *The Game of Princes* to create the totalitarian state that it might be submerged into the New World Order. This is not just another totalitarian state. Rather, it is global in intent. The violation of even one principle of the Law, the bearing of false witness, has historically led to the destruction of a nation. Additionally, the bearing of false witness inevitably leads to gossip, slander, innuendo, and distrust of each other; until no man can any longer judge what is true and what is untrue. This leaves us with little basis upon which to maintain social order. Society then devolves into each man for himself. In such a case, it is impossible to judge wrong from right; the one who does evil, from one who does good. When bearing false witness is condoned: what is good is called evil and what is evil is called good.

The Tenth Commandment

> Thou shalt not covet thy neighbour's house,
> thy shalt not covet thy neighbour's wife,
> nor his manservant, nor his maidservant,
> not his ox, nor his ass,
> nor anything that is thy neighbours.[167]

The Tenth Commandment is one of the longer statements of principle in the Law. There are two versions of this command and both basically say the same thing, with a slightly different wording. The first, as found above, is recorded in Exodus 29:17; the second, found in Deuteronomy 5:21 says,

> Neither shall thou desire thy neighbour's wife, neither shall thou covet thy neighbour's house, his field, or his manservant, nor his maidservant, his ox, nor his ass, or anything that is thine neighbours.

Rushdoony in commenting on this command rightly observes:

> Much has been said by silly triflers about the place of the wife in each of these sentences, before and after the house, and also that she is supposedly on the same level as the ox and the ass. Fools should be left to their folly; the wise will occupy their time with other matters.[168]

There are some, within the church, who believe that the word *covet* applies to a state of mind — and not to a physical action. However, Gerhard Von Rad, in *Deuteronomy, A Commentary,* states:

> If in the last commandment the translation of the verb as "covet" were correct, it would be the only case in which the decalogue deals not with an action, but with an inner impulse, hence with a sin of intention. But the corresponding Hebrew word (*hamad*) has two meanings, both to covet and to take. It includes outward malpractices, meaning seizing for oneself (Josh. 7:21; Micah 2:2, etc).[169]

This is an important distinction, inasmuch as to *covet* means both to wish to have and then to take action to secure. In the United States we see the embodiment of coveting, that is the desire and taking actions to secure one's property for redistribution to another.

The entire welfare system is based on coveting. There were some misguided proponents of the welfare system of noble intent. These individuals saw poverty in the land and wanted with all their heart to fix it. However, the evil that they perpetrated upon America has been long-felt, unjust, and ultimately destructive of society.

It is important to remember that we, as individuals, do have obligations to take care of the poor and the needy. We are personally commanded to have pity on the poor and to "not shut up the bowels of our compassion." But, this is not to be misconstrued as *societal collectivism or governmentalism.* Three important things must be understood about covetousness on a governmental level.

First, it is theft — pure and simple. If while walking down the streets of Washington D.C., I pull out a gun and rob a man, telling him that I am going to give the money to a benevolent society that takes care of crippled children — I am still guilty of theft. If the man is in a $500 suit and has $100 bills hanging out of his back pocket, I am still guilty of theft.

However, by some mystical process, if I walk a bit further down the street to Capital Hill and pass a law which says I can appropriate the funds of a private citizen or individual for some "benevolent" cause, this is perfectly legitimate, and, in fact, even laudable and worthy of praise.

The Founding Fathers knew better than that. Thomas Jefferson said: "to compel a man to furnish contributions of money for the propagation of opinions which he disbelieves is sinful and tyrannical;..."[170]

It is both evil and tyrannical for the government to force us, as taxpayers, to promote pornography, "homo-erotic" and anti-Christian art, as is done through the National Endowment for the Arts (NEA). Proponents of the NEA would say, "Yes, but it's only $180 million dollars, which in the scope of the national budget of $1.5 trillion dollars, is a drop in the bucket."

From a constitutional and Biblical standpoint, the entire concept of the welfare state is abhorrent. Cited earlier were Madison's comments concerning the general welfare clause, but beyond that, to steal from an individual the product of his labor for redistribution of any sort is wrong, sinful, and tyrannical. At the root of the covetous welfare system, is the covetousness of the politicians coveting the rights of citizens, granted by their Creator as unalienable. The politicians, in their coveting, have gone well beyond a state-of-mind, taking draconian actions and making laws which steal our rights to life, liberty and property. Therefore, the command against covetousness is not a vague appendix to the Law; rather, it is the very heart of the Law which keeps our rights unalienable.

In American society, this original system of Law has been replaced by a hybrid of the evils of two systems. The first system, from which we derived much evil, is the Marxist or Socialist State, wherein all are considered to be equal in every way.

As stated earlier, the Marxist principle says, "to each according to his need, from each according to his ability." In one way or another and to varying degrees, all welfare and socialist States hold to this principle. This principle cannot, under any circumstances, be applied justly or equally. Under this socialist concept, violence is done to the productive to reward the unproductive of society.

The second evil which has crept into society is the concept of *Fabian Socialism* (gradual socialism). Its meritocracy system uses tests to gauge the psychological, intellectual, and general aptitude of individuals. But, the Biblical example is far different than this.

> In a family-oriented society, not only do people favor their
> own relatives and their friends, but they add to the special privilege

factor by increasing the advantages of those who are advanced or are hard-working and pleasing. The most offensive statement of special privilege ever made is probably the declaration of Jesus Christ, "For unto every one that hath shall be given, and he shall have abundance: but from him that hath not shall be taken away even that which he hath."[171] This flagrant rewarding of initiative and success is an outrage to many.[172]

In the family-oriented society, each member of the family is given a place; each has a job and a function. In the system of meritocracy, failure is inevitable. Anyone who does not reach the level of the one above him, having gone through supposedly rigorous, scientific testing, must conclude that he is inferior, and thus, the great chasm between the privileged and the inferior ever widens.

Additionally, the system of meritocracy promotes a bureaucracy. It is biased against the entrepreneur, or the free-thinker, whose mind has been freed from the ball-and-chain of mediocrity. Even within the supposedly "all are equal" socialist society, those who rise to the top of the meritocracy are the ruling elite.

However, in our original, Bible-oriented society, built around the family, the State is permitted only a limited role. They are primarily limited to protecting the unalienable rights granted by the Creator and guaranteed by the Constitution. That is, perhaps why the Founding Fathers gave the federal government only seventeen tasks they could perform. Yet, today, the State is involved in every aspect of our lives. As an example, we hear propagated the doctrine of equal pay for equal work.

In the parable of the laborers in the vineyard, Jesus told of the householder who hired men in the morning, midmorning, noon, and afternoon, and then paid them all the same wage. Perhaps there was an economic basis for his action. Often, due to the weather conditions in that region, grapes had to be picked in a single day. As the day progressed, it became more urgent to get the still available workmen before others hired them. The price of labor would tend to rise in such a situation.

The parable does *not* seem to give any ground for such an interpretation. The late arrivals were men who had been standing idle, unemployed. The grape pickers, who had borne the heat of the day, protested at being paid an identical wage to the late arrivals. Their protest was an attack on the special privilege of the late-comers, who received the same pay as they did, even though what they had been paid was fair compensation for a day's work.

253

Jesus' answer is important, both as a religious and an economic principle. "Is it not lawful for me to do what I will with my own? Is thine eye evil because I am good?"[173]

The contract with those first hired had been honestly fulfilled. It was the privilege of the householder to grant whatever he wished to any man. The right to give special privileges is a basic aspect of *freedom* and of *private property.* If the individual's freedom to confer special privileges is denied, then freedom and private property are denied.[174]

Until recently in America, an individual was allowed to pay another individual whatever they thought was fair and appropriate. It was not uncommon for a man with four children, who held a lesser position, to make more than a single man with no children, who was his superior.

Employers understood, because of the Biblical heritage of America, that an employee was a trust to him; that the basis of employment was to benefit the employer. Employers understood that they had an obligation to provide for the needs of the employees and his family. It was his life. He took the liberty of disbursing his property, to his employees — as he decided.

But, the entire concept of "equal pay for equal work" is hinged upon a violation of this Commandment against coveting. This concept of a wage to support a family has been replaced by a wage to support an individual.

Imagine the freedom that it would give to the family, to once again have family-oriented businesses, to be entrepreneurs and inventors, and to again rebuild America to the greatness that she once enjoyed. But a violation of this one command, Thou shalt not covet, has been an effective tool of the Princes in the destruction of the family and the entrepreneurial spirit that was America.

The breaking of the Tenth Commandment of covetousness is now cleverly disguised under such high sounding names as socialism, communism, welfare, fair-share tax programs, and the newest euphemism — economic democracy. But, the results are always the same. History is unmistakable.

Covetousness will always destroy a nation because it undermines the entire law upon which society must be built. Again, remember, if you violate the Law at any point — you have done violence to the whole Law because it is one Law — not laws.

There are those who say that they don't believe that eternal Law applies to society today because we have outgrown such antiquated notions. They would say, "Yahweh is a figment of man's imagination. Man is not made in the image of God — but that God is made in the image of man."

While those who profess such views claim to be enlightened, the facts would support the contrary opinion.

One of the most stunning and telling truths of eternal Law is society as it exists today. The Bible tells us that if we obey the Law, certain blessings will come upon a nation. If we violate the Law, certain curses come upon a nation. In other words, there is a cause and effect relationship between obeying and not obeying the Law of Yahweh.

Deuteronomy 28 says that if we fail to observe His Commandments that we will be cursed in the city and in the fields. Our cities are havens for crime and violence; our fields are failing; our farms are failing and globalist agribusiness is buying them out. In fact, if you want an apt description of America today, read Deuteronomy 28 ... then you decide.

There is a war being waged by the humanistic forces of the New World Order against our historic constitutional and Biblical values. As in any war, there is destruction and there are casualties. What we have seen to this point in time is the destruction of our way of life.

No longer is this "the land of the free and the home of the brave." The free are being imprisoned and the brave often discredited. If they cannot be discredited, they are being silenced. The casualties are all around us.

Each of us lives behind locked doors. Many of us live with bars across our windows. We live in fear of the government at all levels of society. Who among us passes April 15th without the thought crossing our mind, "Will we be audited?"

No longer do any of us really run our own businesses. Instead, we structure our businesses around government rules, regulations, environmental laws, banking laws, quota laws, fair employment acts, and a plethora of other dubious and restrictive laws and regulations that control every aspect of our lives.

Our children are the casualties in these final plays of the Princes' war game. Children can no longer be taught the Ten Commandments in school — but they can be taught safe sex. They can be graphically instructed in the use of condoms and taught that homosexuality is an alternate lifestyle. But they can't be taught: "Thou shalt not commit adultery." After all, the enlightened ones tell us such teachings might be psychologically damaging to the children.

In Ohio, children are being taught that homosexuality is the way people are "born" and not a lifestyle of choice. They are told that many Bible scholars do not see a contradiction between homosexuality and the

255

Bible. There is a homosexual educational phone-in service, which is sponsored by the State of Ohio and the United Way — your tax and charitable dollars at work.

All of us are casualties of the war against the constitutional and Biblical values that were our foundation. We increasingly are becoming the victims of violent crimes such as rape, incest, and sexual molestation. Our children are becoming the victims of pedophiles, who go unpunished or are put into treatment programs. And the war against morality has led to an explosion of sexually transmitted diseases, and finally, to the incurrable and fatal, AIDS. As immorality continues, we are being forced to accept homosexuality as an alternative lifestyle. And HIV-positive and AIDS-infected people have protection under law to work in health care facilities (nurses, doctors, orderlies, and dentists). They are in the food preparation areas of restaurants, cafeterias, and even in the lunchrooms of the schools, where our children attend.

Unfortunately, many of us have not even recognized that we are in a war. Yet, the bodies continue to pile up around us. The collateral damage to our freedom, our property, our unalienable rights goes on at an alarming pace. But make no mistake. There is a war being waged. It is the international elite, who use as their Pawns, schemers and idealistic utopian dreamers; and as their battle weapons the money, power, and influence that they control. From the powerful, humanistic, New World Order lobbyist to the vehemently anti-Christian, anti-liberty, anti-constitutional American Civil Liberties Union; from the television networks and print and electronic media to the FED and the I.R.S.; from the banks with which you deal to every other aspect of your life ... war is being waged.

Finally, we must understand that we are in a fight for the very survival of America. There are ways to win this ideological war and almost certain ways to lose. If we are to be victorious in returning America to the greatness that she was, then we must have a battle plan.

If we continue, over the next half decade with the failed policies of the past, there will be nothing left to defend. There will be no more battles to be fought. There will be no more strategies to be planned or tactics to be employed.

There will be no war to be waged.
It will be too late.
The New World Order is coming upon us very, very quickly.

256

SECTION IV

THE FINAL MOVE

CHEQUE † MATE

Chapter 1

Victory in the Making

For too long now, we have been fighting under the wrong banner and taking orders from the wrong generals. We have taken orders from those who have told us to compromise what we have won in battle and ordered us not to compromise on those things which we have lost. We need to begin the process of uniting under a single banner. I believe that banner is the U.S. Taxpayers Party.

Over the next several years we will see the inevitability of victory or defeat. There is no longer time for wishful thinking. There is no longer time for single-issue political lobbying. There is no longer time for the abandonment theology within the church. **There is only time for action.**

Too many times our lobbying leaders have sold us out for personal gain or aggrandizement. Too many times the "church" has refused to take righteous political action, hiding behind their cowardice of the 501(c)(3) tax status. If this tyrannical designation is more important to the church and its leaders than the preservation of freedom, liberty, and righteousness in America ... these leaders must be abandoned. Their failed policies must be scorned and eschewed.

We must abandon the fatal ideology of Separation of Church and State. It was not the intent of the Founding Fathers to keep the Church from influencing the State. It was their intent to keep the State from influencing the Church. However, the State now controls the Church, but the Church no longer influences the State.

It is important for us to understand that we cannot pass laws forcing people to live righteously. However, we can reimplement the laws to keep them from inflicting evil upon society. That, then, is the goals of the U.S. Taxpayers Party and why I heartily endorse and encourage your participation in the **U.S. Taxpayers Party**.

259

For more information, you may call **703-281-9426,** or write:

U.S. Taxpayers Party
450 Maple Avenue, East
Vienna, VA 22180

Chapter 2

The U.S. Taxpayers Party

Party Platform
Preamble

We, the members of the U.S. Taxpayers Party, gratefully acknowledge the blessings of the Lord God as Creator, Preserver, and Ruler of the Universe and of this Nation. We hereby appeal to Him for aid, comfort, guidance, and the protection of His Divine Providence as we work to restore and preserve this nation as a government of the people, for the people, and by the people.

The U.S. Constitution established a republic under God, rather than a democracy.

Our republic is a nation governed by a Constitution which is rooted in Biblical law, administered by representatives of the Constitution democratically elected by the citizens.

In a republic governed by constitutional law rooted in Biblical law, all life, liberty, and property are safe because law rules.

We affirm the principles of inherent individual rights upon which these United States of America were founded:

- That each individual is endowed by his Creator with certain inalienable rights, that among these are the right to life, liberty, property, and the pursuit of the individual's personal interest so long as such pursuits do not trespass on the equal rights of others;
- That the freedom to own, use, exchange, control, protect, and freely dispose of property is a natural, necessary, and inseparable extension of the individual's inalienable rights;
- That the legitimate function of government is to safeguard those rights through the preservation of domestic tranquility, the maintenance of a strong national defense, and the promotion of equal justice for all;

- That history makes clear that, left unchecked, it is the nature of government to usurp the liberty of its citizens and eventually become a major violator of the people's rights; and
- That, therefore, it is essential to bind government with the chains of the Constitution and carefully divide and jealously limit government's powers to those assigned by the consent of the governed.

The U.S. Taxpayers Party calls on all who love liberty and value their inherent rights to join with us in the pursuit of these goals and the restoration of these founding principles. We speak for the majority of Americans: hardworking, productive, taxpaying men and women who constitute the backbone, and the heart, of the American republic and it economy.

These are the producers; these are the ones who should be "first considered and always remembered." It is on their backs that government is carried and it is out of their pockets that government is financed. Without them and without the product of their skills and their labors, there would be no source to fund the legitimate functions of government and no charity to support the private institutions helping those in need.

No nation can survive if it fails to honorably address the problems which concern these citizens. To these productive but generally forgotten Americans, we offer this platform. It responds to their desires; it is the voice which speaks of them and for them as does that of no other political party.

As did our Founding Fathers, the Platform of the U.S. Taxpayers Party in its opening paragraph "greatfully acknowledge the blessings of the Lord God as Creator, Preserver, and Ruler of the Universe and of this Nation."

Remember, there are only two political systems in the entire world. One is based upon the reasoning of man (humanism) and the other is based upon the principles of eternal Law. The U.S. Taxpayers Party, as stated in the first paragraph, dedicates itself to the restoration and preservation of a government by, for, and of the people — not government *to* the people.

In the second paragraph, it addresses the re-establishment of a republic under God, rather than a democracy. As discussed earlier, the Founding Fathers understood the tyranny of democracy. Our republic is, and can be again, a nation governed by a Constitution which is rooted in Biblical Law.

In such a republic, life, liberty, and property are protected because Law is eternal. Equality then becomes not equality of position, but equality under Law — where both rich and poor are treated with equal justice.

The U.S. Taxpayers Party Platform affirms the principles of inherent, individual rights granted unalienably by a Creator. The State cannot alienate us from those rights. Further, the U.S. Taxpayers Party calls on all those who love liberty and value their unalienable, inherent rights to join with them in the pursuit of those goals. How? Very simply. By electing people of righteousness who will represent right on behalf of the people.

ABORTION

The first duty of the law is to prevent the shedding of innocent blood. America's Founding Fathers emphasized that the Constitution of the United States was ordained and established for "ourselves and our posterity." Article IV of the Constitution guarantees to each state a republican form of government. In a republic, the taking of innocent life may not be authorized by any institution of government — legislative, judicial, or executive. Our right to life may certainly not properly be made dependent upon the vote of a majority of any legislative body. The unborn child is a human person created in Yahweh's image. The duty of civil government is to safeguard from assault each such precious life. We oppose any assignment of federal funds to organizations, domestic or foreign, which advocate, encourage, or participate in the practice of abortion. We will only appoint to the federal judiciary and positions of authority in the Department of Justice qualified individuals who publicly acknowledge the personhood of the unborn child. We support enactment of laws to reverse those statutes and judicial decisions which now provide for abortion on demand.

One might reasonably ask why such a potentially explosive issue as abortion is inserted into the platform of a political party. The answer is simple — **because it is right.** There was a time in this nation when certain types of individuals (particularly Blacks, Indians, and others) were considered non-human — or only partially human. As such, their right to life, liberty, and property was not protected. Supposedly, we ended the tyranny of slavery. However, we reinstituted slavery on all of society in legalizing abortion.

Anyone who believes that abortion is a victimless crime does not know or understand the concept of personhood (life beginning at conception).

263

Today, over 30 million citizens of the United States have been slaughtered. Hitler's holocaust pales in comparison with the slaughter of the innocent.

If our right to life can be made dependent upon the vote of a legislative body, then truly we have become a democratic society as opposed to the republican form of government which our Founding Fathers instituted. If, in fact, the right to life can be snuffed out by a court decision, then we are at best, a civilization of barbarians; at worse, we are the most abhorrent society upon the face of the earth.

Because as we have used and assigned federal funds (your tax dollars) to the slaughtering of unborn children, we through the taxation process, have been forced to participate in the holocaust of the destruction of life — and ultimately — of our nation.

AIDS

The spread of AIDS is attributable to various causes, but principally to promiscuous homosexual conduct and drug abuse. Because of the failure of the federal government to protect the blood supply under its control from corruption, and because of policies which, in fact, encourage illicit sexual conduct and which otherwise place innocent citizens at risk, millions of non-homosexual, non-drug-abusing Americans have been given a death sentence.

Under no circumstances should the federal government continue to subsidize activities which have the effect of encouraging homosexual conduct. In the name of "safe sex," hundreds of millions of tax dollars have been misdirected to organizations which contribute to the spread of AIDS by endorsing, implicitly and explicitly, perverse, unhealthy sexual conduct.

In all federally-funded facilities and institutions, the policy of the United States government should be to protect the uninfected from any avoidable exposure which could place them at risk, not only for the HIV-virus and AIDS, but to all of the diseases which are direct and indirect by-products of promiscuous sexual behavior and drug abuse. We believe that HIV infection is a public health concern, and not a civil rights issue.

Criminal penalties should apply to those willful acts of omission or commission which place members of the public at toxic risk.

There is a price to be paid each time we abridge or pervert eternal Law. There is ample evidence to suggest that AIDS, because it is becoming

264

epidemic in certain areas of the nation, is beginning to be spread in other ways. However, to promote AIDS education in terms of "safe sex" is absolutely abhorrent. It is therefore the position of the U.S. Taxpayers Party that no federal funds should be used to continue to subsidize activities which affect or encourage homosexual conduct under the guise of "safe sex."

For years, certain diseases have been quarantined and not given "civil rights." And while the platform of the U.S. Taxpayers Party does not call for quarantining of AIDS patients, it does, at a minimum, call for the treatment of the wilful spread of AIDS as a criminal act; although, personally I would endorse, as is the case with all other communicable diseases (for instance, small pox, tuberculosis, typhus, and leprosy), the quarantining of HIV- infected persons and AIDS patients.

BRING GOVERNMENT BACK HOME

The closer civil government is to the people, the more responsible, responsive, and accountable it is likely to be. The Tenth Amendment to the Constitution makes clear that the federal government has only those functions which are explicitly assigned to it. All other rights and authorities are reserved to the states and to the people. We pledge to be faithful to this constitutional requirement and to work methodically to restore to the states and to the people control over legislative, judicial, executive, and regulatory functions which are beyond the proper scope of the federal government.

The Founding Fathers gave the federal government only seventeen areas into which they could intervene or inject their power. Washington, when speaking of government, said: "It is not eloquence or reason - it is fire."

Fire properly controlled can warm us and cook our food; uncontrolled it will destroy us. Therefore, the U.S. Taxpayers Party demands that civil government be more responsible, responsive, and accountable. This would be accomplished by restoring individual and state's rights.

CONGRESSIONAL REFORM

The Congress of the United States has become an overpaid, overstaffed, self-serving institution. It confiscates taxpayer funds to finance exorbitant salaries, pensions, and perks. Most members of Congress have become more accountable to the Washington Establishment than to the people in their home districts. Both Houses of Congress are all too often unresponsive and irresponsible, arrogantly placing themselves above the very laws they enact and beyond the control of the citizens they have sworn to represent and serve.

It is time for the American people to renew effective supervision of their employees in public office, to restore right standards, and to take back their government. Congress must once again be accountable to the people.

The U.S. Taxpayers Party calls for the implementation of the following agenda to facilitate such reform:

· Apply to Congress all laws it has enforced upon the private citizens (civil rights, labor laws, environmental laws, etc.);
· Abolish Congressional pensions;
· Abolish federal pay for members of Congress and restore provisions for *per diem* allowances;
· Abolish or severely restrict the franking privilege;
· Abolish the 1974 Federal Election Law and the General Election Commission;
· Make it easier and less expensive for new political parties and candidates to get on the ballot.

We support the opportunity of free citizens to apply term limits to all elected officials and Executive Branch, administrative personnel.

Because of Congress' proven arrogant irresponsibility, they must, like a spoiled child, be subject to close scrutiny. Congress should have applied to it all laws that it has enforced upon the private citizens.

Congressional pensions are an excuse to stay in Congress for a lifetime, as opposed to the concept of a public servant for a short period of time; after which one returns home to live under the laws which they have passed. These should be abolished.

Federal pay for members of Congress should be replaced with a per diem allowance. This too would help end the cycle of professional politicians. For those who think that we need experienced professionals to run such a complex government, I would ask only that they view honestly our current national circumstance. If this is the end result of "professionalism and experience," give me the "unprofessional and inexperienced." They could hardly do worse.

Perhaps we should consider turning off the air-conditioning in the hallowed Halls of Congress. I doubt these purloining demigods would be willing to bear the heat. You would probably find them returning home to their own air conditioned districts in short order. By their spending more time at home, we could begin restricting or eliminating the franking privileges of these elitists. Instead, they could begin speaking to those they represent face to face, a prospect some of them might fear.

By abolishing the Princes-inspired 1974 Federal Election Law and the General Election Commission, we could begin breaking up their political monopoly. These laws were passed supposedly to give us free and open elections. In reality, the opposite has happened. Historically, in excess of 95 percent of all of our federally elected thieves are returned to Washington. This is hardly an open process.

The U.S. Taxpayers Party supports the opportunity of free citizens to apply term limits to all elected officials.

CONSTITUTIONAL CONVENTION

We oppose any attempt to call for a constitutional convention for any purpose whatsoever because it cannot be limited to any single issue and such convention could seriously erode our constitutionally protected inalienable rights.

The idea of a constitutional convention is one planted in the media and in the minds of the public, by those who would immerse us into the New World Order. The Princes know full well that they would be in control of both the agenda of the convention and the news media's reporting of it. Don't be conned by the call for the Con-Con (Constitutional Convention). It would be the death of our free system of government.

It is essential that you work to block or rescind any call for a Con-Con in your state.

COST OF BIG GOVERNMENT

The only legitimate purpose of civil government is to safeguard the God-given rights of its citizens: namely, life, liberty, and property. Only those duties, functions, and programs specifically assigned to the federal government by the Constitution should be funded.

In the past 30 years, federal spending has increased from less than $100 billion a year in 1961, to $1.5 *trillion* for the current fiscal year. Consider this:

- Since 1988, the number of pages required in the federal *Register* to list all new regulations has zoomed from 53,376 pages to 67,716 in 1992.

267

- The number of federal employees involved in issuing and enforcing regulations has increased from 104,360 in 1988, to an all-time high of 124,994 in 1992.
- The amount of taxpayer money the federal leviathan spends each year administering the jungle of regulations has increased from $9.6 billion in 1988, to $11.3 billion in 1992.
- Federal regulations are now costing the American people between $881 billion and $1.65 trillion a year.

The federal government has turned into a tax-and-spend monster which is devouring the people it is supposed to be serving.

As the Declaration of Independence cried out, so it is today: The federal government "has erected a multitude of new offices, and sent hither swarms of officers to harass our people and eat out their substance." Just since 1961, 297 new federal commissions, councils, public corporations, grants, and management programs have been created — in addition to all those which existed beforehand. In addition, more than 60 new boards and commissions were empowered.

The U.S. Taxpayers Party calls on all citizens to join in the drive to restore constitutional government and reduce the cost and controls of the federal leviathan. We must reduce the reach, the grasp, and the take of the federal government. It has grown too big, too expensive, too wasteful, too arrogant. It is a government which has become unaccountable and unresponsive to the people.

We must restore to the states those powers, programs, and sources of revenues which the federal government has usurped.

The U.S. Taxpayers Party calls upon the Congress and the Executive to disapprove and halt all federal expenditures which are not specifically authorized by the Constitution of these United States.

We call for abolition of the Civil Service system which confers a "property right" on jobs as government employees. The President should be able to determine who will carry out - free from subversion or opposition by tax-paid personnel - those programs which he has promised the people to inaugurate and implement.

Turning back the "federal spending clock" by five years will not destroy the economy; in fact, it would revive it. Instead of having these monies confiscated and squandered by politicians and bureaucrats, we would return hundreds of billions of dollars to the taxpayers, so that Americans could spend or invest their own money as they chose. The productive private sector jobs created and the investment capital released would not only put new life in the domestic economy, it would be an important assist in the drive to compete with foreign industries here and in world markets. The return of the people's money would create jobs and investments instead of having it confiscated and spent on non-productive, wasteful programs and pork barrels by politicians and bureaucrats.

Since 1949, the population of the United States has increased by about 90 percent, while the size of government has increased by over 5,000 percent! By restoring the size of constitutional government to constitutional limits, we could shave as much as $1 trillion from the federal budget. Imagine what releasing that $1 trillion into our economy could do. In such an economy, chronic unemployment and underemployment would disappear. No longer would people be hunting for jobs — jobs would be hunting for people. Our economy would far outstrip all other economies of the world, and the myth that America can no longer compete globally, except with governmental intervention, would be forever dispelled.

Government is not capable of creating jobs, security, or anything else. Government only creates more government, which results in tyranny. *Government is not the Creator, it is created by a right of we the people and can be altered only by we the people.*

If we, the citizens, do not immediately take action to restore constitutional government and reduce the tyranny, costs, and controls of the federal leviathan, we will soon find ourselves its prey.

The U.S. Taxpayers Party believes that individuals are more and better able to spend, save, and invest their own money than the federal government. There are, of course, those who would say, "But what about the poor?"

Government cannot solve the problems of the poor. Government programs have been abysmal failures. The Clinton administration talks about empowering people through government programs. The Constitution talks about empowering people by limiting government and denying them the ability to steal the unalienable rights of people.

CRIME

Crime, in most cases, is to be dealt with by state and local governments. To the degree that the federal government, in its legislation, in its judicial actions, in its regulations, and in its Executive Branch activities, interferes with the ability of the people in their communities to apprehend, judge, and penalize accused lawbreakers, it bears responsibility for the climate of crime which has grown more destructive with each passing year.

We favor the unimpeded right of states and localities to execute criminals convicted of capital crimes and to require restitution for the victims of criminals who have not threatened the lives or physical safety of others. Federal interference with local criminal justice processes should be limited to that which is constitutionally required.

In recently televised testimony before the House Judiciary Committee, Justice Anthony Scalea said that he saw no constitutional problem with federalizing more crime. What he did see as a problem was the overloading of the federal Judiciary and the Supreme Court.

In the federalization of more crimes, there is a denial of state and local rights to set the standards for acceptable behavior. Here again, the intent is not to pass laws which will make people *good,* but rather, to enforce law on a local level based upon *the standards of a community,* which will prevent evil.

DEFENSE

It is a primary obligation of the federal government to provide for the common defense, vigilant to deal with significant potential threats and prospective capabilities, as well as with perceived present intentions.

We oppose the unilateral dismantlement and dismemberment of America's defense infrastructure. That which is hastily torn down will not be easily rebuilt.

In order to protect our territory, our armed forces, and our citizenry, we should immediately give the required six-months notice of our withdrawal from the Nixon-Brezhnev Anti-Ballistic Missile Treaty, which restricts full development and deployment of a strategic defense system — the installation of which will be of the highest priority for our party's candidates once elected to office.

Under no circumstances would we commit U.S. forces to serve under any flag but that of the United States of America. We are opposed to any New World Order of the kind conceived by George Bush, and we flatly reject U.S. participation in any New World Army.

The goal of U.S. security policy is to defend the national

security interests of the United States.

We should be the friend of liberty everywhere, but the guarantor and provisioner of ours alone.

We urge the Executive and Legislative Branches to continue to provide for the modernization of our Armed Forces in keeping with advancing technologies and a constantly changing world situation.

We call for the maintenance of a strong, state-of-the-art military on land, sea, and in the air, as well for the development and maintenance of a strong space defense system (which could be to the future defense of this nation what the air and naval power are now).

We support the maintenance of a strong and ready and well-equipped Reserve and National Guard.

We call for talks with the Republic of Panama, intended to restore to the United States control over the operations and security of the Panama Canal, while fully recognizing the autonomy and independence of the Republic of Panama. Under no circumstances should we unilaterally surrender our military base rights in Panama at a time when the people of Panama desire that we continue them.

If the United States is to maintain its sovereignty, it is absolutely necessary that we withdraw from the United Nations and its New World Order treaties which make us a part of a global army or a global community. It is paramount that we understand that the United Nations is a tool of the Princes of the New World Order. The Princes' goal is not to maintain the sovereignty of the United States, but to gain sovereignty over all States globally.

DRUG ABUSE

The U.S. Taxpayers Party will uphold the right of states and localities to restrict access to drugs and to enforce such restrictions in appropriate cases with application of the death penalty. We support legislation to stop the flow of illegal drugs into the United States from foreign sources. As a matter of self-defense, retaliatory policies, including embargoes, sanctions, and tariffs, should be considered.

At the same time, we will take care to prevent violations of the constitutional and civil rights of American citizens. Arbitrary searches and seizures must be prohibited and the presumption of innocence must be preserved.

271

Drug abuse is one of the most serious problems facing the United States today. In addition to being very destructive of society, it has been used as an excuse by the federal government to steal the rights of life, liberty, and property of Americans.

Money laundering and property confiscation laws, which are supposedly passed to stop the flow of money, connected to illicit drugs, have not been used, in most cases, to divert or interdict drug traffic; rather, they are being used as an arm of tyranny for the federal government against the citizens of the United States. In fact, in 1992, the federal government initiated under these laws, over 500,000 confiscations of property. In over 80 percent of these cases, the "victims" were never charged with a crime or, the evidence against them was so weak that the charges had to be dropped. However, the assets ceased in this "legalized" plunder, were not returned (in most cases) to the owners. Under federal law, once assets are ceased, the owner must go to court and prove themselves innocent of a crime, for which in over 80 percent of the cases, they were never charged. How do you prove yourself innocent of a crime for which you were never charged?

In his book, *Red Cocaine,* Dr. Joseph Douglas chronicles, not only the government's knowledge of drug trafficking into this nation, but also details that in many instances the federal government is in complicity with those drug traffickers.

The further health risks of the drug culture in America are now, and will be in the future, catastrophic. Drug and medical treatments have reached astronomical proportions. Further, the spread of communicable diseases, including sexually transmitted diseases, with AIDS at the top of the list, will, if left unchecked, destroy both our medical system and be "the straw that breaks the camel's back" in the bankrupting this nation.

For decades we have followed a failed policy of drug interdiction. Drug trafficking in this nation has not decreased — rather, it has increased dramatically. The last thirty years have proven that these draconian methods of "drug interdiction" have failed.

I believe that taking away the drug traffickers' source of retail outlets is the one thing that will end the proliferation of drug trafficking in the United States and do so almost instantly. McDonald's, without its thousands upon thousands of distribution centers, its retail stores, could not survive financially. Likewise, take away the drug lords' retail establishments, the drug pushers, and you dry up the drug trade in America.

It is, therefore, my recommendation that execution be the penalty for drug trafficking, either on a multi-billion dollar level, or for the street corner

272

or playground level. If the price for selling drugs is too high for the potential profits — there will be less people waiting in line to assume that position.

Liberals, Libertarians, and even some "conservatives" would decry such a plan as unmerciful. However, I would ask, how merciful drug traffickers have been to the millions of people, including children, whose lives have been destroyed as a result of this vile profession. Further, those executed will be permanently discouraged from ever selling drugs to our children again.

As an additional benefit to ending the scourge of drugs in America, the cost of medical care will be radically altered downward. We do not need more drug treatment programs, drug counselling, or education. What we need are laws to take drug dealers off the streets, keep them out of the prisons, and put them where the belong — permanently and irrevocably — out of society.

THE ECONOMY

The big issue of 1992, are jobs and the economy. The reason for economic hard times is that government has grown too big, too burdensome, and too expensive.

During the past 30 years:
- Income tax collections have increased from $41 billion in 1961, to $468 billion in 1991.
- Social Security taxes have gone up from $16 billion in 1961, to $370 billion in 1991.
- Corporate taxes have gone up from $21 billion in 1961, to $98 billion in 1981.

Since 1981, the national debt has quadrupled: from $914 billion to at least $4 trillion.

In two or three years, it will cost more to service the debt than Uncle Sam collects in income taxes.

The situation is not hopeless. A President who knows what needs to be done, who understands how to do it, and who has the courage to act, can turn the crisis around in the space of a single four-year term.

The result will be more jobs, greater prosperity, less inflation, and lower taxes.

The answer is simple. Let's roll the clock back on federal spending to what it was five years ago, where, instead of spending about $1.5 trillion a year, Uncle Sam was spending one-third less.

That kind of cutback in spending can be achieved by a

President willing to use his veto and govern confrontationally against all the special interests which feed at the federal trough.

So much has been said throughout this book on the economy that very little needs to be added to the salient words of the U.S. Taxpayers Party platform. However, I would suggest that you go back and re-read "Cost Of Big Government" in this Section.

EDUCATION

All education is inherently religious, in the sense that all teaching is related to basic assumptions about the nature of God and man. God has invested parents with the responsibility for the nurture and training of the children He has entrusted to them. Education should be parentally accountable.

Education should be free from any federal government subsidy and all government interference. The federal government has no legitimate role in either subsidizing or regulating eduction, except insofar as it relates to members of the Armed Forces and employees of the Executive Branch. Under no circumstances should the federal government involve itself in matters of education curriculum or textbooks.

Again, we see the ugly head of the god-State towering above all of us like a pagan idol, breathing fire, and baring its teeth. Madison warned us of the danger of allowing government into a position of taking care of religion. The false doctrine of Separation of Church and State is now being treated as fact and has been since the 1960s when prayer and Bible reading were removed from the public educational system.

The religion of Humanism, which has been incorporated as a 501(c)(3) religious organization, can, and is, being taught everyday in the classrooms of America. The only religion that has been removed from public education is the religion of Christianity. Christianity and Biblical Law were the foundations of this nation. Therefore, they have removed our foundation for the future, leaving us nothing to build upon for tomorrow.

Education is not the purview of the federal government. Education is the responsibility of parents. Parents may delegate authority to act on their behalf to someone else. But, to have taken that responsibility from them — even by majority vote — is tyranny.

The future of your children, what they will know, and the values they will hold is too important to be entrusted to an inane bureaucracy like

274

the federal government. Therefore, I believe, as much as possible, children should be the product of home education. Remember, if the illegal federal income tax is done away with, the average American would double their spendable income, making home education a good idea and financially possible for almost every family.

However, all education should remain in the private domain of society. By restoring, through proper education the foundation laid by our forefathers, we can march confidently as a free people into the next century.

ELECTION REFORM

The U.S. Taxpayers Party seeks the restoration of an electoral process which is controlled at the state and local level and is beyond manipulation by federal judges and bureaucrats. The federal government has unconstitutionally and unwisely preempted control in matters of district boundaries, electoral procedures, and campaign activities.

Elections should be accountable to the people, not to the government. The Voting Rights Act should be repealed. The Federal Election Commission should be abolished.

Each citizen should have the right to seek public office in accordance with the qualifications set forth in the federal and state Constitutions. Additional restrictions and obligations governing candidate eligibility and campaign procedures unduly burden the fairness and accountability of our political system.

We urge an end to electronic or mechanical voting process-es and a return to the manual counting process overseen by and ac-countable to voters resident in each precinct where the votes are cast.

Election reform laws, as passed by the Congress over the last several decades, have been both unconstitutional and monopolistic. As discussed earlier, while the public relations campaign has been successful in convincing America that this is to protect them from the rich and powerful special interest groups and the elite of society, it has, in fact, done quite the opposite.

The manipulation of elections by the Princes using federal judges and mindless bureaucrats is unconscionable. If control of elections is returned as a right of the states, it greatly diffuses the ability of the Princes to manipulate such elections. The first step in reasserting states' rights in the area of elections is the abolition of the Federal Election Commission and the repealing of the Voting Rights Act.

There are those who would contend that the Voting Rights Act is necessary to protect the right to vote of all peoples — and especially minorities. To those who would make that assertation, I would remind them, there is already constitutional protection concerning the right to vote. Additionally, with less than half of America voting (and an even smaller percentage of "minorities" voting), these laws have had the opposite of their "desired" effect. They have effectively disenfranchised most of America from the electoral process.

There is a time — and that time is now — to bring to light the real purpose of election reform laws. It is to protect the system of the Princes from us — not to protect us from them.

In almost every state, qualification for political parties, except for monopoly "Republicrats," are so draconian as to render unavailable access to the ballot. Many good and responsible candidates are discouraged from seeking public office because of excessive fees, which sometimes amount to 1-5 percent of the annual salary to be paid for the office sought.

Further, with space age technology and the use of computers in counting votes, the ability to electronically rig elections is not only a possibility, but has been a proven reality in many areas. Therefore, a manual counting system needs to be restored with accountability to the people, using judges by and from the people. If access is not restored again soon to the electoral process, two hundred years plus of history, heritage, culture, and freedom will be lost.

ENERGY

We call attention to the continuing need of the United States for a sufficient supply of energy to sustain the nation's standard of living and its agricultural, business, and industrial activities.

Private property rights should be respected and government should not interfere with the development of potential energy sources, including hydroelectric power, solar energy, wind generators, and nuclear energy.

We also encourage the use of coal, shale, and oil sands for the production of power and the conversion of coal, shale, and agricultural products to synthetic fuels.

We oppose any increase in federal fuel taxes and insist that, so long as such taxes are collected in any amount, all of their proceeds should be used exclusively for the maintenance of inter-state highways.

Over the past several decades, America has found itself enslaved by its energy policies. While our government has paid lip service to the development of clean, renewable, domestic energy sources, they have (through subsidies of foreign energy, environmental protectional laws, and oppressive tax penalties) discouraged all independent attempts to develop domestic energy sources. By crushing all independent energy providers, the Princes have managed to gain monopolistic control of all domestic energy production, while maintaining their monopolistic control of foreign energy sources. Through their surrogates and global trusts, even the Arab oil barons and sheiks, have become nothing more than Pawns of the Princes.

If we are to regain control of the energy policy of this nation, we must destroy the tools of the Princes; namely, the Department of Energy, the Environmental Protection Agency, and the legion of other "puppet" bureaucrats, whose craving for power has left us with a power shortage in more ways than one.

ENVIRONMENT

It is a prime responsibility of man to be a prudent, productive, and efficient steward of God's natural resources. In that role, man is commanded to be fruitful, to multiply, to replenish the earth, and develop it — to turn deserts into farms and wastelands into groves. This requires a proper and continuing dynamic balance between development and conservation, between use and preservation.

The proper exercise of stewardship demands that we avoid the extremes; that we escape the deadly hand of government confiscation; that we recognize and preserve the right of the individual to acquire, own, and use his property so long as he does not infringe on the rights of other individuals to do the same.

The progress and well-being of society requires that the best interests of human beings must be accorded preference to so-called animal rights. This is not to say that the preservation and care of the creatures of the forest, field, and water are not part of stewardship — they are; but, when we choose between an owl or a snail darter and the jobs of American citizens and the well-being of their families and children, the families must be valued above plants and animals.

We wholeheartedly support realistic efforts to preserve the environment and reduce pollution — air, water, and land. We reject, however, the argument that this objective ought to be pursued by costly governmental interference, accompanied by multitudes of

277

regulations and the heavy hand of arrogant bureaucrats spurred on by irresponsible pressure groups.

The Constitution of the United States requires that private property owners be compensated for any government "taking" of their property — whether it be through outright confiscation or by the imposition of rules and regulations which preclude the productive use of the property. This mandate must be strictly observed.

We call for the return to the states and to the people all lands which are held by the federal government without authorization by the Constitution.

In the beginning man was given the command to be fruitful, multiply, and have dominion over all of the earth. However, dominion implies stewardship of the earth, not abuse. Untoward regulation is not the answer to our environmental problems. Typically, environmental abuse (as we approach the twenty-first century) is caused — not solved — by regulation. As an example, many of the abuses of small logging companies are caused by environmental regulations which protect the monopolistic interests of the Princes. In order to compete and stay alive financially, many small logging firms have been forced to adopt practices, which in the long term, hurt the environment.

Even with these limited, environmentally damaging practices, it is still a fact, that there are more timbered acres in the United States today than there were fifty years ago. Why? Because it makes good business sense to replant the forests after they have been harvested.

EUTHANASIA

The U.S. Taxpayers Party is on record as recognizing and putting first the sanctity of human life.

Just as we oppose abortion — the taking of an innocent, pre-born life — so we adamantly oppose assisted murder.

We oppose any laws which condone or would legalize euthanasia, the so-called "mercy killing" of the aged, the ailing, the infirm. The concept of euthanasia is a dangerous move toward legalized termination of the non-productive, the unwanted, and the unprotected. A nation which has become inured to the slaughter of some 30 million innocent babies can all too easily slide into the Hitlerian-Sangerite goal of eliminating those it considers misfits, undesirables, or non-productives.

Any physician or nurse who assists in the extinguishment of life is not worthy to be a member of the healing arts profession, which is one of the noblest of all callings.

The sanctity of human life is the underlying principle of the Constitution of the United States. The first unalienable right is that of life. Again remember, there are only two political systems in the entire world. That which protects the sanctity of life, which comes from the Creator. Unfortunately, it seems both historically and currently true, that humanistic law always concentrates its efforts on death.

Biblical eternal Law protects the life of the unborn. Humanistic law give us the "right" of abortion. Eternal Law demands respect and honor for the elderly. Humanistic law seeks to convince society that the life of the infirm and elderly is a life not worth living. It asserts that society has an obligation to assist these individuals in "dying with dignity" (assisted murder). In certain Scandinavian countries, where Euthanasia is the law of the land, the elderly often live in fear, wondering if and when they will be required to "die with dignity." They live in fear of their children and of the government. For these people, euthanasia has not brought dignity — it has brought terror.

The solution is not legalization of murder or the condoning of suicide; nor is it the aborting of thirty million more babies. The solution is to return to eternal principles, and with it, a right understanding of both life and death.

FOREIGN AID

Ever since World War II, the United States has provided military and non-military aid to more than 100 nations. Hundreds of billions of dollars have been poured down that bottomless pit — with little evident benefit to the safety and security of the American people. Not only have we given aid to our "friends," but to "neutrals" by means of which aid we hoped to buy their "friendship." Finally, we are now committing ourselves to send the taxpayers' dollars to those who have been our enemies for years. This must stop!

The Congress and the President have a duty to provide for the defense of this country, but the American people have no similar duty to provide tax dollars for the defense of any foreign nation. Further, the U.S. Government has no right, let alone a duty, to tax the American people to provide aid of any kind to foreign governments.

Therefore, the U.S. Taxpayers Party will:
- Terminate *all* programs of foreign aid, whether military or non-military, to *any* other government.
- Dismantle the Agency for International Development within the Department of State.
- Prevent any dollar of the U.S. taxpayers' money from being spent on aid to the former Soviet Union.

The concept of foreign aid is the same concept that brought us the welfare system and the Great Society programs. Somehow, the government has added to their list of duties and obligations (to the citizenry and to the world at large), making of us and the rest of the world, indentured beggars. This is a globalist wealth redistribution scheme.

Wealth redistribution has failed in the communist countries, in socialist America, and it will fail globally. But it is a part of the Princes plan for a global New World Order. "To each according to his need, from each according to his ability." Foreign aid programs can and must be stopped.

Investment in international markets or business is the purview of private individuals and entrepreneurs willing to take risks for the possibility of gain. Foreign aid has for too long been used as a tool to bring to power the Pawns of the Princes. Through their control of foreign aid policy, they have caused the rise and fall of governments. It is yet another gambit in *Cheque † Mate · The Game of Princes.*

FOREIGN POLICY

The only constitutional purpose and basis of foreign policy is to serve the best interests of the nation. It is not to be the world's policeman or play the world's Santa Claus.

We pledge our allegiance to the American Republic. We say "No!" to any so-called New World Order or one-world government. Not one whit of American autonomy may be given up to any international organization or group of nations.

We oppose entangling foreign alliances. The United States should withdraw from NATO and bring our armed forces home from Europe, as well as from Japan and Korea.

We should review all existing treaties to determine which, if any, are beyond constitutional limits; those which are should be rescinded.

The United States must not enter into agreements which

would have an adverse impact on the security and safety of this nation. We should immediately renounce all economic sanctions and embargoes against the Republic of South Africa.

The U.S. Taxpayers Party calls on the United States to withdraw from the United Nations and to encourage the United Nations to move out of the United States.

We believe that the United States should withdraw from all international monetary and financial institutions and agencies such as the International Monetary Fund (IMF), the World Bank, etc.

Because we have discussed the control of our foreign policy through the Princes' organizations such as the CFR and the Trilateral Commission, we do not need to go into great detail here. Suffice it to say, that like foreign aid, our Foreign Policy should always reflect the interests of these United States. The pundits in the media would have us believe that it is somehow wrong to think of America first. I would simply ask — why?

Washington warned us of the dangers of entangling international military and economic alliances. We should heed those warnings. Foreign policy, like foreign aid, has been yet another tool in *The Game of Princes*. We need to withdraw from entangling international alliances such as NATO, the United Nations, and all treaties linking us to such organizations as the International Monetary Fund and the World Bank.

GUN CONTROL

The right to bear arms is inherent in the right of self defense conferred on the individual by his Creator to safeguard his own life, liberty, and property, and that of his family, as well as to help preserve the independence of the nation.

The right to bear arms is guaranteed by the Second amendment to the Constitution; it may not properly be infringed upon or denied.

The U.S. Taxpayers Party upholds the right of the citizen to keep and bear arms. We oppose attempts to prohibit the ownership of guns by law-abiding citizens, and stand against all laws which would require the registration of guns or ammunition.

We emphasize that when guns are outlawed only the outlaws will have them. In such circumstances, the peaceful citizen's protection against the criminal would be seriously jeopardized.

The right to keep and bear arms is a fundamental right guaranteed by Article II of the Bill of Rights. It is inexorably linked to self-defense. As stated earlier, in many states the militia is defined as "every able-bodied citizen of the state." Article II of the Bill of Rights says that *"A well regulated Militia, being necessary to the security of a free State, the right of the people to keep and bear Arms, shall not be infringed."* According to Webster's dictionary *infringe* means "to break or violate; to encroach on."

In the state in which I reside, I am constitutionally mandated, as a member of the Militia, to keep and bear arms. Yet, my state is the only state in all fifty which has a constitutional Amendment demanding a three day waiting period for the purchase of guns — as if this was going to stop violent crime or criminals from using guns. I sincerely doubt that one out of a thousand violent criminals, the drug lords, or gang members go to their local gun shop to purchase firearms.

The Founding Fathers understood that the national army was a tyranny to the people, but that a well-regulated Militia would secure the freedom of the people and cause the government to be accountable to them — rather than they to it. All law-abiding citizens should be able to have, own, possess, buy, sell, and trade their weapons.

Law-abiding, including those who have committed crimes, but made restitution and are now law-abiding, have a right and an **obligation**, as patriotic Americans, to keep and bear arms. Those who refuse to make restitution, or are guilty of capital crimes, should have been executed. Therefore, only a very small segment of the population would be in a position not to be a part of the Militia, and the general citizenry, whose right and obligation it is to keep and bear arms.

IMMIGRATION

Each year some 400,000 legal immigrants and another 300,000 illegals enter the United States. These immigrants — including illegal aliens — have been made eligible for various kinds of public assistance, including housing, education, Social Security, and legal services, while paying few, if any, taxes. This unconstitutional raid on the federal Treasury is having a severe and adverse impact on our economy, increasing the cost of government at federal and local levels, adding to the tax burden, and stressing the fabric of society.

The U.S. Taxpayers Party demands that the federal government restore immigration policies based on the practice that potential immigrants will be disqualified from admission to the U.S.

if, on grounds of health, criminality, morals, or financial dependency, they would impose an improper burden on persons already resident in the United States.

We oppose bilingual ballots. We insist that those who wish to take part in the electoral process and governance of this nation should be required to read and comprehend basic English.

We insist that each immigrant who is admitted must have a sponsor who is legally, morally, and financially obliged to bear full responsibility for the economic independence of the immigrant, lest the burden be unfairly shifted to other taxpayers.

We also insist that those groups and private agencies which request the admission of immigrants to the U.S. as political refugees or economic hardship cases be required to legally commit themselves to providing housing and sustenance for such immigrants and to post appropriate bonds to seal such covenants.

We support the strengthening of the Immigration and Naturalization Service for the proper screening of immigrants, the apprehending and deportation of illegal aliens, and the protection of our borders.

We oppose the provision of welfare and other taxpayer-supported benefits to illegal aliens and reject the practice of bestowing U.S. citizenship on children born to illegal alien parents while in this country.

Because this nation was built upon immigration, many of us believe that immigration should be free and unrestricted. However, the Founding Fathers dealt with this in the Constitution. They simply set a period of time for which immigration was to be unlimited, after which, understandably, it would be limited depending upon the limits of land, economy, and the ability of immigrants to assimilate into the population.

America has been called the "Great Melting Pot." Melting implies a blending together. The many become one culture. We are Americans. Those who wish to immigrate to this nation need to understand that they are becoming Americans. This is not a *multi-cultural society*. While our culture is diverse, our diversity is blended into a uniquely American culture. A truly merciful and beneficent policy should require individuals, who plan to make this land their home, to adopt this uniquely American culture, based upon life, liberty, and the pursuit of happiness.

We don't need every dead-beat and future welfare recipient in the world coming to our shores. Nor do we need every AIDS-infected individual whose future medical costs will suck from the taxpayers' pockets $100,000-$200,000 before their unavoided and inevitable death. Despite what many liberals and multiculturalists would have us believe, the pursuit of happiness does require pursuit — not idly sitting at some public trough.

INDIVIDUAL RIGHTS

We oppose laws which enforce discrimination (reverse or otherwise) on the basis of race, color, ethic origin, age, or gender.

We oppose quotas imposed by, or applied in, any government or public institution.

Each and every citizen should be free to choose his friends and associates, to offer, seek or refuse employment, and to rent or sell his property to whomever he wishes.

While I agree with the U.S. Taxpayers Party's platform policy on "Individual Rights," I would like to expand this concept to that which I believe the Founding Fathers understood in the concept of "rights."

I believe their understanding of rights was not that which one possesses, but that with which one is endowed. The concept of rights, as explained in a dictionary from 1828 and paraphrased in the "Baker Abridged Version" is this: *rights* are those eternal precepts unalienably or inexorably intertwined in the creation of man.

The concept of rights then, when used in the context of welfare rights, homosexual rights, or abortion rights, is a perversion of the Founding Fathers' understanding of rights. Simply put: all men are created equal because of eternal rights or precepts which are eternally correct, making them equal because they are all judged under Law by the same eternally correct principles or eternally correct things that are right(s).

Therefore, individual rights are those things which are right because they are righteous and are endowed to us by our Creator. They are not something to be grasped or gained — they are eternal and can only be exercised, secured, and protected in a society where *"right"eousness* is the Law of the land.

MONEY AND BANKING

Money is both a medium of exchange and a measure of a nation's morality.

Properly established and guarded, it provides the citizen with

284

an assured standard by which he can trade (exchange) his labors or property for a service or product he desires to acquire. The improper control (manipulation) of the money and banking system destroys the value of the citizen's earnings and investments and brings untold misery upon the people. Indeed, it can spawn rebellion and anarchy which shatters societies and topples governments.

The Founding Fathers established a system of sound and honest money designed to prohibit "improper and wicked" manipulation of the medium of exchange. Its purpose was to guarantee that the purchasing power of the citizen's earnings would not be diminished or degraded between the time income is earned and the time it is spent; that it will not lose its purchasing power between the time it is invested and the time it is withdrawn.

Over the years, the federal government has radically departed from the constitutional principle of money and banking. The present regime of fiat money provides no restraint on the politicians' and the monetary authorities' power to debase the currency. Indeed, today's monetary system is precisely what the Founding Fathers feared most and sought to prohibit constitutionally.

The results of these violations of the Constitution threaten the economic stability and indeed the survival of America's republican form of government. Fundamental reform of the monetary and banking systems of the United States is imperative if this nation is to regain its political integrity and restore its economic health.

The U.S. Taxpayers Party calls for and sees as vital a return to the money and banking provisions set forth in the Constitution. Those rules define a system of money and banking relying on free market principles and prescribe what must be done:

- Restore, as the nation's official medium of exchange, the *type of money* the world has historically favored — commodity money; money capable of being coined or tendered as coin.
- Re-establish the *quality of money* which the international market recognizes as pre-eminent — silver and gold exclusively as the standard of the money of the United States.
- Adopt again, as the *unit of money,* the sound dollar of 371¼ grains (troy) of fine silver, and
- Leave determination of *the ultimate supply of money* up to the free market system of free coinage embodied in Anglo-American common law.

Further, we believe that, to restore integrity, credibility, and stability of the nation's money and banking system, we must:

1. Declare unconstitutional
   - the Federal Reserve Act of 1913,
   - the seizure of gold coins in 1933, and
   - the outlawing in 1934 of private contracts that called for payment in silver and gold.
2. Disestablish the Federal Reserve System.
3. Terminate the status of Federal Reserve Notes as obligations of the United States and as legal tender for all debts.
4. Restore to the constitutional monetary system that gold which was unconstitutionally seized from the American people in 1933, and which is now held by the U.S. Treasury.
5. Revalue in constitutional (silver) dollars all outstanding contracts now payable in Federal Reserve Notes.
6. Resume the "free coinage" of constitutional (silver) dollars and appropriate gold coins.
7. Adopt all monetarily viable foreign silver and gold coins as money in the United States.
8. Prohibit all fraudulent "fractional reserve" banking schemes and related commercial practices.

Our Founding Fathers gave us a unique and workable concept of money. It was based on a constant value set by the federal government, with its foundation being gold. States constitutionally are forbidden from paying their debts in anything but silver or gold. However, there is not one state in the United States that pays its debts with silver or gold.

The money system in this country (controlled and manipulated by the FED) has been one of the most powerful tools of the Princes. Our government has radically departed from the money system described by the Constitution. As a result, we have seen dramatic inflation, recession, and depression; all of which are orchestrated by the Princes to establish their New World Order.

Again, it is important to remind you that the FED is not owned by the federal government. The stock of that corporation is owned privately by a few elitist, globalist families — the same families that own all of the major banking systems in the developed countries of the world.

Therefore, in addition to establishing a constitutional and permanent medium of exchange, we need to declare unconstitutional the Federal Reserve Act of 1913, the seizure of gold coins in 1933, and the outlawing in 1934, of private contracts that called for payment in silver and gold. We need to disestablish and divest of all power the FED. And in the process, we need to defund and defang the Internal Revenue Service, which perpetuates the myth of money issued by the FED.

NEW WORLD ORDER

We say "No" to the so-called New World Order and "Yes!" to the autonomy of these United States of America.

The U.S. Taxpayers Party strongly opposes any alliance or participation in any treaty or agreement which compromises our independence as a nation or which subverts our Constitution by improperly committing us to participation in foreign conflicts or intervention in foreign wars.

We join with other American patriots to steadfastly oppose the surrender of American liberty and autonomy to any form of world government or any organization which works toward that end.

We call upon the President and the Congress to terminate the membership of the United States in the United Nations and its subsidiary and affiliated organizations.

We further call upon the Congress and — if it refuses to act — upon the several states, to move to amend the Constitution to prohibit the United States government from entering into any treaty or other agreement or covenant which in any way commits American armed forces, or tax money, or decision-making authority to agencies beyond direct accountability to the states and the people.

All treaties must be subordinate to the Constitution since the Constitution is the only act which empowers and limits the federal government.

The Framers assumed, as a matters of course, that treaties would be subordinate. In fact, the stated reason for the particular wording of the Constitution concerning treaties was to make sure pre-existing treaties, including the post-Revolutionary peace treaties concluded under the Articles of Confederation, would remain valid.

As pointed out by the late Supreme Court Justice Hugo Black, "The United States is entirely a creature of the Constitution. It can only act in accordance with the limitations imposed by the Constitution.... There is nothing in this language (Article VI) which intimates that treaties and laws enacted pursuant to them do not have to comply with the provisions of the Constitution, nor is there anything in the debates which accompanied the drafting and ratification of the

Constitution which even suggests such a result."

And Thomas Jefferson, addressing the question directly, had this to say: "... Surely the President and Senate can not do by treaty what the whole government is interdicted from doing in any way."

I don't believe this section needs much comment, inasmuch as this entire book is about saying, "NO," to the New World Order. I heartily concur with, endorse, and encourage you in the strongest possible terms, to **insist** that our government adopt the constitutionally and morally correct position of the U.S. Taxpayers Party as concerns the New World Order.

PRIVATIZATION

There is no constitutional basis for the federal government engaging in such enterprises as Amtrak, Conrail, the TVA, or the Oak Ridge uranium enrichment facility.

Further, in violation of Article I, Section 8, Paragraph 17 of the Constitution, the federal government has vast areas of land under federal ownership and control which have nothing to do with the nation's defense or seat of government.

The U.S. Taxpayers Party calls for the federal government to divest itself of operations which are not authorized by the Constitution. We call upon the Congress to get the federal government out of such enterprises which compete with private free enterprise.

In pursuit of these ends, we endorse the ratification of the Liberty Amendment.

We also call for the federal government to divest itself of the millions of acres of lands and natural resources in Alaska and other western states by selling such properties and using the income from such sales only and entirely to reduce the federal debt.

According to the Constitution of the United States, the federal government is to own no lands, except those to be used for the seat of government, magazines, arsenals, and shipyards, and other needful buildings (as defined by the Constitution). In some western states, the government owns as much as 75 percent of the land.

All over the United States your federal government is undertaking a frightening and unconstitutional land grab. At the current rate, if land seizure continues on unabated much longer, they and their masters, the Princes of the New World Order, will own America. Where will that leave us?

It is paramount that we begin electing representatives who will adopt

288

the platform of the U.S. Taxpayers Party, which calls for a divesting by the federal government of all such unconstitutional land holdings and corporations. Preferably, these would be sold to private entrepreneurs, but at least, the federal government constitutionally must divest themselves of these holdings and put in charge (if nothing else) of the several states, in accordance with each state's Constitution.

RELIGIOUS FREEDOM

The preservation of religious freedom, and its protection from the acts of Congress and the infringement of the courts may well become the central civil rights issue of the 1990s.

The federal government (and its agencies and courts) continues to restrict the free exercise and expression of religion. The government openly violates the religious guarantees of the First Amendment:

- It seeks to regulate churches and other religious organizations.
- It has, with the backing of the courts, restricted religious liberty in the area of public and private education.
- It has forbidden non-denominational prayer in the public schools and at educational ceremonies.
- It has prohibited students from reading the Bible on school busses or in classrooms.
- It has refused to permit religious displays on public property such as at Christmas and Chanukah.

And in these violations it has generally been upheld by a majority of the politically appointed Supreme Court.

Further, the Congress, with the approval of the Executive Branch, has subjected churches and their employees to Social Security taxes even though Congress is constitutionally forbidden to make any such law respecting an establishment of religion.

In the strongest tones possible, the U.S. Taxpayers Party calls on the courts, the IRS, and all other federal and state and local governments to uphold religious freedom in this nation. These attacks against freedom of worship must cease and the harassment of religious institutions must halt.

The federal government must stop its attempts to interfere with the encouragement of religious and moral principles by state and local governments.

We assert that any form of taxation on churches and other

religious organizations is a direct and dangerous step toward state control of the church; such intrusion is prohibited by the Constitution and must be halted.

We insist that the original intention of the Framers of the Constitution in regard to the free exercise of religious faith and practice be reasserted.

In the United States we have lost religious freedom. While the federal government is precluded from choosing or establishing a religion, they have, in violation of the Constitution, done just that. Government has, in fact, become the religion of the State. The time has come for each of us to make a determination. Will we continue to serve the god-State or will we again demand religious freedom? Will we choose the liberty that comes with living under eternal Law as opposed to the tyranny that comes in living under humanistic, governmental law?

SOCIALIZED MEDICINE

The U.S. Taxpayers Party opposes the governmentalization and bureaucratization of American medicine. Government regulation and subsidy constitutes a threat to both the quality and the availability of patient-oriented health care and treatment.

Hospitals, doctors, and other health care providers should be accountable to patients — not to politicians.

If the *supply* of medical care is controlled by the federal government, then officers of that government will determine which *demand* is satisfied.

The result will be rationing of services, higher costs, poorer results — and the power of life and death transferred from caring physicians to unaccountable political overseers.

Private solutions must be preferred to partisan posture.

We applaud proposals for employee-controlled "family coverage" health insurance plans based on cash value life insurance principles.

We affirm freedom of choice of practitioner, and treatment for all citizens with any health problem.

For the first time in American history, a poll of the medical professionals has indicated that better than 50 percent of them would instruct or encourage their children *not* to go into the field of medicine. Modern medicine has become a boondoggle. It has no accountability to the patient;

290

rather, all of its accountability is to the federal government and the Judiciary. Every medical procedure has to be weighed against the consequences of erroneous law suits.

As government has become more deeply involved in "medicine" the quality has declined, and will continue to do so. We have at our fingertips easily accessible histories of the governments' running of Amtrak, Conrail, the Post Office, and many other entities — including the federal bookrack. Can you imagine a socialized medical system with these same people in charge?

SOCIAL SECURITY

The Social Security trust should not be a rainy-day fund which politicians can pirate or from which they can borrow to cover their errors and pay for their excesses.

The U.S. Taxpayers Party supports legislation to require that the federal government meet its obligations and protect Social Security funds as a trust which can be used only to fulfill its obligations to those who have contributed to the system.

To protect and enhance the return on payments made by Social Security taxpayers and prevent future defaults, we call for the transfer of all Social Security funds to accounts beyond the reach of politicians who improperly transfer funds from Social Security to help pay the price of other federal programs.

Individuals entering the work force should have the right to choose whether they will sign up for Social Security taxes and benefits, or instead private retirement and pension programs, either at their place of employment or independently.

We call for the removal of earning limitations on persons aged 62 and over, so that they may earn any amount of additional income they choose, without placing their Social Security benefits at risk.

We urge the repeal of those provisions of the Social Security system which penalize those born during the "notch years" between 1917 and 1926 and argue that such persons be placed on the same benefit schedules as all other beneficiaries.

Social Security is yet another boondoggle program of the federal government that was flawed from the very beginning. The idea that someone, other than family, has the responsibility to provide for the elderly in society, is wrong.

Again, humanistic law accents death and burden. The eternal Law of the Lord accents value and honor of the aged. **When government puts itself in a position of being the provider for the people, it assumes the role of god.** It steals the rights and obligations of the individuals and demeans the integrity of those they purportedly serve.

I believe Social Security to be a social evil and not a social good. However, because promises have been made to our elderly, I do not believe that Social Security should be stolen from those who worked their entire lives, dependent upon the lie, that government would provide for them in their old age. However, I also do not believe that the lie should continue for future generations.

We are told in the news media and by our elected thieves, that Social Security is sound. It is not. There is no money in the Social Security system. All monies that happen to be in Social Security have been replaced by a thieving Congress with their worthless I.O.U.s.

Social Security is broke and should be placed in the hands of private enterprise. It should be reconstituted and reformulated to take care of those individuals currently on Social Security and those who are close to retirement age.

However, Social Security can, and must, be phased out. We will have no choice because there will be no money for those under fifty years of age. It is financially, numerically impossible.

By realigning the expectations for the Social Security system for the future, we would be much better able to take care of current Social Security recipients. Under the plan proposed by the U.S. Taxpayers Party, benefits could, and probably would, increase to low income Social Security recipients. Therefore, no one dependent upon the system would in any way be harmed; rather, they would be benefitted by the plan.

By the same token, nobody, below the age of 50 would be harmed by the Social Security phase out, because they would not be living in expectation of Social Security funds, which are not going to exist. In being freed from the false promise of Social Security, they could begin to create, through private investment and retirement programs, provision for their own retirement years — instead of being enslaved by the false notion that the government will provide for them — it will not.

Again, it is important to remember, that many steps need to be taken in concert. While Social Security is being phased out, so would be the I.R.S., giving the average American two or three times their spendable income. Additionally, the prosperity that would be created within the American economy, and the subsequent explosion of job creation (high paying jobs, where the work forces will again be in demand, instead of at the mercy of employers), will put our citizens in a much better position to both save for their future and negotiate for better and more comprehensive retirement programs.

There will, of course, still be those who will foolishly consume all that they have and saved for retirement. The purpose of government is not to protect the foolish from themselves, but to guarantee our right to life, liberty and property. It is both dangerous and presumptuous to perpetuate a lie which says that the government will provide for the citizenry.

Finally, Social Security falsely leads families to believe that they can abandon their responsibility to care for, love, and honor their elders. No civilization or society which refuses to honor their elderly can long survive.

TARIFFS AND TRADE

Article I, Section 8 of the Constitution says the Congress shall have power "to regulate Commerce with foreign Nations,..."

Congress may not abdicate or transfer to others its constitutional functions. We, therefore, oppose the unconstitutional transfer of authority over U.S. trade policy from the Congress to agencies, domestic and foreign, which improperly exercise policy setting functions with respect to U.S. trade policy.

We also favor the abolition of the Office of Special Trade Representative and insist on the withdrawal of the United States from the General Agreement on Tariffs and Trade (GATT) and all other agreements wherein bureaucracies, institutions, or individuals, other than the Congress of the United States, improperly assume responsibility for establishing policies which directly affect the economic well-being of every American citizen.

As indicated in Article I, Section 8, duties, imposts, and excises are legitimate revenue-raising measures on which the United States government may properly rely. As Abraham Lincoln pointed out, the legitimate costs of the federal government can be borne, either by taxes on American citizens and businesses, or by tariffs on foreign companies and products. The latter is preferable to the former.

Similarly, we oppose other international trade agreements which have the effect of diminishing America's economic self-sufficiency and of exporting jobs, the loss of which will impoverish American families, undermine American communities, and diminish America's capacity for economic self-reliance.

We see our country and its workers as more than bargaining

293

chips for multi-national corporations and international banks in their ill-and-evilly-conceived New World Order.

The defense of the American nation and the preservation of its economic integrity is essential to the defense of the liberty and prosperity of every American citizen.

We will recommend strict federal criminal penalties for any officer of the United States government who subsequently hires himself or herself out to represent any foreign government or other entity, public or private, with respect to influencing either public opinion or public policy on matters affecting U.S. trade with any such governments or other entities.

The indebtedness of the American government has dangerously contributed to making our economy more vulnerable to foreign takeover and manipulation. Particularly in the area of national security, foreign interests have thus been abetted in gaining access to America's high-tech secrets under the guise of commercial enterprise.

We reject the concept of Most-Favored-Nation status, especially insofar as it has been used to curry favor with regimes whose domestic and international policies are abhorrent to decent people everywhere and are in fundamental conflict with the vital interests of the United States of America.

As stated in the platform of the U.S. Taxpayers Party, Article I, Section 8 of the U.S. Constitution assigns to the federal government the power to regulate commerce with foreign nations. As Congress advocates its responsibilities to self-serving, self-promoting bureaucracies, and to New World Order organizations, they abdicate their constitutional responsibility.

Abraham Lincoln believed that the legitimate, constitutional costs of federal government can, and should, be born by tariffs on foreign companies and products — as opposed to burdensome taxation on the American people. The concept of "most favored nation" status, as explained earlier, robs us (the American people) of income which should support a constitutional, federal government. Through that robbery, we have allowed government to enslave us with a debt that is not ours.

TAXATION

The Constitution, in Article I, Section 8, gives Congress the power "To lay and collect Taxes, Duties, Imposts, and Excises, to pay the Debts and provide for the common Defence and general Welfare of the United States;..."

In Article I, Section 9, the original document made clear that "No Capitation, or other direct, Tax shall be laid, unless in Proportion to the Census or Enumeration hereinbefore directed to be taken." It is moreover established that "No Tax or Duty shall be laid on Articles exported from any State...."

Since 1913, our constitutional rights to life, liberty, and property have been abridged and diminished by the assumption of direct taxing authority on each of us by the federal government.

We will propose legislation to abolish the Internal Revenue Service and will veto any authorization, appropriation, or continuing resolution which contains any funding whatsoever for that illicit and unconstitutional agency.

Moreover, it is our intention to replace entirely the current tax system of the U.S. government (including income taxes, Social Security taxes, estate taxes, inheritance taxes, corporate taxes, and fuel taxes) with a new approach based on the original design of our Founding Fathers.

To the degree that tariffs on foreign products are insufficient to cover the legitimate constitutional costs of the federal government, we will offer a "state rate tax" in which the responsibility for covering the cost of unmet obligations will be divided among the several states in accordance with their proportion of the total population of the United States, excluding the District of Columbia. Thus, if a state contains 10 percent of the nation's citizens, it will be responsible for assuming payment of 10 percent of the annual deficit.

The effect of this "state rate tax" will be to encourage politicians to argue for less rather than more federal spending.

I probably need to say very little more on this subject. I would remind you that both the Federal Reserve Bank (FED) and the individual personal income tax are tools in the hands of the Princes.

If we are to shake off the shackles of slavery and again live as free people, both the FED and the I.R.S. must be abolished and with them, the stranglehold they have on the economic, moral, and political systems of these United States.

VETO AUTHORITY

Article I, Section 9 of the Constitution says: "No Money shall be drawn from the Treasury, but in Consequence of

295

Appropriations made by Law;...." Appropriations can be made in only two circumstances: a) either a money measure shall be passed by Congress and signed into law by the President, or b) a money measure shall be enacted over a President's veto.

A President who enjoys the support of one-third plus one of the members of either House of Congress, has the constitutional authority to stop unwise and excessive federal spending.

We urge the President of the United States to use his veto power to terminate funding for all federal departments, agencies, and regulatory authorities which exist or operate beyond the bounds of the U.S. Constitution.

We specifically urge the President elected in 1992, to veto any appropriation bill which authorizes outlays in excess of $1 trillion.

Under the current monopolistic system of the Republicrats, we have no chance of ever seeing an effective use of the veto authority of the President of the United States. Remember that both parties, either knowingly or unknowingly, have been co-opted by the Princes of the New World Order.

During the 1992 Presidential elections, we were told by the talking heads in the news media that we had to break the gridlock in Washington. Again, I would ask — why? Gridlock is not necessarily bad. If it is used to stop the tyranny of unconstitutional government, it can be a powerful tool for good. However, we have been led to believe that if Congress is not passing laws, something is wrong. I believe the opposite to be true. I believe that most of our trouble has come as a result of Congress making *too many laws.*

Therefore, the President who has the moral courage and one-third plus one of either House of Congress, can effectively limit government to its constitutional role — legislatively and fiscally.

This is the strategy for victory. Even with only a handful of constitutional, patriotic Congressmen, one man — the Chief Executive — can restore this nation to constitutional government, returning to the people their unalienable rights of "Life, Liberty, and the pursuit of Happiness." **Keeping them, however, is the responsibility of the people.**

WELFARE

The God Who endows us with life, liberty, property, and the right to pursue happiness also charges us to care for the needy, the sick, the homeless, the aged, and those who are otherwise unable to care for themselves.

Charity, and the provision of welfare to those in need, is not a responsibility of the federal government. It may be more efficiently and effectively provided by other entities.

Until the 1960s, it was understood and well recognized that bureaucrats in the nation's capital are unable to make proper decisions concerning welfare policy in communities far distant from them. The more remote the source of charity, the less effective and appropriate the action and the smaller the portion which reaches the needy.

More important, the effect of welfare is determined by the context in which it is delivered. The message of Christian charity is fundamentally at odds with the concept of welfare rights. In many cases, the delivery of welfare by government is not only misdirected, but morally destructive.

To a very great degree, America's welfare crisis is a government-induced crisis. Government social and cultural policies have undermined the work ethic, even as the government's economic and regulatory policies have undermined the ability of our citizens to obtain work.

We encourage individuals and families to fulfill their personal responsibility to help those in need through tithes, offerings, and other acts of charity.

The nation's churches and synagogues should manifest their faith by supporting effective programs to assist those who are in need.

Under no circumstances should the taxpayers of the United States be obliged, under penalty of law and through forced taxation, to assume the cost of providing welfare to able-bodied individuals. Nor should taxpayers be indentured to subsidize welfare for persons who enter the United States illegally.

It is the intended purpose of civil government to safeguard our lives, liberty, and property — not to redistribute our wealth. The Bible commands, "Thou shalt not steal." Theft is wrong, even when it is achieved in elegant surroundings during broad daylight and by majority vote.

Our Founding Fathers told us that to force a man to pay for that which he disbelieves and abhors is sinful and tyrannical. Government has become sinful and tyrannical. The failed welfare policies of the god-State have engendered a dependence upon government and its handouts — as opposed to fostering dependence upon an Almighty, eternal Creator; and the principles which lead to prosperity, liberty, and freedom.

297

History has proven that the failed policies of a welfare state have not, are not, and will not work. They have, are, and will continue to lead to the impoverishment of all, and not to the enrichment of any.

Under such a system, hard work, virtue, and wisdom are punished and taxed. Furthermore, the welfare system is a direct attack on families. It is a system based upon covetousness, and as discussed earlier, is the basis of world socialism: "to each according to his need, from each according to his ability."

In Summation

What has been expressed here in the platform of the U.S. Taxpayers Party is not a radical, new idea of government. It is, in fact, a return to the principles, the foundations given us by our Founding Fathers. The style of government that has been created over the past thirty to forty years is radical. It is a departure from all of the principles so carefully handed down to us by the Founding Fathers.

That which George Bush, Bill Clinton, our Congressmen, Federal Judiciary, and other such traitors have succeeded in foisting upon this nation, unless reversed, will be the ruination of America and the destruction of our unalienable rights to "Life, Liberty, and the pursuit of Happiness."

Reflective of this, **we must, as opposed to merely sitting around and decrying the evil of what has been forced upon us, decide upon a positive action plan.** If we are to keep at bay the forces of the New World Order, to foil their plans, not world-wide, but in our lives and in this once great land, we must chart a course based upon wise principles, such as those given us by the Founding Fathers.

We must return to constitutional government based upon eternal rights - a Biblical understanding.

Chapter 3

The Action Steps

If we are to defeat the Princes who would immerse us into an Orwellian New World Order, it is absolutely crucial that as many people be made aware of this conspiracy as possible. Knowledge of the enemy's plan is perhaps our most important weapon. That is the purpose of *Cheque † Mate · The Game of Princes*. Therefore, it is important that you put this book, this information, into the hands of as many people as possible. Tell your friends, your family, and especially your children what is going on. They need to know.

Read, become familiar, and share with your family the Constitution of the United States, the Declaration of Independence, and the Bill of Rights. Each citizen needs to know and understand what our Founding Fathers gave us. Carry a pocket Constitution with you at all times so that you know your rights.

Understand that most of what you hear on radio, see on television, or read in the print media has been filtered and censored by the propaganda ministers of the New World Order. Learn to look beyond the symptoms of the problems to the root of the problem. Learn the true history and heritage of America and teach it to your children.

Become affiliated with other patriots of like mind. Divorce yourself from the New World Order-controlled parties of the Republicans and Democrats. Become affiliated and involved with and the U.S. Taxpayers Party by becoming a member of the state organization where you live.

Learn and exercise your constitutional and unalienable rights. Get involved in the election process as a candidate or as a member of a campaign team.

Understand the difference between lobbying and electing. Recognize that any lobbying effort in which you participate should be very carefully scrutinized and analyzed. Remember, that most of the lobbying organizations in the "conservative" movement are more concerned with organizational empowerment and fiefdoms than they are with an individual's right to life, liberty, and the pursuit of happiness.

Keep in mind that lobbying those people in government who are diametrically opposed to the principles upon which this nation was founded, has, at best, produced a stalemate, and typically has only managed to slow the rate of loss, not to gain the victory.

Be wise and prudent in your associations with conservative organizations. Be sure that the organizations or groups with whom you are associated do not use patriotism and the right of free association, which is a constitutional right, as an excuse for hatred and racism. There is no room within the precepts of patriotism or Biblical Law for racism. Guard carefully that which you say and do.

Take steps toward financial independence and freedom. Organize a plan to accelerate debt reduction and elimination. Stay out of debt. Create no new debt.

Begin taking steps toward developing financial independence in employment. Begin the process of creating self-governed or cottage industries as a supplement to your income sources.

Make certain that your financial institutions (such as banks, insurance companies, pension funds, etc.) are financially solvent. Order a Weiss Report by writing Martin D. Weiss, 1001 Pennsylvania Avenue, N.W., Washington, D.C. 20004-2599, or calling 202-624-2000.

Invest wisely, prudently, and with great caution in speculative stocks and corporations.

Become a reader. Develop reading sources outside those controlled by the Princes of the New World Order. Recommended reading sources are listed in Appendix B.

Finally, become actively involved in the political processes in your area and demand political accountability from those elected to office from your area. The best and most effective government is local — not state or national.

And in the demanding of accountability, begin now to recognize that there can be only one law system in existence at a time. It will either be Law that leads to Life, Liberty, and the pursuit of Happiness, which is Biblical, eternal Law — or — it will be humanistic law which leads to destruction and is the ultimate tool of the Princes of the New World Order.

We cannot stop the New World Order globally. However, we can individually, in the lives of our families and in this nation, end the tyranny of those who have conspired to steal our sovereignty and our unalienable rights through their conspiracy to submerge us into a New World Order.

This time for action is now. Decisions must be made. But those decisions cannot be made by me — they are left to you, the Reader. As you and I become involved — by the grace of God — together, we can and will be victorious.

In 1777 and in 1778, a beleaguered army filed into Valley Forge. They passed an elongated figure on a horse. Pleasantries were not exchanged — nor were greetings offered — but he was there. Perched high atop his mount, looking over his rag-tagged army, he could see that many of his soldiers were barefoot, often leaving bloody footprints in the snow.

But throughout history, at pregnant junctures or crossroads in the unfolding American pageant, the Creator has raised up the right person, at the right place, at just the right time, and for just the right circumstance. These individuals were foreordained to be personages of courage, vision, valor, and insight. The hand of the Almighty rested on just such a man, as was George Washington.

I believe that God has again raised up the right person, at the right time, at this crucial juncture of history, and that person is YOU.

**The destiny of this nation, held poised in midair,
is waiting for the decision that you will make.
Our children will be free.**

I have confidence in you.

Chapter 4

Here Comes The King

The Princes feel that they have moved all of the pieces into all of the right positions. They are poised to declare, "Cheque," and take control; declaring themselves King, as they establish their New World Order.

But there is yet another Prince coming — The Prince of Peace and it is **He** who has been declared, by and throughout all eternity — King. And it is He, when all the plays have been made, all of the players revealed, who will thunder from Heaven, *"Cheque † Mate!"*

"THAT'S MY KING!"

THE BIBLE SAYS . . .

My King is a seven-way king. He's a king of the Jews, that's a racial king; He's a king of Israel, that's a national king; He's a king of righteousness; He's a king of the ages; He's a king of Heaven; He's a king of glory; He's a king of kings; and He's the Lord of Lords; That's my King!

Well, I wonder do you know Him? David said, "The heavens declare the glory of God and the firmament showeth His handiwork." My King is a sovereign King; no means of measure can define His limitless love; no far-seeing telescope can bring into visibility the coastline of His shoreless supply; no barrier can hinder Him from throwing out His blessings. He's enduringly strong; He's entirely sincere; He's eternally steadfast; He's immortally grateful; He's imperially powerful; He's impartially merciful.

DO YOU KNOW HIM?

He's the greatest phenomenon that has ever crossed the horizon of this world; He's God's Son; He's the sinner's Savior; He's the centerpiece of civilization; He stands in the solitude of Himself; He's august and He's unique; He's unparalleled; He's unprecedented. He is the loftiest idea in literature; He's the highest personality in philosophy; He is the supreme problem in higher criticism; He's the fundamental doctrine of theology; He is the core, the necessity for spiritual religion; He's the miracle of the age; He is the superlative of

303

everything good that you choose to call Him; He's the only one qualified to be an all-sufficient Savior!

I WONDER IF YOU KNOW HIM?

He supplies strength for the weak; He's available for the tempted and the tried; He sympathizes and He saves; He strengthens and sustains; He guards and He guides; He heals the sick; He cleansed the lepers; He forgives sinners; He discharges debtors; He delivers the captives; He defends the feeble; He blesses the young; He serves the unfortunate; He regards the aged; He rewards the diligent and He purifies the meek.

I WONDER IF YOU KNOW HIM?

Well, my King, He is a key to knowledge; He's a wellspring of wisdom; He's a doorway of deliverance; He's a pathway of peace; He's a roadway of righteousness; He's a highway of holiness; He's a gateway of glory.

DO YOU KNOW HIM?

Well, His office is manifold; His promise is sure; His light is matchless; His goodness is limitless; His mercy is everlasting; His love never changes; His Word is enough; His grace is sufficient; His reign is righteousness and His yoke is easy, and His burden is light.

I wish I could describe Him to you! But He's indescribable! He's God. He's incomprehensible; He's invincible; He's irresistible; Well, you can't get Him out of your mind; you can't get Him off your hand; you can't outlive Him and you can't live without Him; the Pharisees couldn't stand Him, but they found out they couldn't stop Him; Pilate couldn't find any fault in Him; the witnesses couldn't get their testimonies to agree; Herod couldn't kill Him; death couldn't handle Him and the grave couldn't hold Him!

YES, THAT'S MY KING! THAT'S MY KING!

And thine is the Kingdom and the power and the glory forever and ever and ever and ever (How long is that?) and ever and ever, and when you get through with all of the forevers, then AMEN, AMEN, AMEN!!!

Dr. S. M. Lockridge

My final words to you, the Reader, are:

And now, let the weak say,
"I am strong ... for He is my King!"

304

Appendix A

Council on Foreign Relations Membership, June 30, 1992
Trilateral Commission - Membership, October 6, 1992
CFR & Skull & Bones
CFR & Trilateral Membership
<u>*Trilateral & Skull & Bones*</u>
<u>***CFR, Trilateral & Skull & Bones***</u>

A
Aaron, David L.
Abboud, A. Robert
Abboud, Labeeb M.
Abdel-Meguid, Tarek
Abegglen, James C.
Abel, Elie
Abram, Morris B.
Abramowitz, Morton I.
Abrams, Elliott
Abshire, David M.
Aburdene, Odeh
Ackerman, Peter
Adams, Gordon M.
Adams, Robert McCormick
Adams, Ruth Salzman
Adelman, Kenneth L.
Aggarwal, Vinod K.
Agnew, Harold M.
Agronsky, Martin
Aguirre, Horacio
Aho, C. Michael
Aidinoff, M. Bernard
Ajami, Fouad
Akers, John F.
Akins, James E.
Albright, Archie E.
Albright, Madeline
Alderman, Michael H.
Aldrich, George H.
Alexander, Robert J.
Alford, William P.
Allaire, Paul A.

Allan, F. Aley
Allard, Nicholas W.
Allbritton, Joe L.
Allen, Lew, Jr.
Allen, Robert E.
Allison, Graham T., Jr.
Allison, Richard C.
Alpern, Alan N.
Altman, Emily
Altman, Roger C.
Altman, Sidney
Altschul, Arthur G.
Alvarado, Donna M.
Ames, Oakes
Amos, Deborah
Andelman, David
Andersen, Harold W.
Anderson, David
Anderson, John B.
Anderson, Lisa
Anderson, Marcus A.
Anderson, Paul F.
Anderson, Robert
Anderson, Robert O.
Andreae, Charles N., III
Andreas, Dwayne O.
Andrews, David R.
Angulo, Manuel R.
Ansour, M. Michael
Anthoine, Robert
Anthony, John Duke
Apgar, David P.
Apodaca, Jerry

Apter, David E.
Araskog, Rand V.
Arciniega, Tomas A.
Arcos, Cresencio S.
Arledge, Roone
Armacost, Michael H.
Armstrong, Anne
Armstrong, C. Michael
Armstrong, DeWitt C., III
Armstrong, John A.
Armstrong, Willis C.
Arnhold, Millard W.
Aron, Adam M.
Aronson, Jonathan D.
Art, Robert J.
Arthurs, Alberta
Artzt, Edwin L.
Asencio, Diego C.
Asher, Robert E.
Asmus, Ronald D.
Aspin, Les
Assevero, Vicky-Ann E.
Assousa, George E.
Atherton, Alfred L., Jr.
Atwood, J. Brian
Auspitz, Josiah Lee
Ausubel, Jesse Huntley
Avedon, John F.
Ayers, H. Brandt

B
Babbitt, Bruce
Bacot, J. Carter

307

Bader, William B.
Baer, M. Delal
Baeza, Mario L.
Bailey, Charles W.
Bains, Leslie Elizabeth
Baird, Charles F.
Baker, Howard H., Jr.
Baker, James E.
Baker, Pauline H.
Balaran, Paul
Baldwin, David A.
Baldwin, H. Furlong
Baldwin, Richard Edward
Baldwin, Robert E.
Baldwin, Robert H. B.
Bales, Carter F.
Balick, Kenneth D.
Ball, David G.
Ball, George W.
Baltimore, David
Banta, Kenneth W.
Barber, Charles F.
Barber, James A., Jr.
Barber, Perry O., Jr.
Barger, Teresa C.
Barker, Robert R.
Barlow, William E.
Barnds, William J.
Barnes, Harry G., Jr.
Barnes, Michael D.
Barnet, Richard J.
Barnett, A. Doak
Barnett, Frank R.
Barnett, Michael N.
Barnett, Robert W.
Baroody, William J., Jr.
Barr, Thomas D.
Barrett, John A.
Barrett, Nancy Smith
Barron, Thomas A.
Barry, Lisa B.
Barry, Thomas C.
Bartholomew, Reginald
Bartlett, Joseph W.
Bartlett, Richard Allen

Bartlett, Thomas A.
Bartley, Robert L.
Barton, Christopher
Barzelay, Michael
Basek, John T.
Bashawaty, Albert C.
Basora, Adrian A.
Bass, James E.
Bassow, Whitman
Batkin, Alan R.
Bator, Francis M.
Battle, Lucius D.
Bauman, Robert P.
Baumann, Carol Edler
Baumann, Roger R.
Bean, Atherton
Beard, Ronald S.
Beattie, Richard I.
Becherer, Hans W.
Beckler, David Z.
Beecher, William
Beeman, Richard E.
Begley, Louis
Behrman, Jack N.
Beim, David O.
Beinecke, William S.
Bell, David E.
Bell, Holley Mack
Bell, J. Bowyer
Bell, Peter D.
Bell, Steve
Bell-Rose, Stephanie
Bellamy, Carol
Bello, Judith Hippler
Benbow, Terence H.
Bender, Gerald J.
Bennet, Douglas J., Jr.
Bennett, Andrew
Bennett, Donald V.
Bennett, J. F.
Bennett, Susan J.
Bennett, W. Tapley, Jr.
Benson, Lucy Wilson
Beplat, Tristan E.
Berger, Marilyn

Berger, Samuel R.
Berger, Suzanne
Bergold, Harry E., Jr.
Bergsten, C. Fred
Berkowitz, Bruce D.
Berman, Howard L.
Bernardin, Joseph Cardinal
Berndt, John E.
Bernstein, Robert L.
Berresford, Susan Vail
Berris, Jan
Beschloss, Michael R.
Bessie, Simon Michael
Best, William A. III
Bestani. Robert M.
Betts, Richard K.
Beyer, John C.
Bialer, Seweryn
Bialkin, Kenneth J.
Bialos, Jeffrey P.
Bicksler, Barbara
Biel, Eric R.
Biemann, Betsy
Bienen, Henry S.
Bierley, John C.
Billington, James H.
Binger, James H.
Binkley, Nicholas B.
Binnendijk, Hans
Birkelund, John P.
Birnbaum, Eugene A.
Bissell, Richard E.
Bissell, Richard M., Jr.
Black, Joseph E.
Black, Shirley Temple
Black, Stanley Warren
Blacker, Coit Dennis
Blackmer, Donald L. M.
Blackwell, James A., Jr.
Blackwill, Robert D.
Blair, Sally Ornesti
Blake, Robert O.
Blake, Vaughn R.
Blank, Stephen
Blechman, Barry M.

Bleier, Edward
Blendon, Robert J.
Blinken, Antony J.
Bliss, Richard M.
Bloch, Julia Chang
Bloom, Evan Todd
Bloomfield, Lincoln P.
Bloomfield, Richard J.
Blum, John A.
Blumenthal, Sidney
Blumenthal, W. Michael
Boardman, Harry
Bobbitt, Philip
Boeker, Paul H.
Boggs, Michael D.
Bohen, Frederick M.
Bohlen, Avis T.
Bohn, John A.
Bolling, Landrum R.
Bolten, Joshua B.
Bond, Robert D.
Bonney, J. Dennis
Bonsal, Dudley B.
Bonsal, Philip W.
Booker, Salih
Bookout, John F.
Boone, Theodore S.
Boren, David Lyle
Boschwitz, Rudy
Bosworth, Stephen W.
Botts, John C.
Bouis, Antonina W.
Bouton, Marshall M.
Bovin, Denis A.
Bowen, William G.
Bower, Joseph L.
Bowie, Robert R.
Bowlin, Mike R.
Bowman, Richard C.
Boyd, Charles G.
Boyer, Ernest L.
Bracken, Paul
Braddock, Richard S.
Brademas, John
Bradford, Zeb

Bradley, Edward R.
Bradley, Tom
Bradley, William L.
Brady, Linda Parrish
Brady, Nicholas F.
Brainard, Lawrence J.
Brainard, S. Lael
Brand, Laurie A.
Branscomb, Lewis M.
Branson, William H.
Breck, Henry R.
Breindel, Eric M.
Bremer, L. Paul, III
Bresnan, John J.
Breyer, Stephen G.
Brimmer, Andrew F.
Brimmer, Esther Diane
Brinkley, David
Brinley, George
Brittenham, Raymond L.
Broad, Robin
Brock, Mitchell
Brock, William E., III
Broda, Frederick C.
Brokaw, Tom
Bromery, Randolph Wilson
Bromley, D. Allen
Bronfman, Edgar M.
Brooke, James B.
Brookins, Carol
Brooks, Harvey
Brower, Charles N.
Brown, Carroll
Brown, David D., IV
Brown, Frederic J.
Brown, Gwendolyn
Brown, Harold
Brown, L. Carl
Brown, L. Dean
Brown, Lester R.
Brown, Richard P., Jr.
Brown, Seyom
Brown, Walter H.
Browne, Robert S.
Bruce, Judith

Bruce, Lawrence, Jr.
Bruemmer, Melissa L. S.
Bruemmer, Russell J.
Bryant, Ralph C.
Bryson, John E.
Brzezinski, Zbigniew
Buchheim, Robert W.
Buchman, Mark E.
Buckley, William F., Jr.
Bucy, J. Fred, Jr.
Buergenthal, Thomas
Bugliarello, George
Bullard, Edward P.
Bullock, Hugh
Bullock, Mary Brown
Bundy, McGeorge
Bundy, William P.
Burgess, John A.
Burke, James E.
Burkhalter, Holly J.
Burley, Anne-Marie
Burlingame, Edward L.
Burns, Haywood
Burns, Patrick Owen
Burns, William G.
Burt, Richard R.
Burton, Daniel Farrell, Jr.
Bushner, Rolland
Bussey, Donald S.
Busuttil, James
Butcher, Goler Teal
Butlker, George Lee
Butler, Samuel C.
Butler, William J.
Buttenheim, Lisa M.
Byrnes, Robert F.
Byrom, Fletcher

C

Cabot, Louis W.
Cabot, Thomas D.
Cabranes, Jose A.
Cahill, Kevin M.
Cahn, Anne H.
Cahouet, Frank V.

Calabia, Dawn T.
Calder, Kent Eyring
Caldwell, Dan
Caldwell, Philip
Calhoun, Michael J.
Califano, Joseph A., Jr.
Calkins, Hugh
Callander, Robert J.
Callen, Michael A.
Calleo, David P.
Calloway, D. Wayne
Callwood, Kevin R.
Campbell, Colin G.
Campbell, John C.
Campbell, Kurt M.
Campbell, W. Glenn
Camps, Miriam
Canal, Carlos M., Jr.
Canavan, Christopher
Canfield, Franklin O.
Cannon, James M.
Cappello, Juan C.
Carbonell, Nestor T.
Carey, Hugh L.
Carey, John
Carey, Sarah C.
Carey, William D.
Carlos, Manuel Luis
Carlson, Robert J.
Carlson, Steven E.
Carlucci, Frank C., III
Carmichael, William D.
Carnesale, Albert
Carothers, Thomas
Carpendale, Andrew Michael
Carrington, Walter C.
Carroll, J. Speed
Carruth, Reba Anne
Carson, C. W., Jr.
Carson, Edward M.
Carswell, Robert
Carter, Ashton B.
Carter, Barry E.
Carter, George E.
Carter, Hodding, III

Carter, Jimmy
Carter, Marshall N.
Case, Robert A.
Casper, Gerhard
Cates, John M., Jr.
Cattarulla, Elliot R.
Catto, Henry E., Jr.
Caulfield, Matthew P.
Cave, Ray
Celeste, Richard F.
Cerjan, Paul G.
Chaffee, John H.
Chace, James
Chafee, John H.
Chain, John T., Jr.
Challenor, Herschelle S.
Chambers, Anne Cox
Chancellor, John
Chanis, Jonathan A.
Chao, Elaine L.
Chapman, Margaret Holt
Charles, Robert B.
Charpie, Robert A.
Chasin, Dana
Chaudhry, Kiren Aziz
Chayes, Abram J.
Chayes, Antonia Handler
Cheever, Daniel S.
Chen, Kimball C.
Chenault, Kenneth I.
Chenery, Hollis B.
Cheney, Richard B.
Cheremeteff, Kyra
Cherne, Leo
Chickering, A. Lawrence
Cholmondeley, Paula H. J.
Choucri, Nazli
Christianson, Geryld B.
Christman, Daniel William
Chrisopher, Robert C.
Christopher, Warren
Chubb, Hendon
Churchill, Buntzie Ellis
Cicconi, James W.
Cisler, Walker L.

Cisneros, Henry G.
Clapp, Priscilla A.
Clarizio, Lynda
Clark, Dick
Clark, Howard L.
Clark, Kenneth B.
Clark, Noreen
Clark, Ralph L.
Clark, Stephen C.
Clark, Susan Lesley
Clark, Wesley K.
Clarke, J. G.
Clendenin, John L.
Cleveland, Harlan
Cleveland, Harold van B.
Clifford, Donald K., Jr.
Cline, Ray S.
Cline, William R.
Clinton, Bill
Cloherty, Patricia M.
Cloud, Stanley Wills
Clough, Michael
Clurman, Richard M.
Cobb, Paul Whitlock, Jr.
Coffey, C. Shelby, III
Coffey, Joseph I.
Cohen, Barbara
Cohen, Benjamin J.
Cohen, Herman J.
Cohen, Jerome Alan
Cohen, Joel E.
Cohen, Patricia
Cohen, Roberta
Cohen, Stephen B.
Cohen, Stephen F.
Cohen, Stephen S.
Cohen, William S.
Colbert, Evelyn
Colby, Jonathan E.
Colby, William E.
Cole, Johnnetta
Coleman, Isobel
Coleman, William T., Jr.
Coles, James Stacy
Collado, Emilio G.

310

Collier, David
Collins, Joseph J.
Collins, Paula J.
Combs, Richard E., Jr.
Comstock, Phil
Condon, Joseph F.
Cone, Sydney M., III
Connolly, Gerald E.
Connor, John T.
Connor, John T., Jr.
Connor, Joseph E.
Considine, Jill M.
Constable, Pamela
Conway, Jill
Cook, Don
Cook, Frances D.
Cook, Gary M.
Cook, Howard A.
Cooke, Goodwin
Cooke, John F.
Coolidge, Nicholas J.
Coolidge, T. J., Jr.
Coombe, George W., Jr.
Coombs, Philip H.
Coon, Jane Abell
Cooney, Joan Ganz
Cooper, Charles A.
Cooper, Chester L.
Cooper, John Milton
Cooper, Kerry
Cooper, Richard N.
Cornelius, Wayne
Corrigan, E. Gerald
Corrigan, Kevin
Cott, Suzanne
Cotter, William
Courtney, William H.
Cowal, Sally Grooms
Cowan, L. Gray
Cowhey, Peter F.
Cowles, John, Jr.
Cox, Edward F.
Cox, Robert G.
Coyne, Thomas A.
Crahan, Margaret E.

Crawford, John F.
Crile, George, III
Crittenden, Ann
Crocker, Chester A.
Cromwell, Adelaide
Cronin, Audrey Kurth
Cross, Devon G.
Cross, June V.
Cross, Sam Y.
Crovitz, Gordon
Crow, Trammell
Crowe, William J., Jr.
Crystal, Lester M.
Cullum, Lee
Culver, John C.
Cumming, Christine
Cummings, Robert L., Jr.
Cummiskey, Frank J.
Cuomo, Mario M.
Curran, R. T.
Currie, Malcolm R.
Curtis, Gerald L.
Cutler, Lloyd N.
Cutler, Walter L.
Cutter, W. Bowman
Cyr, Arthur

D

Dale, William B.
Dalley, George A.
Dallin, Alexander
Dallmeyer, Dorinda
Dalton, James E.
Dam, Kenneth W.
Damrosch, Lori Fisler
Danforth, William H.
Daniel, Ana R.
Daniel, D. Ronald
Danner, Mark
Darman, Richard G.
DaSilva, Russell J.
David, Jack
Davidson, Daniel I.
Davidson, Ralph K.
Davidson, Ralph P.

Davis, Allison S.
Davis, Jacqueline K.
Davis, Jerome
Davis, John Aubrey
Davis, Kathryn W.
Davis, Lynn E.
Davis, Macco N.
Davis, Nathaniel
Davis, Shelby Cullom
Davis, Stephen M.
Davis, Vincent
Davison, Daniel P.
Davison, W. Phillips
Dawisha, Karen Lea
Dawkins, Peter M.
Dawson, Horace G., Jr.
Day, Anthony
Day, Arthur R.
Deagle, Edwin A., Jr.
Dean, Jonathan
Dean, Robert W.
Dean, Thompson
Debevoise, Eli Whitney, II
de Borchgrave, Arnaud
Debs, Barbara Knowles
Debs, Richard A.
DeCrane, Alfred C., Jr.
Decter, Midge
de Cubas, Jose
Dedrick, Fred T.
Dees, Bowen C.
Deffenbaugh, Ralston H., Jr.
Deibel, Terry L.
de Janosi, Peter E.
del Olmo, Frank
de Menil, George
de Menil, Lois Pattison
Deming, Frederick L.
Denison, Robert J.
Dennard, Cleveland I.
Dennis, Everette E.
Denny, Brewster C.
Denoon, David B. H.
Denton, E. Hazel
DePalma, Samuel

311

Dergham, Raghida
Derian, Patricia Murphy
Derryck, Vivian Lowery
De Rubeis, John E.
DeSouza, Patrick J.
Destler, I. M.
Deutch, John M.
Deutch, Michael J.
DeVechhi, Robert P.
Devine, Thomas J.
de Vries, Rimmer
DeWind, Adrian W.
DeYoung, Karen
Dickey, Christopher S.
Dickson, R. Russell, Jr.
Diebold, John
Diebold, William Jr.
Dietel, William M.
Dilenschneider, Robert L.
Dillon, Douglas
Di Martino, Rita
Dine, Thomas A.
Djerejian, Edward P.
de Habsburgo Dobkin,
   Inmaculada
Dodd, Christopher J.
Doetsch, Douglas A.
Doherty, William C., Jr.
Dominguez, Jorge I.
Donahue, Donald J.
Donahue, Thomas R.
Donaldson, Robert H.
Donaldson, William H.
Donnell, Ellsworth
Donnelly, H. C.
Donnelly, Sally B.
Doran, Charles F.
Doty, Paul M., Jr.
Dougan, Diana Lady
Douglas, Paul W.
Douglass, Robert R.
Downie, Leonard, Jr.
Doyle, James S.
Doyle, Michael William
Draper, William H., III

Drayton, William, Jr.
Drell, Sidney D.
Drew, Elizabeth
Dreyfuss, Joel
Drittel, Peter Marc
Drumwright, J. R.
Duberstein, Kenneth M.
Dubow, Arthur M.
DuBrul, Stephen M., Jr.
Duderstadt, James J.
Duersten, Althea L.
Duffey, Joseph
Duggy, Gloria Charmian
Duggy, James H.
Dugan, Michael J.
Dukakis, Michael S.
Duke, Angier Biddle
Dulany, Peggy
Duncan, Charles W., Jr.
Duncan, John C.
Duncan, Richard L.
Dunkerley, Craig G.
Dunlop, Joan Banks
Dunn, Kempton
Dunn, Lewis A.
Dutton, Frederick G.
Raoul-Duval, Michael
Dyke, Nancy Bearg
Dymally, Mervyn M.

E

Eagleburger, Lawrence
Earle, Gordon
Earle, Ralph, II
Easum, Donald B.
Easton, Leonard J., Jr.
Eberle, William D.
Eberstadt, Mary
Ecton, Donna R.
Edelman, Albert I.
Edelman, Gerald M.
Edelman, Marian Wright
Edelstein, Julius C. C.
Edley, Christopher, Jr.
Edwards, Howard L.

Edwards, Robert H.
Ehrlich, Thomas
Eichenberg, Richard C.
Eilts, Hermann Frederick
Eiunaud, Luigi R.
Einaudi, Mario
Einhorn, Jessica P.
Eisendrath, Charles R.
Eliot, Theodore L., Jr.
Elliott, Byron K.
Elliott, Inger McCabe
Elliott, Osborn
Ellis, James R.
Ellis, Patricia
Ellison, Keith P.
Ellsberg, Daniel
Ellsworth, Robert F.
Ely, John Hart
Ely-Raphel, Nancy Halliday
Embree, Ainslie T.
Emerson, Alice F.
Emerson, Steven A.
Enders, Thomas O.
English, Robert D.
Enthoven, Alain
Epstein, David B.
Epstein, Jason
Epstein, Joshua M.
Erb, Guy F.
Erb, Richard D.
Erbsen, Claude E.
Erburu, Robert F.
Ercklentz, Alexander T.
Estabrook, Robert H.
Esty, Daniel C.
Evans, Carol V.
Evans, Gordon W.
Evans, John C.
Evans, Rowland, Jr.
Ewing, William, Jr.
Exter, John

F

Fabian, Larry L.
Fairbanks, Douglas

Fairbanks, Richard M., III
Falco, Mathea
Falk, Pamela S.
Falk, Richard A.
Fanning, Katherine W.
Fanton, Jonathan F.
Farer, Tom J.
Farmer, Thomas L.
Farringrton, Thomas A.
Fascell, Dante B.
Fawaz, Leila
Feaver, Peter D.
Feierstein, Mark
Feiner, Ava S.
Feinstein, Diane
Feissel, Gustave
Feith, Douglas J.
Feldman, Mark B.
Feldstein, Martin S.
Feltman, Jeffrey
Fenster, Steven R.
Ferguson, Charles Henry
Ferguson, Glenn W.
Ferguson, James L.
Ferrari, Frank E.
Ferraro, Geraldine A.
Ferre, Antonio Luis
Ferre, Maurice A.
Fesharaki, Fereidun
Feshbach, Murray
Fessenden, Hart
Fetter, Steve
Fierce, Mildred C.
Fifield, Russell H.
Finberg, Barbara D.
Finger, Seymour Maxwell
Finkelstein, Lawrence S.
Finlayson, Grant Ellison
Finn, James
Finney, Paul B.
Firestone, James A.
Firmage, Edwin B.
Fischer, David J.
Fisher, Cathleen S.
Fisher, Daniel S.

Fisher, Richard W.
Fisher, Roger
Fishlow, Albert
Fitz-Pegado, Lauri J.
FitzGerald, Frances
Fitzgibbons, Harold E.
Flaherty, Peter
Flanagan, Stephen J.
Flanigan, Peter M.
Fletcher, Philip Douglas
Fogleman, Ronald R.
Foley, S. R., Jr.
Foley, Thomas S.
Foote, Edward T., II
Ford, Gerald R.
Forman, Shepard
Forrestal, Robert P.
Forrester, Anne
Fort, Randall M.
Foster, Brenda Lei
Foulon, Mark
Fowler, Henry H.
Fox, Donald T.
Fox, Joseph C.
Franck, Thomas M.
Francke, Albert, III
Frank, Charles R., Jr.
Frank, Isaiah
Frank, Richard A.
Frankel, Andrew V.
Frankel, Francine R.
Frankel, Marvin E.
Frankel, Max
Franklin, Barbara Hackman
Franklin, George S.
Frederick, Robert R.
Fredericks, J. Wayne
Freeman, Bennett
Freeman, Harry L.
Freeman, Orville L.
Freidheim, Cyrus F., Jr.
Frelinghuysen, Peter H. B.
Fremont-Smith, Marion R.
Freund, Gerald
Frey, Donald N.

Freytag, Richard A.
Fribourg, Michel
Fribourg, Paul
Fried, Edward R.
Frieden, Jeffrey A.
Friedman, Benjamin M.
Friedman, David S.
Friedman, Stephen
Friedman, Stephen J.
Friedman, Thomas L.
Friedman, Theodore
Fromkin, David
Fromm, Joseph
Fromuth, Peter
Froot, Kenneth A.
Frost, Ellen L.
Fry, Earl H.
Frye, Alton
Frye, William R.
Fuerbringer, Otto
Fukuyama, Francis
Fuller, Kathryn S.
Fuller, William P.
Fullerton, William Bewick
Funari, John
Furlaud, Richard M.
Futter, Ellen V.

G

Gabriel, Charles A.
Gaddis, John Lewis
Gaer, Felice
Galbraith, Evan G.
Gallagher, Dennis
Gallatin, James P.
Galpin, Timothy J.
Galvin, John R.
Galvis, Carlos
Galvis, Sergio J.
Gann, Pamela
Ganoe, Charles S.
Garber, Larry
Garcia-Passalacqua,
   Juan Manuel
Gard, Robert G., Jr.

Gardels, Nathan P.
Gardner, James A.
Gardner, Nina Luzzatto
Gardner, Richard N.
Garment, Leonard
Garment, Suzanne
Garrison, Mark
Gart, Murray J.
Garten, Jeffrey E.
Garthoff, Raymond L.
Garvin, Clifton C., Jr.
Garwin, Richard L.
Gates, Henry Louis, Jr.
Gates, Philomene A.
Gates, Robert M.
Gati, Charles
Gati, Toby Trister
Gaudiani, Claire Lynn
Gause, F. Gregory, III
Gay, Catherine
Geertz, Clifford
Geiger, Theodore
Gejdenson, Sam
Gelb, Leslie H.
Gelb, Richard L.
Gell-Mann, Murray
Gellman, Barton David
Georgescu, Peter A.
Gephardt, Richard A.
Gerber, Louis
Gergen, David R.
Gerhart, Gail M.
Germain, Adrienne
Gerson, Ralph J.
Gerstner, Louis V., Jr.
Getler, Michael
Geyelin, Philip L.
Geyer, Georgie Anne
Gfoeller, Joachim, Jr.
Ghiglione, Loren
Gibbons, John H.
Gibbs, Nancy Reid
Gibney, Frank B.
Gibney, James Suydam
Giffen, James H.

Gigot, Paul A.
Gil, Andres V.
Gil, Peter P.
Gilbert, Jackson B.
Gilbert, Jarobin, Jr.
Gilbert, S. Parker
Gillespie, Michael J.
Gilmore, Kenneth O.
Gilmore, Richard
Gilpatrick, Roswell L.
Gilpin, Robert G., Jr.
Gingrich, Newton L.
Ginsburg, David
Ginsburg, Jane G.
Ginsburg, Ruth Bader
Glauber, Robert R.
Glazer, Nathan
Glendon, Mary Ann
Gleysteen, William H., Jr.
Globerman, Norma
Gluck, Carol
Godchaux, Frank A., III
Godwin, I. Lamond
Goekjian, Samuel V.
Goheen, Robert F.
Goins, Charlynn
Goizueta, Roberto C.
Goldberg, Andrew C.
Goldberg, Samuel
Goldberger, Marvin L.
Golden, James R.
Golden, William T.
Goldin, Harrison J.
Goldman, Andrew
Goldman, Charles N.
Goldman, Emily O.
Goldman, Guido
Goldman, Marshall I.
Goldman, Merle
Goldmark, Peter C., Jr.
Goldring, Natalie J.
Goldschmidt, Neil
Goldstein, Elizabeth
Goldstein, Jeffrey A.
Golighty Niel L.

Gomory, Ralph E.
Gompert, David C.
Goodby, James E.
Goodman, George J. W.
Goodman, Herbert I.
Goodman, John B.
Goodman, Roy M.
Goodman, Sherri Wasserman
Goodpaster, Andrew J.
Goodsell, James Nelson
Gordon, Albert H.
Gordon, Lincoln
Gordon, Michael R.
Gordon, Philip H.
Gorman, Joseph T.
Gornick, Alan L.
Gotbaum, Victor
Gottfried, Kurt
Gottlieb, Gidon A. G.
Gottsegen, Peter M.
Gould, Peter G.
Gourevitch, Peter A.
Gousseland, Pierre
Grace, J. Peter
Graff, Henry F.
Graff, Robert D.
Graham, Bob
Graham, Katharine
Graham, Thomas, Jr.
Graham, Thomas Wallace
Graham, William R.
Grant, James P.
Grant, Stephen A.
Granville, Maurice F.
Graubard, Stephen R.
Gray, Hanna Holborn
Green, Bill
Green, Carl J.
Green, Jerrold D.
Greenberg, Arthur N.
Greenberg, Maurice R.
Greenberg, Sanford D.
Greene, James C.
Greene, Joseph N., Jr.
Greene, Margaret L.

314

Greene, Wade
Greenfield, James L.
Greenfield, Meg
Greenspan, Alan
Greenswald, Joseph A.
Greenway, H. D. S.
Greenwood, Ted
Gregorian, Vartan
Grenier, Richard
Griffith, Thomas
Griffith, William E.
Grimes, Joseph A., Jr.
Grose, Peter
Gross, Ernest A.
Gross, Patrick W.
Grossman, Gene M.
Grove, Brandon H., Jr.
Groves, Ray J.
Grune, George V.
Grunwald, Henry A.
Guerra-Mondragon, Gabriel
Guest, Michael E.
Guisinger, Stephen E.
Gullion, Edmund A.
Gutfreund, John H.
Guthman, Edwin O.
Gwertzman, Bernard M.
Gwin, Catherine

H
Haas, Peter E.
Haas, Robert D.
Hafner, Joseph A., Jr.
Haig, Alexander M., Jr.
Hakin, Peter
Halaby, Najeeb E.
Haley, John C.
Hallingby, Paul, Jr.
Halperin, Morton H.
Halsted, Thomas A.
Haltzel, Michael
Hamburg, David A.
Hamilton, Ann O.
Hamilton, Charles V.
Hamilton, Daniel

Hamilton, Doug N.
Hamilton, Edward K.
Hamilton, Lee H.
Hamilton, Michael P.
Hamilton, Ruth Simms
Hancock, Ellen
Hanrieder, Wolfram F.
Hansen, Carol Rae
Hansen, Keith Eric
Hanson, Thor
Harari, Maurice
Harding, Harry
Hardt, John P.
Hargrove, John Lawrence
Harleston, Bernard W.
Harman, Sidney
Harpel, James W.
Harper, Conrad K.
Harper, Zenola
Harriman, Pamela C.
Harris, Elisa D.
Harris, Irving B.
Harris, Joseph E.
Harris, Martha Caldwell
Harrison, Selig S.
Harsch, Joseph C.
Hart, Augustin S., Jr.
Hart, Bill, Jr.
Hart, Parker T.
Hartman, Arthur A.
Hartman, J. Lise
Haskell, John H. F., Jr.
Haskins, Caryl P.
Hatfield, Robert S.
Hauge, John R.
Hauser, Rita E.
Hauser, William L.
Hawkins, Ashton
Hayes, Margaret Daly
Hayes, Samuel P.
Haynes, Fred
Haynes, Ulric, Jr.
Hayward, Thomas B.
Hazard, John N.
Healy, Harold H., Jr.

Healy, Melissa
Heard, Alexander
Heck, Charles B.
Heckscher, August
Hedstrom, Mitchell W.
Heep-Richter, Barbara D.
Heginbotham, Stanley J.
Hehir, J. Bryan
Heifetz, Elaine F.
Heimann, John G.
Heimowitz, James B.
Heineman, Benjamin W., Jr.
Heintzen, Harry L.
Helender, Robert C.
Heldring, Frederick
Hellman, F. Warren
Hellmann, Donald C.
Helmboldt, Niles E.
Helms, Richard
Henderson, Lawrence J., Jr.
Henkin, Alice H.
Henkin, Louis
Hennessy, John M.
Henninger, Daniel Paul
Hentges, Harriet
Herberger, Roy A., Jr.
Herbst, Jeffrey
Herling, John
Hermann, Charles F.
Hernandez-Colon, Rafael
Herskovits, Jean
Herter, Christian A., Jr.
Herter, Frederic P.
Hertzberg, Arthur
Hertzberg, Hendrik
Hertz, Barbara
Herzfeld, Charles M.
Herzstein, Jessica
Herzstein, Robert E.
Hesburgh, Theodore M.
Hess, John B.
Hessler, Curtis A.
Hester, James M.
Hewett, Ed
Hewitt, William A.

Hewlett, Sylvia Ann
Heyns, Roger W.
Hicks, Irvin
Higgins, Robert F.
Highet, Keith
Hight, B. Boyd
Hill, J. French
Hillenbrand, Martin J.
Hillgren, Sonja
Hills, Laura Hume
Hilsman, Roger
Hilton, Robert P.
Hinerfeld, Ruth J.
Hines, Gerald D.
Hinshaw, Randall
Hinton, Deane R.
Hirschman, Albert O.
Hoagland, Jim
Hoch, Frank W.
Hodgson, James D.
Hoeber, Amoretta M.
Hoehn, William E., Jr.
Hoenlein, Malcolm
Hoepli, Nancy L.
Hoffman, Adonis Edward
Hoffman, Michael L.
Hoffmann, Stanley
Hoge, James F., Jr.
Hoge, Warren
Hoguet, George R.
Hohenberg, John
Hoinkes, Mary Elizabeth
Holbrooke, Richard C.
Holcomb, M. Staser
Holderman, James B.
Holl, Jane E.
Holland, Mary S.
Hollick, Ann L.
Holmes, H. Allen
Holst, Willem
Holt, Pat M.
Hood, Robert E.
Hooks, Benjamin L.
Hoopes, Townsend W.
Hoover, Herbert W., Jr.

Hope, Judith R.
Horelick, Arnold L.
Horlick, Gary
Hormats, Robert D.
Horn, Garfield H.
Horn, Karen N.
Horn, Sally K.
Horner, Martina S.
Horowtiz, Irving Louis
Horton, Alan W.
Horton, Frank B., III
Horton, Sharon Freeman
Hosmer, Bradley C.
Hoston, Germaine A.
Hottelet, Richard C.
Houghton, Amory, Jr.
Houghton, James R.
House, Karen Elliott
Hovey, Graham
Hovey, J. Allan, Jr.
Howard, John B.
Howard, John R.
Howell, Ernest M.
Hoyt, Mont P.
Huber, Richard L.
Huber, Robert T.
Huberman, Benjamin
Hudson, Manley O., Jr.
Hudson, Michael C.
Huebner, Lee W.
Hufbauer, Gary C.
Huffington, Roy M.
Hufstedler, Shirley
Hughes, Jeffrey L.
Hughes, John
Hughes, Thomas L.
Huglin, Henry C.
Huizenga, John W.
Hume, Ellen
Hummel, Arthur W., Jr.
Hunsberger, Warren S.
Hunter, Robert E.
Hunter, Shireen T.
Hunter-Gault, Charlayne
Huntington, Samuel P.

Hurewitz, J. C.
Hurford, John B.
Hurlock, James B.
Hurst, Robert J.
Hurwitz, Sol
Huyck, Philip M.
Hyde, Henry B.
Hyland, William G.

I

Ignatius, David
Ikle, Fred C.
Ilchman, Alice S.
Inderfurth, Karl F.
Ingersoll, Robert S.
Ink, Dwight
Inman, B. R.
Intriligator, Michael D.
Ireland, R. L., III
Irish, Leon E.
Irvin, Patricia L.
Irwin, John N., II
Isaacson, Walter
Iseline, John Jay
Isenberg, Steven L.
Isham, Christopher
Ispahani, Mahnaz Z.
Issawi, Charles
Istel, Yves-Andre
Izlar, William H., Jr.

J

Jabber, Paul
Jacklin, Nancy P.
Jackson, Bruce P.
Jackson, Jesse L.
Jackson, John H.
Jackson, Lois M.
Jackson, Sarah
Jackson, William E.
Jacob, John E.
Jacobs, Eli S.
Jacobs, Nehama
Jacobs, Norman
Jacobson, Harold K.

Jacobson, Jerome
Jacoby, Tamar
Jaffe, Amy Myers
Jamieson, J. K.
Janis, Mark W.
Janklow, Morton L.
Janow, Merit E.
Jansen, Marius B.
Jaquette, Jane
Jastrow, Robert
Jervis, Robert L.
Jessup, Alpheus W.
Jessup, Philip C., Jr.
Joffe, Robert D.
Johns, Lionel Skipwith
Johnson, Chalmers
Johnson, Howard W.
Johnson, Jerome L.
Johnson, L. Oakley
Johnson, Larry D.
Johnson, Robbin S.
Johnson, Robert H.
Johnson, Samuel C.
Johnson, Suzanne Nora
Johnson, Thomas S.
Johnson, W. Thomas
Johnson, Willard R.
Johnston, Philip
Jones, David C.
Jones, James R.
Jones, Sidney R.
Jones, Thomas V.
Jordan, Amos A.
Jordan, Vernon C.
Jordan, Vernon E., Jr.
Jorden, William J.
Joseph, Geri M.
Joseph, James A.
Joseph, Richard A.
Josephson, William
Joyce, John T.
Junz, Helen B.
Juster, Kenneth I.

K
Kahan, Jerome H.
Kahin, George McT.
Kahler, Miles
Kahn, Harry
Kahn, Tom
Kaiser, Philip M.
Kaiser, Robert G.
Kalb, Bernard
Kalb, Marvin
Kalicki, Jan
Kamarck, Andrew M.
Kaminer, Peter H.
Kaminsky, Howard
Kampelman, Max M.
Kamsky, Virginia A.
Kanak, Donald Perry
Kandell, Jonathan
Kanet, Roger E.
Kann, Peter R.
Kanter, Arnold
Kanter, Rosabeth Moss
Kaplan, Gilbert E.
Kaplan, Harold J.
Kaplan, Helene L.
Kaplan, Mark N.
Kaplan, Stephen S.
Kapp, Robert A.
Karalekas, Anne
Karamanian, Susan L.
Karis, Thomas G.
Karl, Terry Lynn
Karnow, Stanley
Karns, Margaret P.
Kasdin, Robert
Kass, Stephen L.
Kassinger, Theodore W.
Kassof, Allen H.
Katz, Abraham
Katz, Milton
Katz, Ronald S.
Katzenbach, Nicholas deB.
Katzenstein, Peter J.
Kaufman, Henry
Kaufmann, William W.

Kaysen, Carl
Kazemi, Farhad
Kean, Thomas H.
Kearns, David T.
Keel, Alton G., Jr.
Kenne, Lonnie S.
Kenny, Spurgeon M., Jr.
Kelleher, Catherine M.
Kellen, Stephen M.
Keller, Edmond J.
Keller, Kenneth H.
Kellerman, Barbara
Kelley, P. X.
Kelly, James P.
Kelly, John H.
Kelman, Herbert C.
Kemble, Eugenia
Kemp, Geoffrey
Kempe, Frederick
Kempner, Maximilian W.
Kendall, Donald M.
Kenen, Peter B.
Keniston, Kenneth
Kennan, Christopher J.
Kennan, Elizabeth T.
Kennan, George F.
Kennedy, David M.
Kennedy, Donald
Kenney, F. Donald
Keohane, Nannerl O.
Keohane, Robert O.
Keough, Donald R.
Kerr, Ann
Kerry, John F.
Kessler, Martha Neff
Kester, John G.
Ketelsen, James L.
Keydel, John F.
Khalilzad, Zalmay
Khuri, Nicola N.
Kiermaier, John
Kiernan, Robert Edward, III
Kiley, Robert R.
Kimmitt, Robert M.
King, Henry L.

King, John A., Jr.
Kintner, William R.
Kipper, Judith
Kirk, Grayson L.
Kirkland, Lane
Kirkpatrick, Jeane J.
Kisse-Sandoval, Catherine J.
Kissinger, Henry A.
Kitchen, Helen
Kitchen, Jeffrey C.
Kleiman, Robert
Klein, David
Klein, Edward
Klein, Joe
Klissas, Nicholas S.
Klurfeld, James
Knight, Jessie J., Jr.
Knight, Robert Huntington
Knoppers, Antonie T.
Knowlton, William A.
Knowlton, Winthrop
Koch, Wendy
Kolodziej, Edward A.
Kolt, George
Koltai, Steven R.
Kondracke, Morton
Korb, Lawrence J.
Korbonski, Andrzej
Korry, Edward M.
Kotecha, Mahesh K.
Kraar, Louis
Kraemer, Lillian E.
Kramer, Helen M.
Kramer, Jane
Kramer, Michael
Kramer, Steven Philip
Kranenburg, Hendrik J.
Krasner, Stephen D.
Krasno, Richard M.
Krause, Lawrence B.
Krauss, Clifford
Krauthammer, Charles
Kravis, Henry R.
Kreisberg, Paul H.
Krepon, Michael

Kreps, Juanita M.
Krisher, Bernard
Kristol, Irving
Krueger, Anne O.
Kruidenier, David
Kruzel, Joseph
Ku, Charlotte
Kubarych, Roger M.
Kubisch, Jack B.
Kuniholm, Bruce R.
Kuntz, Carol R.
Kupchan, Charles A.
Kupperman, Robert H.
Kurth, James R.
Kurtzer, Daniel C.
Kyle, Robert D.

L

Laber, Jeri
Labrecque, Thomas G.
Lahoud, Nina J.
Lake, W. Anthony
Lake, William T.
Lall, Betty Goetz
Lamb, Denis
Lambeth, Benjamin S.
Lamm, Donald S.
Lamont, Lansing
Lampley, Virginia A.
Lampton, David M.
Lancaster, Carol J.
Landau, Christopher
Landau, George W.
Landers, James M.
Landy, Joanne
Lane, Charles M.
Laney, James T.
Langdon, George D., Jr.
Lansner, Kermit
LaPalombara, Joseph
Lapham, Lewis H.
Lapidus, Gail W.
Larrabee, F. Stephen
Larson, Charles R.
Lary, Hal B.

Lateef, Noel V.
Lauder, Leonard A.
Laudicina, Paul A.
Lauinger, Philip C., Jr.
Laukhuff, Perry
Laventhol, David A.
Lawrence, Richard D.
Lawson, Eugene K.
Layne, Christopher
Lazarus, Steven
Leach, Jim
Leddy, John M.
Lederberg, Joshua
Lederer, Ivo John
Lee, Ernest S.
Lee, Janet
Lee, John M.
Lee, William L.
Lefever, Ernest W.
Leghorn, Richard S.
Legvold, Robert H.
Lehman, John F.
Lehman, John R.
Lehman, Orin
Lehrer, Jim
Leich, John Foster
Leigh, Monroe
Leland, Marc E.
Lelyveld, Joseph
LeMelle, Tilden J.
LeMelle, Wilbert J.
Lempert, Robert J.
Lenzen, Louis C.
LeoGrande, William M.
Leonard, H. Jeffrey
Leonard, James F.
Leonard, James G.
Leone, Richard C.
Lescaze, Lee
Lesch, Ann Mosely
Lesser, Ian O.
Levin, Michael S.
Levine, Irving R.
Levine, Mel
Levine, Susan B.

Levinson, Marc
Levitas, Mitchel
Levy, Marion J., Jr.
Levy, Raymond
Levy, Walter J.
Lewis, Bernard
Lewis, Clifford M.
Lewis, Flora
Lewis, John P.
Lewis, John Wilson
Lewis, Samuel W.
Lewis, Stephen R.
Lewis, W. Walker
Li, Victor H.
Libby, I. Lewis
Lichtblau, John H.
Lichtenstein, Cynthia C.
Lieber, Robert J.
Lieberman, Henry R.
Lieberman, Joseph I.
Lieberman, Nancy A.
Lieberthal, Kenneth
Lief, Louise
Liffers, William A.
Light, Timothy
Lilienthal, Sally
Lincoln, Edward J.
Lind, Michael E.
Lindquist, Warren T.
Lindsay, Franklin A.
Lindsay, George N.
Lindsay, John V.
Lindsay, Robert V.
Link, Troland S.
Linowes, David F.
Linowitz, Sol M.
Lipper, Kenneth
Lipset, Seymour Martin
Lipsky, Seth
Lipson, Leon
Lissakers, Karin M.
Little, David
Litwak, Robert S.
Livingston, Robert Gerald
Llewellyn, J. Bruce

Lockwood, John E.
Lodal, Jan M.
Lodge, George C.
Loeb, John L.
Loeb, Marshall
Loft, George
Logan, Francis D.
Long, Jeffrey W.
Long, T. Dixon
Longstreth, Thomas K.
Loomis, Henry
Loranger, Donald E., Jr.
Lord, Bette Bao
Lord, Winston
Louis, William Roger
Lovdahl, Randall John
Lovejoy, Thomas E.
Lovelace, Jon B.
Low, Stephen
Lowenfeld, Andreas F.
Lowenstein, James G.
Lowenthal, Abraham F.
Lowrey, Dennis Allen
Loy, Frank E.
Lozano, Ignacio E., Jr.
Lubin, Nancy
Lubman, Stanley B.
Lucas, C. Payne
Luce, Charles F.
Luck, Edward C.
Lucy, William
Luers, William H.
Luke, John A., Jr.
Lustick, Ian S.
Luttwak, Edward N.
Lyall, Katharine C.
Lyman, Princeton Nathan
Lynch, Edward S.
Lynn, James T.
Lynn, Laurence E., Jr.
Lynn-Jones, Sean M.
Lyons, Gene M.
Lyons, James E.
Lyons, Richard K.
Lythcott, George I.

M
Ma, Christopher Yi-Wen
MacArthur, Douglas, II
MacCormack, Charles F.
MacDonald, Gordon J.
MacFarquhar, Emily
MacGregor, Douglas A.
MacGregor, Ian K.
MacLaury, Bruce K.
MacMillan, Whitney
Macomber, John D.
Macomber, William B.
Macy, Robert M., Jr.
Madrid, Arturo
Maged, Mark J.
Magowan, Peter A.
Maguire, John D.
Mahoney, Margaret E.
Mahoney, Thomas H., IV
Maier, Charles S.
Makins, Christopher J.
Mako, William P.
Malek, Frederic V.
Malin, Clement B.
Mallery, Richard
Malmgren, Harald B.
Manca, Marie Antoinette
Mandelbaum, Michael E.
Manilow, Lewis
Mann, Michael D.
Mann, Thomas E.
Manning, Bayless
Manning, Robert J.
Marans, J. Eugene
Marcum, John Arthur
Marder, Murrey
Margolis, David I.
Mark, David E.
Mark, Gregory A.
Mark, Hans M.
Marks, Leonard H.
Marks, Paul A.
Marks, Russell E., Jr.
Marlin, Alice Tepper
Marmor, Theodore R.

319

Marr, Phebe A.
Marron, Donald B.
Marshak, Robert E.
Marshall, Andrew W.
Marshall, Anthony D.
Marshall, C. Burton
Marshall, Katherine
Marshall, Ray
Martin, Daniel R.
Martin, Edwin M.
Martin, Lynn
Martin, Malcolm W.
Martin, William F.
Martin, William McC., Jr.
Martin-Brown, Joan
Martinez, Vilma S.
Martinuzzi, Leo S., Jr.
Marton, Kati
Marx, Anthony William
Masin, Michael T.
Mason, Elvis L.
Massie, Suzanne
Mastanduno, Michael
Mathews, Jessica Tuchman
Mathews, Michael S.
Mathias, Charles McC., Jr.
Matlock, Jack F.
Matsui, Robert T.
Matsuoka, Tama
Matteson, William B.
Matthews, Eugene A.
Mattox, Gale A.
Maxwell, Kenneth
Mayu, Ernest R.
Mayer, Gerald M., Jr.
Mayer, Lawrence A.
Mayhew, Alice E.
Maynard, Robert C.
Maynes, Charles William
Mazur, Jay
McAdams, David
McAfee, W. Gage
McAllister, Jef Olivarius
McAuliffe, Jennifer Toolin
McCall, H. Carl

McCann, Edward
McCarthy, James P.
McCarthy, John G.
McCloy, John J., II
McColough, C. Peter
McCormack, Elizabeth J.
McCouch, Donald G.
McCracken, Paul W.
McCurdy, Dave K.
McDonald, Alonzo L.
McDonough, William J.
McDougal, Myres S.
McDougall, Gay J.
McFarlane, Robert C.
McFate, Patricia Ann
McGhee, George C.
McGiffert, David E.
McGillicuddy, John F.
McGovern, George S.
McGowan, Alan
McGrath, Eugene R.
McGuire, Raymond J.
McGale, Thomas R.
McHenry, Donald F.
McKinley, John K.
McKinney, Robert
McLaughlin, David T.
McLean, Sheila Avrin
McLin, Jon B.
McManus, Jason
McNamara, Robert S.
McNeill, John H.
McNeill, Robert L.
McPeak, Merrill A.
McPherson, Harry C., Jr.
McPherson, M. Peter
McQuade, Lawrence C.
Mead, Dana G.
Meagher, Robert F.
Meers, Sharon I.
Mehta, Ved
Meissner, Charles F.
Meissner, Doris M.
Meister, Irene W.
Mello, Judy Hendren

Melloan, George R.
Melville, Richard A.
Mendlovitz, Saul H.
Menke, John R.
Merkling, Christian
Meron, Theodor
Merow, John E.
Merrill, Philip
Merritt, Jack N.
Merszei, Zoltan
Mesa-Lago, Carmelo
Meselson, Matthew
Messner, William Curtis, Jr.
Metcalf, George R.
Mettler, Ruben F.
Meyer, Cord
Meyer, Edward C.
Meyer, John R.
Meyer, Karl E.
Meyerman, Harold J.
Meyerson, Martin
Mickelson, Sig
Mickiewicz, Ellen P.
Midgley, Elizabeth
Midgley, John J., Jr.
Mihaly, Eugene B.
Mikell, Gwendolyn
Miles, Edward L.
Miller, Charles D.
Miller, Christopher D.
Miller, David Charles, Jr.
Miller, Franklin C.
Miller, J. Irwin
Miller, Judith
Miller, Linda B.
Miller, Paul David
Miller, William Green
Millett, Allan R.
Millington, John A.
Mills, Bradford
Mills, Susan
Milner, Helen
Min, Nancy-Ann
Miner, Steven M.
Minow, Newton N.

Mitchell, George J.
Mitchell, Jacqueline A.
Mochizuki, Kiichi
Moe, Sherwood G.
Mondale, Walter F.
Monroe, Hunter
Montgomery, Parker G.
Montgomery, Philip O'B.,III
Moock, Joyce Lewinger
Moody, Jim
Moody, William S.
Moore, John M.
Moore, John Norton
Moore, Jonathan
Moore, Paul, Jr.
Moose, George E.
Moose, Richard M.
Moran, Theodore H.
Morey, David E.
Morgan, Thomas E.
Morgenthau,
  Lucinda L. Franks
Morley, James William
Morrell, Gene P.
Morris, Bailey
Morris, Grinnell
Morris, Max K.
Morris, Milton D.
Morrisett, Lloyd N.
Morse, Edward L.
Morse, F. Bradford
Morse, Kenneth P.
Moses, Alfred H.
Mosettig, Michael
Moss, Ambler H., Jr.
Moss, Richard H.
Motley, Joel W.
Mottahedeh, Roy
Moynihan, Daniel P.
Mroz, John Edwin
Mujal-Leon, Eusebio
Mulford, David C.
Mulholland, William D.
Muller, Henry
Muller, Steven

Mundy, Carl E., Jr.
Munger, Edwin S.
Munroe, George B.
Munroe, Vernon, Jr.
Munyan, Winthrop R.
Murphy, Joseph S.
Murphy, Richard W.
Murphy, Sean David
Murphy, Thomas S.
Murray, Allen E.
Murray, Douglas P.
Murray, Lori Esposito
Muse, Martha T.
Muskie, Edmond S.

N
Nachmanoff, Arnold
Nacht, Michael
Nadiri, M. Ishaq
Nagorski, Andrew
Nagorski, Zygmunt
Najjar, Mitri J.
Namkung, K. A.
Nathan, James A.
Nathan, Robert R.
Natt, Ted M.
Nau, Henry R.
Naylor, Rosamond Lee
Negroponte, John D.
Neier, Aryeh
Nelson, Daniel N.
Nelson, Jack
Nelson, Mark A.
Nelson, Merlin E.
Nenneman, Richard A.
Neustadt, Richard E.
Newburg, Andre W. G.
Newell, Barbara W.
Newhouse, John
Newman, Priscilla A.
Newman, Richard T.
Newsom, David D.
Newton, Quigg
Ney, Edward N.
Nicholas, N. J., Jr.

Nichols, Rodney W.
Nicholson, Jamie E.
Niehuss, John M.
Niehuss,
  Rosemary Neaher
Nielsen, Waldemar A.
Nilsson, A. Kenneth
Nimetz, Matthew
Nitze, Paul H.
Nitze, William A.
Nolan, Janne E.
Nolan, Kimberly
Nolte, Richard H.
Nooter, Robert H.
Norman, William S.
Northrop, Michael F.
Norton, Augustus Richard
Norton, Eleanor Holmes
Novak, Michael
Novicki, Margaret A.
Nuechterlein, Jeffrey D.
Nugent, Walter
Nye, Joseph S., Jr.

O
Oakes, John B.
Oakley, Robert B.
Oberdorfer, Don
O'Brien, Dennis J.
O'Cleireacain, Carol
O'Connell, Mary Ellen
O'Connor, Sandra Day
O'Connor, Walter F.
Odeen, Philip A.
Odell, John
Odom, William E.
O'Donnell, Kevin
Oettinger, Anthony G.
Offit, Morris W.
O'Flaherty, J. Daniel
Ogden, Alfred
Ogden, William S.
O'Hare, Joseph A.
Oksenberg, Michel
Okun, Herbert S.

Oliva, L. Jay
Oliver, April
Oliver, Covey T.
Olmstead, Cecil J.
Olsen, Leif H.
Olson, William C.
Olvey, Lee D.
O'Malley, Cormac K. H.
Omestad, Thomas E.
Ondaatje,
  Elizabeth Heneghan
O'Neill, Michael J.
Opel, John R.
Oppenheimer, Franz M.
Oppenheimer, Michael
Orlins, Stephen A.
Ornstein, Norman J.
Osborn, George K., III
Osborne, Richard de J.
O'Shaughnessy, Elise
Osmer-McQuade, Margaret
Osnos, Peter
Osnos, Susan Sherer
Ostrander, F. Taylor
Overholser, Geneva
Owen, Henry
Owen, Roberts B.
Owens, William A.
Oxman, Stephen A.
Oxnam, Robert B.

P
Packard, George R.
Paine, George C., II
Pais, Abraham
Pakula, Hannah C.
Palmer, Mark
Palmer, Norman D.
Palmer, Ronald D.
Palmieri, Victor H.
Panofsky, Wolfgang K. H.
Parker,
  Barrington Daniels, Jr.
Parker, Jason H.
Parker, Maynard

Parkinson, Roger
Parsky, Gerald L.
Parsons, Richard D.
Passin, Herbert
Patrick, Hugh T.
Patterson, Gardner
Patterson, Hugh B., Jr.
Pauker, Guy J.
Paul, Roland A.
Payne, Donald M.
Pearce, William R.
Pearlstine, Norman
Pearson, John E.
Pedersen, Richard F.
Pederson, Rena
Pelgrift, Kathryn C.
Pell, Claiborne
Pelletreau, Robert H., Jr.
Penfield, James K.
Pennoyer, Robert M.
Percy, Charles H.
Peretz, Don
Perez, Antonio F.
Perkins, Edward J.
Perkins, James A.
Perkins, Roswell B.
Perle, Richard N.
Perlman, Janice E.
Perlmutter, Amos
Peters, Arthur King
Peters, Aulana L.
Petersen, Howard C.
Peterson, Erik R.
Peterson, Peter G.
Peterson, Rudolph A.
Petree, Richard W.
Petree, Richard W., Jr.
Petri, Thomas E.
Petschek, Stephen R.
Petty, John R.
Pezzullo, Lawrence A.
Pfaltzgraff, Robert L., Jr.
Pfeiffer, Jane Cahill
Pfeiffer, Ralph A., Jr.
Pfeiffer, Steven B.

Pharr, Susan J.
Phelan, John J., Jr.
Phillips, Christopher H.
Phillips, Russell A., Jr.
Picker, Harvey
Pickering, Thomas R.
Pieczenik, Steve R.
Piel, Gerard
Pierce, Ponchitta
Pierce, William C.
Piercy, George T.
Pierre, Andrew J.
Pierson, Jeffrey D.
Pifer, Alan
Pigott, Charles M.
Pike, John E.
Pilling, Donald L.
Pilliod, Charles J., Jr.
Pincus, Lionel I.
Pincus, Walter H.
Pinder, Jeanne
Pinkerton, W. Stewart
Pino, John A.
Pipes, Daniel
Pipes, Richard E.
Pitts, Joe W., III
Plank, John N.
Platt, Alan A.
Platt, Nicholas
Plimpton, Calvin H.
Pocalyko, Michael N.
Podhoretz, Norman
Pogue, Richard W.
Polk, William R.
Pollack, Gerald A.
Polsby, Nelson W.
Pond, Elizabeth
Poneman, Daniel B.
Pool, Marquita J.
Popoff, Frank P.
Portes, Richard D.
Porzecanski, Arturo C.
Posen, Barry R.
Posner, Michael H.
Posvar, Wesley W.

Potter, William C.
Powell, Colin L.
Powell, Robert
Power, Philip H.
Powers, Thomas Moore
Powers, William F., Jr.
Pranger, Robert J.
Precht, Henry
Press, Frank
Pressler, Larry
Preston, Lewis T.
Prewitt, Kenneth
Price, Daniel M.
Price, Hugh
Price, John R., Jr.
Price, Robert
Puchala, Donald J.
Puckett, Allen R.
Pugh, Richard C.
Purcell, Susan Kaufman
Pursley, Robert E.
Pusey, Nathan M.
Pustay, John S.
Putnam, Robert D.
Pye, Lucian W.
Pyle, Cassandra A.
Pyle, Kenneth B.

Q
Quandt, William B.
Quewster, George H.
Quigley, Kevin F. F.
Quigley, Leonard V.

R
Rabb, Maxwell M.
Rabinowitch, Alexander
Rabinowitch, Victor
Radenmaker, Stephen
Radway, Laurence I.
Ragone, David V.
Raines, Franklin D.
Ramirez, Lilia L.
Ramo, Simon
Rangel, Charles B.

Ranis, Gustav
Rashish, Myer
Rather, Dan
Rathjens, George W.
Rattner, Steven L.
Rauch, Rudolph S.
Raul, Alan Charles
Ravenal, Earl C.
Ravenholt, Albert
Ravitch, Richard
Rawl, Lawrence G.
Raymond, Jack
Raymond, Lee R.
Read, Bejamin H.
Reback, Sanford C.
Reed, Charles B.
Reed, John S.
Reed, Joseph Verner
Reeves, Jay B. L.
Reichert, Douglas D.
Reid, Ogden
Reid, Whitelaw
Reinhardt, John E.
Reisman, W. M.
Reiss, Mitchell B.
Renfrew, Charles B.
Reppy, Judith V.
Resor, Stanley R.
Revesz, Richard L.
Rey, Nicholas A.
Reynolds, A. William
Rhinelander, John B.
Rhinesmith, Stephen H.
Rhodes, Edward
Rhodes, Franklin H. T.
Rhodes, John B., Sr.
Rhodes, Thomas L.
Rhodes, William R.
Ribicoff, Abraham A.
Rice, Condoleezza
Rice, Donald B.
Rice, Joseph A.
Rice, Susan Elizabeth
Rich, John H., Jr.
Rich, Michael D.

Richards, Paul G.
Richardson, David N.
Richardson, Elliot L.
Richardson, Frank H.
Richardson, Henry J., III
Richardson, John
Richardson, Richard W.
Richardson, William B.
Richardson, William R.
Richman, Joan F.
Rickard, Stephen A.
Riddell, Malcolm
Ridgway, Rozanne L.
Riellly, John E.
Ries, Hans A.
Riesel, Victor
Rindskopf, Elizabeth R.
Ritch, John B., III
Rivers, Richard R.
Rivkin, Donald H.
Rivlin, Alice M.
Rizk, Nayla M.
Rizopouloa, Nicholas X.
Robb, Charles S.
Robbins, Carla Anne
Roberts, Brad
Roberts, Chalmers M.
Roberts, John J.
Roberts, Richard W.
Roberts, Walter R.
Robinson, Charles W.
Robinson, David Z.
Robinson, Davis R.
Robinson, Elizabeth L.
Robinson, James D., III
Robinson, Leonard H., Jr.
Robinson, Linda S.
Robinson, Marshall A.
Robinson, Pearl T.
Robinson, Randall
Robison, Olin C.
Roche, James G.
Roche, John P.
Roche, Mark D.
Rockefeller, David

323

Rockefeller, David, Jr.
Rockefeller, John D., IV
Rockefeller, Rodman C.
Rockwell, Hays H.
Rodman, Peter W.
Rodriguez, Rita M.
Rodriguez, Vincent
Roett, Riordan
Roff, J. Hugh, Jr.
Rogers, Bernard W.
Rogers, William D.
Rogers, William P.
Rogovin, Mitchell
Rohatyn, Felix G.
Rohlen, Thomas P.
Rokke, Ervin J.
Romberg, Alan D.
Romero-Barcelo, Carlos
Roney, John H.
Roosa, Robert V.
Roosa, Ruth AmEnde
Rosberg, Carl G.
Rose, Daniel
Rose, Elihu
Rose, Frederick P.
Rosecrance, Richard
Rosen, Arthur H.,
Rosen, Jane K.
Rosenberg, Tina
Rosenblatt, Peter R.
Rosenblith, Walter A.
Rosenblum, Mort
Rosenfield, Stephen S.
Rosenfield, Patricia A.
Rosenstock, Robert
Rosenthal, A. M.
Rosenthal, Douglas E.
Rosenthal, Jack
Rosenzweig, Robert M.
Rosin, Axel G.
Roskens, Ronald W.
Rosovsky, Henry
Ross, Arthur
Ross, Dennis B.
Ross, Roger

Ross, Thomas B.
Rosso, David J.
Rossotti, Charles O.
Rostow, Elspeth Davies
Rostow, Eugene V.
Rostow, Nicholas
Rostow, Walt W.
Rotberg, Robert I.
Roth, Stanley Owen
Roth, William M.
Roth, William V., Jr.
Rothkopf, David J.
Rovine, Arthur W.
Rowen, Henry S.
Rowny, Edward L.
Rubin, James P.
Rubin, Nancy H.
Rubin, Seymour J.
Rubin, Trudy
Ruckelshaus, William D.
Rudenstine, Neil L.
Rudman, Warren B.
Rudolph, Barbara
Rudolph, Lloyd I.
Rudolph, Susanne Hoeber
Ruebhausen, Oscar M.
Ruenitz, Robert M.
Ruffie, John F.
Ruina, J. P.
Runge, Carlisle Ford
Rush, Kenneth
Rusk, Dean
Russell, Thomas W., Jr.
Rustow, Dankwart A.
Ruttan, Vernon W.
Ryan, John T., Jr.
Ryan, John T., III

S

Sacks, Paul M.
Safran, Nadav
Sagan, Carl
Sagan, Scott D.
Said, Edward
Sakoian, Carol

Salacuse, Jeswald W.
Salisbury, Harrison E.
Salk, Jonas
Salomon, Richard E.
Salomon, William R.
Sample, Steven B.
Samuel, Howard D.
Samuels, Barbara C., II
Samuels, Michael A.
Samuels, Nathaniel
Samuels, Richard J.
Sanchez, Nestor D.
Sanders, Edward G.
Sanford, Charles S., Jr.
Sanford, Terry
Santos, Miriam
Sapiro, Miriam
Sarro, Dale M.
Sato, Kumi
Saul, Ralph
Saunders, Harold H.
Savage, Frank
Sawhill, John E.
Sawyer, Diane
Sawyer, John E.
Saylor, Lynne S.
Scalapino, Robert A.
Scali, John A.
Schacht, Henry B.
Schachter, Oscar
Schaetzel, J. Robert
Schaffer, Howard B.
Schake, Kori Naomi
Schaufele, William E., Jr.
Schecter, Jerrold
Scheffer, David J.
Scheinman, Lawrence
Schiff, Frank W.
Schilling, Warner R.
Schlesinger, Arthur, Jr.
Schlesinger, James R.
Schlosser, Herbert S.
Schmertz, Herbert
Schmidt, Benno, Jr.
Schmoke, Kurt L.

324

Scmults, Edward C.
Scneider, Jan
Schneider, William
Schneier, Arthur
Schienbaum, Thomas John
Schoettle, Enid C. B.
Schorr, Daniel L.
Schreyer, William A.
Schroeder, Patricia
Schubert, Richard F.
Schub, G. Edward
Schulhof, Michael P.
Schuyler, C. V. R.
Schwab, Susan C.
Schwab, William B.
Schwartz, Eric Paul
Schwartz, Harry
Schwartz, Thomas Alan
Schwartz, Frederick A.O., Jr.
Schwarzer, William W.
Schwarzman, Stephen A.
Schwebel, Stephen M.
Sciolino, Elaine F.
Scowcroft, Brent
Scranton, William W.
Seaborg, Glenn T.
Seagrave, Norman P.
Seamans, Robert C., Jr.
Seely, Carolyn T.
Segal, Sheldon J.
Segal, Susan L.
Seib, Gerald
Seibold, Frederick C., Jr.
Seidman, Herta Lande
Seigenthaler, John L.
Seigle, John W.
Seignoous, George M.
Seitz, Frederick
Selin, Ivan
Semple, Robert B., Jr.
Setear, John K.
Sewall, John O. B.
Sewall, Sarah Buckeley
Sewall, John W.
Sexton, William C.

Shafer, D. Michael
Shaffer, Gail S.
Shalala, Donna E.
Shanker, Albert
Shapiro, Eli
Shapiro, Harold T.
Shapiro, Isaac
Sharp, Daniel A.
Shayne, Herbert M.
Sheeline, Paul C.
Sheffield, James R.
Sheffield, Jill W.
Sheinbaum, Stanley K.
Sheldon, Eleanor Bernert
Shelley, Sally Swing
Shelp, Ronald K.
Shelton, Joanna Reed
Shelton-Colby, Sally A.
Shenk, George H.
Shenk, George L.
Sherwood, Ben
Sherwood, Elizabeth D.
Sherwood, Richard E.
Shestack, Jerome J.
Shiner, Josette
Shinn, Richard R.
Shipley, Walter V.
Shirer, William L.
Shirk, Susan L.
Shlaes, Amity
Shoemaker, Alvin V.
Shoemaker, Christopher Cole
Shoemaker, Don
Shriver, Donald W., Jr.
Shubert, Gustave H.
Shulman, Colette
Shulman, Marshall D.
Shultz, George P.
Sick, Gary G.
Siegman, Henry
Sifton, Elisabeth
Sigal, Leon V.
Sigmund, Paul E.
Silas, C. J.
Silberman, Laurence H.

Silk, Leonard S.
Silkenat, James R.
Silvers, Robert B.
Simes, Dimitri K.
Simmons, Adele Smith
Simon, William E.
Sims, Albert G.
Singer, Christine Eibs
Sisco, Joseph J.
Sitrick, James B.
Skarzynski, Michael P.
Skidmore, Thomas E.
Skinner, Elliott P.
Skolnikoff, Eugene B.
Slade, David R.
Slater, Joseph E.
Slawson, Paul S.
Sloan, David M.
Sloane, Ann Brownell
Slocombe, Walter N.
Slocum, John J.
Sloss, Leon
Small, Lawrence M.
Smalley, Patricia T.
Smart, S. Bruce, Jr.
Smith, Carleton Sprague
Smith, Clint E.
Smith, Datus C., Jr.
Smith, David S.
Smith, DeWitt C., Jr.
Smith, Edwin M.
Smith, Gaddis
Smith, Gare A.
Smith, Gerard C.
Smith, Hedrick L.
Smith, Jeffrey H.
Smith, John T., II
Smith, Larry
Smith, Leighton W., Jr.
Smith, Malcom B.
Smith, Michael B.
Smith, Perry M.
Smith, Peter B.
Smith, Peter Hopkinson
Smith, R. Jeffrey

Smith, Richard M.
Smith, Stephen G.
Smith, Theodore M.
Smith, Tony
Smith, W. Y.
Smith, Wayne S.
Smythe, Mabel M.
Snow, Robert Anthony
Snowe, Olympia J.
Snyder, Craig
Snyder, David M.
Snyder, Jack L.
Snyder, Jed C.
Snyder, Richard E.
Sobol, Dorothy Meadow
Soderberg, Nancy E.
Sofaer, Abraham David
Sohn, Louis B.
Solarz, Stephen J.
Solbert, Peter O. A.
Solomon, Anne G. K.
Solomon, Anthony M.
Solomon, Peter J.
Solomon, Richard H.
Solomon, Robert
Sonenshine, H. Marshall
Sonenshine, Tara
Sonne, Christian R.
Sonnenfeldt, Helmut
Sonnenfeldt, Richard W.
Sorensen, Theodore C.
Soros, George
Soros, Paul
Southern, Ronald
Sovern, Michael I.
Spain, James W.
Spalter, Jonathan
Spang, Kenneth M.
Spector, Leonard S.
Spencer, Edson W.
Spencer, John H.
Spencer, William C.
Spencer, William U.
Spero, Joan Edelman
Speth, James Gustave

Speyer, Jerry I.
Spiers, Ronald I.
Spiro, David E.
Spiro, Herbert J.
Spiro, Peter J.
Spratt, John M., Jr.
Squadron, Howard M.
Stackpole, Stephen H.
Stacks, John
Staheli, Donald L.
Stalson, Helena
Stamas, Stephen
Stankard, Francis X.
Stanley, Peter W.
Stanley, Timothy W.
Stanton, Frank
Stanton, R. John, Jr.
Staples, Eugene S.
Starobin, Herman
Starr, Jeffrey M.
Starr, S. Frederick
Stassen, Harold E.
Steadman, Richard C.
Stebbins, James H.
Steel, Ronald
Stegemeier, Richard J.
Steiger, Paul E.
Stein, Elliot, Jr.
Stein, Eric
Stein, Jonathan B.
Steinberg, David J.
Steinberg, James B.
Steinbruner, John D.
Steiner, Daniel
Stengel, Richard
Stent, Angela E.
Stepan, Alfred C.
Stephanopoulos, George
Stern, Ernest
Stern, Fritz
Stern, H. Peter
Stern, Paula
Sterner, Michael E.
Sternlight, David
Stevens, Charles R.

Stevens, James W.
Stevens, Norton
Stevens, Paul Schott
Stevenson, Adlai E., III
Stevenson, Charles A.
Stevenson, John R.
Stewart, Donald M.
Stewart, Gordon
Stewart, Patricia Carry
Stewart, Ruth Ann
Sticht, J. Paul
Stiehm, Judith Hicks
Stifel, Laurence D.
Stobaugh, Robert B.
Stockman, David A.
Stockton, Paul Noble
Stoessinger, John G.
Stoga, Alan
Stokes, Bruce
Stokes, Donald E.
Stokes, Louis
Stone, Jeremy J.
Stone, Michael P. W.
Stone, Roger D.
Stookey, John Hoyt
Stratton, Julius A.
Straus, Donald B.
Straus, Oscar S.
Straus, R. Peter
Straus, Ralph I.
Straus, Robert K.
Strauss, Simon D.
Strausz-Hupe, Robert
Stremlau, John J.
Strock, James M.
Stromseth, Jane E.
Stroud, Joe E.
Studeman, William O.
Styron, Rose
Sudarkasa, Michael E. M.
Sudarkasa, Niara
Suits, Christopher D.
Suleiman, Ezra N.
Sullivan, Gordon Russell
Sullivan, Leon H.

Sullivan, Margaret C.
Sullivan, Roger W.
Sullivan, William H.
Summers, Harry F., Jr.
Summers, Lawrence H.
Sunderland, Jack B.
Suslow, Leo A.
Sutterlin, James S.
Sutton, Francis X.
Swank, Emory C.
Swanson, David H.
Sweitzer, Brandon W.
Swenson, Eric P.
Swid, Stephen C.
Swiers, Peter Bird
Swigert, James W.
Swing, John Temple
Szanton, Peter L.

T

Taft, William H., IV
Tahir-Kheli, Shirin R.
Talbot, Phillips
Talbot, Strobe
Tang, David K. Y.
Tanham, George K.
Tannenwald, Theodore, Jr.
Tanner, Harold
Tanter, Raymond
Tapia, Raul R.
Tarnoff, Peter
Tasco, Frank J.
Taubman, William
Taylor, Arthur R.
Taylor, George E.
Taylor, William J., Jr.
Teece, David J.
Teeters, Nancy H.
Teitelbaum, Michael S.
Telhami, Shibley
Tempelsman, Maurice
Tennyson, Leonard B.
Terracciano, Anthony B.
Terry, Sarah M.
Thayer, A. Bronson

Theobald, Thomas C.
Thery, Jane L. Barber
Thoman, G. Richard
Thomas, Barbara S.
Thomas, Brooks
Thomas, Evan W., III
Thomas, Franklin A.
Thomas, Lee B., Jr.
Thomas, Lewis
Thompson, W. Scott
Thomson, James A.
Thomson, James C., Jr.
Thornburgh, Dick
Thronell, Richard P.
Thornton, Thomas P.
Thoron, Louisa
Thorup, Cathryn L.
Thurman, M. R.
Thurow, Lester C.
Tigert, Ricki Rhodarmer
Tillinghast, David R.
Tillman, Seth P.
Timothy-Lankester, Kristen
Timpson, Sarah L.
Tisch, Laurence A.
Tobias, Randall L.
Todaro, Michael P.
Todd, Maurice Linwood
Todman, Terence A.
Tolbert, Kathryn
Toll, Maynard J., Jr.
Tomlinson, Alexander C.
Topping, Seymour
Torres, Art
Toth, Robert C.
Townley, Preston
Townsend, Alair
Trachtenberg, Stephen Joel
Train, Harry D. H.
Train, John
Train, Russell E.
Trainor, Bernard E.
Trani, Eugene P.
Travers, Peter J.
Travis, Martin B., Jr.

Treat, John Elting
Trebat, Thomas J.
Treverton, Gregory F.
Trewhitt, Henry L.
Trezise, Philip H.
Trifflin, Robert
Trojan, Vera
Trooboff, Peter D.
Trowbridge, Alexander B.
Truitt, Marion Dawson
Truman, Edwin M.
Tsipis, Kosta
Tu, Lawrence P.
Tucher, H. Anton
Tuck, Edward Hallam
Tucker, Nancy Bernkopf
Tucker, Richard F.
Tucker, Robert W.
Tung, Ko-Yung
Turck, Nancy B.
Turkevich, John
Turner, J. Michael
Turner, Robert F.
Turner, Stansfield
Turner, William C.
Tuthill, John Wills
Tyrrell, R. Emmett, Jr.
Tyson, Laura D'Andrea

U

Udovitch, A. L.
Uhlig, Mark
Ullman, Richard H.
Ulman, Cornelius M.
Ungar, Sanford J.
Ungeheuer, Frederick
Unger, David
Unger, Leonard
Urfer, Richard P.
Usher, William R.
Utgoff, Victor A.
Utley, Garrick
Utton, Albert E.

327

V
Vagliano, Alexander M.
Vagliano, Sara
Vaky, Viron P.
Valdez, Abelardo Lopez
Valenta, Jiri
Valentine, Debra A.
Valenzuela, Arturo
Vance, Cyrus R.
van den Haag, Ernest
vanden Heuvel, Katrina
vanden Heuvel, William
van der Vink, Gregory
Van Dusen, Michael H.
Van Dyk, Ted
Van Evera, Stephen W.
Van Fleet, James A.
Van Vlierden, Constant
van Voorst, L. Bruce
Veblen, Tom C.
Vecchio, Mark S.
Veit, Carol M.
Veit, Lawrence A.
Veliotes, Nicholas A.
Vermilye, Peter H.
Vernon, Raymond
Verville, Elizabeth G.
Vessey, John W.
Vest, George S.
Viederman, Stephen
Viets, Richard Noyes
Vila, Adis Maria
Villa, Arturo
Vine, Richard D.
Viorst, Milton
Viscusi, Enzo
Vitale, Alberto
Voell, Richard A.
Vogel, Ezra F.
Vogelgesang, Sandy
Vojta, George J.
Volcker, Paul A.
Von Klemperer, Alfred
von Mehren, Robert B.
Votaw, Carmen Delgado

Vuono, Carl E.

W
Wachner, Linda Joy
Waddell, Rick
Wadsworth-Darby, Mary
Wahl, Nicholas
Wakeman, Frederic F., Jr.
Wales, Jane
Walinsky, Adam
Walter, Charles E.
Walker, G. R.
Walker, John L.
Walker, Joseph, Jr.
Walker, Mary Lynn
Walker, William N.
Wallander, Celeste A.
Wallerstein, Mitchel B.
Wallison, Peter J.
Walters, Barbara
Walton, Anthony J.
Waltz, Kenneth N.
Ward, F. Champion
Ward, John W.
Ward, Patrick Joseph
Ware, Carl
Warner, Edward L., III
Warnke, Paul C.
Warren, Gerald L.
Washburn, Abbot M.
Washburn, John L.
Wasserstein, Bruce
Waterbury, John
Waters, Cherri D.
Watson, Alexander F.
Watson, Thomas J., Jr.
Wattenberg, Ben J.
Watts, Glenn E.
Watts, John H.
Watts, William
Way, Alva O.
Weatherstone, Dennis
Weaver, David R.
Weaver, George L. P.
Weber, Steven

Webster, William H.
Wedgwood, Ruth
Wehrle, Leroy S.
Weidenbaum, Murray L.
Weigel, George
Weiksner, George B., Jr.
Weil, Frank A.
Weinberg, John L.
Weinberg, Steven
Weinberger, Caspar W.
Weiner, Myron
Weinert, Richard S.
Weinrod, W. Bruce
Weinstein, Michael M.
Weintraub, Sidney
Weiss, Charles, Jr.
Weiss, Cora
Weiss, Edith Brown
Weiss, Seymour
Weiss, Thomas G.
Welch, Jasper A., Jr.
Welch, John F., Jr.
Welch, Larry D.
Weller, Ralph A.
Wells, Damon, Jr.
Wells, Herman B.
Wells, Samuel F., Jr.
Wender, Ira T.
Wendt, E. Allan
Wendt, Henry
Wertheim, Mitzi M.
Wesely, Edwin J.
Wessel, Michael R.
West, J. Robinson
Weston, Burns H.
Westphal, Albert C. F.
Wexler, Anne
Weymouth, Elizabeth
Whalen, Charles W., Jr.
Whalen, Richard J.
Wharton, Clifton R., Jr.
Wheat, Francis M.
Wheeler, John K.
Wheelon, Albert D.
Whipple, Taffart

Whitaker, C. S.
Whitaker, Jennifer Seymour
Whitaker, Mark
White, John P.
White, Julia A.
White, P. Maureen
White, Peter C.
White, Robert J.
White, Robert M.
Whitehead, John C.
Whitehouse, Charles S.
Whiting, Allen S.
Whitman, Marina v.N.
Whitney, Craig R.
Whittemore, Frederick B.
Wiarda, Howard J.
Wickham, John A., Jr.
Widner, Jennifer
Wiener, Malcolm H.
Wieseltier, Leon
Wiesner, Jerome B.
Wilbur, Brayton, Jr.
Wildavsky, Aaron
Wilds, Walter
Wiley, Richard A.
Wiley, W. Bradford
Wilhelm, Harry E.
Wilhelm, Robert E.
Wilkie, Edith B.
Wilkins, Roger W.
Wilkinson, Sharon
Willey, Fay
Williams, Avon N., III
Williams, Earle C.
Williams, Eddie Nathan
Williams, Harold M.
Williams, Haydn
Williams, Joseph H.
Williams, Karen Hastie
Williams, Maurice J.
Williamson, Irving A.
Williamson, Thomas S., Jr.
Willrich, Mason
Wilmers, Robert G.
Wilson, Donald M.

Wilson, Ernest James, III
Wilson, Heather A.
Wilson, John D.
Wimpfheimer, Jacques D.
Winokur, Herbert S., Jr.
Winship, Thomas
Winslow, Richard S.
Winston, Michael R.
Winterer, Philip S.
Winters, Francis X.
Winters, Robert C.
Wirth, David A.
Wirth, John D.
Wirth, Timothy E.
Wisner, Frank G., II
Witunski, Michael
Woerner, Fred F.
Wofford, Harris L.
Wohlforth, William C.
Wohlstetter, Albert
Wohlstetter, Roberta
Wolf, Charles, Jr.
Wolf, Milton A.
Wolfensohn, James D.
Wolff, Alan Wm.
Wolfowitz, Paul D.
Wolpe, Howard
Woolf, Harry
Woolsey, R. James
Wray, Cecil, Jr.
Wriggins, W. Howard
Wright, Robin
Wright-Carozza, Paolo G.
Wyman, Thomas H.

Y
Yalman, Nur
Yankelovich, Daniel
Yarmolinsky, Adam
Yeo, Edwin H., III
Yergin, Daniel H.
Yochelson, John N.
Yoffie, David B.
Yost, Casimir A.
Young, Alice

Young, Andrew
Young, Edgar B.
Young, Joan P.
Young, M. Crawford
Young, Nancy
Young, Stephen B.
Youngman, William S.
Yu, Frederick T. C.
Yudkin, Richard A.

Z
Zagoria, Donald S.
Zakheim, Dov S.
Zarb, Frank G.
Zartman, I. William
Zeidenstein, George
Zelikow, Philip D.
Zelnick, C. Robert
Zilkha, Ezra K.
Zimmerman, Edwin M.
Zimmerman, Peter D.
Zimmerman, William
Zimmermann, Warren
Zinberg, Dorothy S.
Zinder, Norton D.
Zoellick, Robert B.
Zogby, James J.
Zolberg, Aristide R.
Zonis, Marvin
Zorthian, Barry
Zraket, Charles A.
Zuckerman, Harriet
Zuckerman, Mortimer B.
Zumwalt, Elmo R., Jr.
Zwick, Charles J.
Zysman, John

Appendix B

Recommended Reading List

46 Angry Men
46 Civilian Doctors of Elisabethville
- Western Islands

Abortion: Pro-Life By Conviction, Pro-Choice By Default
Richard Exley - Honor Books

AIDS Coverup?, The
Gene Antonio - Ignatius Press

AIDS: Rage & Reality
Gene Antonio - Anchor Books

AIDS: The Unnecessary Epidemic
Dr. Stanley Monteith - Covenant House

AIDS: What The Government Isn't Telling You
Dr. Lorraine Day - Rockford Press

America, Oil & The Islamic Mind
Michael Youssef - Zondervan

America's Secret Establishment
Antony C. Sutton - Liberty House

Annals of America
Encyclopedia Britannica

Apocalypse Next
William R. Goetz - Horizon House

Art of War, The
Sun Tzu - Oxford University Press

Betrayal of America
David Funderburke - Larry McDonald Foundation

Born Again Republic
Red Beckman - Freedom Church

Call It Conspiracy
Larry Abraham - Double A

Committee of 300
Dr. John Coleman - Joseph Publishing

Deadly Deception
Shaw & McKenney - Huntington House

Deceived By The New Age
Will Baron - Pacific Press

Philip Dru: Administrator
E. M. House

En Route To Global Occupation
Gary Kah - Huntington House

Fearful Master, The
G. Edward Griffin - Western Islands

Foreign Affairs
Council on Foreign Relations

Global Tyranny
William F. Jasper - Western Islands

High Cost Of Free Love
Al Haffner - Here's Life Publishers

Hitler & The New Age
Bob Rosio - Huntington House

Hollywood vs. America
Michael Medved - Harper Collins

Holy Bible

How To Create Your Own Unit Study
(For Homeschoolers) - Valerie Bendt

*I'd Speak Out On The Issues If Only
I Knew The Answers*
Jane Chastain - Regal Books

Institutes of Biblical Law, The
Rousas J. Rushdoony - Craig Press

Invisible Government, The
Dan Smoot - The Dan Smoot Report

Keys Of This Blood, The
Malachi Martin - Touchstone

Kinsey, Sex & Fraud
Dr. Judith Reisman - Huntington
House

*Last Crusader: The Untold Story of
Christopher Columbus*
George Grant - Crossway Books

Law And Society
Rousas J. Rushdoony - Ross House

Law That Never Was, The
Benson & Beckman - Constitution
Research Center

Light and The Glory, The
Marshall & Manuel - Fleming H.
Revell

Light That Was Dark, The
Warren Smith - Northfield Publishing

Masters of Deceit
J. Edgar Hoover - Pocket Books

Mountain Of Lies
Kirby Ferris - Rapid Lightning Press

Naked Capitalist, The
W. Cleon Skousen - The Reviewer
1-800-388-4512 Orders

New Lies For Old
Anatoliy Golitsyn - Dodd, Mead

New World Order
Pat Robertson - Word

Next Four Years, The
Howard Phillips - Adroit Press

New World Order
Ralph Epperson - Publius Press

*New World Order: The Ancient Plan
of Secret Societies*
William Still - Huntington House

One World Under Antichrist
Peter LaLonde - Harvest House

Perestroika
Mikhail S. Gorbachev - Harper Row

Proofs of A Conspiracy
John Robinson - Western Islands

Quick And The Dead, The
George Grant - Crossway Books

332

Rebirth of America
Arthur S. DeMoss Foundation - *Free when you call 215-254-5500*

Rebuilding The Walls
Peter Waldron - Wogelmuth Hyatt

Red Cocaine
Joseph D. Douglas, Jr. - Clarion

Saturday Morning Mind Control
Phil Phillips - Oliver Nelson

Shadows In The Land
William Dannemeyer - Ignatius Press

Shadows Of Power
James Perloff - Western Islands

Soft Porn Plays Hardball
Dr. Judith Reisman - Huntington House

Teens And Devil-Worship
Charles G. B. Evans - Huntington House

Too Old Too Soon
Doug Fields - Harvest House

Tragedy & Hope
Carroll Quigley - MacMillan Co.

Two Babylons, The
Alexander Hislop - Loizeaux Brothers

U.S. Constitution and Bill of Rights

U.S. Taxpayers Party Platform

Unanimous Declaration of Independence

Unhappy Gays, The
Tim LaHaye - Tyndale House

Unseen Hand, The
Ralph Epperson - Publius Press

Whatever Happened To The Human Race?
Koop & Schaeffer - Crossway Books

When Is It Right To Die?
Joni Eareckson Tada - Zondervan

When The World Will Be As One
Tal Brooke - Harvest House

Who Will Rock The Cradle?
Phyllis Schlafly - Word

World Without Tyrrany
Dean C. Curry - Crossway Books

Recommended Newsletters:

ADI News
1055 N. Fairfax St., Suite 200
Alexandria, VA 22314

Aid & Abeit Police Newsletter
1001 N. 43rd Ave. E-84
Phoenix, AZ 85009

The Baker Report
Jeff Baker
4275 - 34th Street, South #150
St. Petersburg, FL 33711

The California Statesman
William K. Shearer
8158 Palm Street
Lemon Grove, CA 91945

Chalcedon Report
R.J. Rushdoony
P.O. Box 158
Vallecito, CA 95251

The Christian World Report
Omega - Letter, Inc.
P.O. Box 1440
Niagara Falls, NY 14302

The Eco-Profiteer
Larry Abraham
1350 Center Dr. #100
Dunwoody, GA 30338

Family Research Report
Dr. Paul Cameron
P.O. Box 2091
Washington, D.C. 20013

Flashpoint
Texe Marrs
1708 Patterson Road
Austin, TX 78733-6507

Foundations of Liberty
900 46th Avenue
E. Moline, IL 61244

The Goodloe Report
P.O. Box 25736
Seattle, WA 98125-1236

The Insider Report
Larry Abraham
P.O. Box 467939
Atlanta, GA 30346-7939
1-800-728-2288

The McAlvany Intelligence Advisor
Don S. McAlvany
P.O. Box 84904
Phoenix, AZ 85071

Gary North's Remnant Review
Gary North, Ph.D.
P.O. Box 84906
Phoenix, AZ 85071

The Ron Paul Survival Report
18333 Egret Bay Blvd.
Suite 265
Houston, TX 77058

*The Howard Phillips Issues &
Strategies Bulletin*
Policy Analysis, Inc.
9520 Bent Creek Lane
Vienna, VA 22182

The Weaver Report
Mark Weaver
U.S. Taxpayers Party
450 Maple Avenue, East
Vienna, CA 22180

World News Digest
Larry Abraham
1350 Center Dr. #100
Dunwoody, GA 30338
1-800-728-2288

Endnotes

1   President George Bush's speech before Congress on September 11, 1990.
2   President George Bush's speech before Congress on October 30, 1990.
3   Mikhail Gorbachev, before the Supreme Soviet Politiburo on November 2, 1987.
4   *St. Petersburg Times* (April 10, 1993).
5   *St. Petersburg Times* (April 9, 1993).
6   Malachi Martin, *The Keys Of This Blood* (New York: Touchstone, 1990), p. 16.
7   President George Bush's speech before Congress on March 6, 1991.
8   *Katanga* (Westlake Village, CA: American Media).
9   Genesis 11:4, Holy Bible, King James Version.
10   Michael Youssef, *America, Oil & The Islamic Mind: The Real Crisis Is The Gulf Between Our Ways of Thinking* (Grand Rapids, MI: Zondervan Publishing House, 1983), p. 9.
11   Malachi Martin, *The Keys Of This Blood* (New York: Touchstone, 1990), p. 21.
12   Joseph Wechsberg, *The Merchant Bankers* (New York: Pocket Books, 1966), p. 10.
13   Don Bell, "Who Are Our Rulers?," *American Mercury,* (September, 1960), p. 136.
14   *F.D.R.: His Personal Letters* (New York: Duell, Sloan and Pearce, 1950), p. 373.
15   Phoebe and Kent Courtney, *America's Unelected Rulers: The Council on Foreign Relations* (New Orleans, LA: Conservative Society of America, 1962), p. 92..
16   Peter LaLonde, *One World Under Antichrist* (Eugene, OR: Harvest House Publishers, 1992), p. 239.
17   William R. Goetz, *Apocalypse Next* (Camp Hill, PA: Horizon House Publishers, 1992), p. 239.
18   Loraine Boettner, *Roman Catholicism* (Philadelphia, PA: The Presbyterian and Reformed Publishing Co., 1962), pp. 241-242.
19   Ibid.
20   Malachi Martin, *The Keys Of This Blood* (New York: Touchstone, 1990), p. 17.
21   Ibid, p. 41.
22   Larry Abraham, *Call It Conspiracy* (Wuana, WA: Double A Publications, 1971), p. 107.
23   Antony C. Sutton, *America's Secret Establishment: An Introduction to the Order of Skull & Bones* (Billings, MT: Liberty House Press, 1986), p. 6.
24   Ibid, pp. 213-214.
25   Ibid, p. 29.
26   Ibid, p. 27.
27   Ibid, p. 25.
28   William T. Still, *New World Order: The Ancient Plan of Secret Societies* (Lafayette, LA: Huntington House, 1990), p. 39.
29   Ralph Epperson, *The New World Order* (Tucson, AZ: Publius Press, 1990), p. 66.
30   Alexander Hislop, *The Two Babylons* (Neptune, NJ: Loizeaux Brothers).
31   Ralph Epperson, *The Unseen Hand* (Tucson, AZ: Publius Press, 1985), p. 84.
32   Ibid, p. 79.
33   Ibid, p. 79.

34   Ibid, p. 81.

35   Ibid.

36   Nesta Webster, *World Revolution* (London: Constable and Company, 1921), p. 18.

37   Ibid, p. 14.

38   Ralph Epperson, *The Unseen Hand,* p. 82.

39   William T. Still, *New World Order: The Ancient Plan of Secret Societies,* p. 23.

40   Genesis 6:12, 13, 17, Holy Bible, King James Version.

41   William T. Still, *New World Order: The Ancient Plan of Secret Societies,* p. 42.

42   Ibid, pp. 42-43.

43   Ralph Epperson, *The New World Order,* pp. 63-64.

44   Ibid, pp. 66-67.

45   Ralph Epperson, *The Unseen Hand* (Tucson, AZ: Publius Press, 1985), p. 85.

46   Ibid, p. 86.

47   Ibid.

48   John Robinson, A.M., *Proofs of a Conspiracy* (Boston, MA: Western Islands, 1967), p. 7

49   Tal Brooke, *When the World Will Be As One,* (Eugene, OR: Harvest House Publishers, Inc., 1989), p. 248.

50   Don S. McAlvany, *McAlvany Intelligence Adivsor,* (Phoenix, AZ, November, 1992), pp. 5-6.

51   Supreme Court Justice David J. Brewer, *America, A Christian Nation,* "Unanimous Opinion" (Phoenix, AZ: Lord's Covenant Church, February 29, 1892).

52   Don S. McAlvany, *McAlvany Intelligence Adivsor,* (November, 1992), pp. 5-6.

53   Howard Phillips, *Issues and Strategies Bulletin,* (Vienna, VA: Policy Analysis, Inc., October 26, 1992).

54   Howard Phillips, *U.S. Taxpayers Party Quarterly Review,* Vol. 1, Issue 1 (Spring, 1993), p. 4.

55   Howard Phillips, *The Next Four Years* (Franklin, TN: Adroit Press, 1991), p. 151.

56   Nord Davis, Jr., *Desert Shield And The New World Order* (Topton, NC: Northpoint Tactical Teams), p. 20.

57   *McCall's,* telephone conversation with Barbara Luttresll's assistant on April 12, 1993.

58   *New American* (November 2, 1992), pp. 7-10.

59   *"W" Magazine* (New York: Fairchild Publications, August 4-11, 1978), p. 4.

60   *The CFR/Trilateral Connection* (Kerrville, TX: F.R.E.E.).

61   Antony C. Sutton, *America's Secret Establishment: An Introduction to The Order of Skull and Bones,* p. 25.

62   *Council on Foreign Relations, Annual Report* (July 1, 1991, - June 30, 1992), pp. 174-175.

63   Ibid, p. 5.

64   William F. Jasper, *Global Tyranny... Step By Step* (Appleton, WI: Western Islands, 1992), pp. 49-50.

65   James Perloff, *Shadows of Power* (Appleton, WI: Western Islands, 1988), pp. 8-9.

66   Phyllis Schlafly and Chester Ward, *Kissinger on the Couch* (New Rochelle, NY: Arlington House, 1975), p. 151.

67   Larry Abraham, *Insider Report,* "The Clinton Clique" (Wuana, WA: January, 1993).

68   Howard Phillips, *Issues and Strategies Bulletin* (February 28, 1993).
69   Larry Abraham, *Call It Conspiracy,* p. 155.
70   James Perloff, *Shadows of Power,* p. 14.
71   Arthur Schlesinger, Jr., *A Thousand Days* (Boston, MA: Houghton Mifflin, 1965), p. 128.
72   Carroll Quigley, *Tragedy and Hope: A History Of The World In Our Time* (New York: MacMillan Company, 1966), p. 130, Special Collections Division, Georgetown University Library.
73   W. Cleon Skousen, *The Naked Capitalist* (Salt Lake City, UT: The Reviewer, 1970), p. 26.
74   Ibid, pp. 26-27.
75   Ibid, p. 27.
7€   Ibid, pp. 27-28.
77   U.S. Taxpayers Party of Florida, *The Constitution and The Declaration of Independence* (Tampa, FL: 1991), p. 8.
78   Carrol Quigley, *Tragedy and Hope: A History Of The World In Our Time,* p. 130.
79   Ibid, pp. 130-131.
80   Ibid, p. 131.
81   Ibid.
82   Ibid, p. 132.
83   Ibid.
84   Ibid, p. 950.
85   Governor Bill Clinton, Acceptance Speech to the Democratic National Convention, 1992.
86   Carroll Quigley, *Tragedy and Hope: A History Of The World In Our Time,* p. 950.
87   Ibid, pp. 951-952.
88   Ibid, p. 954.
89   Malachi Martin, *The Keys of This Blood,* p. 278.
90   Don S. McAlvany, *McAlvany Intelligence Advisor* (September, 1992), p. 2.
91   Al Gore, *Earth In The Balance: Ecology And The Human Spirit* (Boston: Houghton Mifflin Co., 1992), p. 121.
92   Bill Benson and M. J. "Red" Beckman, *The Law That Never Was* (South Holland, IL: Constitutional Research Assoc., 1985), pp. 10-11.
93   *St. Petersburg Times* (April 10, 1993).
94   J.S. Mill, *American State Papers: The Federalist* (Chicago: Encyclopedia Britannica, Inc., 1952), p. 100.
95   G. Edward Griffin, *The Fearful Master* (Boston: Western Islands Press, 1964), p. 45.
96   Senator Thomas Dodd entered into the Congressional Record (September 8, 1961).
97   Ibid.
98   G. Edward Griffin, *The Fearful Master,* p. 3-64.
99   The 46 Civilian Doctors of Elisabethville, *46 Angry Men* (Belmont, MA: American Opinion, 1962), pp. 92.
100 *World Press* (December 6, 1961).
101 G. Edward Griffin, *The Fearful Master,* p. 60.

102 The 46 Civilian Doctors of Elisabethville, *46 Angry Men,* pp. 91-92.

103 G. Edward Griffin, *The Fearful Master*, p. 64.

104 Frank Vanderlip, "Farm Boy To Financier," *Saturday Evening Post,* (February 9, 1935), p. 25, 70. Also: Ralph Epperson, *The Unseen Hand,* p. 170.

105 Congressional Record (December 22, 1913, Vol. 51), p. 1446.

106 Congressional Record (1934), pp. 24-25. Also Ralph Epperson, *The Unseen Hand*, p. 182.

107 *Christian American* (January 1993), p. 7.

108 Michael Medved, *Hollywood vs. America* (New York: Harper Collins, Zondervan, 1992), p. 286.

109 Ibid, pp. 286-288.

110 Ibid, pp. 290-291.

111 Ibid, pp. 296-297.

112 Ibid, p. 15

113 Jane Chastain, *I'd Speak Out On The Issues If Only I Knew What To Say* (Ventura, CA: Regal Books, 1987), p. 153.

114 Dr. John Seale, "Problems Associated With Aids," p. 144.

115 Phil Phillips, *Saturday Morning Mind Control* (Nashville: Oliver-Nelson Books, a division of Thomas Nelson, Inc., 1991), p. 19.

116 Ibid, p. 109.

117 Ibid, p. 123.

118 George Grant, *The Last Crusader: The Untold Story of Christopher Columbus* (Wheaton, IL: Crossway Books, 1992), p. xiv.

119 Ibid, p. 66.

120 *The Annals of America - Vol. I - 1433-1754, Discovering The New World* (Chicago: Encyclopedia Britannica, Inc., 1968), pp. 2-3.

121 George Grant, *The Last Crusader*, p. 22.

122 *Rebirth of America* (Philadelphia, PA: Arthur S. DeMoss Foundation, 1986).

123 Ibid, p. 31.

124 Ibid.

125 Ibid, p. 37.

126 Barnes & Noble, *American Historical Documents,* pp. 34-38.

127 *The Annals of America - Vol. 3 - 1784-1786,* pp. 493-495.

128 Ibid, pp. 3-48.

129 Ibid, pp. 162-169.

130 Ibid, pp. 612-613.

131 Ibid, p. 613

132 Ibid.

133 Ibid, p. 614.

134 Ibid, p. 612.

135 Ibid, p. 610.

136 Chuck Noel: Typed statement given in person to Jeffrey A. Baker on November 6, 1992.

137 *Rebirth of America*, p. 90.

138 Judith A. Reisman, Ph.D., *"Soft Port" Plays Hardball: Its Tragic Effects on Women,*

Children & The Family (Lafayette, LA: Huntington House Publishers, 1991), p. 52.

139   Col. Ronald D. Ray, USMCR, "Military Necessity & Homosexuality" (Louisville, KY: First Principles, Inc., 1992).

140   Proverbs 31:10-31, The Holy Bible, King James Version.

141   *Christian American* (May/June, 1991).

142   Exodus 20:1-3, The Holy Bible, King James Version.

143   Deuteronomy 12:8, The Holy Bible, King James Version.

144   Exodus 20:4-6; Deuteronomy 5:8-10, The Holy Bible, King James Version.

145   Exodus 20:7; Deuteronomy 5:11, The Holy Bible, King James Version.

146   Rousas J. Rushdoony, *The Institutes of Biblical Law*, p. 102.

147   Ibid, pp. 105-106.

148   Ibid, pp. 107-108.

149   Ibid, p. 108.

150   Ibid, p. 109.

151   Exodus 20:7, The Holy Bible, King James Version.

152   George Washington's Farewell Address, *Annals of America, Vol 3, pp. 606-615.*

153   Exodus 21:16, The Holy Bible, King James Version.

154   Exodus 21:17, The Holy Bible, King James Version.

155   Exodus 20:8-11, The Holy Bible, King James Version.

156   Isaiah 57:20-21, The Holy Bible, King James Version.

157   Exodus 20:12, The Holy Bible, King James Version.

158   E. Adamson Hoebel, *Man in the Primitive World*, p. 448.

159   Exodus 20:13, The Holy Bible, King James Version.

160   Deuteronomy 19:16-21, The Holy Bible, King James Version.

161   People v Rosen (1937) 20 Cal. App. 2nd 445, 66, P2d 1208, 1210 (McComb J); Rousas J. Rushdoony, *The Institutes of Biblical Law* (The Craig Press, 1973), p. 571.

162   Exodus 20:14, The Holy Bible, King James Version.

163   Exodus 20:15, The Holy Bible, King James Version.

164   Rousas J. Rushdoony, *Institutes of Biblical Law*, p. 452.

165   Exodus 20:16, The Holy Bible, King James Version.

166   Rousas J. Rushdoony, *Institutes of Biblical Law*, p. 543.

167   Exodus 20:17, The Holy Bible, King James Version.

168   Rousas J. Rushdoony, *Institutes of Biblical Law*, p. 632.

169   Gerhard Von Rad, *Deuteronomy, A Commmentary* (Philadelphia: Westminster Press, 1966), p. 59.

170   *The Annals of America, Vol. 3*, pp. 53-54.

171   Matthew 25:29, The Holy Bible, King James Version.

172   Rousas J. Rushdoony, *Institutes of Biblical Law*, p. 642.

173   Matthew 20:15, The Holy Bible, King James Version.

174   Rousas J. Rushdoony, *Institutes of Biblical Law*, p. 643.